Easy AutoCAD® Release 13 for Windows

With Reference to DOS

John D. Hood

McGraw-Hill

New York San Francisco Washington, D.C. Auckland Bogotá
Caracas Lisbon London Madrid Mexico City Milan
Montreal New Delhi San Juan Singapore
Sydney Tokyo Toronto

McGraw-Hill

A Division of The McGraw·Hill Companies

Library of Congress Cataloging-in-Publication Data

Hood, John D.
  Easy AutoCAD release 13 for Windows: with reference to DOS / by
John D. Hood.
      p.   cm.
  Includes index.
  ISBN 0-07-029790-8 (pbk.)
  1. Computer graphics.   2. AutoCAD for Windows. 3. MS-DOS
(Computer file) 4. PC-DOS (Computer file)   I. Title.
T385.H689 1996
620'.0042'02855369--dc20   95-46483
                                                      CIP

 2 3 4 5 6 7 8 9 FGR/FGR 9 0 0 9 8 7 6

ISBN 0-07-029790-8

The supervising editor for this book was Marjorie Spencer. The book ed-
itor was Kellie Hagan, and the executive editor was Robert E. Ostrander.
The production supervisor was Katherine G. Brown. This book was set
in ITC Century Light. It was composed in Blue Ridge Summit, Pa.

Printed and bound by Quebecor Fairfield, PA.

McGraw-Hill books are available at special quantity discounts to use as
premiums and sales promotions, or for use in corporate training programs. For
more information, please write to the Director of Special Sales, McGraw-Hill,
11 West 19th Street, New York, NY 10011. Or contact your local bookstore.

To Shirley, Allen, and Carmel.

Contents

Acknowledgments

I want to thank the people at Autodesk for their outstanding support, through their Registered Developer Program. Without their support in providing prerelease copies of AutoCAD software, it would be extremely difficult to write a book that keeps up with the latest release of AutoCAD. Over the years many students have helped make this a better book by offering suggestions and by finding the "bugs." Their patience and assistance is greatly appreciated.

Thanks also to those who used early copies of this book, especially Bill Este, who patiently reviewed much of the manuscript and helped eliminate many of the bugs, and Randy Halverson, who has made many helpful suggestions over the years.

Preface

I wrote *Easy AutoCAD for Windows* to provide you with the necessary skills and knowledge to use AutoCAD Release 13 in order to construct and plot production-quality drawings. This book covers everything you need to know, from basic drawing to multiscale, multiview, and three-dimensional drawing. *Easy AutoCAD for Windows* is a tutorial that allows you to step through each chapter, learning to use AutoCAD by drawing, dimensioning, editing, and plotting industry-standard drawings. If you're a beginner with no CAD experience, you'll find the book easy to follow and arranged in an orderly manner in order to bring you up to speed as a CAD operator in little time. Experienced CAD operators who want to learn AutoCAD 13 for both Windows and DOS will find the book informative and comprehensive. You'll learn how to write custom menus, use model and paper space, use external references, produce multiscale and multiview production drawings with borders and title blocks, complete a slide show, draw solid three-dimensional models, write AutoLISP programs, and employ features of the Windows environment.

Easy AutoCAD for Windows is written for Release 13 of AutoCAD for Windows, with references to the DOS version where commands are different. If you're working only in DOS, you'll be able to follow the exercises. AutoCAD drafters converting from DOS to Windows will find the text of particular value because of the reference to DOS and the complete listing of AutoCAD DOS menu tables in appendix G, as well as the complete listing of AutoCAD for Windows toolbar menus in appendix A.

What makes this book unique is that you're immediately involved in the drawing process. I've found that serious students are quickly bored with drawing lines, circle, boxes, and strange shapes. The industry requires that CAD drafters handle a total project, which involves mastering drawing skills and also being able to calculate text heights, dimension scales, hatch scales, and linetype scales. Once all these skills are mastered, you're much better prepared to be a CAD drafter.

Introduction

Practice is the only way to learn a skill. My purpose in writing this book is to provide a set of tutorial notes that supplement the *AutoCAD User's Guide*, which is supplied with the AutoCAD program. AutoCAD also has an excellent Help program that provides detailed information about using AutoCAD menus, toolbars, commands, and dialog boxes. Help procedures are discussed in appendix D of this book. I recommend that you read that section and become familiar with AutoCAD's Help menu before you tackle the exercises in the book. The *AutoCAD User's Guide* and AutoCAD's Help program, however, do little to demonstrate actually using AutoCAD to produce integrated drafting projects. It's my objective to provide you with those skills.

In this book, I emphasize using AutoCAD to efficiently complete drawings in a number of disciplines, using practical drawing projects. Although the primary emphasis is on AutoCAD for Windows, I'll refer to the DOS version of AutoCAD in each application to assist drafters transitioning from DOS to Windows.

Having taught CAD, it has been my observation that the biggest problem both students and experienced drafters have when starting to use CAD is that they lack the confidence to sit down in front of the computer and begin a drawing. It's really a simple thing to do: you just start at the beginning and work toward the end. In this book, therefore, I provide a set of projects that allow you to do just that.

I.1 The AutoCAD Program

AutoCAD is a computer-aided drafting program from Autodesk Inc. It's written in the C programming language, which is machine-independent and composed of an intricate set of drawing and editing capabilities.

The program is written to run on 80386/80486/Pentium-based microcomputers. Drawings made with the Windows and DOS versions of AutoCAD are compatible, and drawings done in one version can be edited or completed in the other. Drawings done with AutoCAD 13 can also be saved in Release 12 format. AutoCAD for Windows users can employ features of the Windows environment, such as linking AutoCAD drawings with word-processing and spreadsheet applications. AutoCAD has become the de facto standard of microcomputer CAD programs in industry and education.

AutoCAD 13 is shipped with a multiplatform license, which allows you to install and use AutoCAD for DOS, Windows, Windows 95, and Windows NT on a single PC. This feature is particularly useful for drafters transitioning from DOS to Windows, and it's an objective of this book to make that transition easier.

The AutoCAD program is both tool/icon- and menu-driven. This means that you don't have to remember complex commands, just where to locate a command's tool or menu. Appendix A illustrates all the toolbars for AutoCAD for Windows, with an alphabetized listing of the tools so you can find the appropriate figure for each tool. You can also enter all the commands by typing them on the keyboard.

I.2 How To Use This Book

This book is composed of a series of tutorial projects, each about three hours in length, which are designed to bring novice users, with no CAD or other computer experience, to the level of a fully trained CAD operator in a short period of time. Experienced CAD operators will find the text invaluable because it demonstrates how to efficiently use AutoCAD commands to complete complex drafting procedures.

The tutorials are written to complement the *AutoCAD User's Guide* supplied with the AutoCAD software. Commands aren't introduced in a specific order, but rather as required to complete specific drawing projects. Refer to the *AutoCAD User's Guide, AutoCAD Command Reference*, and the Help menu when using Easy Auto-CAD if you need more information about a command.

I recommend that new users start at the beginning of this book and complete all the projects. Although there's sufficient repetition of instruction in the projects, I assume that you've completed prior projects and understand the application of commands used in earlier chapters. There are two exceptions to this general rule. The process of plotting isn't discussed until chapter 7, and using AutoCAD in the Windows environment is covered in chapter 19. This usually works best in the classroom, but you might want to read those chapters earlier.

The AutoCAD for Windows drawing screen is illustrated in Figure I.1. The drawing name (UNNAMED in this case) is shown in the *title bar* at the top of the screen. Drawing commands and settings can be chosen from the *menu bar*, the *Standard toolbar*, and other *toolbars*. You can dock toolbars, as shown in Figure I.1, or have them float (be located anywhere on the screen). You can also enter commands from the keyboard. The AutoCAD for DOS drawing screen is shown in Figure I.2.

In Figure I.1, the Line command has been invoked with the Line tool in the Draw toolbar. You do this by moving the cursor with the *pointing device* (a mouse or digitizer puck) into the Draw toolbar, shown in its docked position at the top of the screen in Figure I.1 and illustrated in section A.3 of appendix A). Your Draw toolbar can be in another location or not visible on your screen. The procedure for displaying toolbars is discussed later in Chapter 1. When the cursor (displayed on the screen as a small arrow) is placed on a tool, a rectangular *Tooltips* box with the name of the tool is displayed below the cursor. Place the cursor on the Line tool (Figure I.3) and press and release the <pick> button (usually the left or 1 button) on the pointing device to invoke the Line command. (For the location of AutoCAD for DOS commands, refer to appendix G.)

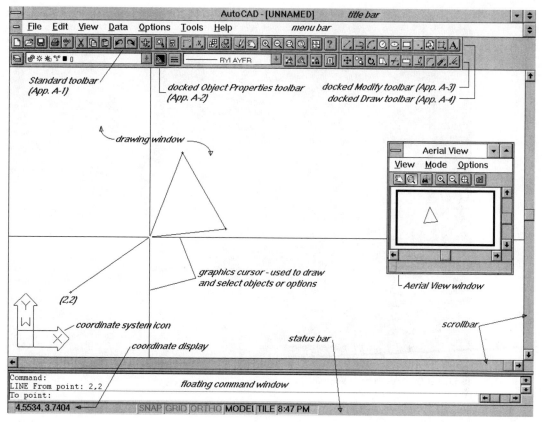

Figure I.1 Drawing screen.

Tools with a small black triangle have *flyouts*. If a tool has a flyout, the last tool invoked can be displayed in the tool's position on the toolbar. The flyout for the Line tool group is displayed in Figure I.4 and sections A.3 and A.3.1 of appendix A. If, for example, the Xline tool (see sections A.3 and A.3.1) rather than the Line tool is displayed in the Draw toolbar, you can locate the Line tool by moving the cursor onto the Xline tool and pressing and holding down the <pick> button on the mouse to display the Line flyout. Continuing to hold the <pick> button, move the pointing device along the Line flyout onto the Line tool and, when the pointing device is on the Line tool, release the <pick> button to invoke the Line command. As the cursor is moved along a flyout, the name of each tool is displayed in the Tooltips box under the cursor as it passes over the tool. Appendix A contains a listing of all AutoCAD for Windows toolbars, along with an alphabetized listing of the tools. Refer to this when you need to locate a tool for a command.

Click on the Line tool in the Draw toolbar to invoke the Line command. (In DOS, the Line command is in the Draw menu):

Draw <toolbar> Line <pick>

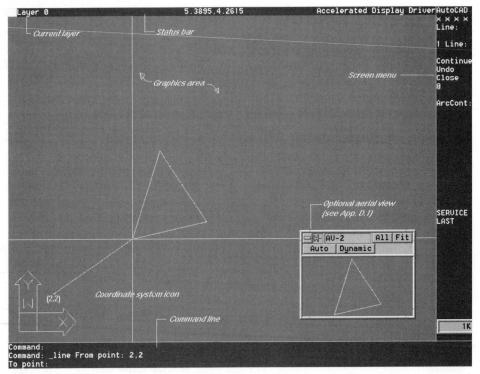

Figure I.2 DOS drawing screen.

Figure I.3 Line Tool.

Figure I.4 Line flyout.

In Windows, Draw <toolbar> refers to the toolbar containing the tool; in DOS, Draw refers to the Draw menu, which contains the Line command. When the Windows toolbar name and the DOS menu name are different, each will be shown.

AutoCAD displays commands in the Command window at the bottom of the monitor as they're entered (refer back to Figure I.1). When the Line command is chosen, the command line displays the following request:

```
Line from point:
```

You need to enter the start point of the line. In some cases you'll enter data by typing it on the keyboard. As is the convention used in this book, the AutoCAD request or prompt is in computer type, the data you're to type is in bold, and names of keys and mouse buttons are contained in angle brackets. Menu names and menu items, as well as any explanatory text, are in regular type. To draw a line starting at coordinate 2,2:

`Line from point:` **2,2** <return>

In other words, AutoCAD will prompt you with `Line from point:` and you type **2,2** and press either the <return> key on the keyboard or the <return> button on the mouse (the middle or 2 button). AutoCAD will respond in the (floating) Command window with:

`To point:`

Now you need to enter the next point for the line, either from the keyboard, as previously illustrated, or by moving the cursor (crosshairs) on the screen to the desired point and pressing the <pick> button. This is referred to as *digitizing* the point. If you want to attach the line from point 2,2 to the left corner of the triangle on the screen (refer back to Figure I.1), move the cursor to the point:

`To point:` Move the cursor to the left side of the triangle and digitize the point. <pick>

In other words, AutoCAD will prompt you with `To point:`, then you perform the specified function and press the <pick> button. AutoCAD will draw the line and respond with:

`To point:`

If you don't want to continue drawing lines, you can exit the command by pressing the <return> button on the mouse or the <return> key on the keyboard without entering a value. If you do:

`To point:` Move the cursor to the left side of the triangle and digitize the point. <pick> `To point:` <return>

You could have entered the Line command by typing **line** from the keyboard instead of selecting it from the toolbar or menu. When typing in commands, you can use either uppercase or lowercase letters, and enter the command by pressing <return>. Note that all the AutoCAD commands in this book use the following format:

- Data you are to type is in boldface.
- Keys on either the mouse or keyboard are enclosed in angle brackets, like <return> and <pick>. The word <toolbar> is also in angle brackets, to show that the previous item is the name of a toolbar and not a menu item.

- AutoCAD responses or requests are printed in computer type.

- Instructions you are to follow are in text type.

I.3 CAD Hardware

AutoCAD 13 is written for 80386/486 and Pentium microcomputers. In order to run AutoCAD for Windows, your microcomputer should have 16 megabytes of random-access memory (RAM). You'll also need a math coprocessor, a floppy drive, and hard disk drive with at least a 120-megabyte capacity. AutoCAD is written to operate with DOS 5.0 or later, and the Windows version requires Windows 3.1 running in enhanced mode, Windows for Workgroups version 3.1 or later, or Windows 95.

You'll also need a graphics monitor to display the drawing. The monitor can be black and white, monochrome, or color. You'll need a Windows-compatible color/graphics adapter to display the graphics.

The standard resolution for a video graphics display monitor is 600 × 480 pixels, which means a screen resolution of 600 positions horizontally and 480 positions vertically on the screen (normally a higher-resolution monitor is used for CAD). A diagonal line will be "jaggy" on this type of monitor in that it will appear as a stepped line because of the lower resolution of the screen. (While all diagonal lines are composed of a number of short horizontal and vertical lines, the lower the resolution of the screen, the more apparent they are.) This makes it more difficult to read drawings on the screen, but doesn't affect the paper plot of the drawing, where the line will appear as a uniform line.

I.3.1 Pointing devices

You can use the keyboard to move the cursor around the screen to draw lines, select points, and choose icons and menu commands. If you do anything beyond a very minimal amount of drawing, however, you'll need some kind of pointing device. AutoCAD for Windows can be configured for a mouse, a digitizing tablet, or both a mouse and a digitizer.

A mouse is a locating device that uses relative motion to move the cursor on the screen as the mouse is moved about a flat area. A mouse has a small ball in its base that rotates as the mouse is moved along a smooth surface, causing the cursor to move on the screen. A trackball functions as an upside-down mouse; it sits stationary on the desk and you move the ball with your fingers. The mouse has buttons on its surface that you use to pick points on the monitor or choose items from a menu or tool box. A mouse usually costs around $100 and is one of the cheaper pointing devices available. It's limited, however, because it's a relative-motion device and can't be used to trace over paper drawings and transfer points into an AutoCAD drawing.

A digitizing tablet can be used as an absolute screen-pointing device. This means that you can set the digitizer to allow points on its surface to relate directly to points on the screen, so paper drawings can be fastened to the digitizer and traced with the digitizer puck to transfer them into a drawing. You can also use the digitizer as a mouse to choose tools and commands from AutoCAD toolbars and menus, or with tablet templates to select commands from the template on the digitizer.

I.4 Dialog Boxes

Dialog boxes are an important part of AutoCAD. If you don't get a dialog box when this book says you should, enter the following at the command line with the keyboard to get dialog boxes for reading and writing files:

```
Command: filedia <return>
New value for FILEDIA <0>: 1 <return>
```

To get dialog boxes for plotting:

```
Command: cmddia <return>
New value for CMDDIA <0>: 1 <return>
```

I.5 Using the Appendices

Appendix A displays the toolbar menus for AutoCAD for Windows. Appendix D gives troubleshooting hints and demonstrates how to use AutoCAD's Help function. You might want to look at that section as you begin chapter 2. This book is primarily aimed at using AutoCAD with Windows, but, to assist those working with DOS or converting from DOS to Windows, appendix G lists AutoCAD for DOS menus. Appendix H outlines the procedure for using AutoCAD in the Windows 95 environment. Other appendices are referred to throughout the book; review them when they're mentioned.

1

First Steps

First turn on all peripherals, e.g., a plotter, printer, and a digitizing tablet. Then turn on the computer. To run any programs, the microcomputer must first have a copy of the disk operating system, referred to as DOS, loaded into it. To run AutoCAD for Windows, you must also have Windows loaded on your computer. DOS is loaded when the computer is turned on (booted), and the DOS prompt, C:\>, is displayed. Your system can be set up to start Windows automatically. If Window isn't started when the computer is turned on, enter the following command at the DOS prompt:

C:\> **Win** <return>

1.1 Handling Floppy Disks

If your system has two floppy drives, usually the left or upper drive is drive A and the right or lower drive is drive B. The drives will be for either 3.5-inch or 5.25-inch diskettes.

To insert a floppy diskette into the drive, open the drive latch (for a 5.25-inch drive) and slowly insert the disk into the drive, with the label on the disk pointing up and under your thumb when grasping the disk. Do not under any circumstances touch the magnetic surface of the disk or you might lose data that's stored on it. Disks shouldn't be inserted or removed from the disk drive when the red disk operation light is on. If the disk light is on, wait until it goes off (indicating that the drive isn't reading or writing information) and then insert or remove the disk.

1.2 Windows Operations (for Windows 95, see appendix H)

When Windows is started, the Program Manager appears on the screen with various application windows, as illustrated in Figure 1.1. Depending on how Windows is set up, your system might have more or fewer application windows than illustrated. If you're starting Windows for the first time, refer to your *Windows User's Guide* and *Reference Manual* for instructions on how to set up Windows.

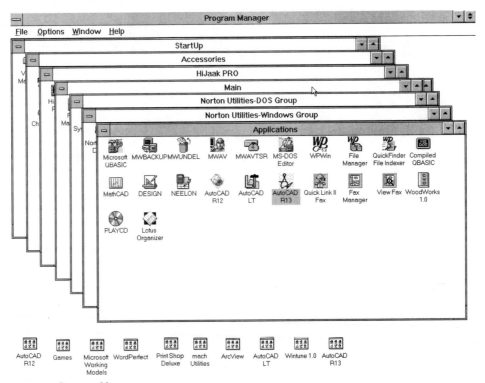

Figure 1.1 Program Manager.

Application windows display program icons, which are small pictures representing applications you can start from Windows. The Applications window illustrated in Figure 1.1 includes program icons for AutoCAD R13, AutoCAD LT, and Design.

1.2.1 File Manager

The Windows File Manager is an application that helps you organize files. Start it as follows:

1. Boot up DOS and start Windows (see the preceding section).

2. Choose the Main application window by placing the mouse pointer on its window, as illustrated by the arrow in Figure 1.1, and quickly pressing and releasing the <pick> button (usually the left or 1 button) on the mouse. The Main application window is displayed on the desktop in front of the other windows, as shown in Figure 1.2.

3. Choose the File Manager by placing the mouse pointer on its icon, as illustrated in Figure 1.2, and quickly pressing the <pick> button twice. Alternatively, you can press <pick> on the icon and then choose Run from the File menu. This is discussed later in the chapter.

4. The File Manager dialog box shown in Figure 1.3 will be displayed.

1.2.2 Preparing a data disk

You must prepare new blank disks that don't contain any programs or data for use. This is called *formatting*. You must format a disk only before its first use. If it's reformatted after data is stored on it, the data will be lost.

When using AutoCAD in a classroom setting, your drawings will usually be stored on a data disk in a floppy drive. In the instructions in this book, drive A (usually the left or upper drive) will be used. Format a disk for use as follows:

1. Insert a new blank disk into the proper floppy drive, as outlined in section 1.1.
2. Choose Disk from the File Manager window menu bar by placing the cursor on it, as illustrated in Figure 1.4, and pressing the <pick> button on the mouse. The Disk menu will be displayed.
3. From the Disk menu, choose Format Disk... to display the dialog box shown in Figure 1.5.
4. Place the mouse pointer on the arrow at the right of the Disk In selection box, as illustrated in Figure 1.5, and press the <pick> button. This will display a drop-down list box. Select the drive containing the disk to be formatted by choosing it from the drop-down box.
5. If necessary, choose the drive capacity from the drop-down Capacity list box. The capacity of a high-density 3.5-inch disk is 1.44MB, and that of a high-density 5.25-inch disk is 1.2MB.
6. Press the OK button by clicking it with the mouse, as illustrated in Figure 1.6, to start the diskette formatting process. Windows will display a Confirm Format Disk box, shown in Figure 1.7. Select Yes.
7. When the formatting process is complete, you're asked if you want to format another diskette. If you do, select Yes. If you're finished, select No.
8. Close the Print Manager window by clicking on the Control menu box containing the single dash, –, in the top left corner of the window, shown in Figure 1.8. Select the Close option.

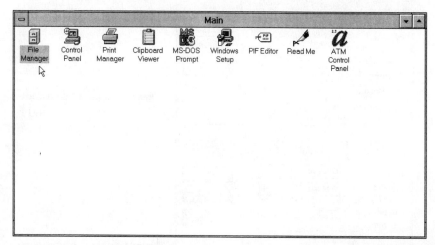

Figure 1.2 Main application window.

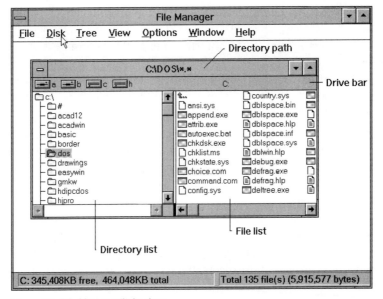

Figure 1.3 File Manager dialog box.

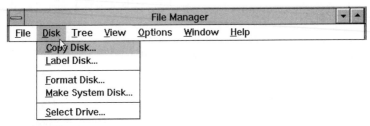

Figure 1.4 Disk menu.

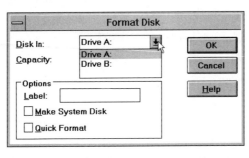

Figure 1.5 Format Disk dialog box.

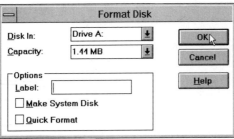

Figure 1.6 Start format.

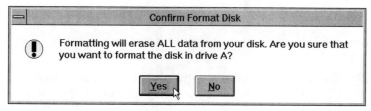

Figure 1.7 Confirm Format Disk box.

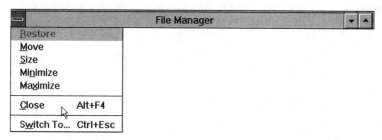

Figure 1.8 Closing a window.

If you want to place the windows back in their original order, refer back to Figure 1.1. Click on each window starting with the one to be in the back of the pack, and proceed sequentially to the front. This will put each window in order. The last one selected remains on top.

1.2.3 Displaying a disk directory

The files stored on a disk are listed in the disk directory. A hard drive will also have subdirectories; floppy disks do sometimes, but less often because they have a much smaller capacity. A subdirectory is similar to a drawer in a file cabinet. It allows you to store files in a more orderly manner. The subdirectory can also have sub-subdirectories, and so on. This is similar to using file folders in file drawer in a file cabinet, and further subdividing data in the file folders.

A file is the primary unit of storage. A file might be a drawing produced with AutoCAD, or a letter produced with a word processor. Every file must have a name. File and directory names follow certain rules. They:

- Can be up to eight characters long, and can also have an extension up to three characters long. The name is separated from the extension with a period, e.g., HOUSE.DWG.
- Can be entered in upper- or lowercase letters.
- Can be composed of letters A through Z, numbers 0 through 9, and the following special characters: &, -, _, ^, ~, !, #, %, {, }, ', @, ", (, and).
- Cannot contain spaces, commas, backslashes, or periods (except the period that separates the name from the extension).
- Cannot be identical to the name of another file or subdirectory in the same directory.

You can display the directory of a disk as follows:

1. Choose the File Manager from the Main application window, as illustrated back in Figure 1.2.

2. The Directory window is the rectangular window displayed inside the File Manager window, illustrated back in Figure 1.3. In Figure 1.3, the default drive is C: and the displayed subdirectory is DOS. This directory path is shown at the top of the Directory window as C:\DOS*.*.

The asterisk, *, is used as a wildcard character when specifying file or directory names. In the preceding file path, *.* indicates that all files (with any name and extension) are listed for the directory C:\DOS.

On the left side of the Directory window, closed file-folder icons indicate directories on the default drive. The current directory icon is displayed as an open file folder, and the icon and directory name, dos, are shaded, as shown back in Figure 1.3. The right-hand side of the Directory window shows a list of the files in the current directory.

You can change the default directory by moving the cursor pointer onto the directory icon, e.g., acad13, in the directory list of the Directory window and pressing the <pick> button. The files for that directory will be displayed in the file list of the Directory window.

You can change the default drive by clicking on the icon in the drive bar at the top of the Directory window. This is discussed further in following sections. If you want to close the File Manager window, select Close from the Control Menu box (see section 1.2.2).

1.2.4 Making a subdirectory

Create a new subdirectory on drive C: named Drawings as follows:

1. If the File Manager window isn't open, follow the procedure to open it, outlined in section 1.2.1.

2. Using the mouse, choose the icon for drive C: by placing the mouse cursor on the icon, illustrated in Figure 1.9. Then press the <pick> button.

3. If the path at the top of the Directory window isn't C:*.*, place the mouse pointer on the file folder icon for C:\ in the directory list of the Directory window and press the <pick> button.

4. Choose File from the File Manager window bar to display the pull-down File menu.

5. Choose Create Directory... from the File menu by placing the mouse cursor on the command, as illustrated in Figure 1.10, and pressing the <pick> button.

6. Enter the directory name, Drawings, in the Name box of the Create Directory window, illustrated in Figure 1.11. Then move the mouse cursor onto the OK button in the box and press the <pick> button on the mouse. This is referred to as pressing OK. The box is removed from the screen and the directory is created as

a subdirectory on drive C:, and it's listed in the directory list of the Directory window (refer back to Figure 1.9).

7. Close the File Manager window by selecting Close in the Control Menu box (see section 1.2.2).

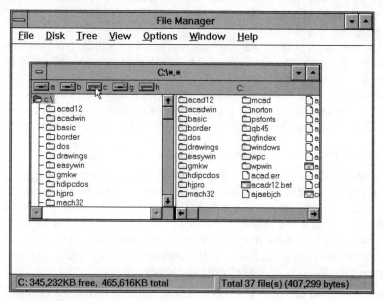

Figure 1.9 Selecting a default drive.

Figure 1.10 Create Directory option.

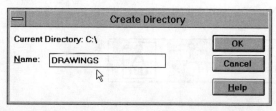

Figure 1.11 Create Directory dialog box.

1.3   Starting AutoCAD (for Windows 95, see Appendix H)

Before running AutoCAD, you must install the software onto your hard disk. Refer to your *AutoCAD Installation Guide* for the procedure to transfer the program from the diskettes supplied by AutoCAD to your hard disk.

When you install AutoCAD on your microcomputer, the installation program provided with AutoCAD asks for a directory name for the AutoCAD files. The default name provided is Acadr13.

The installation program will also ask you to select a program item icon for Auto-CAD in the Program Manager group. The available icons are shown in Figure 1.12, and the icon used in this book is shaded.

The following instructions assume you've created the subdirectory Drawings on drive C:, as outlined in section 1.2.4, and you'll save drawings either in that directory or on a floppy diskette in drive A:. Start AutoCAD for Windows as follows:

1.   Start Windows, as outlined in section 1.2.

2.   Your AutoCAD program item icon will be displayed in a window named AutoCAD or in the Applications window. Select the window that contains your AutoCAD R13 icon by clicking on the window. (Refer to your *Windows User's Guide* and *Reference Manual* if you want to move the AutoCAD R13 icon to the Applications window. If you do that, you'll reduce the AutoCAD window to an application icon (relocate it to a small icon at the bottom of the screen, as illustrated back in Figure 1.1). This eliminates clutter on the screen.

3.   Place the cursor on the AutoCAD R13 program icon with the mouse, as illustrated in Figure 1.13, and quickly press the <pick> button on the mouse twice.

4.   AutoCAD will boot, briefly displaying the text window with some messages, and the Graphics window will appear.

The AutoCAD graphics screen is illustrated in Figure I.4. Your screen might appear slightly different because of screen resolution. You can start AutoCAD for DOS by entering the name of the AutoCAD batch file, for example:

C:\> **acadr13** <return>

1.3.1   Beginning a new drawing

If you're starting a new drawing, you can name the drawing either at the beginning of the drawing session with the New command, or any time during the session with the Save As command. Normally you'll name the drawing before beginning drawing.

Move the cursor to the top of the screen into the Standard toolbar by using the mouse, and choose the New file tool by clicking on it once, as illustrated in Figure

Figure 1.12   AutoCAD icons.

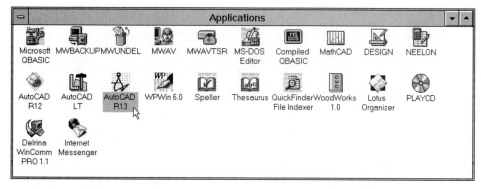

Figure 1.13 Starting AutoCAD for Windows.

1.14 (also see section A.1.2 in appendix A). You can also select the New command from the File menu in the menu bar. The Create New Drawing dialog box illustrated in Figure 1.15 will be displayed. (With DOS, select the New command in the pull-down File menu.)

The drawing is to be stored in the C:\Drawings directory created in section 1.2.4. (If you want to save your drawing on drive A:, read on but don't enter these commands.) Change to C:\ by clicking on New Drawing Name... in the New Drawing Name dialog box, as illustrated in Figure 1.15. (Command or selection options followed by an ellipsis (...) indicate that a dialog box will be displayed.) The Directories list box illustrated in Figure 1.16 is displayed. Choose drive C:\ in the directory list box by moving the cursor onto its icon and clicking the <pick> button twice, <pick> <pick>. Then choose the Drawings directory, as shown in Figure 1.17, by clicking twice on its icon. If the Drawings directory isn't visible in the Directories box, you might have to use the slider bar located on the right side of the box to scroll the list up or down.

Figure 1.14 Opening a new file.

Create New Drawing

Prototype...   acad.dwg

☐ No Prototype
☐ Retain as Default

New Drawing Name...

OK   Cancel

Figure 1.15 Create New Drawing dialog box.

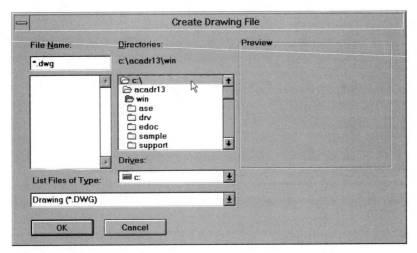

Figure 1.16 Directories list box.

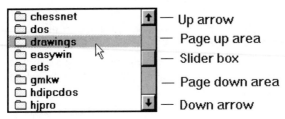

Figure 1.17 Choosing a directory.

Clicking the up or down arrow on the slider bar (see Figure 1.17) scrolls the list down or up by one item. To scroll the list one page at a time, select a point in the page up or page down area (above or below the slider box). To scroll through the list, move the cursor onto the slider box and hold the <pick> button down. You can then drag the slider box up or down to scroll the list. Release the <pick> button when the slider box is in the position you want.

The File Name entry box back in Figure 1.16 shows the filename as *.dwg. Auto-CAD drawings always have the extension .dwg. The current drawing is to be named Proj-1.dwg. Move the cursor into the File Name entry box and type **Proj-1**, as shown in Figure 1.18. (It isn't necessary to enter the extension because it's the default in the List Files of Type box.) Press the OK button to exit the dialog box by moving the cursor onto it and pressing the <pick> button. The Create New Drawing dialog box will be redisplayed with the drawing name, C:\Drawings\Proj-1.dwg, entered in the New Drawing Name box, shown in Figure 1.19.

If you want to save the drawing on a floppy diskette, for example on drive A: instead of C:\Drawings, select the drive from the drop-down Drives: list box located below the Directories list box back in Figure 1.16. Then enter the drawing name in the File Name: box, as explained previously.

1.3.2 Entering commands

You can enter AutoCAD commands by typing them or selecting them from the menu bar, toolbar, or toolbox. In this book, I'll usually show commands being selected from tool boxes. Appendix A displays all the tool bars, along with their associated actions.

To select commands in the toolbar, move the cursor arrow onto the desired tool with the mouse, as illustrated in Figure 1.20. If the desired toolbar (Draw, in this case) isn't displayed, read section 1.3.3. When the cursor is on the tool, a Tooltips box with the name of the tool is displayed, as shown in Figure 1.20. Press the <pick> button on the mouse once to invoke the command asssociated with the tool. Choose the Line command in the Draw toolbox. In the DOS version of AutoCAD, select the Line command from the Draw menu at the top of the screen.

The command window at the bottom of the monitor should now display Line from point:, which means that AutoCAD has invoked the Line command and is waiting for you to enter some data. Move the cursor into the drawing area of the

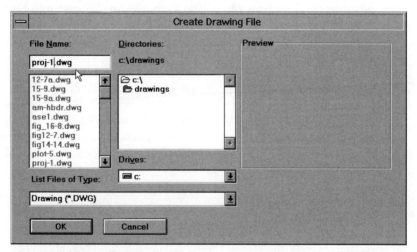

Figure 1.18 Naming a drawing.

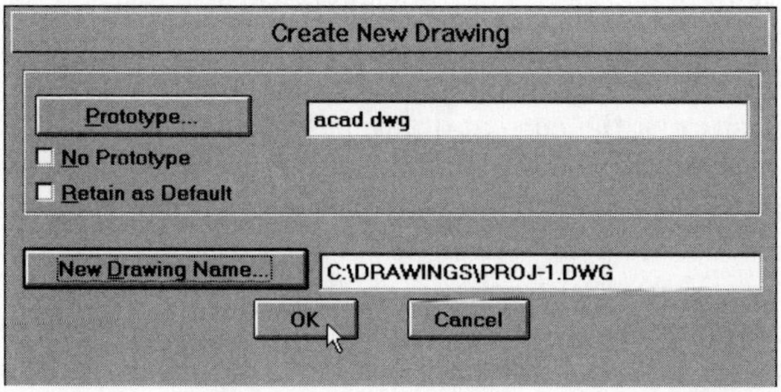

Figure 1.19 New drawing name.

Figure 1.20 Selecting a tool.

 Figure 1.21 Save tool.

screen and digitize a point by pressing the <pick> button on the mouse. The command window should now show To point:.

Move the cursor to another point and press the <pick> button on the mouse. Notice the command window. Move the cursor to another point, extending a line at an angle to the previous point, and pick that point. Now type a **c** in response to the command and press the <return> key on the keyboard, or the <return> button on the mouse (usually the middle or the 2 button), as follows:

To point: **c** <return>

Notice how the line segments close onto the first point and the Command window is no longer prompting for a point.

You have now completed your first drawing. Before continuing, save the drawing by choosing the Save tool (Figure 1.21) in the Standard toolbar (see section A.1.3 in appendix A). In the DOS version of AutoCAD, Save... is located in the File menu of the menu bar at the top of the screen:

Save <pick> (Windows)
File <pick> Save... <pick> (DOS)

The Save tool invokes the Qsave (quick save) command, which saves the current named drawing without requesting a filename. You can also specify Qsave by typing it from the keyboard. If the current drawing hasn't been named (see section 1.3.3), you'll be asked to enter a filename. This drawing is C:\DRAWINGS\PROJ-1.DWG or A:\PROJ-1.DWG, which was entered with the New tool when the drawing was started (refer back to Figure 1.19).

Save (Qsave) doesn't exit the current drawing, so you can continue the drawing. It's a good habit to save your drawing whenever you've drawn enough that you wouldn't want to have to redraw it if the system crashed. If that happens, you could reboot AutoCAD and continue the drawing from what was saved the last time with Qsave.

Each time the drawing is saved, AutoCAD makes a backup copy of the previous version by changing the file extension from .dwg to .bak, and saves the new copy of the drawing with a .dwg extension. So you always have two copies of a drawing. The latest copy is Proj-1.dwg and the previous copy is Proj-1.bak. If you save a drawing a third time, the .bak copy is deleted, the .dwg is renamed .bak, and the current version is saved with the extension .dwg.

1.3.3 Displaying toolbars

If a toolbar isn't visible on the screen in AutoCAD for Windows, you can bring it to the screen by choosing its tool in the Tool Windows flyout (see section A.1.11 in appendix A). For instance, to display the Draw toolbar, move the cursor onto the Tool Window tool (see section A.1 in appendix A) and press and hold the <pick> button. Then move the cursor into the Tool Windows flyout onto the Line tool and release the <pick> button, as illustrated in Figure 1.22. The Draw tool will then be displayed.

The toolbar is initally floating on the monitor, but you can "dock" it at the top, bottom, left, or right side of the monitor by moving the cursor onto the title of the toolbar and pressing and holding the <pick> button. Then move the cursor to the desired location using the mouse and release the <pick> button. As you move the toolbar, it might change shape, showing how it will look in the new location. To move a docked toolbar, place the cursor on the toolbar slightly above a tool (the grab area of the toolbar), then slide the toolbar to the desired location.

Figure 1.22 Displaying a toolbar.

You can change the shape of a floating toolbar by placing the cursor on its border where the cursor changes to a double sided arrow, as shown in Figure 1.23, and dragging the toolbar into the desired shape.

1.3.4 Canceling a command

After issuing an AutoCAD command, you can cancel it by pressing either the <esc> or, with DOS, the <ctrl> and C keys together on the keyboard.

1.3.5 Exiting AutoCAD

You've completed your first AutoCAD drawing. Exit the drawing editor and save your drawing by clicking on the File command in the Menu bar and choosing the Exit command, as illustrated in Figure 1.24 and shown here:

File <pick> Exit... <pick>

If you've already saved the drawing and not made any changes since the last save, you'll exit AutoCAD. If you haven't saved the drawing or have made changes since the last save, the Drawing Modifications options box shown in Figure 1.25 will be displayed. Select Save Changes... to save the drawing and exit AutoCAD.

1.4 Copying a File in Windows (for Windows 95, see appendix H)

If you've exited AutoCAD, you can copy file in Windows by using the File Manager window. As outlined in section 1.2.1, bring the Main application window to the desktop and then choose the File Manager icon to display the File Manager dialog box, illustrated back in Figure 1.3. Highlight the file to be copied following the procedure discussed earlier in this chapter. Then choose the File menu (refer back to Figure 1.4) and select Copy Disk... to display the Copy dialog box, illustrated in Figure 1.26. Note the current directory and drawing name in the From: box. Enter the location to copy the file to, e.g., A:\, as shown in Figure 1.26.

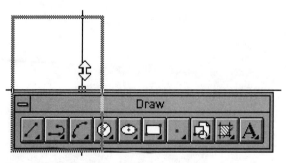

Figure 1.23 Modifying a toolbar shape.

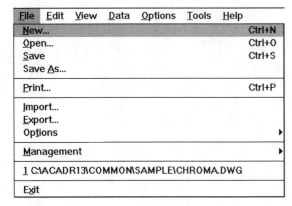

Figure 1.24 File menu.

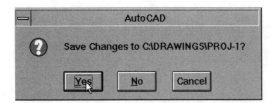

Figure 1.25 Drawing Modifications options box.

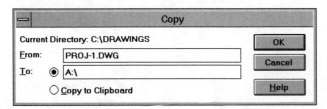

Figure 1.26   Copy File dialog box.

1.5   Renaming a File in Windows (for Windows 95, see appendix H)

To rename a file in Windows, choose the File Manager window, as described in section 1.2.1. Highlight the file to be renamed, as shown previously. Then choose Rename... in the File menu. A Rename dialog box similar to the one in Figure 1.26 will be displayed. Enter the new filename in the To: box.

2

Drawing Construction

Objective: Begin a new drawing (set limits, units, and precision), use draw commands (Line, Circle, Point, and Fillet), edit a drawing (Erase, Oops, Break, and Cancel), use display controls (Zoom all, extents, previous, and window), and use the Exit and Save commands.

Drawing: Start by booting AutoCAD as outlined in chapter 1, section 1.3. The procedure to draw the trapezoid illustrated in Figure 2.1 is outlined in the following text.

2.1 Load AutoCAD

Start AutoCAD for Windows by clicking on its icon as outlined in chapter 1, section 1.3. With DOS, at the DOS prompt enter the AutoCAD batch file, e.g., acadr13, and press <return>. AutoCAD's graphic window illustrated in Figure I.1 appears.

2.1.1 Beginning a new drawing

Although you can immediately begin drawing and name the drawing later using the Save As command, it's usually best to name a new drawing at the start of the session. Choose the New File tool in the Standard toolbar by moving the mouse onto its tool (see Figure 1.14) and pressing the <pick> button on the mouse. (With DOS select the New... command in the pull-down File menu.)

The Create New drawing dialog box illustrated in Figure 1.15 will be displayed. Click on the New Drawing Name... command button to display the Create Drawing File dialog box illustrated in Figure 1.16. Click twice quickly on c:\ in the Directories list box, as shown by the open arrow in Figure 1.16. Then select the Drawings subdirectory by clicking its name in the Directories list box, as illustrated in Figure 1.17.

Move the cursor to the File Name: entry box and press the <pick> button, and type the filename as **Proj-2**. Close the dialog box by clicking on OK. The Create New

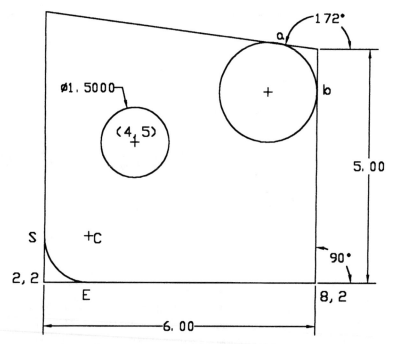

Figure 2.1 Project 2.

Drawing dialog box (Figure 1.19) will be redisplayed showing the new drawing name as C:\DRAWINGS\PROJ-2.DWG. If the drawing name is correct, click on the OK button to open the drawing file. If the name is incorrect, click on New Drawing Name... and repeat the procedure outlined above.

2.2 Screen Limits

Choose the following from the menu bar, as illustrated in Figure 2.2:

Data <pick> Drawing Limits <pick> ON/OFF/<Lower left corner> <0.0000, 0.0000>: Select the default coordinates of 0,0 displayed in the wedge brackets. <return> Upper right corner <12.0000,9.0000>: Use the default coordinates of 12 units horizontal and 9 units vertical. <return>

You can invoke the Limits command, like all standard AutoCAD commands, by typing **limits** and pressing <return> at the AutoCAD command prompt:

Command: **limits** <return>

2.3 Set Units and Precision

The drawing is to be done in decimal units, so select the following from the menu bar:

Data <pick> Units... <pick>

The Units Control dialog box illustrated in Figure 2.3 is displayed. The available units are:

Type	Example
1. Scientific	1.67E+01
2. Decimal	16.70
3. Engineering	1'–4.5
4. Architectural	1'–4½
5. Fractional	16½

The circles next to the options in the Units and Angles boxes are referred to as *radio buttons*. When a radio button is pressed (turned on), its center is filled, and only one radio button in a box can be on at a time. You turn on a radio button by clicking on it with the mouse. Turning on a new button will turn the previous one off.

Select the Units Decimal button, and the Angles Decimal degrees button, as shown in Figure 2.3.

The units should be precise to two digits to the right of the decimal. Click on the downward-pointing arrow on the right side of the Precision box at the bottom of the Units box to display the pop-up list box showing the precision options, illustrated in Figure 2.4. If the 0.00 precision isn't displayed, scroll the list up or down using the slider bar, as outlined in chapter 1, section 1.3.1, and select 0.00.

You can change the coordinate system used for designating angles. You'll usually want to use the Cartesian coordinate system illustrated in Figure 2.5. The angle 0 direction is east and positive angles are measured in a counterclockwise direction. Click on the Direction... command button in the Angles box and set the appropriate radio buttons, as illustrated in Figure 2.6, and press the OK button.

You can invoke the Units command from the command prompt by entering units.

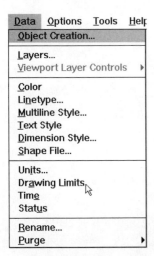

Figure 2.2 Data menu.

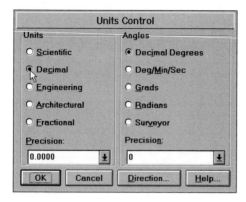

Figure 2.3 Units Control dialog box.

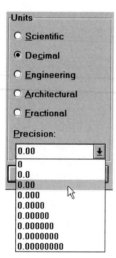

Figure 2.4 Units Precision drop down box.

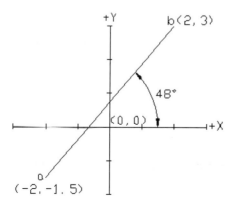

Figure 2.5 Cartesian coordinate system.

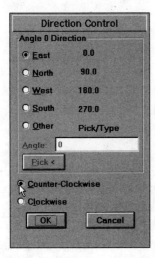

Figure 2.6 Direction Control dialog box.

2.4 Lines and the Cartesian Coordinate System

Two-dimensional points on the AutoCAD drawing screen are located based on the Cartesian coordinate system, illustrated back in Figure 2.5. In the Cartesian coordinate system, horizontal lines drawn from left to right are said to be along the X axis in a positive direction. Vertical lines drawn in an upward direction are said to be along the Y axis in a positive direction. Positive angles are measured from the positive X axis in a counterclockwise direction. In Figure 2.5, the coordinates of point b are 2,3 (2 along the positive X axis and 3 along the positive Y axis). The coordinates of point a are –2,–1.5. Line a-b is at an angle of 48 degrees. (Refer to chapter 15 for three-dimensional drawings.)

Lines. To draw a line, select the Line command from the Draw toolbar (in DOS, select Draw from the men bar, then Line):

Draw <toolbar> Line <pick>

The trapezoid shown back in Figure 2.1 will be drawn using the four available methods of drawing lines.

Lines by real coordinates. You can locate a point on the drawing by entering the screen coordinates of the point:

Line from point: **2,2** <return>

Lines by relative X Y distances. You can specify a point by entering its distances relative to the last point entered. To draw a line from coordinate 2,2 to coordinate 8,2, as illustrated in Figure 2.7, the relative distances from point 2,2 are 6.00 units in the X direction and 0 units in the Y direction. To draw the line using relative coordinates:

To point: **@6,0** <return>

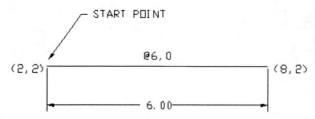

Figure 2.7 Line 1.

The @ symbol tells AutoCAD that the point is relative to the last point entered. In this case, the point is 6 units to the right and 0 units above the previous point. Points to the right of the previous point are positive and points above the previous point are positive. Negative points can be entered for relative points.

Lines by relative distance and angle. You can also locate points by giving their relative distance and angle with respect to the last point. To draw Line 2, in Figure 2.8:

To point: **@5<90** <return>

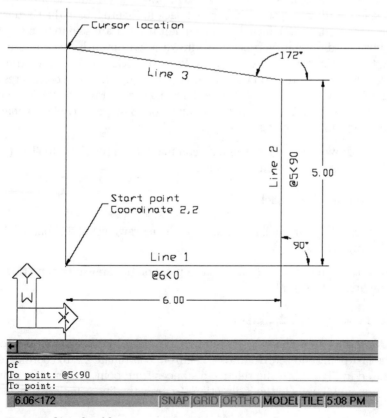

Figure 2.8 Lines 2 and 3.

The @ symbol tells AutoCAD that the point is relative to the last point entered. The < indicates that the next value is the angle of the line. Angles are based on rectangular Cartesian coordinates, where angles are positive if rotation from the X axis is counterclockwise and negative if rotation from the X axis is clockwise. Angles are always measured from the horizontal in degrees (unless you redefine the location of 0 degrees when defining the angle units; see the previous section on setting units and precision).

Lines by digitized points. You can enter points by locating them on the drawing screen using the cursor control keys, a mouse, or a digitizing tablet. First, press <ctrl>–D (hold down the <ctrl> key and press the D key) to turn on the display of the current screen coordinates, located in the left corner of the status bar, shown in Figure 2.8. (In DOS, it's located at the top of the screen.) Move the cursor around on the screen. If the coordinates displayed in the coordinate display window don't change as the cursor moves, press <ctrl>–D again.

You can display coordinates as X-Y (e.g., 5.25,3.10) or distance<angle (e.g., 4.10<56) by toggling <ctrl>–D. Toggle <ctrl>–D until distance<angle is displayed, and move the cursor on the screen until the distance to the next point is shown as 6.06<172. The vertical cursor should be lined up with the start point, 2,2, as illustrated in Figure 2.8. To locate the point accurately, move the cursor close to the desired point using the mouse. Then use the four arrow keys on the keyboard to locate the point precisely. When the coordinates display 6.06<172 and the vertical cursor line is aligned with the start point, press the <return> key on the keyboard (not on the mouse).

Close command. You can close a set of lines on the first point in the set by entering **C** from the keyboard:

To point: **C** <return>

If the trapezoid didn't close properly, the following section will help you resolve the problem.

2.5 Undo, Redo, and Cancel Commands

If you started the set of lines that were just completed from a new point (rather than the original start point), the last line drawn will close on the new start point. If the trapezoid didn't close on coordinate 2,2 (the start point), choose Undo (Figure 2.9) from the Standard toolbar. Redraw the line and close it on the coordinate 2,2. If you press Undo and you then want to undo the undo, press redo (Figure 2.10). If you don't end the Line command with Close, AutoCAD will request the next point. Press the <esc> key on the keyboard to cancel the command (in DOS, press Ctrl–C).

Figure 2.9 Undo tool.

Figure 2.10 Redo tool.

2.6 Circle Command

A circle that's 1.5 units in diameter is to be drawn with its center point at coordinates 4,5, as shown in Figure 2.11. Move the cursor onto the Circle tool in the Draw toolbar, as illustrated in Figure 2.12 (also see A.3 in appendix A). Press and hold the <pick> button on the mouse and slide the cursor along the flyout onto the Circle Center Diameter tool. Release the <pick> button to invoke the command. In DOS, the Circle command is located in the Draw menu. The commands are as follows:

Draw <toolbar> Circle Center Diameter <pick> 3P/2P/TTR <center point>: **4,5** <return> Diameter: **1.5** <return>

Now draw a circle using the Circle 3 Point command:

Draw <toolbar> Circle 3 Point <pick> 3P First point: Digitize point a, as shown in Figure 2.11. <pick> Second point: Digitize point b. <pick> Third point: Using the cursor, drag the third point of the circle to draw a circle similar to that shown in the figure. <pick>

Other circle commands are discussed in later chapters.

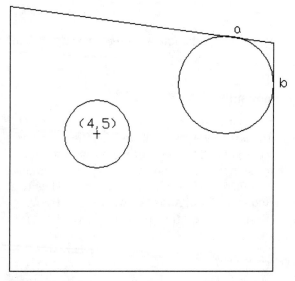

Figure 2.11 Circles.

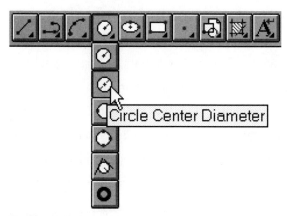

Figure 2.12 Circle tool flyout.

  Figure 2.13 Point tool.

2.7 Point Command

The point command places a point on the drawing. The command repeats, so you must cancel to exit. Choose the Point tool (Figure 2.13) in the Draw toolbar, or Draw menu in DOS:

Draw <toolbar> Point <pick> `Point:` Digitize a point on the drawing. <pick> `Point:` Press <esc> on the keyboard to cancel the command.

The default point style is Dot, but you can set other point styles from the Options menu (Figure 2.14) in the menu bar, as follows:

Options <pick> Display <pick> Point Style... <pick>

The Point Style dialog box illustrated in Figure 2.15 will be displayed. The default dot point is in the upper-left corner selection box. Select another point style by clicking on its selection box and then pressing OK. Retry the point command, then return the point style to Dot.

2.8 Arc Command

A number of arc options are available in AutoCAD:

3 point. Specifies three points on the arc.

Start Center End. Specifies the start, center, and endpoints.

Start Center Angle. Specifies the start point, center point, and included angle.

Start Center Length. Specifies the start point, center point, and length of chord.

Start End Angle. Specifies the start and endpoints and included angle.

Start End Direction. Specifies the start and endpoints and arc tangent direction.

Start End Radius. Specifies the start and endpoints and radius.

Center Start End. Specifies the center, start, and endpoints.

Center Start Angle. Specifies the center and start points and included angle.

Center Start Length. Specifies the center and start points and length of chord.

Arc Continue. Uses the first point of the arc at the last point entered on the drawing.

Choose the Start Center End tool in the Arc flyout of the Draw toolbar, as illustrated in Figure 2.16. In DOS, the Arc commands are in the Draw menu. The commands to draw the arc with a radius of 1, illustrated in Figure 2.17, are:

Draw <toolbar> Arc Start Center End <pick> arc Center/<Startpoint>: **2,3** <return> Center/End/<Second point>: _c Center: **@1<0** <return> Angle/Length of Chord <End point>: **@1<270** <return>

Notice that the start point was entered as real coordinates and the other points were entered as relative distance angles. The points could have been entered with any of the methods discussed for line drawing. Practice using some of the other arc commands, noting the following:

- Enter @ or choose Arc Continue to start the arc on the last point drawn.

- Arcs are always drawn counterclockwise.

- AutoCAD sets the drag mode for the last point, allowing you to visualize the arc as you move the cursor to select the last point.

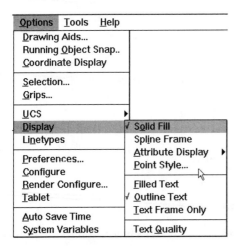

Figure 2.14 Options menu.

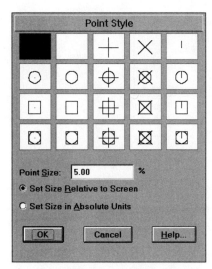

Figure 2.15 Point Style dialog box.

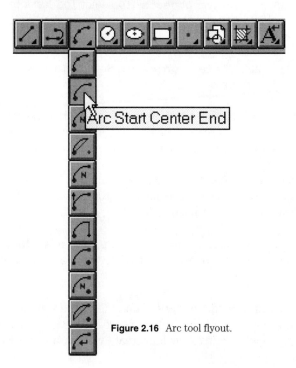

Figure 2.16 Arc tool flyout.

2.9 Erase and Oops Commands

Use the Erase command to erase whole entities. If a line has been drawn, you can use the Erase command to remove the entire line from the drawing. If a portion of the line is to be removed, use the Break command. The Erase command is in the Modify toolbox (the Modify menu for DOS). Load the Modify toolbox by choosing its tool in

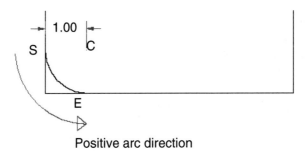

Positive arc direction

Figure 2.17 Arc.

the Tool Windows flyout, as outlined in chapter 1, section 1.3.3, and illustrated in Figure 2.18. Dock the Modify toolbar at the top of the screen (refer to chapter 1, section 1.3.3).

In the following, the last object drawn is erased. When the Erase tool (Figure 2.19) is chosen, AutoCAD requests `Select objects`. To select the last object drawn, choose the Select Last tool in the Select tool flyout, as shown in Figure 2.20 (in DOS, Last is in the Assist menu):

Modify <toolbar> Erase <pick> `Select objects:` Select <toolbar> Select Last <pick> `Select objects:` <return>

Note that the last object drawn, the arc, became dotted when Select Last was pressed, and was erased from the screen when the <return> key was pressed to exit the Erase command. You can enter Last from the keyboard as **L** in place of using the Select Last button.

Use the Oops command to cancel the last Erase command. The Oops tool is located in the Miscellaneous toolbar. The Miscellaneous toolbar isn't in the Tool Windows flyout, so you must load it from the command line, as follows:

`Command:` **toolbar** <return> `Toolbar name (or ALL):` **miscellaneous** <return> `Show/Hide/Left/Right/Top/Bottom/Float <Show>:` **r** <return> `Position <0,0>:` <return>

The Miscellaneous toolbar is docked along the right side of the screen. Choose the Oops button illustrated in Figure 2.21 to restore the arc. In DOS, Oops is located in the Modify menu. Oops should be invoked immediately following the Erase command. Choose the following:

Modify <toolbar> Erase <pick> `Select objects:` Place the cursor selection box on the circumference of the large circle <pick> `Select objects:` click on the bottom horizontal line of the trapezoid <return> `Select objects:` <return>

Notice that the selected objects became dotted when picked, indicating they were in the selection set, but they weren't removed from the screen until the final <return>

was pressed to exit the Erase command. Restore the erased objects using the Oops command.

Window selection box. Another method of selecting objects to be erased is using a window selection box. Enter the following commands:

Modify <toolbar> Erase <pick> Select objects: Move the cursor so the horizontal cursor line is slightly below the bottom of the large circle and the vertical cursor line is slightly to the left of the circle (Figure 2.22). <pick> Other corner: Move the cursor upward and to the right so the window created completely encloses the circle. <pick> Select objects: <return>

In a window selection box, the second point selected defining the box is always to the right of the first point, e.g., in Figure 2.22 the lower left corner is picked first and the upper right corner is picked second. Also, the first point of the window must *not* be on any object. Notice that, although the top line and the right side of the trapezoid were included in the window, they weren't erased. Only the circle that was entirely enclosed by the window was erased. In a window selection box, only whole objects are added to the selection set. When prompted by AutoCAD to Select objects:, entering **w** (window) from the keyboard also puts AutoCAD into the window box selection mode.

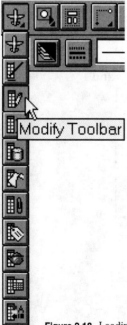

Figure 2.18 Loading the Modify toolbar.

Figure 2.19 Erase tool.

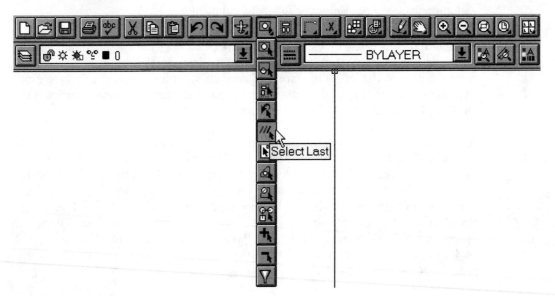

Figure 2.20 Select flyout.

Figure 2.21 Oops button.

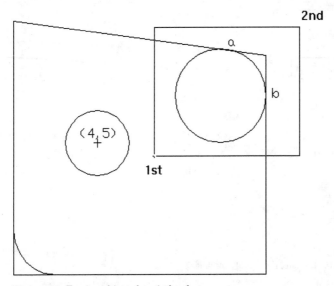

Figure 2.22 Erasing objects by window box.

Alternatively, you can select the Select Window button in the Select flyout. You'll then be asked to select the first and second points defining the window box. You can select these points from left to right or right to left, and they can fall on a drawing object. You could do this in a cluttered drawing where the first point defining the window box could fall on another object. Use the Oops command to restore the erased objects, and then choose the following:

Modify <toolbox> Erase <pick> `Select objects:` **w** <return> `Window First corner:` Select a corner of the window box to enclose the object to be erased. <pick> `Other corner:` Select the other corner of the window box. <pick> `Select objects:` <return>

Crossing selection box. All objects enclosed or cutting through a crossing selection box are added to the selection set. In a crossing selection box, the second point defining the selection box is always to the left of the first point. As with a window selection box, the first point used to start the box must not be on any object. Use the Oops option to restore the previously erased objects and repeat the Erase commands entered previously for the window selection box, but start the selection box by picking the upper right corner of the box first (see Figure 2.22). When the commands are completed, the circle and the top and right side lines of the trapezoid will be erased.

You can also invoke a crossing box by entering **c** (crossing) or choosing the Select Crossing tool in response to the `Select objects:` prompt. In this case, the order of selecting the defining points for the crossing box isn't crucial, and the points can fall on drawing objects. Restore the erased entities by using the Oops command, and use c to invoke a crossing box to select entities to be erased. Restore any erased objects. (You can invoke the Erase command by entering Erase at the command prompt.)

Remove and Add. Objects added to the selection set to be erased become dotted on the monitor. If you've selected an object and want to remove it from the selection set, choose the Select Remove button in the Select flyout (or enter **r**) in response to AutoCAD's `Select objects:` prompt. Any selected objects following that entry will be removed from the selection set. To return to the add mode, choose the Select Add button or enter **a** in response to `Select objects:`.

2.10 Redraw

Phantom lines and dots often remain on the screen after entities are erased or selected with other commands. You can clean up the screen at any time by choosing the Redraw tool in Figure 2.23, located in the Standard toolbar. Redraw is in the View menu in DOS. You can also enter Redraw at the command line by typing **redraw**.

2.11 Zoom

Use the Zoom command to enlarge or shrink the view of a portion of the drawing. The Standard toolbar (see section A.1 in appendix A) has tools for Zoom In, Zoom

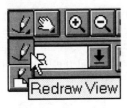

Figure 2.23 Redraw flyout.

Out, Zoom Window, and Zoom. Move the cursor onto the Zoom tool and display the flyout, as shown in Figure 2.24, and choose the Zoom Scale tool (in DOS, Zoom is located in the View menu):

Zoom <pick> Zoom Scale <pick> `All/Centre/Extents/Previous/Window/` `<Scale(X/XP)>:` **2** <return>

Entering a scale value of 2 will display the object twice as large as the full view. Press the <spacebar> or <return> key to recall the ZOOM command, and enter **0.5** for the zoom scale. Notice that the object is one-half as large as the full view. You can use the <spacebar> or <return> key to recall the previous command. To return the object to its original size, invoke the Zoom command and enter the scale as **2X**. This will zoom the screen to twice the size of the current screen. You can also enter **zoom** from the keyboard. To select Zoom Window in the Standard toolbar:

Zoom Window <pick> `First corner:` Digitize a corner of a window box to include points a and b (refer back to Figure 2.1). <pick> `Other corner:` Digitize the other corner of the window box. <pick>

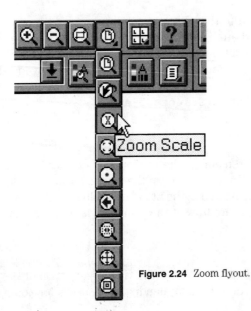

Figure 2.24 Zoom flyout.

Viewing the zoomed area, how accurate were you able to place the circle along the top of the line? I'll discuss a more precise method of placing lines tangent to circles in later projects. This exercise should demonstrate the difficulty of placing entities on a drawing without assistance from AutoCAD.

Try the Previous and Extents options of the Zoom command, noting the effect on the view. Also try the Zoom options listed below. Restore the original view based on the drawing limits by choosing the following:

Zoom <pick> Zoom All <pick>

The options of the Zoom command are as follows (their application is illustrated in later chapters):

Zoom In. Zooms the display to twice the current view.

Zoom Out. Zoom the display to half the current view.

Zoom Window. Zooms on an area defined by a selection window.

Zoom All. Zooms to display the entire drawing.

Zoom Previous. Zooms to display the previous view.

Zoom Scale. Zooms the display at a specified scale factor.

Zoom Dynamic. You define the zoom area using a view box.

Zoom Center. You specify the center and magnification value or height of a zoom window.

Zoom Left. You specify the left corner and magnification value or height of a zoom window.

Zoom Extents. Zooms to display the drawing extents.

Zoom Vmax. Zooms as far as possible without forcing a regeneration of the drawing.

2.12 Break

Use this command to delete a portion of an entity. Select the following from the Modify toolbar (in DOS, Break is in the Modify menu):

Modify <toolbar> Break 2 Points (Figure 2.25) <pick> Select object: Digitize a point on the top line of the trapezoid near the left end of the line. <pick> Enter second point (of F for first point): Digitize a point on the same line about 0.5 inches from the previous point. <pick>

A gap is made in the line between the selection point and the break point. Select Undo (refer back to Figure 2.9) in the Standard toolbar to undo the break, restoring the original line. Undo is in the Edit menu in DOS. You can also enter a single undo by typing **u** at the command line. The Undo command must be used immediately fol-

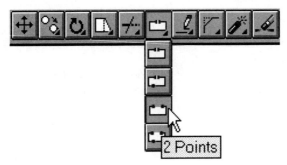

Figure 2.25 Break flyout.

lowing the command to be undone. You could restore Break by using the Redo tool (refer back to Figure 2.10), which undoes the last Undo.

Now you'll use the Break command to form a fillet by deleting the corner of the trapezoid from a to b (refer back to Figure 2.1) and the lower part of the circle from a to b. Select the following from the Modify toolbar:

Modify <toolbar> Break 2 Points Select <pick> Select object: Digitize a point on the top line of the trapezoid well to the left of the circle so AutoCAD is clear about what item is being selected (Figure 2.26). <pick> Enter second point (or F for First point): **f** Enter first point: Digitize the intersection point of the circle and the top side of the trapezoid, the first point. <pick> Enter second point: Digitize the end of the top line on the trapezoid at the top right corner of the trapezoid, the second point. <pick>

In the preceding commands, the 2 Points Select tool allows you to pick the object and then pick a first and second point of the break. Compare this with the Break command, where the point used to select the object and the first point of the break were the same. If the first point of the break falls on two entities, such as the circle and the line, AutoCAD must be told first which entity is to be used for the break.

Using the same procedure, break the line on the right side of the trapezoid from point b (refer back to Figure 2.1) to the top corner. When breaking a circle or arc, AutoCAD always breaks the entity in a counterclockwise direction between the first and second point. Select the following to break the circle from a to b (refer back to Figure 2.1):

Modify <toolbar> Break 2 Points Select <pick> Select object: Digitize a point on the circumference of the circle, clear of any of the lines (Figure 2.27). <pick> Enter second point (of F for first point): f Enter first point: Digitize the first point. <pick> Enter second point: Digitize the second point. <pick>

You can also enter the Break command by typing **break** at the command line. The break tools are:

1 Point. Breaks the object at the selection point.

1 Point Select. Requests selection of the object and a break point, and breaks the object at the break point.

2 Points. Uses the selection point as the first point of the break and requests the second break point.

2 Points select. Requests selection of the object and two break points, and breaks the object between the two break points.

2.13   Exiting a Drawing

Save the drawing by choosing the Save button (see Figure 1.21) located in the Standard toolbar. This enters the Save command, which saves the drawing using the name and file path specified when the drawing was opened. For DOS, use the Save... option in the File menu. The following commands in the File menu (see Figure 1.24) are used to save and exit a drawing:

Save..... Saves the drawing using the current drawing name without exiting the drawing. You can enter this command from the keyboard as **QSAVE.**

Save as..... Saves the drawing allowing you to enter the filename. You can enter this command from the keyboard as **SAVE.**

Exit.. Exits AutoCAD. If the drawing file hasn't been saved and changes have been made to the drawing, the Drawing Modifications options box (Figure 1.25) will be displayed, asking if you want to save the drawing before exiting. You can enter the **QUIT** command from the keyboard to exit a drawing without saving changes.

This drawing was named C:\Drawings\Proj-2.Dwg in section 2.1.1. Choose the Save... command in the File menu to save the drawing.

   Get in the habit of saving a backup copy of your drawings. To save a copy on a floppy diskette, place a formatted diskette in drive A: and select the following:

File <pick> Save as... <pick>

The Save Drawing As dialog box illustrated in Figure 2.28 will be displayed. Display the drop-down Drives menu and select drive A:, as shown. This will change the di-

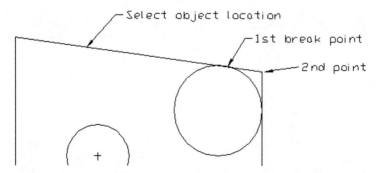

Figure 2.26 Break points on line.

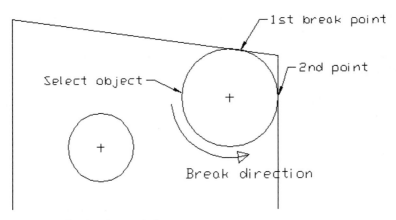

Figure 2.27 Break points on circle.

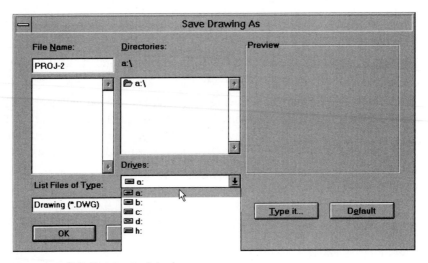

Figure 2.28 Save Drawing As dialog box.

rectory to A:\. the filename is shown as Proj-2. Press OK to save the file on the floppy in drive A:.

The Type it option allows you to type the drawing directory and name from the command line. Choose the Exit option in the File menu to exit AutoCAD.

3

Relocating Objects

Objective: Practice commands from the previous project; use grips to edit an object; use Move, Offset, and Copy commands; draw circles using Tangent Tangent Radius; draw center ticks and center lines for circles; save drawings.

Drawing: Boot AutoCAD and begin a new drawing (review chapter 2, section 2.1.1) with the name c:\ drawings\proj-3. Draw the V-box illustrated in Figure 3.1 using the procedures outlined in this chapter.

3.1 Set Units and Precision

Set the drawing units to decimal, with two digits to the right of the decimal point. Refer back to chapter 2, section 2.3 for the procedure. Press <ctrl>–D or F6 to turn the cursor position coordinate display on.

3.2 Drawing Screen Limits

The V box will require a space of about 6 × 5 units. The default AutoCAD screen limits are 0,0 (lower left corner) and 12,9 (upper right corner). AutoCAD drawings are always drawn in 1:1 scale on the monitor. If scaling needs to be done, it will be done when the drawing is plotted. The screen "size" will be reduced to 6,5. In order to start the lower left corner of the V box at 0,0, the lower left corner of the screen will be set as –1,–1 and the upper right corner will be 5,4. The commands are:

Data <pick> Drawing Limits <pick> Lower left corner <0.0000,0.0000>:
–1,–1 <return> Upper right corner <12.0000,9.0000>: **5,4** <return>

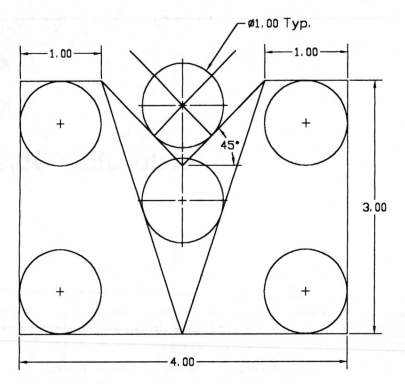

Figure 3.1 Project 3.

A tick will appear on the screen locating the new limits. Use the Zoom All tool in the Standard toolbar (refer back to Figure 2.24) to reset the monitor view to the new limits (In DOS, Zoom is in the View menu):

Zoom All <pick>

Note: Each time the screen limits are changed, you must use the Zoom All tool to reset the monitor to the new limits.

3.3 V-Box Drawing

Draw the perimeter of the V box. Select the Line tool in the Draw toolbar and start the lower left corner of the V box at coordinate 0,0. Draw the V box in a counterclockwise direction. Try to draw the lines for the object without looking at the commands following this paragraph. If you draw a line and want to change it, select the Undo tool immediately after the line is drawn to undo it. If Undo is invoked during a line sequence, only the last line will be undone. If Undo is invoked after you exit the Line command, all lines drawn in the sequence will be undone. To undo an Undo, invoke Redo. Refer to chapter 2, section 2.5.

Draw <toolbox> Line <pick> From point: **0,0** <return> To point: **@3<90** <return> Undo <pick> To point: **@4<0** <return> To point: **@3<90** <return> To point: **@1<180** <return> To point: **@–1,–1** <return> To point: **@–1,1** <return> To point: **@1<180** <return> To point: **c** <return>

The @–1,–1 coordinates specify that the bottom of the V is 1 unit to the left (positive) and 1 unit below (negative) the top right side of the V. The relative coordinates to draw the line from the bottom of the V to the top left end are @–1,1. Notice how the Undo tool was used to correct an input error in the sequence.

Save your drawing prior to continuing so you won't lose the work you've done up to this point if the computer crashes for any reason. Refer to chapter 2, section 2.13.

3.4 Moving Objects

A circle one unit in diameter is to be drawn in the V at the top of the V box. In order to demonstrate a number of commands, four different methods will be used to locate the circle in the V. The circle is initially drawn above the V in the initial position illustrated in Figure 3.2:

Draw <toolbar> Circle Center Diameter <pick> Circle 3P/2P/TTR <center point>: Using the cursor, pick the initial center point of the circle (Figure 3.2). <pick> Diameter: **1** <return>

Prior to moving the circle into the V, the working area is zoomed. Choose the Zoom Window tool in the Standard toolbar (see section A.1 in appendix A) to enlarge the area defined by the window box in Figure 3.2. In DOS, Zoom is in the View menu.

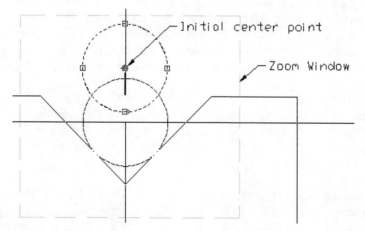

Figure 3.2 Moving objects.

3.4.1 Move command

Click on the Move tool in the Modify toolbar (see section A.4 in appendix A). In DOS, Move is in the Modify Menu:

Modify <toolbar> Move <pick> Select objects: Click on the circumference of the circle. <pick> Select objects: <return> Base point or displacement: Digitize a point on the bottom of the circle directly above the V. <pick> Second point of displacement: Using the mouse, drag the circle down until its sides are tangent to the sides of the V. <pick>

In the Move command, you can either drag the second point into place or enter a numeric coordinate or relative coordinate value. Notice that the original circle isn't erased until the second point is entered. If a shadow of the original circle is left on the drawing, press the Redraw tool in the Standard toolbar to redraw the screen.

Use the Undo tool (Figure 2.9) to undo the Move command, returning the circle to its original position. If you used Redraw, you might have to use Undo twice. In DOS, Undo is in the Assist menu.

3.4.2 Grips

Pick a point on the circumference of the circle. The circle becomes highlighted and small blue boxes, called *grips*, appear on the circumference and at the center of the circle, as illustrated in Figure 3.2. Highlighted entities can be manipulated with the grips. If the grips didn't appear, set the Grips system variable to 1, as follows, and retry the previous procedure:

Command: **grips**
New value for GRIPS <0>: **1** <return>

The cursor will have a small target box at its intersection, indicating that the Grips system variable is set to 1. Move the target box onto the grip at the center of the circle and press the <pick> button. The grip will fill in, becoming hot (red) indicating it will serve as the basis for editing. The first grip mode is Stretch. Press the <return> key on either the keyboard or the mouse to change the grip mode to Move:

STRETCH
<Stretch to point>/Base point/Copy/Undo/eXit: <return>
MOVE
<Move to point>/Base point/Copy/Undo/eXit: Drag the circle into the V using the mouse. <pick>

Grip commands toggle through Stretch, Move, Rotate, Scale, and Mirror when you press <return>. Click on a grip on the circle circumference and try stretching it. Then use the Undo tool to undo the stretch. Turn the grips off by pressing the <esc> key on the keyboard. (Refer to appendix D for more information on using grips.)

3.5 Offset

Use the Erase tool to erase the original circle. The next procedure to draw the circle in the V demonstrates the Offset command. Since the circle has a radius of 0.5 units, lines drawn 0.5 units parallel to the sides of the V will cross at the center of the circle, as illustrated in Figure 3.3. The Offset command is in the Copy flyout (see Figure 3.4 and section A.4.2 in appendix A) of the Modify toolbar (Offset is in the Modify menu in DOS):

Modify <toolbar> Offset <pick> Offset distance or Through <Through>: **0.5** <return> Select object to offset: Click on one of the V lines. <pick> Side to offset: Click on the side V where the line is to be offset. <pick> Select object to offset: Click on one of the V lines. <pick> Side to offset: Click on the side V where the line is to be offset. <pick> Select object to offset: <return>

Draw a 1.0-diameter circle, selecting the crossing point of the offset lines as the center. Use the Erase tool in the Modify toolbar (Erase is in the Modify menu in DOS) to erase the offset lines. Then save your drawing.

3.6 Copy

The Copy tool is located in the Modify toolbar's Copy flyout (see Figure 3.4 and section A.4.2 in appendix A). Practice using the Copy command to copy the circle:

Modify <toolbar> Copy <pick> Select objects: Digitize the circumference of the circle. <pick> Select objects: <return> <Base point or displacement>/ Multiple: Digitize a point on the circle. <pick> Second point of displacement: Drag a copy of circle to the desired location. <pick>

Use the Undo tool to undo the copy. Press the spacebar to repeat the Copy command:

Select objects: Digitize the circumference of the circle. <pick> Select objects: <return> <Base point or displacement>/Multiple: **m** <return> Base point: Digitize a point on the circle. <pick> Second point of displacement: Drag a copy of circle to the top left corner of the V box. <pick> Second point of displacement: Drag a copy of the circle to each of the other corners. <pick> Second point of displacement: <return>

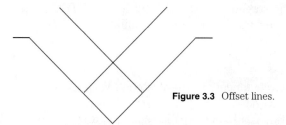

Figure 3.3 Offset lines.

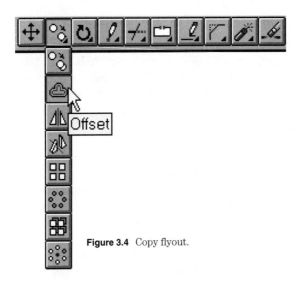

Figure 3.4 Copy flyout.

3.7 Stretch and Copy with Grips

Click twice on ORTHO in the status line at the bottom of the screen (see Figure 3.5), turning the orthogonal mode on. Ortho is on when its text is no longer grayed out. Ortho constrains movement of the cursor in a vertical or horizontal direction when drawing or modifying objects.

Click on the two 1-unit horizontal lines at the top of the V box and the two lines forming the V, turning on their grips, as shown in Figure 3.5. Then click on the grip at the bottom of the V, making it the hot (red) controlling grip. If the Stretch mode isn't the current mode (see the Command window at the bottom of the screen), press <return> until it is current. Enter **c** from the keyboard to set stretch to copy. The command window will display the text shown in Figure 3.5, indicating stretch is in the multiple stretch (copy) mode. This is similar to the multiple copy mode used in the previous set of commands. Move the cursor to the bottom line of the V box, stretching a copy of the V, as shown in Figure 3.5. Notice how Ortho makes it easier to set the cursor on the line since you don't have to worry about moving the cursor at an angle. When the tip of the V is on the bottom line of the V box, press the <pick> button. Press <return> to exit the multiple Stretch command. Notice that the original V remains in position because Stretch was in the copy mode.

Press the <esc> key on the keyboard twice to turn the grips off. Then use the Redraw tool to clean up the screen. Finally, click twice on ORTHO in the status bar, turning Ortho off. Save your drawing before continuing.

3.8 Drawing Circles Using TTR

Draw a 1-unit diameter circle tangent to the stretched V:

Draw <toolbar> Circle Tan Tan Radius <pick> Enter Tangent spec: Digitize a point on one side of the stretched V. <pick> Enter second Tangent spec: Digitize the other side of the stretched V. <pick> `Radius <0.5>:` **0.5** (if it isn't shown as the default value; otherwise, press <return> to accept the default)

Notice how easy and precise it is to place a circle tangent to two lines using this command.

3.9   Drawing Center Marks and Lines

The style and size of circle center marks are governed by the number stored in the dimension variable Dimcen. If the number stored in Dimcen is zero, no center marks are drawn. If a positive number is stored, center ticks are used. If a negative number is stored in Dimcen, then center lines are used. The default value of Dimcen is 0.09. You can set these values at the command line or by using the Dimension Styles dialog box.

Load the Dimension toolbar by choosing the Dim toolbar in the Tool Window, as illustrated in Figure 3.6 (also refer back to section 1.3.3 in chapter 1). Dock the Di-

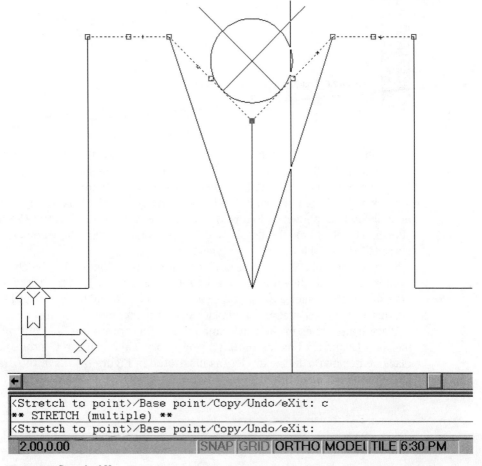

```
<Stretch to point>/Base point/Copy/Undo/eXit: c
** STRETCH (multiple) **
<Stretch to point>/Base point/Copy/Undo/eXit:
```

2.00,0.00 |SNAP|GRID|ORTHO|MODEL|TILE|6:30 PM

Figure 3.5 Stretched V.

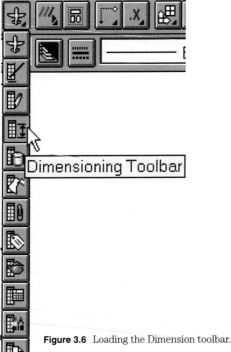

Figure 3.6 Loading the Dimension toolbar.

mension toolbar on the left side of the screen. Choose the Dimension Styles tool, shown in Figure 3.7, to display the Dimension Styles dialog box, illustrated in Figure 3.8. In DOS, the Dimension Style selection is in the Data menu.

Click on the Geometry bar in the Dimension Styles dialog box to display the Geometry dialog box, shown in Figure 3.9. Press the Mark button in the Center box, as shown. The Size box should show 0.09. Press OK to exit the Geometry box, and press OK to exit the Dimension Styles box.

Place center marks in corner circles (refer back to Figure 3.1) by clicking on the Center Mark tool, shown in Figure 3.10. In DOS, Center is in the Dim menu. When choosing a circle, click a point on its circumference. Recall the command by pressing <return> or the <spacebar>, and place center marks in each of the corner circles.

Place center lines in the remaining circles. First press the Line button in the dimension Geometry box, as outlined previously. Then use the Center Mark tool to place center marks in the circles, as illustrated in Figure 3.1. Save the drawing and also save a backup of the drawing. Then Exit AutoCAD.

Figure 3.7 Dimension Styles tool.

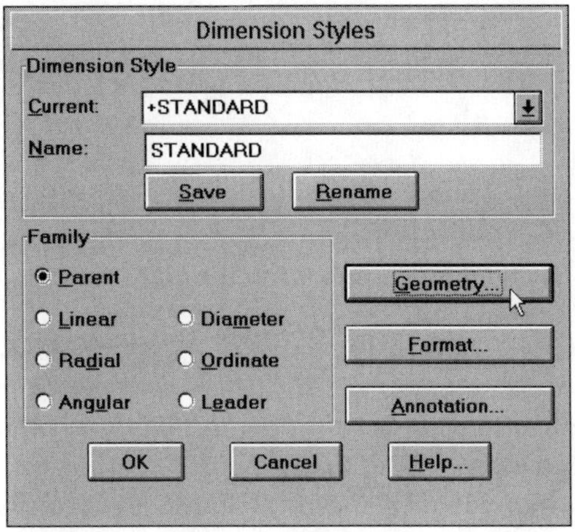

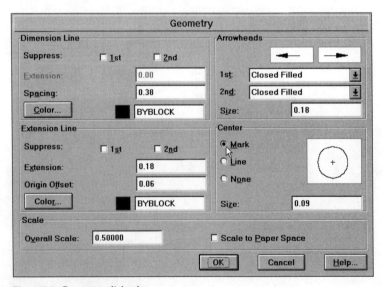

Figure 3.8 Dimension Styles dialog box.

Figure 3.9 Geometry dialog box.

Figure 3.10 Center Mark tool.

4

Dimensioning

Objective: Dimension a drawing; calculate and set dimension scale; set dimension controls; use linear, angular, and radius dimensioning; use last point and the arc command; and calculate text scale.

Drawing: Boot AutoCAD and start a new drawing named c:\drawings\proj-4. Complete the drawing shown in Figure 4.1, including all dimensions and text, following the procedures outlined in this chapter.

4.1 Set Drawing Limits and Units

Set the drawing units to decimal, with one digit to the right of the decimal. Refer to chapter 3 if you have trouble. Set the limits of the monitor so that a 14 × 10-unit object will fit the screen and also allow room for dimensions. The lower-left corner of the object will be started at coordinate 0,0, so that corner of the monitor will need negative coordinates. The limits can be reset at any time during the drawing process.

4.2 Drawing Lines and Arcs

Begin drawing the perimeter using the lower-left corner as coordinate 0,0, and draw in a counterclockwise direction:

Draw <toolbar> Line <pick> `Line from point:` **0,0** <return> `To point:` **@8<0** <return> `To point:` **@1<90** <return> `To point:` **@4<0** <return>

4.2.1 Last point

Draw an arc starting from the end of the last line drawn. That point is the last point drawn by AutoCAD, and is referred to as *last point*. When AutoCAD requests a point

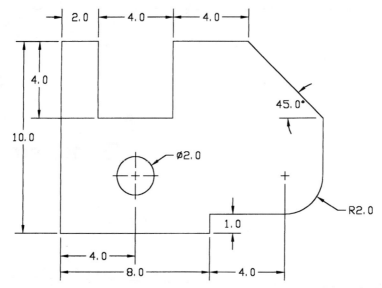

Figure 4.1 Project 4.

and the point is the same as the last point drawn, you can indicate that the last point is to be used by entering **@** at the keyboard. There is also an arc tool named Arc Continue, which uses the last point as the start point of the arc.

To draw the arc with a radius of 2 units and starting at the last point, use the Arc Continue tool in the Arc flyout (refer back to Figure 2.16 in chapter 2) of the Draw toolbar (in DOS, Arc Continue is in the Draw, Arc menu). AutoCAD uses the last point as the start point of the arc and requests the second point of the arc. Arcs are drawn in a counterclockwise direction by AutoCAD. The center of the arc is 2 units directly above the start point, and the end of the arc is 2 units directly to the right of its center (see Figure 4.1). The relative coordinate of the end of the arc from the start point is then @2,2:

Draw <toolbar> Arc Continue <pick> Center/<Start point>: End point: **@2,2** <return>

Draw the remainder of the perimeter of the object. If you draw a line incorrectly, use the Undo tool to undo it and then redraw the line. To start the line sequence at the end of arc—the last point drawn—use the relative @ command. When drawing the diagonal line, use relative coordinates to locate the next point. Enter real coordinates of 0,0 to close the perimeter on the first point. Then press <return> to exit the Line command:

Line <pick> From point: **@** <return> To point: **@3<90** <return> To point: **@–4,4** <return> (etc.)

Draw the circle two units in diameter with its center at coordinate 4,3. Save your drawing before continuing.

4.3 Set Text Scale

When using AutoCAD, height or size refers to the number of drawing units. The number of units used for the size of text and dimension variables must reflect either the drawing limits set or the size desired for the text and dimensions on the plotted drawing. We'll consider two methods to calculate the text height: the first based on a drawing not plotted to scale, and the second based on a scaled plot.

4.3.1 Method 1: a drawing not plotted to scale

To calculate the text height, assume the following specifications for this drawing:

- Limits are set as –3, –3, and 17,13, giving a drawing size of 20 × 16 units.
- Plot size is to be an A-size sheet (11 by 8.5 inches).
- Text height desired on the plotted sheet is $\frac{3}{16}$ inch (0.1875 inch).

AutoCAD lettering height, h, is calculated by setting up a ratio of:

$$\frac{\text{screen text height}}{\text{screen dimension}} = \frac{\text{plot text height}}{\text{plot dimension}}$$

Based on the drawing height, h/16 = 0.1875/8.5, giving h = 0.35. Based on the drawing width, h/20 = 0.1875/11, giving h = 0.34. The larger value governs, so for lettering set h = 0.35. When text is inserted into a drawing, AutoCAD requests the text height. If the drawing isn't to be plotted to scale, enter 0.35.

4.3.2 Method 2: a drawing plotted to scale

If the drawing is to be plotted to scale, the text height is calculated based on the plot scale. Assume this drawing is drawn in inch units and is to be plotted on an A-size sheet (8.5 by 11 inches). A drawing plot scale of 1 inch = 2 inches, or ½ scale, should be satisfactory. If the text height on the plotted drawing is to be $\frac{3}{16}$ (0.1875 inch), the height (h) of the text on the monitor is calculated as ½ × h = 0.1875, giving h = 0.375 drawing units (inches).

Text won't be added to this drawing, but the text height of 0.375 units will be used to calculate the height of dimension text and other dimension variables.

4.4 Dimension Scale

You can set dimension variables (arrow size, dimension text height, extension line offsets, circle and arc center lines or marks, etc.) individually or set the scale factor for all dimensions (Dimscale). The default value for Dimscale is 1. AutoCAD's default size for dimension text is 0.18 drawing units, assuming AutoCAD's measurement system is set to English units (refer to section 6.13 in chapter 6) multiplied by Dimscale, which has a default setting of 1.

In section 4.3.2 it was determined that the text should be 0.375 units high on the monitor to obtain ³⁄₁₆-inch text on the plotted drawing. Dimscale is calculated with the following formula:

$$\text{Dimscale} \times 0.18 = \text{Text height}$$
$$\text{Dimscale} \times 0.18 = 0.375, \text{ giving Dimscale} = 2.1$$

4.5   Setting Dimension Variables

The Dimension toolbar was loaded for Proj-3 and should be docked on the right side of the monitor. If it isn't loaded, follow the process outlined in section 1.3.3 in chapter 1. Click on the Dimension Styles tool to display the Dimension Styles dialog box, shown back in Figure 3.8 in chapter 3. In DOS, select Data, then Dimension Style.

The Parent button in the family box, should be pressed on. This indicates that the settings to be made are generic for all dimension types. Click the Geometry... command button to display the Geometry dialog box illustrated in Figure 4.2.

In the Scale box of the Geometry dialog box, set the scale to 2.1, as illustrated in Figure 4.2. Then click the Line radio button in the Center box. The circle marks in the display will change to center lines, as shown. Click the OK button to exit the Geometry box and return to the Dimension Styles dialog box.

Click the Annotation... command button to display the Annotation dialog box, illustrated in Figure 4.3. Then click on the Units... command button in the Primary Units box to display the Primary units dialog box, shown in Figure 4.4. Click on the

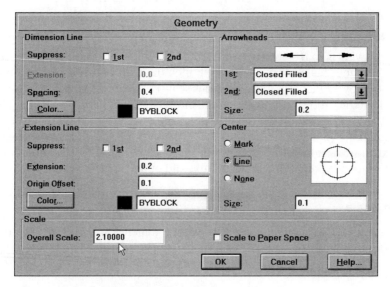

Figure 4.2 Geometry (dimension) dialog box.

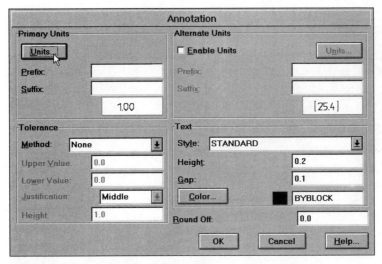

Figure 4.3 Annotation (dimension) dialog box.

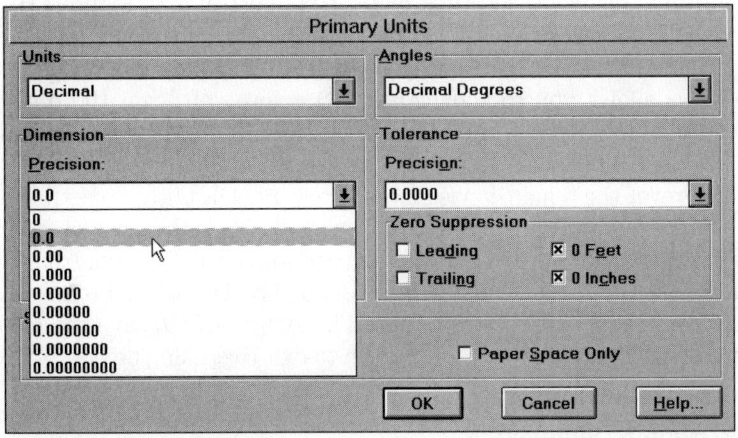

Figure 4.4 Primary Units dialog box.

down arrow to the right of the Precision box to display the precision drop-down box, as illustrated in Figure 4.4. Choose a precision of 0.0 for all dimensions, as shown. Press the OK button to return to the Annotation dialog box (Figure 4.3). Press the OK button to return to the Dimension Styles dialog box.

4.5.1 Radial and diameter variables

The Dimension Style dialog box is currently on the screen. Specific settings will be made for radial (diameter, radius) dimensioning. Click the Radial radio button in the Family box. The changes to be made affect the current dimension style, which is named Standard. Consequently, AutoCAD displays an Alert box, shown in Figure 4.5, asking if you want to save the changes to the current style. Press the Yes button

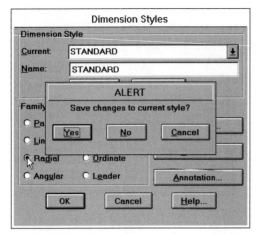

Figure 4.5 Alert box.

to save the changes to the Standard style. The Alert box will be removed from the screen and the Dimension Style dialog box will be visible. Click the Format... command button to display the Format dialog box, illustrated in Figure 4.6.

The radial dimensions are to be drawn as leaders, as shown in Figure 4.1. In the Format dialog box, click the User Defined box on (it's on when there's an × in it). This options allows you to show AutoCAD where you want the dimension to be placed during placement of the radial dimension. Display the drop-down Fit box, as shown in Figure 4.6, and choose Text and Arrows so the text and arrows are kept together wherever the dimension is placed. Press the OK button to exit the dialog box.

The Dimension style dialog box is displayed. Click the Diameter button in the Family box and make the same setting as used for radial. When the diameter settings are completed and the Dimension Style dialog box is returned to the screen, press the Save command button, as illustrated in Figure 4.7, to save the changes to the Standard style. Then press the OK button to exit the dialog box.

4.6 Diameter and Radius Dimensions

Set the drawing limits to –3,–3 and 17,13 to allow room for dimensions. Remember to Zoom All to set the monitor to the new drawing limits. Choose the Diameter Dimension tool from the Dimensioning toolbar, as shown in Figure 4.8 (in DOS, choose Dimensioning, then Radial, then Diameter):

Dimensioning <toolbar> Diameter Dimensioning <pick> Select arc or circle: Digitize a point on the top right side of the circumference of the 2.0 diameter circle where you want the arrow head for the diameter dimension to start (Figure 4.1). <pick> Dimension line location (Text/Angle): Digitize the leader length by moving the cursor to draw the leader. <Pick>

If the default value isn't what you want, enter **t** (text) in response to Dimension line location (Text/Angle): and AutoCAD will request the text value.

The 2.0-radius arc is to have center marks. Display the Dimension Style dialog box, press the Radial family button, and then press the Geometry... command button. Change the center style to Mark in the Center box of the Geometry dialog box (refer back to Figure 4.2). Press OK to exit the Geometry dialog box. Press Save command button in the Dimension Style dialog box and then press OK to exit.

Choose the Radius Diameter tool in the Dimensioning toolbar and dimension the arc, as shown back in Figure 4.1. Save the drawing before continuing.

4.7 Linear Dimensioning

Linear dimensioning can be horizontal, vertical, aligned (parallel to a diagonal line), or rotated (drawn at a specified angle, not necessarily parallel to the item being dimensioned).

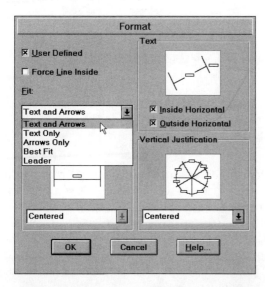

Figure 4.6 Format dialog box.

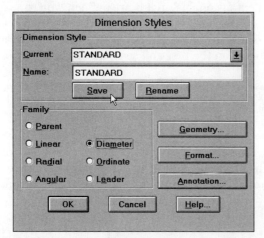

Figure 4.7 Saving the changes.

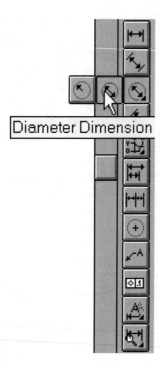

Figure 4.8 Radial Dimension flyout.

When linear dimension commands are invoked, AutoCAD requests the `First extension line origin or RETURN to select:`. If you select a point, it's taken as the first extension line origin (see Figure 4.9) and you're then asked to select the second extension line origin. If you press <return> instead, AutoCAD will respond with `Select line, arc, or circle:`. If a line or arc is selected, the first and second extension line origins will automatically be taken by AutoCAD as the endpoints of the line or arc. If a circle is selected, the diameter will be used for the first and second extension line origins.

Once the first and second extension line origins are defined, you're asked for the `Dimension line location`. The point entered is where the dimension line will be drawn (see Figure 4.9). AutoCAD then prompts you to enter the dimension text, using the distance measured between the first and second extension line origins as a default dimension.

Add the dimensions along the top of the figure, as follows (in DOS, from the Draw menu choose Dimensioning, then Linear):

Dimensioning <toolbar> Linear Dimension (Figure 4.10) <pick> `First extension line origin or RETURN to select:` <return> `Select line, arc or circle:` Pick a point on line a-b (Figure 4.11) close to end a. <pick> `Dimension line location (Text/Angle/Horizontal/Vertical/Rotated):` Pick point c. <pick>

The dimension is placed where specified with a value of 2.0. If a different dimension text is to be used than that shown by AutoCAD while the dimension line is being selected, enter **t** (text) in response to Dimension line location (Text/Angle/ Horizontal/Vertical/Rotated):, and AutoCAD will request the text value. Other options will be discussed later.

In the dimensioning, <return> was pressed when AutoCAD prompted for First extension line origin or RETURN to select:. This forced AutoCAD into its automatic extension line mode and you were asked to select the line, arc, or circle to be dimensioned. By selecting line a-b near end a, you told AutoCAD to use end a as the first extension line origin. This is necessary because the Continue option is to be used to continue the dimension string and Continue uses the second extension line origin in the dimension to be continued, point b in this case, as its first extension line origin.

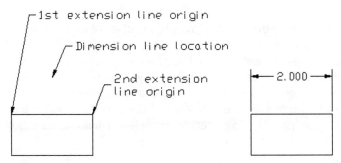

Figure 4.9 Dimensioning.

Figure 4.10 Linear Dimension tool.

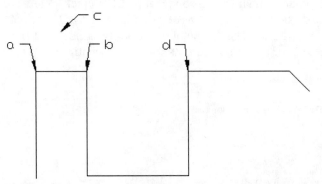

Figure 4.11 Dimension selection points.

4.7.1 Continuous dimensions

When dimensions are continuous on top of the drawn plate, you can use the Continue Dimension tool (Figure 4.12) to complete the string of dimensions (for DOS, use Draw, then Dimension, then Continue):

Dimensioning <toolbar> Continue Dimension <pick> `Second extension line origin or RETURN to select:` Pick point d. <pick> `Second extension line origin or RETURN to select:` Pick the next point. <Pick> `Second extension line origin or RETURN to select:` <return> <return>

Note that you must press <return> twice to exit the Continue Dimension command. AutoCAD doesn't allow you to enter specific dimension text (also see appendix D, section D.3).

4.7.2 Undo

If a dimension is inserted incorrectly, Press the Undo tool to undo the dimension. If you undo the wrong dimension, use Redo to restore the Undo. Undo won't function during the Dimension Continue option. Exit the command and then press Undo and retry the dimension. For more information on Undo, refer to appendix D.

If you want to change dimension text, enter **dimedit** at the command line and then enter **n** (new) and the new text. If you selected the wrong extension line origin, you can stretch the dimension to the correct location (see chapter 13, section 13.2.5).

4.7.3 Baseline dimensions

Use the Baseline Dimension tool (Figure 4.13) to draw a series of dimensions from a baseline, such as the 4.0- and 8.0-unit dimensions along the base of the object (refer back to Figure 4.1). Both use the left side of the object as a baseline (for DOS, choose Draw, then Dimension, then Baseline):

Dimensioning <toolbar> Linear Dimension (Figure 4.10) <pick> `First extension line origin or RETURN to select:` Digitize point a. (Figure 4.14) <pick> `Second extension line:` Digitize point b. <pick> `Dimension line location (Text/Angle/Horizontal/Vertical/Rotated):` Digitize point c. <pick>

Figure 4.12 Continue Dimension tool.

Figure 4.13 Baseline Dimension tool.

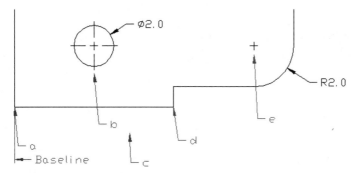

Figure 4.14 Dimensioning selection points.

Dimensioning <toolbar> Baseline Dimension <pick> Second extension line origin or RETURN to select: Digitize point d. <pick> Dimensioning <toolbar> Continue Dimension <pick> Second extension line origin or RETURN to select: Digitize point e. <pick> Second extension line origin or RETURN to select: <return> <return>

Dimension the left side of the plate (see Figure 4.1) The baseline is at the top of the plate, so you should begin the dimension string from there. Also add the 1.0-unit dimension, as shown back in Figure 4.1. Save the drawing before continuing.

4.8 Angular Dimension

An angular dimension is required for the slope of the right side of the figure. A horizontal extension line must be constructed with the angular dimension. Indicate this by pressing <return> when asked to Select arc, circle, line, or RETURN: (in DOS, choose Draw, then Dimensioning, then Angular):

Dimensioning <toolbar> Angular Dimension (Figure 4.15) <pick> Select arc, circle, line or RETURN: <return> Angle vertex: Digitize point a (Figure 4.16). <pick> First angle endpoint: Click twice on ORTHO (orthogonal mode) in the status bar, turning it on (in DOS, select Ortho from the Assist menu or press <ctrl>–O). Digitize point b (slightly to the left of a). <pick> Second angle endpoint: Digitize point c. <pick> Dimension arc line location (Text/Angle): Turn ORTHO off and then digitize the point where you want the dimension line to be located. The angular dimension is visible and moves with the cursor. <pick>

Entering **t** (text) in response to Dimension arc line location (Text/Angle): allows you to specify the text. Entering a (angle) allows you to specify the text angle. Save the drawing to c:\Drawings\Proj-4.Dwg and to a floppy diskette as a backup. Exit AutoCAD.

Figure 4.15 Angular Dimension tool.

Figure 4.16 Angular dimensioning.

Drawing with Precision

Objective: Use object snaps to select the nearest point, tangents, intersections, and apparent intersections; use the Aerial View window; trim objects; mirror objects; set dimension styles; dimension; use XYZ point filters; add text to a drawing; change text styles; and open a drawing for editing.

Drawing: Boot up AutoCAD and start a new drawing named c:\drawings\proj-5.dwg. Draw the control block illustrated in Figure 5.1, following the procedures outlined in this chapter. Set the drawing units to decimal with two digits to the right of the decimal. This project is longer than previous ones, so you might have to complete it in two stages. If you do, refer to section 5.18 for the procedure to save and open a drawing for editing.

5.1 Drawing Construction

New CAD drafters often don't know where to begin drawing and are often confused as to what coordinates to use for screen limits. The easiest way to determine drawing limits is to use a pencil and paper, and sketch boxes outlining the objects to be drawn. Remember that the drawing units are irrelevant at this point. The total drawing space is based on the space taken up by items on the drawing, relative to the numerical size of the object to be drawn. Examine the drawing in Figure 5.1, noting that the length of the object is 4.7 units. Allow 1 unit on each side for dimensioning, and another 4 units for text, giving a total required drawing width of approximately 11 units. Using a similar estimation, the required height on the screen is about 9 units. If the lower left corner of the front view of the object to be drawn is at coordinates 0,0, the lower left corner of the screen will be set to –1,–1. Using the required width, height space of 11,9, the upper right coordinates should then be 10,8. Set the drawing limits at –1,–1 and 10,8. Remember to Zoom All to set the monitor to the new limits. You can modify the limits at any time, so it isn't crucial they be exact right now.

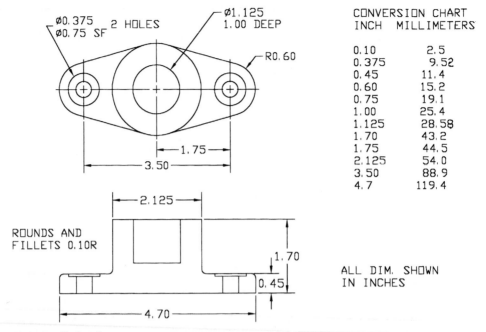

Figure 5.1 Project 5.

The circles and arcs in the top view define the front view, so you'll draw the top view first. The center of the top view will be located at coordinates 3,5:

Draw <toolbar> Circle Center Diameter <pick> 3P/2P/TTR/<Center point>: **3,5** <return> Diameter/<Radius>: d_ Diameter: **2.125** <return> <spacebar> Circle 3P/2P/TTR/<Center point>: **@** <return> Diameter/<Radius>: **d** <return> Diameter: **1.125** <return>

AutoCAD command prompts show the default value to be entered in angle brackets, < >, unless the prompt is followed by another prompt, e.g., Diameter/<Radius>: d_ Diameter:. The second prompt, d_ Diameter:, immediately follows the first prompt, so you should enter the circle diameter.

In the previous command sequence, the <spacebar> recalls the previous command. When the command is recalled, the prompt is Diameter/<Radius>:. Although the original command requests the circle *diameter*, when the command is recalled (using the <spacebar> or <return> key), the default entry is the circle *radius*. In order to enter the alternate response, enter **d** and press <return>, forcing AutoCAD to request the circle diameter. Always watch the command line to ensure you're entering the value AutoCAD is requesting, not what you think is being requested.

In the previous set of commands, the center of the second circle has the same coordinates as the center of the first circle: the last point entered. Consequently, when the center of the second circle is requested, @ indicates the last point.

Draw three circles to the left of the block. The center of the circles is 1.75 units to the left of the center circle (see Figure 5.1), giving a drawing coordinate of 1.25,5. The inner circle should have a diameter of 0.375 units, the next circle a diameter of 0.75 units, and the outer circle a radius of 0.6 units. Save the drawing before continuing.

5.2 Object Snaps

Object snap is a mode that lets you refer to points already on the drawing, such as the endpoint and middle points of a line, center of a circle, and apparent intersection of two lines. You can turn object snaps on temporarily to assist in locating a point on the drawing by entering the Object Snap command when AutoCAD requests the point. Or you can set a running object snap, which will be applied to all points selected until the object snap is turned off. You can turn the running object snap off temporarily by entering the None object snap command. When object snap is on, an aperture (box) is added to the intersection of the cursor crosshairs. To snap onto a line or other element, place the aperture on the line or elements. AutoCAD will then use the lines or elements within the aperture to search for the object snap location. The object snap aperture appears only when a point, such as the start point of a line, is to be located on the monitor.

In the drawing you're doing in this chapter, tangent lines join the center circle, which is 2.125 units in diameter, and a side circle, which is 0.6 units in radius. Auto-CAD has an object snap command Tangent, which will be used to place the lines tangent to the circles. Prior to drawing the tangent lines, enlarge the top view by using the Zoom Window tool in the Standard toolbar (in DOS, select View, then Zoom, then Window):

Zoom Window <pick> First corner: Digitize a point slightly to the left and below the top view. <pick> Second corner: Move the cursor up and to the right so the window encloses the top view, allowing room for the circles to be drawn to the right of the center circle. <pick>

You can set a tangent running object snap by choosing the Running Object Snap tool in the Object Snap flyout, as illustrated in Figure 5.2 (in DOS, select Options, then Running Object Snap). The Running Object Snap dialog box illustrated in Figure 5.3 will be displayed. Set the Tangent object snap by placing the cursor in the Tangent box and pressing the <pick> button. A × will appear in the Tangent box. Press the OK button to exit.

With the help of the Tangent object snap, the line joining the two circles can be drawn tangent to the circles with minimum effort:

Draw <toolbox> Line <pick> From point: The cursor should now display a rectangular aperture box, which is the object snap target. Place the aperture box on the top of the 2.10 unit diameter center circle (Figure 5.4). <pick> To point: Place the object snap aperture box on the top of the right side circle (Figure 5.4). The tangency line will be visible. <pick>

Figure 5.2 Object Snap flyout.

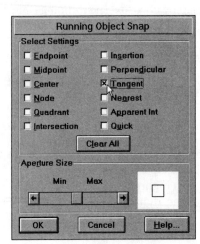

Figure 5.3 Running Object Snap dialog box.

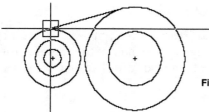

Figure 5.4 Tangent object snap location.

Figure 5.5 Trim tool.

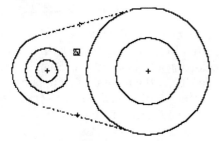

Figure 5.6 Trimmed circle.

Notice that AutoCAD draws a line tangent to the two circles. You should always use object snaps when a line is to connect onto an object. Never attempt to locate points by "eye" on an AutoCAD drawing. They might appear correct on the screen, but will invariably be off the desired point. Press <return> to exit the Line command.

Recall the Line command and add a line tangent to the bottom of the same two circles. If you have problems, use the Undo command and try again.

When you've completed the lines, use the Running Object Snap tool to display the Running Object Snap dialog box illustrated in Figure 5.3. Turn off the tangent object snap by placing the cursor in the Tangent box and pressing the <pick> button. The × will be removed, indicating that the object snap is off. Press the OK button to exit. *Always* turn running object snaps off when they're no longer required.

5.3 Trim Command

The circle that's 0.6 units in radius is to have the portion of its circumference inside the object removed (refer back to Figure 5.1). Use the Trim command to cut objects precisely at an edge defined by one or more objects. Choose the Trim tool (Figure 5.5) in the Trim flyout of the Modify toolbar (in DOS, select Modify, then Trim):

Modify <toolbar> Trim <pick> `Select cutting edges: (Projmode = UCS, edgemode = No extend) Select objects:` Click on the top tangency line. <pick> `Select objects:` Click on the bottom tangency line. <pick> `Select objects:` <return> `Select objects to trim/Project/Edge/Undo:` Click on the section of the circle to be trimmed (Figure 5.6). <pick> `Select objects to trim/Project/Edge/Undo:` <return>

5.4 Mirror Command and Temporary Object Snap

The right side of the top view will be created when you use the Mirror command to mirror the objects on the left side, about the center of the view. Choose the mirror tool (Figure 5.7) in the Copy flyout of the Modify toolbar (in DOS, select Construct, then Mirror):

Modify <toolbar> Copy <flyout> Mirror <pick> Select objects: Select the tangent lines and the left side circles using a crossing window, illustrated by the dotted line (Figure 5.8). You'll start a crossing window by picking a right-side corner of the window box. <pick> Other corner: Pick the opposite corner on the left side of the crossing box. <pick> 5 found Select objects: <return> First point of mirror line:

Use the Center object snap to select the center of the middle circles. Since the object snap is required for only one selection, a temporary object snap will be used. You can set a temporary object snap by selecting it from the Object Snap cursor menu, illustrated in Figure 5.9. To display the Object Snap cursor menu, press the <shift> key and right button of the mouse together, indicated as <shift>–<right> in the following, and then select Center from the Object Snap menu:

First point of mirror line: <shift>–<right> Center <pick> of Place the center object snap aperture on the circumference of the large center circle. <pick> Second point: Click twice on ORTHO in the status bar to turn Ortho (orthogonal mode) on (in DOS, select Assist, then Ortho). Then pick the second point of the mirror directly below the first point selected. <pick> Delete old objects. <N>: <return>

Turn Ortho off before continuing. Notice how Ortho was used to facilitate the selecting of a vertical mirror line.

Figure 5.7 Mirror tool.

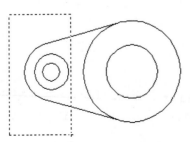

Figure 5.8 Crossing window.

From
Endpoint
Midpoint
Intersection
Apparent Intersection
Center
Quadrant
Perpendicular
Tangent
Node
Insertion
Nearest
Quick,
None
.X
.Y
.Z
.XZ
.YZ
.XY

Figure 5.9 Object Snap cursor menu.

5.5 Calculate Text Height and Dimscale

The plot will be done on an A-size sheet (8.5 by 11 inches) using a plot scale of ¾ inches = 1 inch. If the desired text height on the plotted drawing is ⅛ in (0.125), the text height (h) on the monitor should be:

$$\text{¾} \times h = 0.125 \text{ inch, which gives } h = 0.17$$

Dimscale is then calculated using equation 4.2:

$$\text{Dimscale} \times 0.18 = 0.17, \text{ which gives Dimscale} = 0.94$$

5.6 Set Dimension Variables

If the Dimensioning toolbar isn't loaded, load it following the procedure outlined in chapter 1, section 1.3.3. Then choose the Dimension Style tool to display the Dimension Style dialog box. The Parent button should be on in the Family box, indicating that the settings to be made relate to all dimensioning.

Click Geometry... to display the Geometry dialog box. Set the Overall Scale in the Scale box to the Dimscale setting of **0.94**. Then click the Line button in the Center box, setting center marks to center lines. Press the OK button to return to the Dimension Style dialog box.

Click Annotation... to display the Annotation dialog box illustrated in Figure 4.3. Click the Units... command button in the Primary Units box to display the Primary Units dialog box. Set the units precision to **0.00** and then press the OK button to return to the Annotation dialog box. Press the OK button to return to the Dimension Style dialog box.

You need specific settings for diameter and radial dimensioning that are different than the Family settings. Click the Diameter button on in the Family box. AutoCAD will display an Alert box prompting you if you want to save the changes to be made to the current style. Press the Yes button. Then press the Format... command button to display the Format dialog box.

Diameter dimension format settings will allow you to specify where diameter dimensions are to be located when the dimensions are being done. Press the User Defined button and then Select Text and Arrows in the Fit box. Press OK to exit and return to the Dimension Style dialog box. Press the Radial Family button and set the radial dimension family to the same settings used for the diameter family.

When the special settings for radial and diameter dimensions are completed, press the Save command button in the Dimension Styles box, saving the settings with the name STANDARD. Then press OK to exit.

Following the procedure used in chapter 3, section 3.9, add center lines to each of the set of circles (refer back to Figure 5.1). When selecting the side circles, pick a point on the arc so the center lines extend to the arc. For the middle set of circles, pick a point on the circumference of the larger circle.

5.7 Aerial View Window

The aerial view window is available only in Windows. If you're using DOS, either skip to section 5.8 or see appendix D, section D.1, item 50 on how to display an aerial view window in DOS.

Prior to dimensioning the top view, you must change the size of the view on the screen in order to provide room to add dimensions. The Aerial View window allows you to see the entire drawing in a separate window, locate a specific area, and move to that area quickly. You can also zoom in on an area, change the magnification, and match the view in the graphics window to the one in the Aerial View window, or vice versa. If the Aerial View window isn't already displayed on your screen, click on the Aerial View tool (Figure 5.10) in the Tool Windows flyout of the Standard toolbar (see section A.1.11 in appendix A).

The Aerial View window illustrated in Figure 5.11 will be displayed on the screen. You can move the window anywhere on the screen by moving the cursor into the window's title box, holding down the <pick> button, and moving the cursor, dragging the window across the screen. Release the <pick> button when you have the window in the desired location.

5.7.1 Zoom using the Aerial View

1. Choose the Zoom tool in the Aerial View window toolbar (Figure 5.12).

2. Move the cursor into the Aerial View screen and click one corner of a zoom window (see the dotted rectangle in Figure 5.11).

3. Click the other corner of the zoom window.

Figure 5.10 Aerial View button.

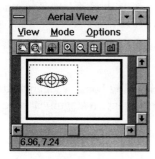

Figure 5.11 Aerial View window.

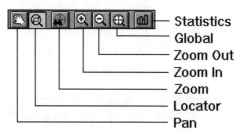

Figure 5.12 Aerial View toolbar.

The object will zoom on the graphics screen to suit the zoom window selected. A solid view box will appear around the object in the Aerial View window, defining the zoom window selected.

5.7.2 Pan using the Aerial View

Panning an object in AutoCAD is similar to moving a camera while viewing an object through the view finder; the object slides across the screen to a new location.

1. Choose the Pan tool in the Aerial View tool bar (Figure 5.12). The pan box will appear to be the same size as the current zoom window box (created previously with the zoom command). If you can't see the outline of the pan box, it's because it's the same size as the Aerial View window.

2. Drag the pan box with the cursor and press the <pick> button when the object is panned to the desired area. You can use the Aerial View window's scrollbars to reposition the image in the Aerial View window.

The graphics window will display the selected area.

5.7.3 Panning and zooming using Aerial View's Locator tool

1. Choose the Locator tool in the Aerial View toolbar (Figure 5.12). Hold down the <pick> button and drag the locator onto the graphics area.
2. As you move the cursor on the object, the view inside the dotted rectangle is displayed in the Aerial View window (see Figure 5.13).
3. Release the <pick> button to display the magnified view in AutoCAD's graphics window.

You can change the Locator magnification by choosing Locator Magnification in the Options menu of the Aerial View Window, which displays a Magnification dialog box.

5.7.4 Changing the Size of the Aerial View Image

The following tools (refer back to Figure 5.12) change the size image in the Aerial View window *without* affecting the view in the graphics window:

- The Global tool displays the entire drawing in the Aerial View window.
- The Zoom In tool incrementally decreases the size of the view in the window.
- The Zoom Out tool incrementally enlarges the view in the window.

You can use the Aerial View window transparently without canceling AutoCAD commands that request the selection of points or entities. This is extremely useful in complex drawings. For instance, you could invoke the Line command and use the Aerial View window to zoom in and select the first point of the line. When requested for the next point of the line, you could once again use the Aerial View window to zoom into another part of the drawing and select the point. In each case, the Line command would not be interrupted.

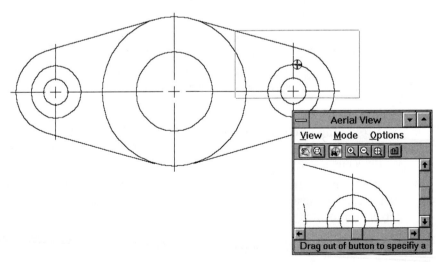

Figure 5.13 Using Locator.

Prior to dimensioning the top view, it's necessary to enlarge the size of the view on the screen to allow room to display the dimensions as they're drawn. Use the Aerial View window to zoom the view on the graphics screen, as defined by the dotted rectangle back in Figure 5.11.

5.8 Dynamic Zoom

With DOS, use Dynamic Zoom to enlarge the top view for dimensioning (this is also available in Windows):

View <pick> Zoom <pick> Dynamic <pick>

(If Zoom dynamic doesn't work, enter **Viewers** and then **yes** to turn on the Fast Zoom mode.)

AutoCAD will clear the screen and display the dynamic zoom screen illustrated in Figure 5.14. The drawing extents box (white or black) shows the larger of either the area occupied by the drawing or the drawing limits. The generated area limits within the red corners indicates the portion of the drawing AutoCAD can generate at high speed without a regeneration of the drawing. The View box allows you to select the desired view to be displayed on the graphics screen when the command is exited. When the View box has an × in it (see Figure 5.14) you use it as a *pan* box, sliding it across the screen to select the desired view. Pressing the <pick> button changes the View box to a *zoom* box with an arrow in it, as shown in Figure 5.15. Moving the cursor enlarges or shrinks the View box. The <pick> button toggles the View box between the pan and zoom modes. Select a view, illustrated by the dotted Current view box in Figure 5.14, and press <return>.

5.9 Horizontal Dimensions

The horizontal dimensions in the top view originate from a baseline at the center of the circles on the right side of the view. When dimensioning from a center line, the dimension extension lines should originate from and act as an extension to the circle center line. Use the endpoint object snap, which you can select from the Object Snap cursor menu (refer back to Figure 5.9) by holding down the <shift> button and pressing the second button on the mouse, illustrated as <shift>–<right> in the following (in DOS, Dimensioning is in the Draw menu):

Dimensioning <toolbar> Linear Dimension (Figure 4.10) <pick> `First extension line origin:` <shift>–<right> Endpoint <pick> of Place the endpoint object snap aperture box on the bottom end of the center line of the right-side circle. <pick> `Second extension line origin:` <shift>–<right> Endpoint <pick> of Place the endpoint object snap aperture box on the bottom end of the center line of the center circle. If more than one object is in the object snap aperture box, AutoCAD will search for the end of the object located closest to the cursor crosshairs. <pick> `Dimension line location (Text/Angle/Horizontal/Vertical/Rotated):` Digitize the desired location of the dimension line. If the text illustrated in the dimension line be-

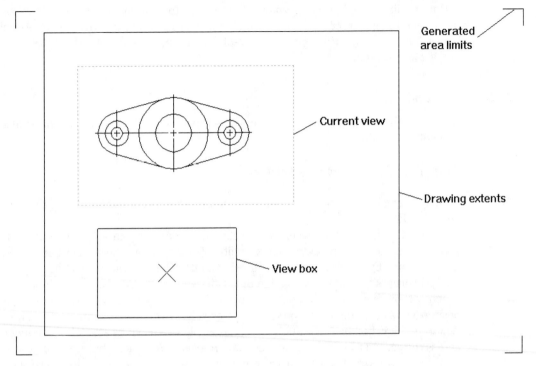

Generated
area limits

Current view

Drawing extents

View box

Figure 5.14 Dynamic zoom.

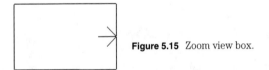

Figure 5.15 Zoom view box.

ing dragged into location is incorrect, you can enter **T** so AutoCAD will request the text value. <pick> Dimensioning <toolbar> Baseline <pick> Second extension line or RETURN to select: <shift>–<right> Endpoint <pick> of Place the endpoint object snap aperture box on the bottom end of the center line of the left-side circle. <pick> Second extension line or RETURN to select: <return> Select base line: <return>

5.10 Dimension Style Setting

Center marks are normally added to the object when the circle is dimensioned. In this drawing, center marks are required for the horizontal dimensions added to the drawing prior to dimensioning the circles. In order to not duplicate the center marks, they'll be set to None in the Dimension Styles' Format dialog box; however, if a dimension style is modified at any time, all dimensions done previously with that style also change based on the new settings. The initial dimension style is named Standard (default) by AutoCAD. A new dimension style named Standard1, with the center marks set to none, is created as follows:

Dimensioning <toolbar> Dimension Style <pick>

The Dimension Style dialog box (see Figure 5.16) will be displayed. Move the cursor into the Dimension Style Name box, as shown in Figure 5.16, change the name to Standard1, and then press the Save command button to save Standard1 as the current style. AutoCAD indicates that settings from the Standard style are used as default settings in the new style.

Press the Diameter Family button and then press the Geometry... command button to display the Geometry dialog box illustrated in Figure 4.2. Set the center mark to None and then press the OK button. Repeat the procedure for the Radial Family. When the Alert box is displayed, enter **y** (yes) to save the changes to the current style. When the Diameter and Radial dimension settings are completed, press the Save command button in the Dimension Style dialog box to save the changes made to the Standard1 style, and return to the drawing screen.

5.10.1 Overriding Dimension Settings

Use the Radius Dimension tool and add the 0.60 R radius to the arc on the right side, as shown back in Figure 5.1. Next, dimension the center circle using the Diameter Dimension tool. The dimension is to be a 1.125 diameter but, because the dimension accuracy is set to two digits to the right of the decimal, it appears as 1.13. Press Esc during the command sequence to exit the command, or use Undo to undo the dimension after it's done. You can use an override setting to override the dimension, as follows:

Dimensioning <toolbar> Dimension Style <pick>

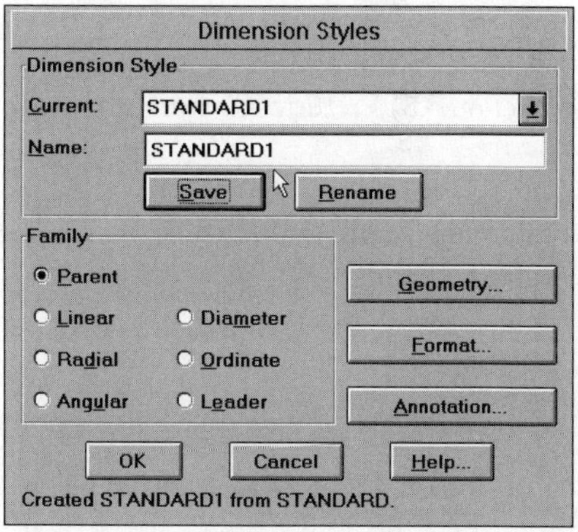

Figure 5.16 Creating a Dimension Style.

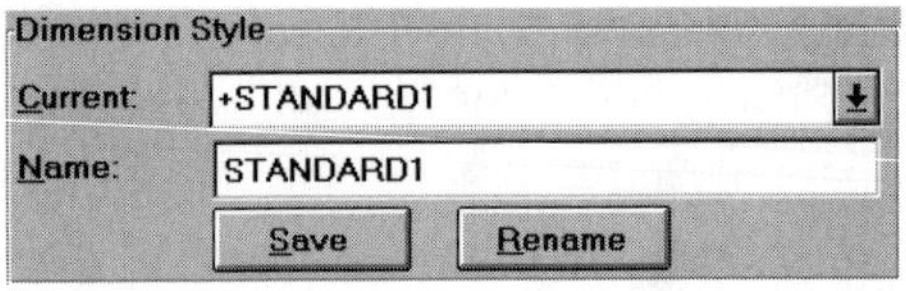

Figure 5.17 Overriding dimension style.

The Dimension style dialog box (see Figure 5.16) is displayed. Note that the family is Parent. Overrides can be done only to the Parent family. Press the Annotation... command button to display the Annotation dialog box. Then press the Primary Units command button and set the Units precision to 0.000. Exit the dialog boxes by pressing OK. Do *not* save the dimension style.

Dimension the center circle using Diameter Dimension tool, noting that the default dimension is now 1.125.

Redisplay the Dimension Style dialog box. Note that the dimension in the current box is +Standard1. The plus sign indicates that the current style is a dimension override. Display the drop-down Current Style box, as illustrated in Figure 5.17, and choose Standard1 as the current style. Redisplay the drop-down list, noting that since +Standard was an override it's no longer available in the list.

5.11 Single-Line Text

You can add the 1.00 Deep text to the drawing with either the Text (single-line text) or Dtext (dynamic text) command. When the Text command is invoked, you enter the text at the command line and AutoCAD places it on the drawing screen when the Text command is exited. The Dtext command is similar to text, but the text appears on the screen as it's entered and Dtext allows you to enter multiple lines of text. Invoke the Text command as follows (in DOS, select Draw, then Text, then Single-Line text):

Draw <toolbar> Single-Line Text (Figure 5.18) <pick> Justify/Style/<Start point>: Digitize the lower left corner of the text location on the screen. <pick> Height <0.20>: **0.17** (see section 5.5) <return> Rotation angle <0>: <return> Text: **1.00 DEEP** <return>

If you enter **j** in response to the prompt Justify/Style/<Start point>, Auto-CAD will prompt:

Align/Fit/Center/Middle/Right/TL/TC/TR/ML/MR/BL/BC/BR:

The options are:

Align. You enter two points. AutoCAD adjusts the text height and length to fit between the points.

Fit. You enter two points and the text height. AutoCAD fits the text between the points and uses the text height entered.

Center. Aligns the text on a point entered as the center of the baseline of the text.

Middle. Aligns the text on a point entered as the middle of the text.

Right. Right-justifies the text on its baseline using a point entered.

TL. (top left) left-justifies the text on its baseline using a point entered.

TC. (top center) Centers the text at a point entered for the top of the text.

TR. (top right) Right-justifies text at a point entered for the top of the text.

ML. (middle left) Left-justifies text at a point entered for the middle of the text.

MC. (middle center) Centers text horizontally and vertically at the middle of a point entered.

MR. (middle right) Right-justifies text at a point entered for the baseline.

BL. (bottom left) Left-justifies text at a point entered for the baseline.

BC. (bottom center) Centers text at a point entered for the baseline.

BR. (bottom right) Right-justifies text at a point entered for the baseline.

5.12 Leader and Mtext

The diameter dimension for the circle on the left side is to have a leader leaning to the left with the dimension on its right side (refer back to Figure 5.1). The diameter dimension command places the text on the side to which the leader leans so the Leader command will be used. Normally, the Leader command also places the text on the side to which the leader leans, but you can trick it by placing a short horizontal line at the end of the leader. The Leader command uses Mtext (multiline text) for text input (also see section D.4 in appendix D). You can put special characters in the text using the format \U+nnn, where nnn is a code listed in Table 5.1 (the U must be uppercase).

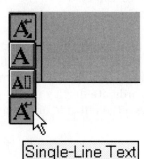

Figure 5.18 Text flyout.

TABLE 5.1 Unicode characters

Character	Unicode	Example	
Ø	\U+22050.375	\U+22050.375	Ø0.375
°	\U+00B0	12\U+00B0	12°
±	\U+00B1	\U+00B13.5	±3.5
\	\\	c:\\drawings	c:\drawings
overline	\L...\O	\O2\O	$\overline{2}$
underline	\L...\L	\L2\L	$\underline{2}$

The leader is drawn as follows (in DOS, select Draw, then Dimensioning, then Leader):

Dimensioning <toolbar> Leader <pick> From point: Digitize the tip of the arrow of the leader. <pick> To point: Digitize the end of the first segment of the leader. <pick> To point (Format/Annotation/Undo): Digitize a short horizontal line on the right side of the leader. To point (Format/Annotation/Undo): **a** (annotation) <return> Annotation or RETURN for options: **\U+22050.375** <return> Mtext: **\U+22050.75 SF** <return> Mtext: <return>

If you pressed <return> instead of drawing the short horizontal line, the leader command would have drawn a short horizontal line on the side toward which the leader leaned (left) and placed the text on that side. If you entered **f** (format) in response to To point (Format/Annotation/Undo), AutoCAD would allow you to draw the leader as a curved spline. You can also specify if an arrow is to be used or not at the start point of the leader. Use the Text (single-line text) command to add the text 2 HOLES.

5.13 Front View

Select Zoom All in the Standard toolbar. Then use the Aerial View window or the Dynamic Zoom command to zoom on the drawing from slightly above the horizontal center line in the top view to the base of the drawing screen below it (see Figure 5.19). This is done so the front view will be as large as possible on the monitor, and a sufficient amount of the top view is displayed so lines can be extended down to locate elements on the front view.

The top-left corner of the shaft 2.125 units in diameter in the front view will have a Y coordinate (vertical) of 2, which you can determine by visually locating the screen cursor at the approximate vertical position desired and reading the vertical coordinate of that position from the coordinate display in the status bar. The X coordinate (horizontal) is to be in line with the left side of the circle in the top view.

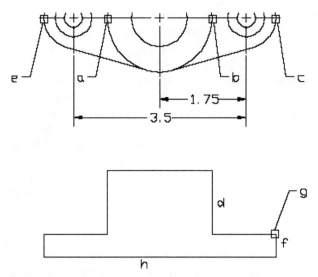

Figure 5.19 Front view.

5.13.1 X/Y/Z point filters

When AutoCAD requests coordinates, you can selectively enter them with XYZ point filters. The format of XYZ point filters is .coordinate. The point filter coordinate is any one or two of the letters X, Y, and Z. This lets you build a two- or three-dimensional coordinate by entering coordinate values that are independent of each other. For example, you can enter a three-dimensional point by selecting the X,Y coordinates. Then snap onto the endpoint of an existing line and enter the Z value from the keyboard. You can select the .X and .Y filters from the Standard toolbar Point Filters flyout (see section A.1.15 in appendix A) and from the floating cursor menu illustrated in Figure 5.9. To display the cursor menu, hold down the <shift> key and press the second button on the mouse (shown in the following as <shift>–<right>). Using filters is illustrated here:

Draw <toolbar> Line <pick> Line From point: <shift>–<right> <pick> .XZ <pick> of Intersection <pick> of Locate the intersection object snap aperture box over point a (Figure 5.19). <pick>

You've used an XZ point filter to locate the x,z coordinates. You also used the Intersection object snap to accurately select the intersection. The x coordinate is on the horizontal plane of the monitor, and the z coordinate is 0 because this is a two-dimensional drawing. AutoCAD now requests the y coordinate, which was decided earlier to be 2:

(need Y): **2** <return>

XYZ point filters are used in the continuation of the Line command. Note that *both* .XY and .XZ filters are used in the following:

To point: <shift>–<right> .XZ <pick> of <shift>–<right> Intersection <pick> of Place the aperture box over the intersecting entities at b (Figure 5.19). <pick> (need Y): **2** <return> To point: **@1.25<270** <return> To point: <shift>–<right> .XZ <pick> of <shift>–<right> Intersection <pick> of Place the aperture box over the intersecting entities at c. <pick> (need Y): <shift>–<right> Endpoint <pick> of Place the aperture box near the bottom end of line d. <pick> To point: **@0.45<270** <return> To point: <shift>–<right> .XZ <pick> of Intersection <pick> of Place the aperture box over intersection e. <pick> (need Y): <shift>–<right> Endpoint <pick> of Place the aperture box near the lower end of line f. <pick> To point: <shift>–<right> .YZ (Note YZ) <pick> of <shift>–<right> Intersection <pick> of Place the aperture box over the intersection at point g. <pick> (need X): <shift>–<right> Endpoint <pick> of Place the aperture box near the left end of line h. <pick> To point: <shift>–<right> .YZ <pick> of <shift>–<right> Intersection <pick> of Select intersection g. <pick> (need X) <shift>–<right> Intersection <pick> of Select intersection a. <pick> To point: **c** (Close) <return>

Draw the 1.125-diameter hole in the 2.125-diameter shaft in the front view. The lines are to be continuous, rather than hidden, because the solid portion of the front view is to be hatched in chapter 7, section 7.4. Start the hole as follows:

Draw <toolbar> Line <pick> From point: <shift>–<right> .XZ <pick> Intersection <pick> of Place the aperture target on the intersection on the left-side intersection of the 1.125-diameter hole and the center line in the top view. <pick> (need Y): <shift>–<right> Endpoint <pick> of Place the object snap aperture box on the top of the shaft in the front view. <pick> To point: **@1<270** <return> (etc.)

When drawing the bolt and countersunk hole in the front view, it's important that the lines exactly meet the object lines because of the hatching to be done later. Use the Nearest object snap to snap onto a line, arc, or circle that's closest to the center of the object snap aperture box, as follows:

Draw <toolbar> Line <pick> From point: <shift>–<right> .XZ <pick> Intersection <pick> of Place the target on the intersection of the side of the countersunk hole and the center line in the top view. <pick> (need Y): <shift>–<right> Nearest <pick> of Place the object snap target on the top of the plate in the front view where the countersunk hole is to start. <pick> To point:

Draw the depth of the countersunk hole by eye. Continue the bolt holes in the front view. Use the .XZ point filter to locate the x coordinate in the top view when required, and the Nearest object snap to ensure that the y coordinate is selected exactly on an object line. Alternatively, draw the lines past the surface lines of the object and use the Trim command to trim the lines. When the bolt hole is completed on one side, use the Copy command to copy it 3.5 inches horizontally to the other side (or use the Mirror command).

5.14 Fillet Command

You can add fillets by editing the drawing. When using the Fillet command for the first time, you must set the radius by entering the **r** (radius) option, as illustrated below. Once you enter the radius, you don't have to reenter it unless the fillet radius is to be changed. Draw the fillet, then, recall the Fillet command and digitize the two lines that are to be joined by the fillet (for DOS, select Construct, then Fillet) See section A.5 in appendix A:

Modify <toolbar> Fillet (Figure 5.20) <pick> `Polyline/Radius/Trim/<Select first object>:` **r** (radius) <return> `Enter fillet radius <0.00>:` **0.1** <return> <return> `Fillet Polyline/Radius/Trim/<Select first object>:` Digitize one of the lines at the corner to be filleted (Figure 5.1). <pick> `Select second object:` Digitize the other line at the corner. <pick>

Recall the Fillet command by pressing <return>, and fillet the other corners. Note that the default radius is now 0.1. If the trim option is used, the corner will be filleted without trimming off the edges.

5.15 Dimension the Front View

You calculate the horizontal dimension on the bottom of the front view by using AutoCAD's automatic extension line process (in DOS, select Draw, then Dimensioning, then Linear):

Dimensioning <toolbar> Linear <pick> `First extension line origin or RETURN to select:` <return> `Select line, arc, or circle:` Pick the bottom horizontal line in the front view. <pick> `Dimension line location (Text/Angle/Horizontal/Vertical/Rotated):` Drag the dimension to the desired location, noting the default text. If the text is otherwise, enter **T** to allow input of the text. <pick>

Add the dimensions along the right side of the front view, as illustrated in Figure 5.21. Note the use of the Apparent Intersection object snap to locate the intersection of the two lines at the fillet:

Dimensioning <toolbar> Linear <pick> `First extension line origin or RETURN to select:` <shift>–<right> Intersection <pick> of Place the intersection aperture box on the lower right corner of the front view. <pick> `Second exten-`

Figure 5.20 Fillet tool.

sion line origin: <shift>–<right> Apparent Intersection <pick> of Place the aperture box on the short horizontal line (Figure 5.12). <pick> Dimension line location (Text/Angle/Horizontal/Vertical/Rotated): Drag the dimension to the desired location. If the text isn't 0.45, press <esc> and try again. <pick>

Use the Baseline Dimension tool to add the 1.70 dimension, as shown in Figure 5.21.

Start the 2.125 horizontal dimension at the top of the shaft (refer back to Figure 5.1), noting that AutoCAD reads the dimension as 2.13. Press Esc to cancel the dimension, and then use a dimension styles override, as outlined in section 5.10.1, to set the Dimension Precision to 0.000. (When exiting the Dimension Style dialog, choose OK—*not* Save—so this change is an override and is not saved in the Standard1 style.) Now redo the dimension as 2.125 units. When the dimension is complete, change the dimension style back to Standard1.

5.16 Dtext Command

The Dtext command is similar to the text command, but it allows you to enter multiline text and view the text in the graphics window as it's entered (in DOS, select Draw, then Text, then Dynamic Text):

Draw <toolbar> Dynamic Text (Figure 5.18) <pick> Justify/Style/<Start point>: Digitize the lower location of the left corner of the first line of text. <Pick> Height <0.20>: **0.17** (section 5.5) <return> Rotation angle <0>: <return> Text: **ROUNDS AND** <return> Text: **FILLETS 0.10R** <return> Text: <return>

If you enter **j** (justify), the text justification options are the same as those listed in section 5.11. As you enter the text, it's displayed on the screen. When you press the second <return> at the end of the entry, AutoCAD regenerates the text to the screen, interpreting any control codes in the text. Codes can be Unicode characters, outlined back in Table 5.1, or AutoCAD text control codes, listed here (in the Dtext

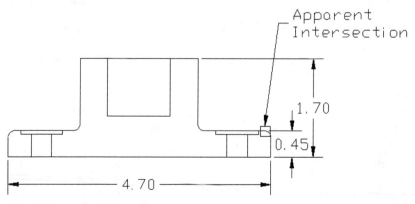

Figure 5.21 Apparent intersection.

command codes, such as %%c, are initially shown in code format, e.g., %%c, and translated when the text is regenerated):

Text (single-line text) and Dtext (dynamic text) commands use the following control codes to input characters (the Unicode characters listed back in Table 5.1 can also be used):

%%nnn. Draws the character with the ASCII code *nnn*.

%%u. Toggles underscore mode on/off.

%%d. Draws the degree symbol.

%%p. Draws the plus/minus tolerance symbol.

%%c. Draws the diameter dimensioning symbol.

%%%. Draws the single percent sign.

5.17 Text Styles

The data in the conversion chart should have the decimal points aligned vertically. The standard text font in AutoCAD is the TXT font, which uses variable spaces for letters, making it impossible to align decimals vertically in the conversion chart. The MONOTXT font uses the same amount of space for each character, so it will be used for the text in the chart. Change the text style with the Style command in the Data menu of the menu bar:

Data <pick> Text Style <pick> `Text style name (or ?) <Standard>:` **mono** <return> `New Style`

AutoCAD will display the Select Font file dialog box, shown in Figure 5.22. Select the monotxt.shx file, as shown, and then press OK to load the file. AutoCAD will continue with:

`Select monotxt.shx New style. Height <0.00>:` <return> `Width factor <1.00>:` <return> `Obliquing angle <0>:` <return> `Backwards? <N>:` <return> `Upside-down?<N>:` <return> `Vertical? <N>:` <return> `Mono is now the current text style.`

Note that all the default options were selected. If the height, for instance, was entered, it will become the default text height for all text with this style and you won't be able to enter a text height when using the Text or Dtext command.

Use dynamic text (Dtext) to enter the conversion chart (<*n*sb> means press the space bar on the keyboard *n* times):

Draw <toolbar> Dtext <pick> `Justify/Style/<Start point>:` Digitize the start point for the text <pick> `Height <0.17>:` <return> `Rotation angle <0>:` <return> `Text:` **CONVERSION CHART** <return> `Text:` **INCH**<3sb>**MILLIMETER** <return> `Text:` <1sb><return> `Text:` **0.10**<6sb>**2.5** <return> `Text:` **0.375** <6sb>**9.52** <return> `Text:` **0.45**<5sb>**11.4** <return>, etc.

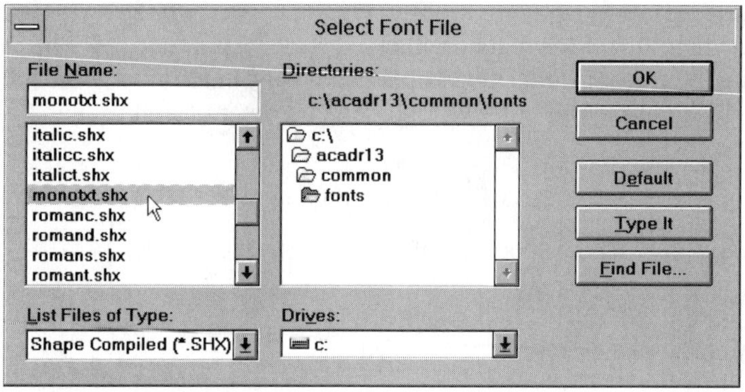

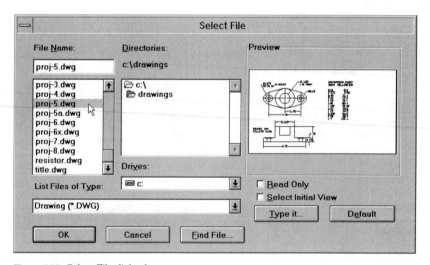

Figure 5.22 Select Font File dialog box.

Figure 5.23 Select File dialog box.

Complete the chart and press <return> twice at the end to exit the Dtext command. Recall the Dtext command and enter **s** (style) in response to `Justify/Style/ <Start point>:`. AutoCAD will then request the style. Enter **standard** to reset the style back. Then add the remaining text to the drawing.

Move the cursor to the top left corner of an imaginary box on the screen outlining the object and text, and read the coordinates in the coordinate display of the status bar. If the coordinates exceed the original limits of 10,8 (as set in section 5.1), then reset the limits; for example, reset the limits to 11,8 and then choose Zoom All. If the drawing area falls within the limits of 10,8, the limits don't have to be reset. Save the drawing.

5.18 Editing an Existing Drawing

If you exit a drawing and want to edit it, choose the Open tool in the Standard tool-bar (see section A.1 in appendix A). In DOS, select File, then Open. AutoCAD will display the Select File dialog box illustrated in Figure 5.23. Set the desired directory in the Directory box. Then choose the drawing file in the File list box, as shown. You can preview release 13 drawings in the Preview box. Press OK to load the drawing file for editing.

6

Metric Measurement System

Objective: Draw using AutoCAD's metric measurement system, use Layers and surveyor's units, set hatch and line type scale factors, hatch objects, set dimension variables, edit dimensions, and use the Snap command.

Drawing: Boot up AutoCAD. The drawing to be completed is shown in Figure 6.1. It will be done in AutoCAD's metric system of units. The system of measurement will be set before you name the drawing.

6.1 AutoCAD's Measurement System

Previous chapters used AutoCAD's English measurement system. The drawing in this chapter will be done in metric units. Set the metric measurement system by selecting the following in the menu bar:

Options <pick> Preferences... <pick>

The Preferences dialog box, illustrated in Figure 6.2, will be displayed. Choose International, as shown, to display the International dialog box in Figure 6.3. Press the Metric Measurement button, and set the Drawing Type to METRIC.ISO Size A3. Press OK to exit the dialog box. When a new drawing is loaded, the default limits are 297 × 420 and the default dimension text height is 2.5 units. Default scale factors are based on 1 unit per 1 mm of plotted drawing. This changes the equation back in chapter 4 from:

$$\text{Dimscale} \times 0.18 = \text{Text height}$$

to:

$$\text{Dimscale} \times 2.5 = \text{Text Height}$$

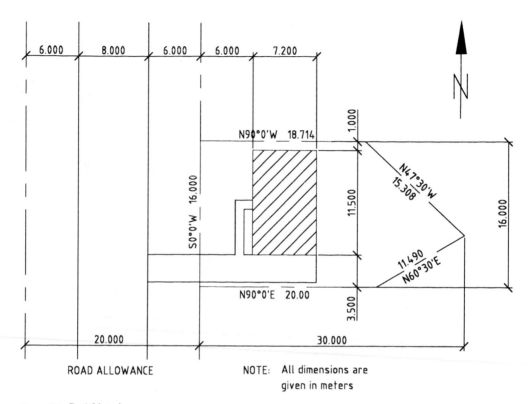

Figure 6.1 Proj-6 lot plan.

Figure 6.2 Preferences dialog box.

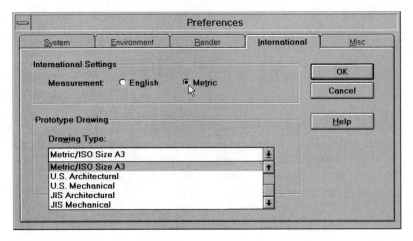

Figure 6.3 Setting measurement type.

You can create metric drawings with AutoCAD set for English measurement. The measurement system is irrelevant since a unit of measurement in AutoCAD is whatever unit you want it to be. When the default measurement system is set to English, AutoCAD loads a prototype drawing named ACAD.DWG (created back in chapter 1), and when set to Metric, AutoCAD loads a prototype drawing named ACADISO.DWG. These prototype drawings have different line type, hatch, and dimension factors, and different values for items such as text height. Otherwise, the drawing process is the same.

6.2 Beginning a New Drawing

Begin a new drawing with the name c:\drawings\proj-6. Set the drawing units to decimal with three digits to the right of the decimal, and the screen limits to 0,0 and 70,50. Note that, with the metric system of measurement, the default limits are 0,0 and 420,297. With the English system of measurement, the limits are 0,0 and 11,9. Zoom All to the new limits.

6.3 Using Layers

The concept of layering in CAD is similar to text overlays, where various components are drawn on transparent sheets and can be viewed individually or with any number overlaid to view the intersection of the parts. In AutoCAD, you can use any number of layers. The layers all have the same drawing limits, coordinate system, and units. Zoom factors apply to all layers in a drawing. You can view individual layers or any number or sequence of layers at once. You can freeze a layer so it isn't regenerated by AutoCAD, and you can lock it to protect it from being edited. Any one layer can be designated as the current layer on which new items will reside.

The drafter designates a color and line type for each layer. All items on a layer will have the same color and line type. You can use the Object Creation Modes dialog box in the Object Properties menu (section A.2 in appendix A) to set different colors for objects residing on the same layer. I recommend, however, that you don't mix the two methods—colors by layer and also by object—to prevent confusion.

The plotter uses the color of a layer to select pens. When plotting, you can give each color a pen number. As the colors change in the drawing, the plotter will select the pen number designated for that color. The pens can have different colors and/or nib widths. This allows you to control the line widths and colors on a plotted drawing. The colors can be displayed with a color monitor.

You can change the layer on which an item resides at any time. If an item is moved to a layer with a different line type or color, the item's line type and color will change to match that of the new layer.

6.3.1 Line types

Each layer is associated with a specific line type. A sample of line types supplied with AutoCAD is illustrated in Figure 6.4. The default line type for a layer is continuous.

6.3.2 Colors

Each layer is assigned a specific color number, an integer between 1 and 255. The first seven color numbers are associated with the following colors:

1   Red
2   Yellow
3   Green
4   Cyan
5   Blue
6   Magenta
7   White or black

AutoCAD creates objects with the color of the current layer if the color is set to BYLAYER. If objects drawn on a layer don't appear in the color of the layer, set the color to BYLAYER as follows: (in DOS, select Data, the Object Creation):

Object Properties <toolbar> Properties (Figure 6.5) <pick>

AutoCAD will display the Object Creation Modes dialog box, illustrated in Figure 6.6. Press the Color... command button to display the Select Color dialog box shown in Figure 6.7. Set the color to BYLAYER, as described.

Although the colors can't display on a monochrome monitor, you might want to use specific color numbers for layers to control the selection of pens by the plotter. When plotting, each color number can be associated with a specific pen number. The pens might vary in color and/or nib widths, thereby giving you control over the lines in the plotted drawing. The default color number for a layer is 7 (white or black).

```
     Name             Description
---------------   -------------------
BORDER            __ __ . __ __ . __ __ . __ __ . __ __ .
BORDER2           _._.._._.._._.._._.._._.._._.._._.._._
BORDERX2          ___ ___ . ___ ___ . ___ . ___ ___ . ___ .
CENTER            ___ _ ___ ___ _ ___ ___ _ ___ ___ _ ___
CENTER2           __ _ __ __ _ __ __ _ __ __ _ __ __ _ __

CENTERX2          _____ __ _____ _____ __ _____ __ _____
DASHDOT           __ . __ . __ . __ . __ . __ . __ . __ .
DASHDOT2          _._._._._._._._._._._._._._._._._._._
DASHDOTX2         ___ . ___ . ___ . ___ . ___ . ___ . ___
DASHED            __ . __ . __ . __ . __ . __ . __ . __ .

DASHED2           _ _ _ _ _ _ _ _ _ _ _ _ _ _ _ _ _ _ _
DASHEDX2          ___ ___ ___ ___ ___ ___ ___ ___
DIVIDE            ___ . . ___ . . ___ . . ___ . . ___ . .
DIVIDE2           _._.._._.._._.._._.._._.._._.._._.._._.
DIVIDEX2             . .        . .           . .

DOT               . . . . . . . . . . . . . . . . . . .
DOT2              .....................................
DOTX2             .  .  .  .  .  .  .  .  .  .  .  .  .
HIDDEN            _ _ _ _ _ _ _ _ _ _ _ _ _ _ _ _ _ _ _
HIDDEN2           - - - - - - - - - - - - - - - - - - -

HIDDENX2          ___ ___ ___ ___ ___ ___ ___ ___
PHANTOM           ___ _ _ ___ _ _ ___ _ _ ___ _ _
PHANTOM2          __ _ _ __ _ _ __ _ _ __ _ _ __ _ _
PHANTOMX2         _____    ___    ___    _____
```

Figure 6.4 AutoCAD line types.

Figure 6.5 Properties tool.

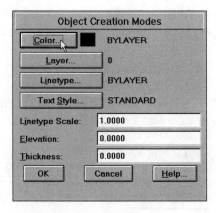

Figure 6.6 Object Creation Modes dialog box.

6.3.3 Layer names

You must give each layer an individual name. It can be up to 31 characters long and can contain letters, digits, and the special characters $, _, and –. Don't include spaces in the layer name. It's better to pick descriptive names for a layer, such as roof or 1sfloor, but the names can be as simple as 1, 2, or 3.

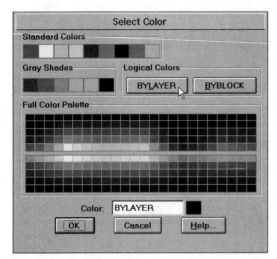

Figure 6.7　Select Color dialog box.

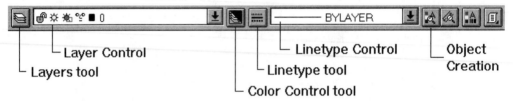

Figure 6.8　Object Properties toolbar.

When AutoCAD is started, a layer named 0 is created with a continuous line type and a color number 7. This layer has specific properties, which are discussed in chapter 10, and it cannot be deleted or renamed as other layers can.

6.4　Setting Layer Specifications

The lot plan to be drawn is to have five layers, as specified in Table 6.1. The current layer name is displayed in the Layer Control box of the Object Properties toolbar, illustrated in Figure 6.8 as layer 0. Any new objects drawn will be displayed on that layer. The default layer set by AutoCAD is 0. The current line type is displayed in the Linetype Control box as continuous (indicated by the solid line in Figure 6.8) and BYLAYER.

TABLE 6.1　Layer Specifications

Object	Layer name	Color	Line type
Road and walkway	0	Black	Continuous
Road allowance	Center	Blue	Center
House	House	Red	Continuous
Dimensions and text	Dimens	Black	Continuous
Property	Property	Red	Center

6.4.1 Creating new layers

Prior to doing anything with layers, you must first create them. Layer 0 doesn't have to be created because it's the default layer and so is created when AutoCAD is booted. You can create new layers at any time during the drawing process, either individually as they're required or together as a group. You'll create all the required layers for this drawing now. In DOS, select Data, then Layers.

Object Properties <toolbar> Layers (Figure 6.8) <pick>

The Layer Control Dialog box, illustrated in Figure 6.9, will be displayed. Type the names in the name box, as shown, and then press the New button to enter the names in the Layer Name list box, as shown in Figure 6.10. Note that, in the list of layer names, the names are separated with a comma and there are no spaces in the list. Click on Layer 0 in the list box, highlighting it, and then press the Current button, making layer 0 current. Any new objects drawn will reside on layer 0.

6.4.2 Setting the line type for each layer

The default line type for layers when they're created is Continuous. Entities drawn on layers Center and Property are to have a Center line type. Choose layers Center and Property by clicking their names in the Layer Name list box. If layer 0 is highlighted, click on it to deselect it. Highlight the layer names as shown in Figure 6.11.

Until you choose a layer to work on, buttons on the right side of the Layer Control dialog box, such as On and Off, are grayed (see Figure 6.9) and thus inactive. These buttons become active after a layer or layers are selected in the Layer Name list box (see Figure 6.10). Click on the Set Ltype... command box to display the Select Linetype dialog box, shown in Figure 6.12.

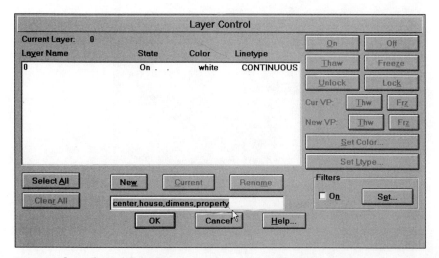

Figure 6.9 Layer Control dialog box.

Layer Control
Current Layer: 0
Layer Name
State
Color
Linetype
0 On . . white CONTINUOUS
CENTER On . . white CONTINUOUS
HOUSE On . . white CONTINUOUS
DIMENS On . . white CONTINUOUS
PROPERTY On . . white CONTINUOUS
On
Off
Thaw
Freeze
Unlock
Lock
Cur VP:
Thw
Frz
New VP:
Thw
Frz
Set Color...
Set Ltype...
Select All
Clear All
New
Current
Rename
0
Filters
On
Set...
OK
Cancel
Help...

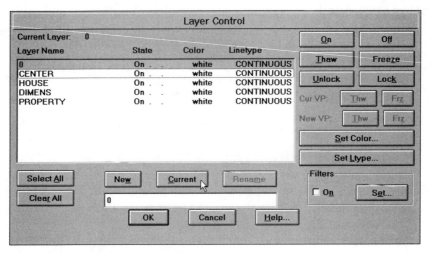

Figure 6.10 Setting the current layer.

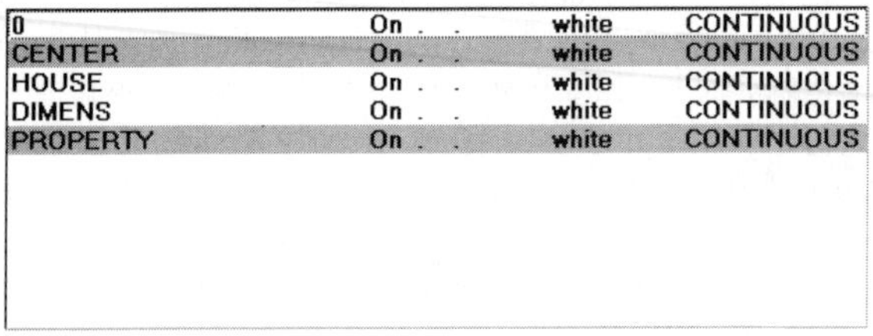

0 On . . white CONTINUOUS
CENTER On . . white CONTINUOUS
HOUSE On . . white CONTINUOUS
DIMENS On . . white CONTINUOUS
PROPERTY On . . white CONTINUOUS

Figure 6.11 Choosing layers.

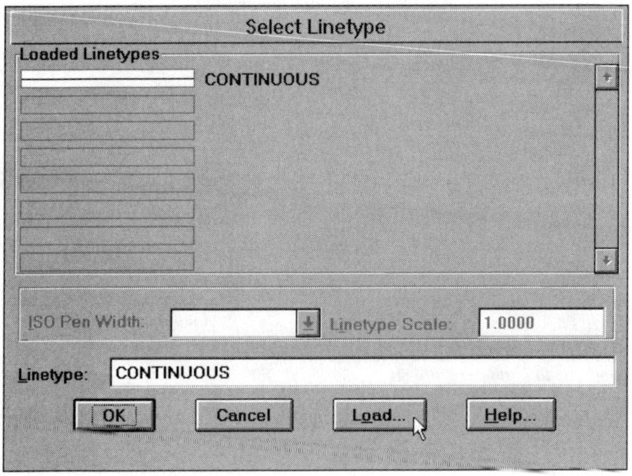

Select Linetype
Loaded Linetypes
CONTINUOUS
ISO Pen Width:
Linetype Scale:
1.0000
Linetype:
CONTINUOUS
OK
Cancel
Load...
Help...

Figure 6.12 Select Linetype dialog box.

As indicated in Figure 6.12, only the Continuous line type is currently loaded. To load the Center line type, press the Load... command box to display the Load or Reload Linetypes dialog box, illustrated in Figure 6.13. Select the Center line type, as shown, and then press the OK button to load the Center line type and return to the Select Linetype dialog box. Note that you can highlight any number of line types to be loaded, or press the Select All command button to select all available line types.

The loaded line types, Center and Continuous, are displayed in the Select Linetype box. Select the Center line type, as illustrated in Figure 6.14, and press OK to exit the dialog box.

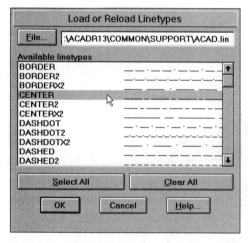

Figure 6.13 Loading a line type.

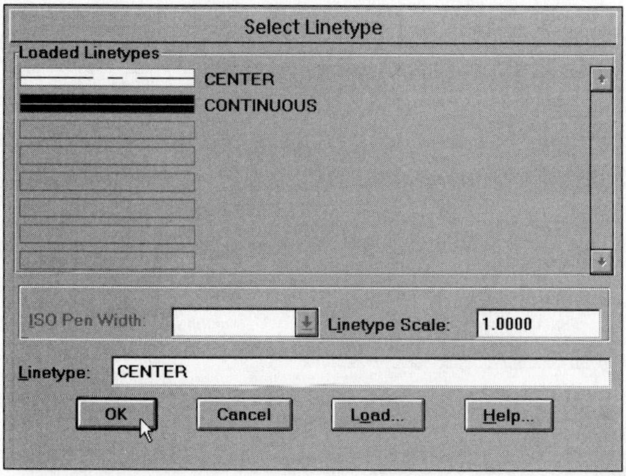

Figure 6.14 Selecting a line type.

6.4.3 Setting the color for each layer

The color for each layer needs to be defined. Remember that, even if you don't have a color monitor, the Color command is used because it instructs the plotter to select a different pen for each color in the drawing. Entities drawn on layer Center are to be blue. Currently, layers Center and Property are highlighted. Deselect layer Property by clicking on its name in the Layer Names list box. Only layer Center is to be highlighted. Click on the Set Color... button to display the Select Color dialog box, illustrated in Figure 6.15. Then select the blue box in the Standard Colors box. The color will be listed in the Color box at the bottom of the dialog box. Press the OK button.

Set the remaining layer colors, as illustrated in Figure 6.16. Note that the current layer is shown as 0 in Figure 6.16 and its color is displayed in the Current Color box of the toolbar. Press the OK button to exit the Layer Control dialog box.

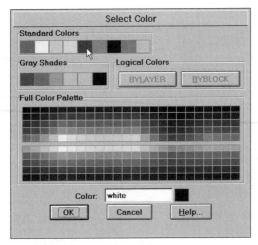

Figure 6.15 Selecting a layer color.

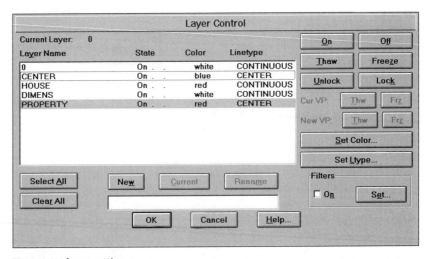

Figure 6.16 Layer setting.

6.4.4 Other layer options

Other layer options available are:

On. Layers turned on are displayed on the monitor.

Off. Layers turned off are not displayed.

Freeze. Frozen layers are ignored in drawing regenerations, thereby speeding up the drawing. Frozen layers are not displayed.

Thaw. Turns the frozen state for a layer off.

Lock. Entities on a locked layer are visible, but cannot be edited.

Unlock. Unlocks a layer to allow editing.

Set. Used with the Layer command at the command line to set a current drawing layer.

Make. Used with the Layer command at the command line to create a new layer and make it the current layer.

New. Used with the Layer command at the command line to create a new layer.

6.5 Snap Command

Decimal units have been set with three digits to the right of the decimal for this drawing. For actual drawing purposes, however, only one digit to the right of the decimal is required (see Figure 6.1). Snap will be set to 0.1 so the smallest movement of the cursor will be on an imaginary grid with spaces at 0.1 apart. Snap sets the fine movement of the cursor. You can still make larger steps, and turn off or re-set snap at any time. Choose the following in the menu bar:

Options <Pick> Drawing Aids... <pick>

The Drawing Aids dialog box illustrated in Figure 6.17 will be displayed. Move the cursor into the Snap X Spacing edit box and enter **0.1**. Press the <return> button and AutoCAD will set the X spacing to 0.1. Turn Snap on by clicking the On check box, which displays an ✕ when on. Turn the Ortho (orthogonal) mode on by clicking its check box in the Modes block. Press the OK button to exit the dialog box.

You can turn Snap on or off at any time by pressing the SNAP button in the status bar at the bottom of the Windows screen. In DOS, you can turn a Windows snap on or off by using <ctrl>–B (holding down <ctrl> and pressing B) or the F9 function key. You can toggle Ortho on and off by using the ORTHO button in the status bar or pressing <ctrl>–L (Windows), <ctrl>–O (DOS), or the F8 function key.

6.6 Drawing the Road and Driveway

You'll draw the road and driveway on Layer 0 (see section 6.2.1), which is the current layer, as indicated in the Layer Control box (refer back to Figure 6.8). The line

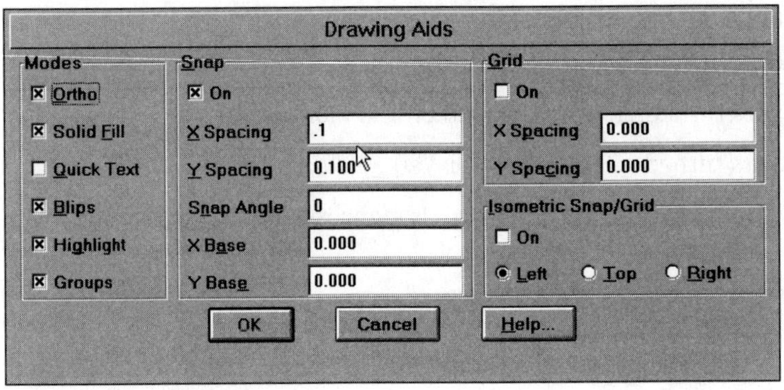

Figure 6.17 Drawing Aids dialog box.

type for layer 0 is continuous, so continuous lines are drawn on the monitor. The co-ordinates of the lower-left corner of the road are assumed as 7,8:

Draw <toolbox> Line <pick> From point: **7,8** <return> To point: Move the cursor vertical to about 7,45 and digitize the point. If the coordinate display in the status bar at the bottom of the screen doesn't change as the cursor is moved, press <ctrl>–D; if the coordinate display shows relative distance < angle, press <ctrl>–D again until it displays screen coordinates as the cursor moves. <pick> To point: <return>

In the previous set of commands, you should have noted that during the line command the Ortho mode made it easier to locate a point orthogonal to (directly above) the previous point. Also, <ctrl>–D or F6 is a toggle switch used to:

- Activate or deactivate the coordinate display.
- Set the coordinate display to relative distance < angle.
- Set the coordinate display to current screen coordinates.

Recall the Line command by pressing <return> or <spacebar>. The other side of the road is to start from a point 8 units to the right of the last point:

<return> Line From point: **@8<0** <return> Move the cursor down and select a point parallel with the first line. <pick> To point: <return>

Draw the driveway. The coordinates of the lower-left corner of the driveway are assumed as 15,16.5 (see Figure 6.18), and the driveway is 3 units wide:

<return> Line from point: **15,16.5** <return> To point: **@19.2<0** <return> To point: **@3<90** <return> To point: <return>

Draw the remainder of the driveway and walkway as shown in Figure 6.18. Do not place any driveway lines along the house lines because, when you plot this drawing in chapter 7, you'll use a different pen color for the house and driveway.

6.7 Changing a Layer

The current working layer shown in the Layer Control box (refer back to Figure 6.8) is layer 0. The house is to be drawn on layer House, so the current layer needs to be changed to layer House. You can do this by using the Layer Control dialog box (refer back to Figure 6.10), which is the method to use with DOS. With Windows, you can click on the Layer Control box, displaying the drop-down Layer Control box, illustrated in Figure 6.19. Note that the color of each layer is displayed beside its name in the drop-down box. You can change the layer's visibility on/off, freeze/thaw, and lock/unlock status by selecting the appropriate icon in the drop-down box list. Click on House in the list to make it current.

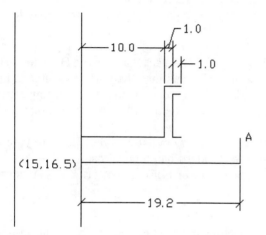

Figure 6.18 Driveway and walk.

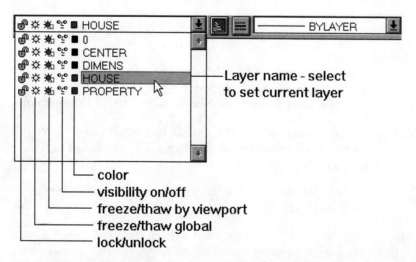

Figure 6.19 Layer Control box.

House is now displayed in the Layer Control box. Presently, all layers are on, but House is the layer on which new items will be drawn. Draw the house lines starting at point A in Figure 6.18. Use the Endpoint object snap to snap the start point on A.

6.8 Hatching

AutoCAD Release 13 provides two distinct options for hatching. The Hatch command invokes release-12 nonassociative hatching. The Bhatch command invokes associative hatching.

Associative hatching, which is invoked by the Bhatch command, is updated when the hatch boundary is modified. For example, the house lines in Figure 6.1 define a rectangular boundary measuring 7.2 m × 11.5 m that is to be hatched. In Chapter 13, the house will be stretched to 8.0 m × 11.5 m. If associative hatching is used, when the house is stretched the hatching is updated by AutoCAD to match the revised house dimensions defining the hatch boundary.

You can invoke the Bhatch command (associative hatching) by selecting the Hatch tool in the Draw toolbar (from DOS, select Hatch in the Draw menu) or by entering Bhatch at the command line. You can invoke the Hatch command (nonassociative hatching) by entering Hatch at the command line. Consequently, selecting Hatch from a toolbar or menu will invoke the Bhatch command, which is used throughout this book.

AutoCAD is supplied with a good library of hatch styles. Refer to your *AutoCAD User's Guide* for a listing of the standard hatch patterns available. You can create your own hatch pattern libraries, but I won't discuss pattern creation here.

6.8.1 Hatch scale factor

All AutoCAD's hatch patterns are drawn based on a factor of 1 unit per inch; hence the measurement system used does not affect the Hatch scale. The following formula is used to determine AutoCAD's Hatch scale factor:

$$\text{Plot scale} \times \text{Hatch} = 1 \text{ inch} \times \text{conversion}$$

where:

$$\text{Plot scale} = \text{scale at which drawing is to be plotted}$$
$$\text{Hatch} = \text{hatch scale factor}$$
$$\text{conversion} = \text{factor to convert inch units to the drawing units.}$$

This drawing is done in meter units and will be plotted using a scale of 1:300 on an A4 size sheet, which is measured in millimeters at 210 by 297. The Hatch scale is calculated using equation 6.2:

$$\tfrac{1}{300} \times \text{Hatch} = 1 \text{ inch} \times (25.4 \text{ mm} / 1 \text{ inch} \times 1 \text{ m} / 1000 \text{ mm})$$
$$\text{Hatch} = 7.62$$

A Hatch scale factor of 7.62 is then used. (Hatch scale factors are listed in appendix C, Table C.3, item A, Drawing Units: Meters shows the Hatch scale factor of 7.62 for a drawing in meter units with a plot scale of 1:300.)

6.8.2 Hatching the house

The house is hatched using the Ansi (American National Standards Institute) 31 hatch pattern. Invoke the Bhatch command, which does associative hatching, as follows (in DOS, select Draw, then Hatch...):

Draw <toolbar> Hatch <Pick>

The Boundary Hatch dialog box illustrated in Figure 6.21 will be displayed. Choose the ANSI31 pattern, as illustrated. Then enter the Hatch scale of **7.62** in the Scale box, as shown in Figure 6.22. The default Angle of 0 is to be used. Ensure that the Associative box is on (it should have an × in it).

You can select the object to be hatched by defining its boundary lines or by selecting an internal point and letting AutoCAD determine the boundary of that point. Press the Pick Point < command button. AutoCAD will remove the Boundary Hatch dialog button from the graphics screen, and continue at the command line with:

`Select internal point:` Pick a point inside the house walls. `<pick> Selecting everything... Selecting everything visible.... Select internal point: <return>`

If a box with the message "Nothing was found to make a boundary out of" is displayed on the screen, then AutoCAD couldn't locate a closed boundary to be

Figure 6.20 Hatch tool.

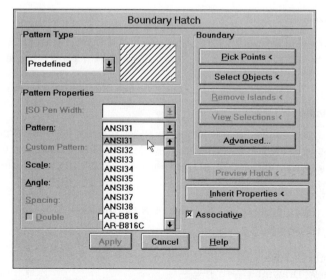

Figure 6.21 Select the hatch pattern.

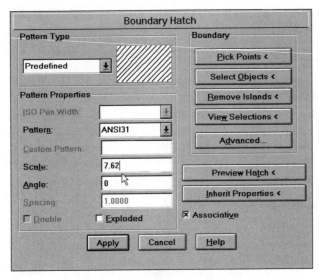

Figure 6.22 Boundary Hatch dialog box.

hatched. In that case, press <esc> and check that the area to be hatched has a closed boundary.

If a closed boundary was found, The Boundary Hatch dialog box will be returned to the screen when you press <return>. Press the Preview Hatch < command button (see Figure 6.22), and AutoCAD will remove the dialog box from the screen and display the hatching to be done. Press the Continue button to exit the preview and return to the Boundary Hatch dialog box. If the previewed hatch was correct, press the Apply button to complete the hatching.

6.9 Drawing Property Lines

Set the current layer to Property. When the layer is set correctly, the Layer Control box will display the name Property in it. Refer to section 6.7 for the procedure used to set a new current layer.

6.9.1 Setting the line type scale

The center line type is used for the Property layer. Because the line type is not a solid line, it must be scaled to suit the drawing. AutoCAD line types are based on a factor of 1 unit per inch, so the measurement system set doesn't affect the line type scale. The line type scale (Ltscale) is calculated as follows:

$$\text{Plot scale} \times \text{Ltscale} = 1 \text{ inch} \times \text{conversion} \times \tfrac{3}{4}$$

where:

Plot scale = scale at which drawing is to be plotted
Hatch = hatch scale factor
conversion = factor to convert inch units to the drawing units.

The ¾ factor in the equation simply gives a better line on the drawing. The drawing is in meter units and is to be plotted using a scale of 1:300:

$$\frac{1}{300} \times \text{Ltscale} = 1 \text{ inch} \times (25.4 \text{ mm} / 1 \text{ inch} \times 1 \text{ m} / 1000 \text{ mm}) \times \frac{3}{4}$$
$$\text{Ltscale} = 5.7$$

You can set line type scales globally by using the Ltscale command or by object with the Celtscale command (to be discussed in another chapter). Set the global line type scale (Ltscale) as follows (in DOS, select Data, then Linetype):

Object properties (Figure 6.8) <toolbar> Linetype <pick>

The Select Linetype dialog box illustrated in Figure 6.23 will be displayed. Note that the Linetype is Bylayer. Set the Linetype Scale to 5.7, as shown, and press OK to exit.

6.9.2 Surveyor's units

Property lines are defined in surveyor's units, as shown back in Figure 6.1. Bearing angles are always specified from either north or south toward the east or west. For instance a 45-degree angle is shown as N45°E, a 125-degree angle is shown as N35°W, and a 200-degree angle is shown as S70°W.

Because the degree symbol (°) isn't available on the keyboard, the letter D (upper- or lowercase) is used in place of the degree symbol when entering angles in Auto-CAD, so an angle is entered as 70d35'30". This same angle entered as a bearing is N70D35'30"E. Angle units are set to surveyor's units as follows:

Data <pick> Units <pick>

The Units Control dialog box illustrated in Figure 6.24 will be displayed. Click the Surveyor button on in the Angles box. Then click on the down arrow in the Precision

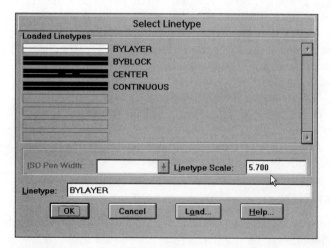

Figure 6.23 Setting the line type scale.

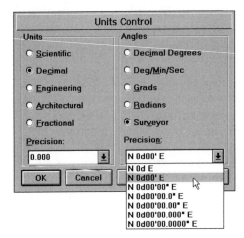

Figure 6.24 Surveyor angle units.

box to display the drop-down Precision box. Set the precision to N0d00'E, so angles are displayed to the nearest minute. North is to be at 12 o'clock, placing East at 3 o'-clock. Click on the Direction Control... box to display Direction Control dialog box. Press the East radio button, setting the East direction at 3 o'clock. Choosing North would place East at 12 o'clock (where North normally is), and choosing West would place East at 9 o'clock (where West normally is). Press the Counterclockwise radio button so positive angles are measured in a counterclockwise direction. Exit the dialog box by clicking on OK.

Turn the orthogonal mode off by clicking the ORTHO button in the status bar or pressing <ctrl>–O. Orthogonal is off when the ORTHO button is shaded. The legal survey description for the lot name Easy is: commencing at the Southwest corner of Easy property, then Easterly along a line 20.000 meters N90°0"E, then Northerly 11.490 meters along a line N60°30'E, then Northerly 15.308 meters along a line N47°30'W, then Westerly 18.714 meters along a line N90°0'W, then Southerly 16.000 meters along a line S0°0"W to the BEGINNING.

The Southwest corner of the lot is at coordinates 21,16 on the monitor. Enter the lot data following the legal survey description:

Draw <toolbox> Line <pick> From point: **21,16** <return> To point: **@20<N90D0'E** (or E) <return> To point: **@11.490<N60D30'E** <return> etc.

When AutoCAD surveyor's units are used, angles can be entered as angles (e.g., 90) or as bearings (e.g., N), as illustrated in this exercise.

6.10 Drawing the Road Allowance

The road allowance is to be drawn on the Center layer. Set Center as the current drawing layer. The line type scale doesn't have to be set again. Draw the road allowance as shown in Figure 6.25. Do not overlap the previously drawn property line because a different color is used for the property line. Start the far left property line using the From object snap, which allows you to specify a "last point" from which to measure a distance. In this case, the left property boundary is to start @6<180 from the lower left corner of the road—point A in Figure 6.25. Enter the following (<shift>–<right> means to press the <shift> and 2nd mouse button together to display the floating object snap menu):

Draw <toolbar> Line <pick> From point: <shift>–<right> From <pick> from Base point: <shift>–<right> Endpoint <pick> of Place the endpoint object snap aperture on the bottom left end of the road line (point A in Figure 6.25). <pick> <Offset>: **@6<180** <return>, etc.

6.11 Text Height

The text height is calculated assuming the drawing will be plotted on an A4-size sheet (210×297 mm) using a scale of 1:300 (1 mm = 300 mm, or 0.3 m). The drawing units are meters, and the desired height of text on the plotted drawing is 3 mm. The monitor text height (h) is then calculated as follows (also see appendix C, Table C.3):

$$\tfrac{1}{300} \times h = 3 \text{ mm}$$
$$h = 900 \text{ mm, or } 0.9 \text{ m}$$

6.12 Dimensioning

Dimensioning is to be done on the Dimens layer. Set Dimens as the current drawing layer. The dimension scale Dimscale is calculated based on the default AutoCAD value for dimension text height of 2.5 mm in the metric measurement system, and the text height, h, for text on the monitor calculated as 0.9 in the previous section. Dimscale is calculated using the first equation in the chapter, as follows (also see appendix C, Table C.3):

$$\text{Dimscale} \times 2.5 = \text{Text Height}$$
$$\text{Dimscale} \times 2.5 = 0.9$$
$$\text{Dimscale} = 0.36$$

6.12.1 Setting dimension variables

Display the Dimension Style dialog box, illustrated in Figure 6.26. Note that the default dimension style in AutoCAD's metric measurement setting is ISO-25. Click on Geometry... to display the Geometry dialog box (Figure 6.27) and set the Overall Scale to the Dimscale value calculated in the previous section as 0.36. Then set the Arrowheads to Oblique. AutoCAD multiplies all numerical dimension variables, such as the size of arrowheads, by the Overall Scale factor (Dimscale) as they're used in the drawing, so they don't have to be modified. Press the OK button to return to the Dimension Style dialog box.

Press the Format... command button to display the Format dialog box illustrated in Figure 6.28. Turn the User Defined box off (no × in it) initially. If User Defined is off, you

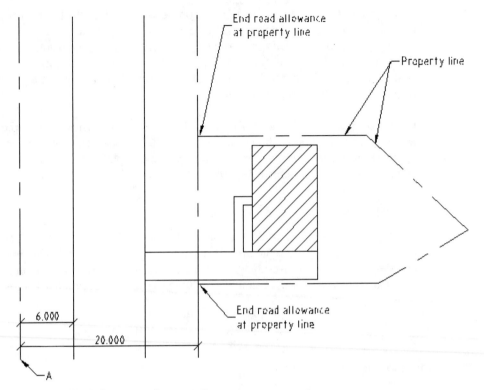

Figure 6.25 Road allowance and property lines.

can specify where the text is to be automatically located in the Horizontal Justification box. Try some of the Horizontal Justification settings to see what they look like. You can also specify the fit for the text (Best Fit is displayed in Figure 6.28). If the space is available, AutoCAD will place text and arrowheads between the extension lines. If there isn't enough space for both, the following settings govern how text and arrows fit:

Best Fit. When enough space is available for text, it's placed between the extension lines, and arrowheads are placed outside the extension lines. When there's enough space for arrowheads, they're placed between the extension lines, and the text is placed outside the extension lines. When space is available for neither, AutoCAD places both outside the extension lines.

Text and Arrows. If there's not enough space for both text and arrowheads between the Arrows extension lines, both are placed outside the extension lines.

Text Only. When space is available, AutoCAD places the text between the extension lines, and places the arrowheads outside. When no space is available, both text and arrowheads are placed outside the extension lines.

Turn the User Defined box on (there should be an × in it), which allows you to locate the dimension text where you want it as you do the dimension, e.g., centered between the extension lines, to the left of the extension lines, or to the right of the

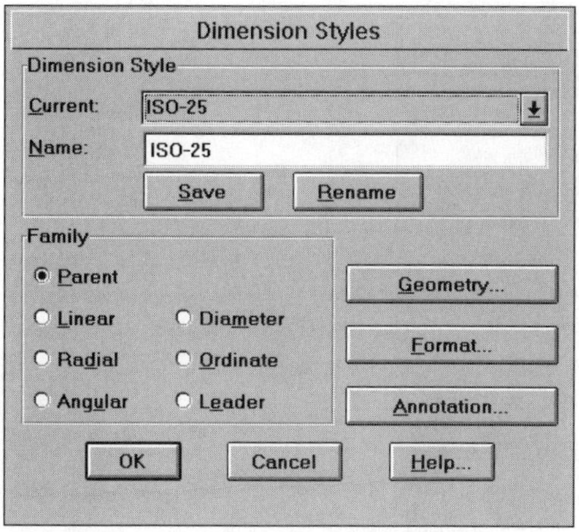

Figure 6.26 Metric dimension style.

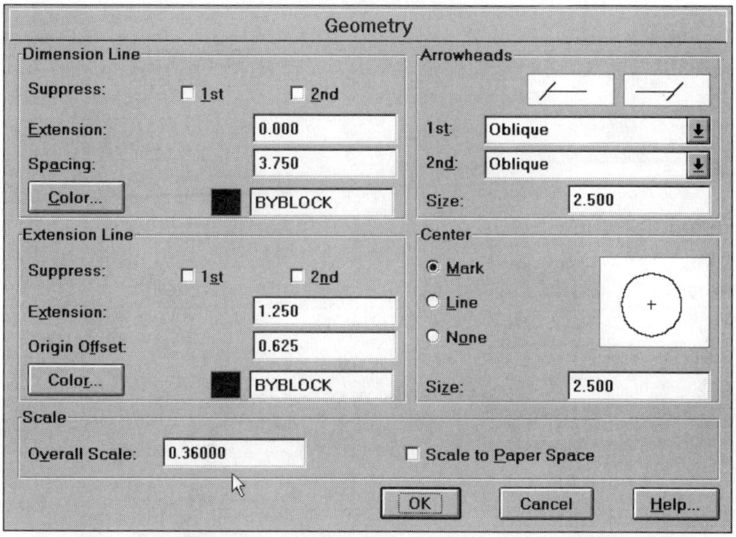

Figure 6.27 Geometry settings.

extension lines. Set the Vertical Justification to Above so the dimensions are placed above the dimension line. Complete the other settings, as illustrated in Figure 6.29, and press the OK button to return to the Dimension Style dialog box.

Press the Annotations... command button to display the Annotations dialog box illustrated in Figure 6.29. Note that you can change the text style, set alternate units to be displayed with the dimension, and set tolerances to be displayed. Also note the default dimension text height of 2.5 (see section 6.12). This value isn't changed because the actual dimension text height on the monitor is the product of this value and the Overall Scale (Dimscale) of 0.36. Press the Units... command button to display the Primary Units dialog box, illustrated in Figure 6.30. Set the Precision to

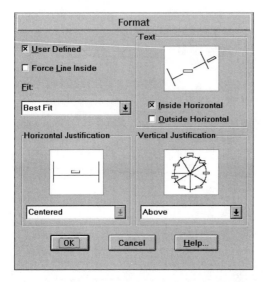

Figure 6.28 Format Settings.

Figure 6.29 Annotation settings.

0.000. Then turn the Trailing Zero Suppression button off. If it's on, dimensions such as 3.600 will appear as 3.6, e.g., the trailing zeros will be suppressed. Also turn the Leading Zero Suppression off (no × in it). If it's on, 0.36 will appear as .36. Press OK to return to the Annotation dialog box, and press OK to return to the Dimension Style dialog box illustrated in Figure 6.26.

Press the Save button to save the changes in the settings to the ISO-25 dimension style. Then press OK to return to the graphics screen.

6.12.2 Associative dimensioning

Associate dimensioning (Dimaso) is on by default. When associative dimensioning is on, dimension lines, text, arrowheads, etc. are drawn as a single object. Enter the following at the command line to see if Dimaso is on:

`Command:` **dimaso** `<return> New value for Dimaso <on>: <return>`

6.12.3 Linear dimensions

Add the horizontal dimension across the bottom of the lot plan:

Dimensioning <toolbar> Linear Dimension <pick> `First extension line origin or RETURN to select:` <shift>–<right> Nearest <pick> to Place the Nearest aperture box over the bottom left side of the road allowance, where you want the 20.000 dimension line to start. <pick> `Second extension line origin:` <shift>–<right> Nearest <pick> to Place the aperture over the right side of the road allowance, in line with the last point entered. <pick> `Dimension line location (Text/Angle/Horizontal/Vertical/Rotated):` Keeping the cursor along the same line as the two points picked, move it to the right and left, noting how the dimension text moves with it. This is because the User Defined box is on in the dimension Format dialog box. Move the cursor to place the text in the middle of the two points picked. <pick>

Draw the 20.000 dimension text as specified (refer back to Figure 6.1). If you make a mistake, press Undo and try again. Continue the dimension:

Dimensioning <toolbar> Continue Dimension <pick> `Second extension line or RETURN to select:` <shift>–<right> Intersect <pick> of Place the Intersection aperture over the intersection point on the right side of the lot. <pick> `Second extension line or RETURN to select:` <return> <return>

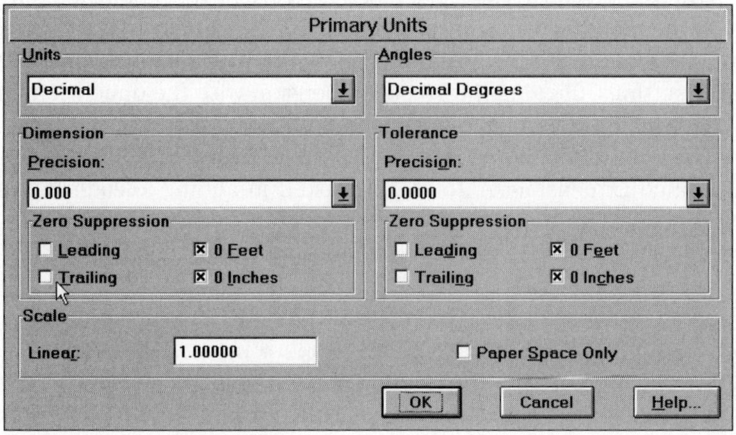

Figure 6.30 Units settings.

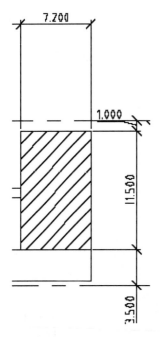

Figure 6.31 Continued dimension.

Draw the 30.000 dimension text as specified (refer back to Figure 6.1). Complete the dimension string across the top of the property. Remember to use object snaps to locate the extension line points accurately.

Add the 16.000 dimension on the right side of the property. Note that the dimension text is placed horizontally by AutoCAD, not aligned with the dimension line, as shown back in Figure 6.1. To align the dimension, display the dimension Format dialog box illustrated back in Figure 6.28. In the Text box, turn the Inside Horizontal box off (no × in it). The Outside Horizontal box should also be off. Then press OK to return to the Dimension Style dialog box. Press the Save... command box to save the settings to the ISO-25 style, and then press OK. The dimensions will be regenerated by AutoCAD, and all ISO-25 style dimensions (all your dimensions) will be redrawn to the new settings, aligning the 16.000 dimension with the dimension line.

Add the remaining vertical dimensions on the right side of the house, shown in Figure 6.31. I had difficulty with the 1.000 dimension at the top of the house when using Continue Dimension; AutoCAD persisted in adding a leader and placing the text horizontally. This might be corrected in later versions of AutoCAD. Fix the dimension by using the Erase tool to erase the dimension, then replace the dimension:

Dimensioning <toolbar> Linear Dimension <pick> `First extension line origin or RETURN to select:` <shift>–<right> Intersection <pick> Place the Intersection aperture box over the intersection of the dimension and extension line of the 11.500 dimension, where the oblique arrowhead is. <pick> `Second extension line origin:` <shift>–<right> Nearest <pick> Place the aperture over the property line, in line with the last point entered. <pick> `Dimension line location`

(Text/Angle/Horizontal/ Vertical/Rotated): Keeping the cursor along the same line as the two points picked, move it to the right so the 1.00 dimension text falls (Figure 6.1). <pick>

6.12.4 Editing associative dimensions

Because associative dimensioning is on, you can edit the dimensions as single entities. For example, the 3.500 dimension on the right side of the house is placed outside the extension lines. It can be homed (placed inside the extension lines), as follows (in DOS, Select Draw, then Dimensioning, then Home):

Dimensioning <toolbar> Home <pick> select dimension: Select the 3.500 text. <pick> Enter text location (Left/Right/Home/Angle): **h**

The 3.500 dimension text is now homed between the extension lines. Try some of the other options, such as Rotate. Press Undo to return to the original dimension in each case.

6.13 Text

The text is to be on layer Dimens, which should be the current layer. In section 6.11, the text height was calculated as 0.9 screen units. Normally, you select the start point when entering text. To center the bearing text above a lot line, use the center option, which allows entry of the bottom center point for the text (refer to chapter 5, section 5.11).

The bearing requires a degree symbol, which you can enter by using the unified code \U+00B0 (see Table 5.1 back in chapter 5) or the text control code %%d (see chapter 5, section 5.16). Enter the N60°30'E bearing as follows:

Draw <toolbar> Single-line text <pick> Justify/Style/<Start point>: **j** (Justify) <return> Align/Fit/Center/Middle/Right/TL/TC/TL/ML/MC/MR/BL/ BC/BR: **tc** <return> Pick the top center point for the N60°30'E text below the sloping lot line (Figure 6.1). <pick> Height <0.900>: <return> Rotation Angle <E>: Pick a point so the "rubber band" cursor line is parallel with the lot line. <pick> Text: **N60%%d30'E** <return>

Add the remaining text to the drawing, using appropriate justification for placing the text on the drawing. If you forget the bearing or length of a line, you can invoke the List command to display the line data, as follows (in DOS, select Inquiry, as shown in Figure 6.32, then List:

Object Properties <toolbar> List <pick> Select objects: Pick a line for which you want to view the data. <pick> Select objects: <return>

The data for the N60°30'E bearing line is as follows:

```
Select objects:
              LINE        Layer: PROPERTY
                          Space: Model space
              Handle = 23D
```

```
    from point, X=   51.000   Y=   21.658   Z=    0.000
      to point, X=   39.714   Y=   32.000   Z=    0.000
Length =    15.308,   Angle in XY Plane = N 47d30' W
        Delta X =  -11.286, Delta Y =    10.342, Delta Z = 0.000
```

6.14 North Arrow

Use the leader command to draw the north arrow. Display the Dimension Style dialog box (Figure 6.27) and press the Leader family button on. Then press the Geometry... command button to display the Geometry dialog box (Figure 6.28). Set the Overall Scale in the Scale box to 1.5, then change the Arrowheads to Closed Filled. Press the OK button to return to the Dimension Style dialog box.

In the Dimension Style Name box, enter the name **Arrow** from the keyboard, and then press the Save command button to make Arrow the current style. Arrow is the same as ISO-25, except for the changes made in the Leader family. Press OK to exit. Use the Leader tool to draw the arrow:

Dimensioning <toolbar> Leader <pick> From point: Pick the tip of the arrow. <pick> To point: Pick the end of the shaft. <pick> To point: <return> Annotation (or RETURN for options): <return> Tolerance/Copy/Block/ None/<Mtext>: **n** <return>

Now use the single-line text to add the N. Use a text height of 3. Recall the Dimension Style dialog box and set the Dimension Style back to ISO-25. Save the drawing and exit AutoCAD.

Figure 6.32 Inquiry flyout.

Configuring AutoCAD and Plotting/Printing

Objective: Configure AutoCAD for graphics hardware, set plot specifications and plot drawings, set a system printer using Windows Print Manager, and hatch complex objects.

Drawing: Plot Proj-5.dwg and Proj-6.dwg.

7.1 Configuring AutoCAD

The configuration procedure tailors AutoCAD to the graphics devices connected to your computer, such as a plotter, printer, mouse, digitizing tablet, and video display. For instance, if you want to plot your drawings, you must configure AutoCAD to communicate with your plotter. This communication requires driver information, which gives AutoCAD technical information about the type of plotter you have. AutoCAD uses AutoCAD device interface (ADI) drivers to communicate with peripheral hardware. Some ADI drivers come with AutoCAD. If a driver for your device (e.g., a plotter) isn't listed with AutoCAD's drivers, you'll have to obtain one from the manufacturer of the device.

When installing AutoCAD, you must configure it. I assume that AutoCAD is installed on your system, and the purpose of this chapter is to assist you in installing new devices or change existing devices. The configuration procedures discussed are limited to more common configurations. Refer to your *AutoCAD Installation Guide* for configurations of a more complex nature.

To change the configuration of a graphics device or add a new graphics device to your configuration, choose the following in the menu bar:

Options <pick> Configure <pick>

AutoCAD will display the current configuration for your system and request `Press RETURN to continue`. Do so now. AutoCAD will then display copyright information and the serial number for your copy of release 13, and the following Configuration menu:

```
Configuration menu:

0. Exit to drawing editor
1. Show current configuration
2. Allow detailed configuration
3. Configure video display
4. Configure digitizer
5. Configure plotter
6. Configure system console
7. Configure operating parameters.

Enter selection <0>:
```

You can select a task by typing the number associated with the task and pressing <return>. When the selected task is finished, AutoCAD will return to the Configuration menu.

7.1.1 Exit to main menu

When the configuration process is completed, enter **0**, Exit to Main Menu. AutoCAD will ask if you want to save the configuration changes you made. If you answer **N**, the original configuration will be used and the changes will be deleted. A **Y** answer will cause AutoCAD to save the new configuration and use that configuration both in the current drawing and each time AutoCAD is booted.

7.1.2 Show current configuration

To see what AutoCAD is configured for, enter **1**, Show Current Configuration. AutoCAD will list the hardware it's presently configured for.

7.1.3 Allow detailed configuration

If you want to specify additional parameters during the configuration of devices, press **2**, Allow Detailed Device Configuration, and then enter **Y**. AutoCAD will respond with `Additional questions will be asked during device configuration`, and you'll be returned to the Configuration menu. Entering **N** will return you to the Configuration menu.

7.1.4 Configure video display

This task, option 3 in the Configuration menu, lets you tailor AutoCAD to your particular video display components. The available video displays are listed and you're asked to select one. A series of questions about the device are then displayed. Respond to each prompt.

On some screens, the dot density isn't the same in the horizontal and vertical axes. The ratio of horizontal and vertical dots per inch is called the *dot aspect ratio*. The display driver file contains a factor that should correct the dot aspect ratio. If circles appear as ovals on your screen, you might want to make a further correction during the video display configuration task. AutoCAD will prompt:

```
If you have previously measured the height and width of a "square" on your
graphics screen, you may use these measurements to correct the aspect ratio. Would
you like to do so? <N>:
```

If you've made the specified measurements and want to make the dot aspect ratio correction, enter **Y**. If not, enter **N**.

7.1.5 Configure digitizer

Choose item 4 in the Configuration menu to configure a pointing device or digitizer. With Windows, if you don't have a digitizer, select Current System Pointing Device to use the Windows system pointer.

7.1.6 Configure plotter

Choose item 5 in the Configuration menu to install a printer or plotter. AutoCAD will display the following menu:

```
Plotter configuration menu

0. Exit to configuration menu
1. Add a plotter configuration
2. Delete a plotter configuration
3. Change a plotter configuration
4. Rename a plotter configuration

Enter selection, 0 to 4 <0>:
```

If you enter 1, a list of supported devices will be displayed and you'll be asked to select one. Follow the prompts for information about the selected device. If you're using a single-pen plotter, you'll be asked `Do you want to change pens while plotting?` If you answer **Y** (yes), the plotter will pause during plotting to allow you to change pens for each different screen color in the drawing.

You can configure AutoCAD for a number of plotters, or have more than one configuration for the same plotter by entering a unique descriptor for each configuration. AutoCAD will prompt:

```
Enter a description for this plotter:
```

Enter a unique descriptor and press <return>. AutoCAD will then return to the Plotter Configuration menu. To return to the Configuration menu, enter **0**.

7.1.7 Configure operating parameters

Option 7 in the Configuration menu displays the following menu:

```
Operating Parameters menu

0. Exit to configuration menu
1. Alarm on error
2. Initial drawing setup
3. Default plot file name
4. Plot spooler directory
5. Placement of temporary files
6. Network node name
7. Automatic-save feature
8. Full-time CRC values
9. Automatic audit after AXFIN or DXBIN
10. Login name
11. File-locking

Enter selection <0>:
```

The options in this menu are as follows:

Alarm on Error. Causes an alarm to beep when AutoCAD detects an invalid entry.

Initial Drawing Setup. Allows you to specify a default prototype for new drawings. The default is acad.dwg. This option allows you to create a drawing with specific settings that are the default whenever a new drawing is started.

Default Plot File Name. If you plot to a file, this name will be used as the default name for the file.

Placement of Temporary Files. During the drawing process, AutoCAD writes temporary working files to RAM. If available RAM is exceeded, it will store the files to disk. These files are normally written to the drawing file directory. This option allows you to specify another directory.

Automatic Save Feature. This allows you to specify the time interval for automatic saves and the filename.

File Locking. If you aren't working on a network file, disable locking.

7.2 Plotting Drawings

You can plot/print drawings by choosing either Print... from the File menu in the menu bar or the print tool in the Standard toolbar. AutoCAD will display the Plot Configuration dialog box, shown in Figure 7.1.

7.2.1 Device and default selection

Click on the Device and Default Selection... command box to display the Device and Default selection box illustrated in Figure 7.2. To choose a device, select it from the list box. If your plotter/printer isn't listed, follow the configuration procedure outlined in section 7.1. The System Printer shown in the device list in Figure 7.2 is the

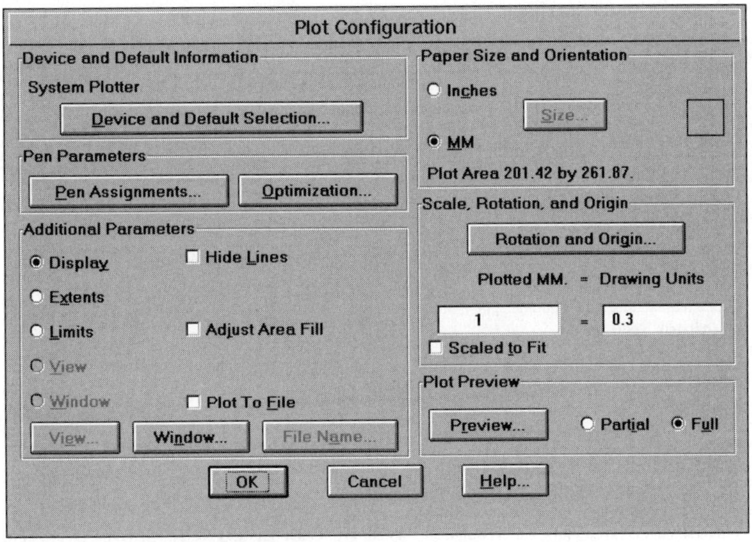

Figure 7.1   Plot Configuration dialog box.

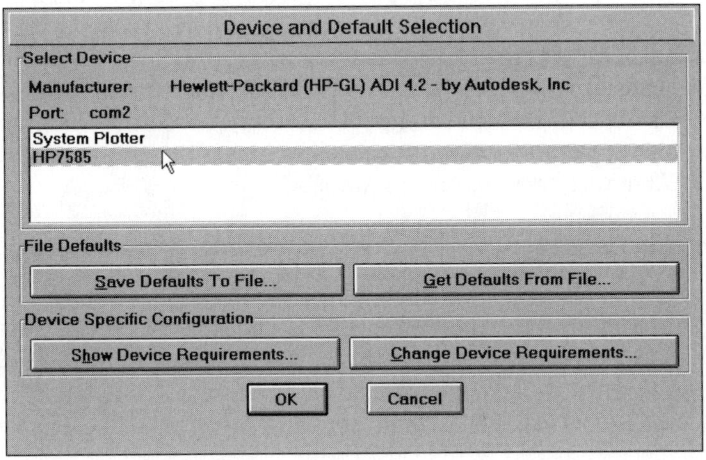

Figure 7.2   Device selection.

printer installed with the Windows Print Manager. The procedure for installing a printer through Windows Print Manager is outlined in the following section.

7.3 Windows Print Manager

To install a system printer through the Windows Print Manager, exit AutoCAD to the Windows Program Manager (for Windows 95 see appendix H). Bring the Main Window group to the front by clicking on it, and then choose the Print Manager icon. The

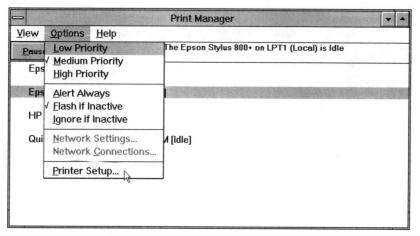

Figure 7.3 Windows Print Manager.

Print Manager Window (Figure 7.3) will be displayed. Choose Printer Setup... from the menu, and the Printer selection box shown in Figure 7.4 will be displayed.

Click the Add >> button in the Printer selection box to display the list of printers shown in Figure 7.4. Then select the printer/plotter you want to add from the drop-down box. Install the device by clicking Install. You might be asked to insert the disk that contains the printer driver file. This is one of your original Windows diskettes or a diskette provided by your printer manufacturer. If you're prompted for other files, insert the diskette and then press the OK button. Choose the Close button when through installing printers/plotters. You can now access the printer/plotter you've installed as a Windows system printer in AutoCAD.

7.4 Plotting/Printing the Drawing

Boot AutoCAD and choose either Open... from the File menu or the Open tool in the Standard toolbar to display the Select File dialog box. Open drawing C:\DRAW-INGS\PROJ-6 for editing. The full drawing should be displayed on the screen. If not, enter the Zoom and All commands. Select Print... in the File menu or toolbar. The Plot Configuration dialog box illustrated back in Figure 7.1 will be displayed.

7.4.1 Choosing a plotter/printer

If you're using a printer other than the one listed in the Device and Default Information box, click on the Device and Default Selection... command button to display the Device & Default Selection dialog box, shown back in Figure 7.2. Choose the desired printer from the device list box and then press OK to return to the Plot Configuration dialog box.

7.4.2 Paper size and orientation

Proj-6 is drawn in meter units, so the paper size used is to be in millimeters. Press the MM radio button in the top right corner of the Plot Configuration dialog box. Then click on the Size... command button to display the Paper Size dialog box illustrated in

Figure 7.5. The size list box on the left side of the dialog box lists the plot sizes available for the configured plotter/printer. To choose a listed size, such as MAX, move the cursor onto it and press the <pick> button. You can enter other sizes in the User input boxes. Assuming this plot is to be done on an 11 × 8.5-inch sheet converted to 280 × 215 mm, Click on the User Width box and enter **280**. Then click the Height box and enter **215** and press <return>. When you press the <return> key, the User size is listed and highlighted in the list box. Press the OK button. If you're using a Windows system printer, the paper size and orientation is set in the Print Manager. To change the size, toggle to Print Manager and choose Setup in the Printers Window (Figure 7.4).

7.4.3 Plot rotation and orientation

In the Plot Configuration box, click on the Rotation and Origin... command box to display the Plot and Rotation dialog box, shown in Figure 7.6. Press the **0** Plot Rota-

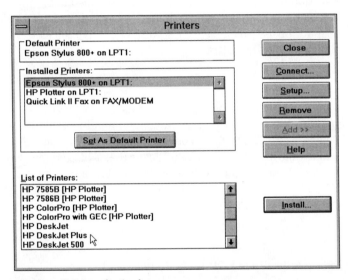

Figure 7.4 Printer selection box.

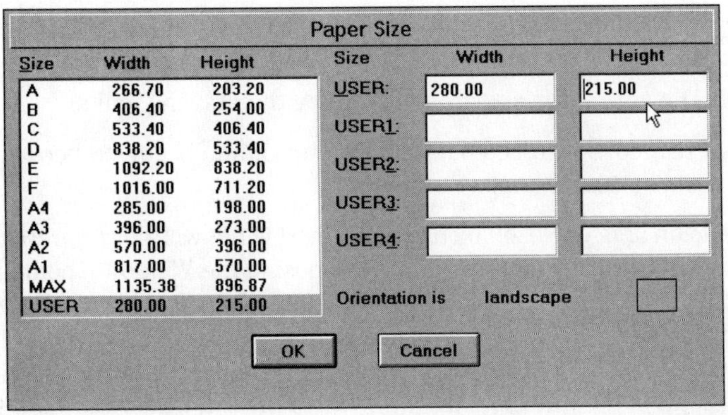

Figure 7.5 Setting the paper size.

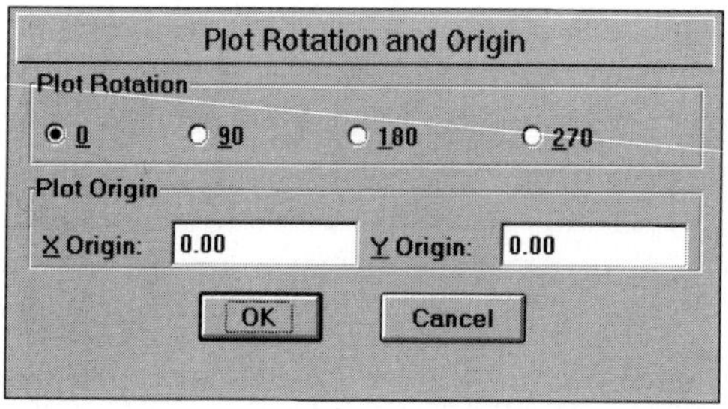

Figure 7.6 Setting the plot rotation and origin.

tion button (with a standard printer, you might have to rotate the plot 90 or 270 degrees). 0.00 X Origin and 0.00 Y Origin will be accepted. If you want to start the plot at some other location on the sheet, measure the X and Y distance from the plotter's home position using the paper size units (mm in this case) and enter the desired coordinates in the input boxes. You'll have to experiment with your plotter to see what settings are best. Press the OK button.

7.4.4 Plot scale

Proj-6 is drawn in meter units, and is to be plotted using a scale of 1:300. This means that 1 millimeter (mm) of the plot is to be equal 300 mm of the drawing. Since the drawing is in meter (m) units, you must convert 300 mm to drawing units by dividing by 1000 (1 m = 1000 mm), giving 0.3 m. This means that 1 plotted mm = 0.3 drawing units (meters). Enter **1** and **0.3** in the Plotted MM = Drawing Units entry boxes, as shown back in Figure 7.1. If the drawing isn't going to be plotted to scale, you can select the Scale to Fit box to have AutoCAD plot the drawing to fit the paper size entered.

7.4.5 What to plot

The available plot options in the Plot Configuration box are:

Display. Plots all of the entity currently visible on the monitor.

Extents. Plots the largest view available of the drawing that contains all the drawing entities.

Limits. Plots the entire drawing area defined by the drawing limits.

View. Plots a named view (see chapter 15). This option is grayed because there are no named views in this drawing.

Window. Plots an area enclosed by a user-defined window. Prior to pressing the Window button, you must define a window by choosing the Window... command button to display the dialog box shown in Figure 7.7. You can define the window to enclose the plotted area in two ways: by entering a First Corner X and Y coordinate and a Second Corner X and Y coordinate in the input boxes, or by clicking the Pick< button, which displays the drawing, allowing you to place a window around the plotted area using the cursor.

Press the Display radio button to plot the view currently displayed on the monitor. Press the OK button to exit.

7.4.6 Pen assignments

The Plot Configuration box (Figure 7.1) is displayed. Click on the Pen Assignments... box to display the Pen Assignments dialog box, illustrated in Figure 7.8. The pen list box shows the following (if you're using a printer you might not have any options available, or you might be able to set dots/mm depending on your printer):

Color. The color of an object on the drawing, defined by the layer or object color.

Pen No. The number of a pen slot in the pen holder of the plotter. Setting this number tells AutoCAD what pen to select for a specified object color.

Linetype. The linetype defined by the plotter. The linetype of objects is normally controlled by the layer linetype setting in AutoCAD, and the plotter line type is set to 0, which is a continuous linetype. Mixing linetypes, such as using a center line type on a layer and setting a dotted linetype on the plotter, will give you unexpected results. To list the line types available on the plotter and their associated number, click on the Feature Legend... box.

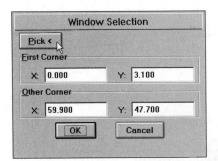

Figure 7.7 Defining a plot using a window.

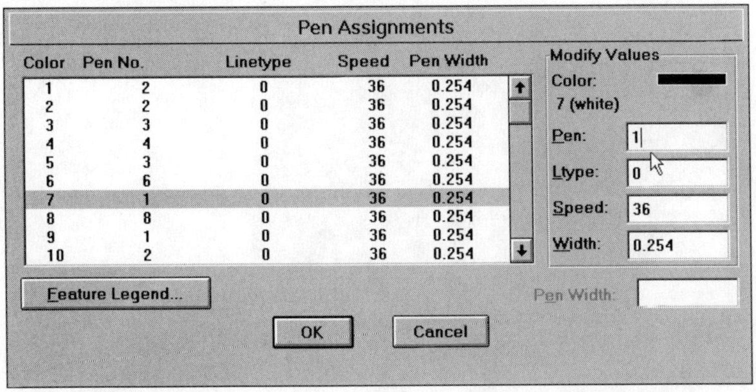

Figure 7.8 Setting pen assignments.

Pen speed. The speed of the plotter. You might want to reduce the pen speed for a pen that skips.

Pen Width. The width of the pen being defined. This is crucial when an object is being filled (see chapter 10) since it tells AutoCAD how far apart to place the strokes of the pen to fill something in. The number on a pen, e.g., .3, is usually in millimeters. Setting a pen width too large, such as 0.3 (mm) rather than 0.01 (inches) for Imperial unit drawing, will often cause strange output from the plotter.

The layer colors used in Proj-6 (see section 6.3 in chapter 6) are black (7), blue (5), and red (1). Set the pens for those colors, as illustrated in Figure 7.8. For example, to set color 7, move the cursor onto color 7 and press <pick>, highlighting that color in the selection box. When a color's data is highlighted in the list box, you can modify its pen number, line type, etc., with the Modify Value entry boxes on the right side of the dialog box. The color box will change to black, and 7 (black) will be printed.

Move the cursor into the Pen: entry box, type **1**, and press <return>. Set the Ltype to 0, Speed to 36 (or default), and Width to 0.254 (or 0.3), as shown. As the values are entered, they change in the list box. Click color 7 in the list box to deselect it, and then click color 5. Color 5 will be highlighted and the Modify Values color box will change to blue. Modify the settings for color 5, as shown in Figure 7.8, then deselect color 5, select color 1 (red), and modify its settings. Since no other colors are used in the drawing, you don't need any other settings. When the plot is being done, the plotter will select pen 1 for red entities, pen 2 for blue entities, and pen 1 for white entities. The pens in these holders can be whatever color or width of pen you want to be selected for each color. Press the OK button when through.

7.4.7 Plot preview

You can obtain a preview of the plot prior to the actual plotting. To obtain a partial preview, illustrated in Figure 7.9, press the Partial radio button in the Plot Preview

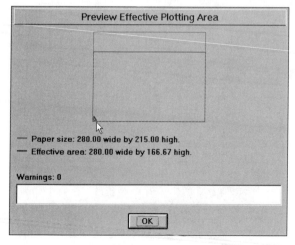

Figure 7.9 Partial plot preview.

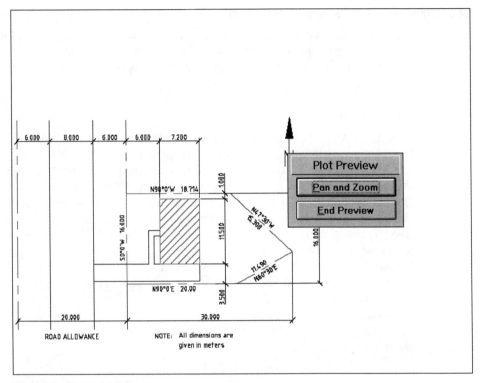

Figure 7.10 Full plot preview.

box of the Plot Configuration dialog box (refer back to Figure 7.1) and then click the Preview... command button. The rotation icon (pointed to in Figure 7.9) marks the lower left corner of your drawing. Since the rotation of the drawing was set to 0 degrees, it appears in the lower left corner of the display. If the plot is rotated 90 degrees (clockwise), the rotation icon would appear in the upper left corner, etc. If the plot isn't orientated correctly on the paper, exit and click the Rotation and Origin... box and rotate the plot 90 degrees. Press the OK button.

To obtain a full preview, illustrated in Figure 7.10, press the Full radio button and then click on the Preview... command button. Try the Pan and Zoom options, which are similar to Zoom Dynamic (refer back to chapter 5, section 5.8), and then end the preview by clicking the End Preview box. Change the plot origin to better center the plot on the sheet by clicking on the Rotation and Origin... box. Preview the plot, and if necessary reset the plot origin again.

7.4.8 Readying the plotter

When the plot is centered properly and all the plot settings are completed, send the drawing to the plotter by pressing the OK button of the Plot Configuration dialog box. AutoCAD will show the plot area and request that you position the paper and Press RETURN to continue or S to Stop for hardware setup. Press <return> and the drawing will be plotted. You can pause the plot at any time by pressing **S**.

7.4.9 Multipen Plotting on a Single Pen Plotter

If you're using a single-pen plotter and you configured your system to plot different colors with different pens (refer back to section 7.1.6), the plotter will pause when necessary during the plotting to allow you to change pens.

7.5 Hatching the Drawing

Boot AutoCAD and open the drawing C::\DRAWINGS\PROJ-5 for editing. Display the Layer Control dialog box by clicking on the Layers tool in the Object Properties toolbar. In DOS, select Data, then Layers. Following the procedures in chapter 6 to create a new layer for the hatching named Hatch, colored red, with a Continuous linetype. Then click on Hatch in the Layer Name list box so its row is highlighted. (If other rows are highlighted, click on them to deselect them.) Set Hatch as the current layer by pressing the Current button. The layer named DEFPOINTS in the Layer Name list box contains AutoCAD definition points for associative dimensions (see chapter 6, section 6.12.2). Items on the layer DEFPOINTS might be visible on the monitor but not plotted, so you should never make this the current layer. Press OK to exit the Layer Control dialog box.

The Layer Control box in the Object Properties toolbar should show Hatch as the current layer and its color as red. If not, display the Layer Control dialog box and check the layer settings.

7.5.1 Hatching the front view

The hatch scale is calculated using the second equation back in chapter 6, and the object is to be plotted on an A-size sheet using a ¾ scale:

$$\text{Plot Scale} \times \text{Hatch} = 1 \text{ inch} \times \text{Conversion}$$
$$\tfrac{3}{4} \times \text{Hatch} = 1 \times 1$$
$$\text{Hatch} = 1.33$$

Invoke the Bhatch command by choosing the Hatch tool in the Draw toolbox (in DOS, select Draw, then Hatch) to display the Boundary Hatch dialog box. Choose the ANSI31 pattern. Then enter the hatch scale of 1.31 in the Scale box. Ensure that the Associative box is on (it should have an × in it).

The Pick Points < command button allows you to select points in enclosed areas to be hatched. If Island Detection is enabled in the Advanced Option dialog box (it's on by default), AutoCAD will use objects within the outermost boundary as islands that are hatched as specified by the hatch style. Press Advanced... to display the Advanced Options dialog box, illustrated in Figure 7.11. Turn Island Detection on. Display the drop-down Style box and try each of the styles, noting how they appear in the image tile to the right of the box. Then set the style to Normal. Press OK to return to the Boundary Hatch dialog box.

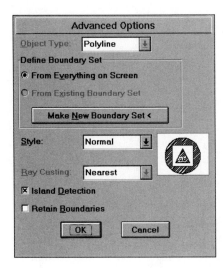

Figure 7.11 Advanced Options dialog box.

Press the Pick Points < command button. AutoCAD will continue at the command line with:

`bhatch Select internal point:` Pick one of the points in an area to be hatched (Figure 7.12). `<pick> Selecting everything... Selecting everything visible... Analyzing the selected data. Analyzing Internal Islands Select internal point:` Pick the next (second) area to be hatched. `<pick> Select Internal point:` Select the third area to be hatched. `<pick> Select internal point: <return>`

If you select a wrong area, you can enter **u** (undo) when asked to `Select internal point`. Note that the boundary of the area selected is drawn hatched in the color of the current layer. When <return> is pressed, the Boundary Hatch dialog box is returned to the screen.

Press the Preview Hatch < command button to preview the hatch. (If the hatch isn't correct, you might have lines that don't intersect at corners; you'll have to cancel the hatch and fix them.) Press Continue to exit the preview.

Press the Apply command button to hatch the object. The hatch should appear as shown in Figure 12.10. Save the drawing.

7.6 Plotting the Drawing

Choose the Plot tool in the Standard toolbar, or Print... from the File menu. The Plot Configuration dialog box with the settings for plotting Proj-5 is illustrated in Figure 7.13. Choose the plotter to be used, as outlined in section 7.2.1.

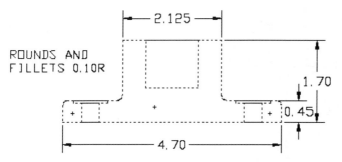

Figure 7.12 Defining the hatch boundaries.

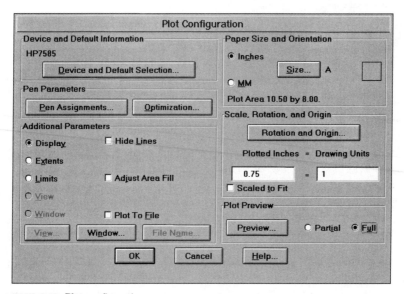

Figure 7.13 Plot configuration.

The plot scale to fit Proj-5 on an A-size sheet (11 × 8.5 inches) is ¾ inch = 1 inch. Set the plot configuration as illustrated in Figure 7.13, using inch units and an A-size sheet. Press the Size... command button and set the sheet size to A-size (10.5 × 8.0 inches). Only black and red colors are used in the drawing. Press the Pen Assignments... command button and set the pens (refer back to Figure 7.8) as: color 1 (red) for pen number 2, and color 7 (black) for pen 1. Press OK to return to the Plot Configuration Dialog box. Place a black pen in your pen holder slot 1, and a red pen in your pen holder slot 2. Preview... the plot before pressing OK. If the paper orientation is incorrect, press Rotation and Origin... and rotate the paper 90 degrees. Press OK when the settings are correct and the plot is executed.

8

Isometric Drawing

Objective: Use AutoCAD's Isometric drawing mode, set isoplanes and an isometric ellipse (isocircle), set drawing aids (snap and grid), and edit with the Trim command.

Drawing: Boot AutoCAD. Prior to beginning this drawing, following the procedures in chapter 6, section 6.1, to set AutoCAD's measurement system to English units.

Begin a new drawing named C:\DRAWINGS\PROJ-8. Set the screen limits to –6, –0.5, and 6,8.5 (remember to Zoom All), so the coordinates of the lower front corner of the bracket are 0,0. Use decimal units with 2 digits to the right of the decimal. You'll be drawing the 4 unit × 4 unit "isobracket" illustrated in Figure 8.1.

8.1 Isometric Snap/Grid

You'll use the Snap command to align cursor movements to an invisible grid. The snap resolution defines the spacing of the grid points. When Snap is on, the smallest movement of the cursor is from grid point to grid point. There are two snap styles to select from: standard and isometric. In standard mode, the invisible grid is on a rectangular x,y plane. In isometric mode, the grid is rotated to a 30-degree isometric plane.

When the snap style is set to isometric, the cursor movements vary depending on whether you're drawing on the top, front, or right side view of an object. When isometric "left" snap is activated, the isoplane is the left side of the cube. As the cursor is moved about the drawing screen, the movements is either in a vertical direction or along a line 150 degrees to the horizontal, as illustrated in Figure 8.2.

You can change the isoplane by selecting a new plane from the screen menu or by pressing <ctrl>–E or F5. The new plane will be shown in the Command window at the bottom of the drawing screen.

When isoplane "right" is activated, the cursor movements are in a vertical direction or along a line at 30 degrees to the horizontal, as illustrated in Figure 8.2. In the

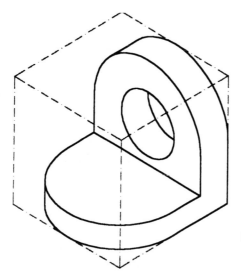

Figure 8.1 Proj-8 Isobracket.

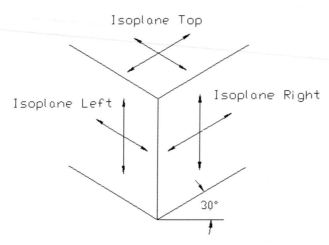

Figure 8.2 Isometric snap cursor movement.

isoplane "top" mode, the cursor movements are along a line at 30 degrees to the horizontal or a line at 150 degrees to the horizontal, also shown in Figure 8.2.

The isometric mode can help you to draw isometric views, and has no other effect on the drawing. You can reset AutoCAD to the standard mode at any time and continue drawing with the cursor movements acting along the standard horizontal and vertical lines. Set the snap style to isometric by selecting the following from the menu bar:

Options <pick> Drawing Aids... <Pick>

The Drawing Aids dialog box illustrated in Figure 8.3 will be displayed. Press the On button in the Isometric Snap/Grid box to set the isometric mode on. An × will appear in the box when isometric is on. You can set the Isoplane to Left, Top, or Right by pressing the appropriate radio button. You can also toggle Isoplanes from the drawing window by pressing either <ctrl>–E or F5. Press the Left radio button. Do *not* press OK.

8.1.1 Snap

The snap setting defines the smallest numerical movement of the cursor on the monitor, and defines the accuracy of the drawing. For this drawing, we'll use a snap setting of 0.1. In the standard (nonisometric) mode, X and Y snaps can have different values defining a rectangular invisible grid. In the isometric mode, however, you enter the Y axis snap value (90 degrees) and AutoCAD calculates the X value based on the isometric angle of 30 degrees. Consequently, when a value of 0.1 is entered for the Y snap (see Figure 8.3) AutoCAD enters a value of 0.17 for the X snap. Click on the Snap On box to turn Snap on, and enter the Y snap value of **0.1**. Auto-CAD will enter the X snap value of 0.17. You can toggle Snap on and off from the drawing editor by pressing SNAP on in the status bar at the bottom of the monitor, or by pressing <ctrl>–B or F9. Do *not* press OK yet.

The Snap Angle entry box allow you to rotate the 0 base angle. The X Base and Y Base entry boxes allow you to define the base point for the rotated snap.

8.1.2 Grid

The Grid settings allow you to define a reference grid of dots with a specified spacing on the drawing editor screen. The grid is visible only on the monitor and is not plotted with the drawing. When isometric is on, the grid follows the isometric planes. If the grid spacing is too dense, AutoCAD will display a message indicating this and the grid won't be drawn. The grid is drawn only within the screen limits. Like snap, you can enter different X and Y grid values in the standard (nonisometric) mode. In the isometric mode, you enter the Y value and AutoCAD calculates the X (30 degree)

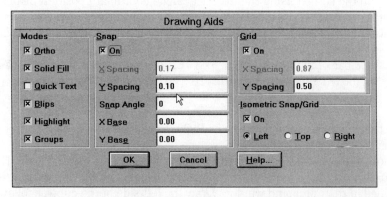

Figure 8.3 Drawing aids settings.

value. Click on the Grid On box to turn Grid on, and enter the Y grid value of **0.5**. AutoCAD will enter the X grid value of 0.87. You can toggle Grid on and off from the drawing editor by pressing GRID on in the status bar or <ctrl>–G or F7. Do *not* press OK yet.

8.1.3 Ortho (orthogonal) mode

When the Ortho mode is turned on, lines are snapped to the drawing planes. This means that, if the snap mode is set to standard and Ortho is on, all lines will snap to either a vertical or horizontal axis. In the isometric mode, the lines snap along a vertical or 30-degree, or 150-degree axis, depending on the current isoplane. Click on the Ortho On box to turn Ortho on. You can toggle Ortho on and off from the drawing editor by pressing ORTHO on in the status bar, or <ctrl>–L or F8. When your settings are the same as those in Figure 8.3, press OK to exit the Drawing Aids dialog box.

The screen will now display a grid of dots 0.5 units c/c on an isometric grid. Move the cursor around the screen noting that the X,Y coordinate values in the Coordinate Display box in the status bar show the cursor moving along an invisible grid with steps of 0.1—the snap setting. If the values in the Coordinate Display Window do not change as the cursor moves, press <ctrl>–D or F6. Also note that the SNAP, GRID, and ORTHO buttons in the status bar are pressed (on).

8.2 Drawing the Cube

The bracket object lines are to be drawn on layer 0, and the construction lines on layer Constr. Using the Layer Control dialog box, complete the following layer settings:

Object	Name	Color	Linetype
Bracket object lines	0	White	Continuous
Construction lines	Constr	Yellow	Continuous

Set Constr as the current layer. If the current isoplane isn't the right-side plane, toggle <ctrl>–E to set the isoplane. Draw the right side of the cube using the following commands—you can enter data via the keyboard, as illustrated, or by digitizing the points on the screen using the distance<angle coordinate position displayed at the top of the screen. If the curser coordinate display in the status bar doesn't display the distance<angle as the cursor is moved, toggle <ctrl>–D until it's displayed.

Draw <toolbar> Line <pick> From point: **0,0** <return> To point: **@4<30** <return> To point: **@4<90** <return> To point: **@4<210** <return> To point: **c** <return>

Note that, when drawing on Isoplane Right, the cursor moves along a 30-degree and 90-degree line on the right-side view.

Prior to drawing the lines for the left side of the cube, toggle <ctrl>–E (or press the F5 function key) to set the snap plane to Isoplane Left. The current isoplane is specified in the Command window. Draw the left side of the cube as follows:

Line <toolbar> From point: <shift>–<right> Intersect <pick> of Place the intersection object snap on the lower front corner of the current right-side view. <pick>
To point: **@4<150** <return> To point: **@4<90** <return> To point: <shift>–
<right> Intersect <pick> of Close the left-side view by placing the object snap tar-
get on the top front corner of the right-side view. <pick> To point: <return>

Use the <ctrl>–E (or F5) toggle switch to set the snap style on Isoplane Top, and
draw the top view of the cube. Use a temporary object snap to start the lines from a
corner of the cube.

8.3 Ellipse Command

When drawing an ellipse, you must enter the center point of the ellipse. Toggle to
Isoplane Left and draw the lines shown in Figure 8.4 to locate the center of the back
side of the cube—Ortho must be on:

Line <pick> From point: <shift>–<right> Midpoint <pick> of Place the target on
one of the midpoints indicated in Figure 8.4. To point: Draw the line as illustrated.
To point: <pick> <return> <return> Line from point: Draw the next Midpoint
line.

Toggle to Isoplane Top and draw the construction lines to locate the center point of
the bottom of the cube.

The Pellipse system variable is set to 0 by default so AutoCAD draws a true ellipse.
A setting of 1 draws a polyline representation of an ellipse. This drawing requires
that lines be drawn tangent to the sides of the ellipse (see Figure 8.5). Unfortu-
nately, the tangent object snap won't snap onto the true ellipse for the start point of
the line (with the release of AutoCAD 13 I'm using). Consequently, the polyline rep-

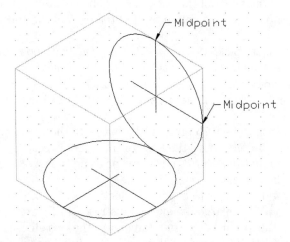

Figure 8.4 Ellipse.

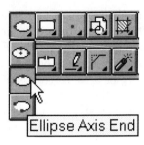

Ellipse Axis End

Figure 8.5 Ellipse flyout.

resentation of the ellipse will be used. (Autodesk states that the next release of AutoCAD won't support the polyline ellipse.) You might want to proceed with Pellipse set to 0. Then if you can't snap onto the ellipse, erase the ellipses, set Pellipse to 1, and redraw the ellipses. The process is the same for drawing a true ellipse or a polyline representation of the ellipse. Set Pellipse to 1, as follows:

Command: **pellipse** <return> New value for PELLIPSE <0>: **1** <return>

Prior to drawing the ellipses, set the current layer to 0. The ellipse is drawn on the bottom of the cube as follows—the current plane should be isoplane top, and the layer should be 0 (in DOS, select Draw, then Ellipse):

Draw <toolbar> Ellipse Axis End <pick> Arc/Center/Isocircle/<Axis endpoint 1>: **i** (Isocircle) <return> Center of circle: <shift>–<right> Intersection <pick> of Place the target on the midpoint intersecting lines in the bottom view of the cube. <pick> <Circle Radius>/Diameter: **2** (the radius of the ellipse) <return>

Toggle <ctrl>–E (or F5) until the isoplane is the left side, and draw the ellipse on the back face of the cube. The thickness of the back of the cube is 1 unit. Use the Copy command to draw a second ellipse one unit in front of the back of the cube:

Modify <toolbar> Copy Object <pick> Select objects: Digitize a point on the circumference of the ellipse, which is on the back of the cube. <pick> Select objects: <return> Base point or displacement>/Multiple: Pick a point on the ellipse. <pick> Second point of displacement: **@1<210** <return>

The bottom of the bracket is to be 0.75 units thick. Toggle to the top isoplane and copy the bottom ellipse 0.75 units above the base of the cube. Freeze layer Constr using the global freeze icon in the Layer Control box, or using the Layer Control dialog box. Layer 0 should be current.

   Use the Aerial View window (refer to chapter 5, section 5.7) or Zoom Dynamic (see chapter 5, section 5.8) to enlarge a view, as illustrated in Figure 8.6. In Isoplane Left, draw line a in the upper-left corner, tangent to the two ellipses by using the Tangent object snap to pick each point. If AutoCAD indicates that a tangency couldn't be found, press <esc> (or <ctrl>–C in DOS) and redo the line, placing the

Tangent object snap target closer to where the point of tangency should be. This might happen because the ellipse is drawn as a polyline (see chapter 15) with four arc segments, and the tangent target might not be on the proper segment. Toggle to Isoplane Right and draw lines b and c (Figure 8.6), as follows:

Draw <toolbox> Line <pick> From point: <shift>–<right> Tangent <pick> to Digitize the tangency point for line b. <pick> To point: **@2<270** <return> To point: <return> <return> Line from point: <shift>–<right> Tangent <pick> to Digitize the tangency point for line c. <pick> To point: **@2<30** <return> To point: <return>

The angle for the second point must be entered from the keyboard because Auto-CAD disables orthogonal mode for the second point when the Tangent object snap is used for the first point.

8.4 Trimming Lines

You'll use the Trim command to trim lines to a specified cutting edge. Lines b and c in Figure 8.6 are to meet at a point, hence each line acts as a cutting edge for the other. Trim the lines as follows:

Modify <toolbar> Trim <pick> Select cutting edges... Select objects: Select the cutting edge for line b (Figure 8.6). <pick> Select objects: <return> Select object to trim: Select the end of the line b to trim (Figure 8.6). <return>

Repeat the Trim command to trim line c. Line b is the cutting edge. When picking the object to be trimmed, remember to pick the side of line c that is to be trimmed off. If

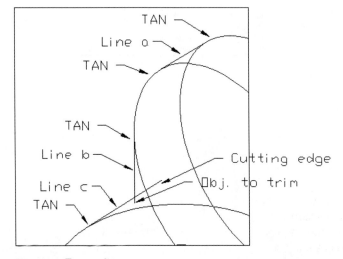

Figure 8.6 Tangent lines.

you make a mistake and trim the wrong side, use the Undo command to fix the mistake and try again. Zoom the back and right side of the lower right corner of the cube and add in the necessary lines, following the same procedures.

You must now remove sections of the ellipses. Zoom on a view, as illustrated in Figure 8.7. To trim the ellipse on the front of the vertical portion of the bracket, select two cutting edges, also shown in Figure 8.7. The object to trim is then the bottom of the ellipse. When trimming the ellipse at the back of the cube, the cutting edges are line a, shown in Figure 8.6, and the vertical line in the lower right corner of the back of the cube.

Complete the cube as shown in Figure 8.1. The hole in the back upright is 2 units in diameter (1-unit radius). You'll have to turn layer Constr on to draw the hole. When the drawing is complete, turn the Constr layer off and plot the drawing using a scale of ½ = 1.

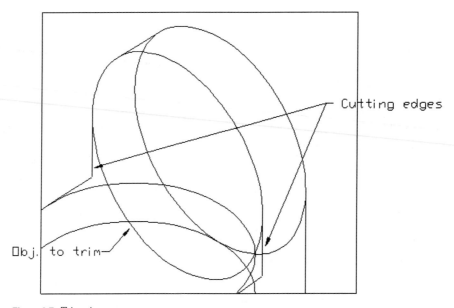

Figure 8.7 Trimming.

9

Object Controls

Objective: Use object controls Move, Copy, Array, and Mirror; rotate objects; change the layer on which an object resides; set grid and snap mode; work with chamfer objects; set a linetype scale by object; use center, midpoint, and from object snaps; select objects using a window polygon; use the Rectang command; set dimension variables; and plot.

Drawing: Draw and dimension the octagonal and rectangular plates shown in Figure 9.1. Begin a new drawing named C:\DRAWINGS\PROJ-9. Set the screen limits to 0,0 and 13,9 (don't forget to Zoom All). Use decimal units with 2 digits to the right of the decimal. The measurement system should be set to English, before naming the drawing.

9.1 Defining Layers

The drawing in this chapter requires four layers with the following specifications:

Item	Name	Color	Linetype
Objects	0	White	Continuous
Construction lines	Construc	Green	Continuous
Center lines	Center	Blue	Center
Dimensions & text	Dimens	Red	Continuous

Using the Layer Control dialog box, create the new layers and set their colors and linetypes (see chapter 6). Set layer 0 as current.

9.2 Setting Snap and Grid

Display the Drawing Aids dialog box illustrated in Figure 9.2 and set snap and grid, as shown. Enter a Snap X spacing of **0.1**. AutoCAD automatically uses the same

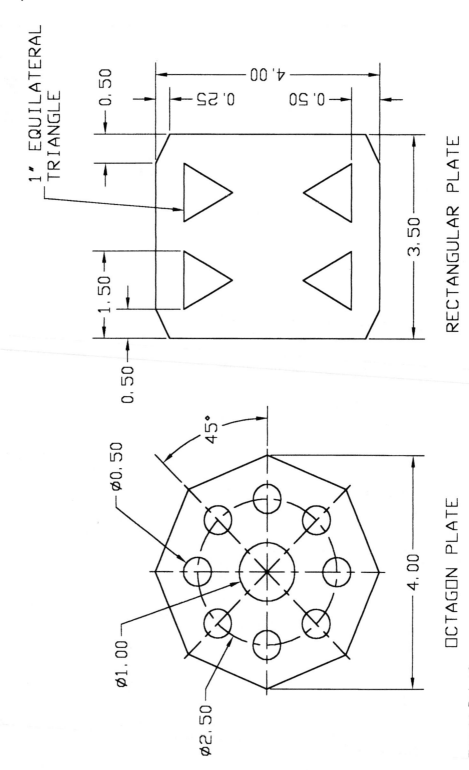

Figure 9.1 Project 9.

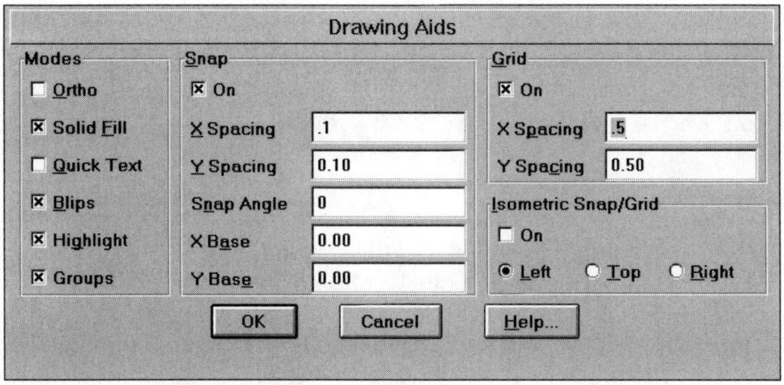

Figure 9.2 Setting snap and grid.

value for the Snap Y spacing. If you needed a different value for the Y snap, you could enter it. Enter a Grid X spacing of **0.5**. Press the Snap and Grid buttons on, and press OK to exit the dialog box.

9.3 Setting the Linetype Scale Factor

Since a center linetype is being used, you'll have to set the linetype scale (Ltscale) to suit the final plot size of this drawing. I assume that the drawing units are inches, and that the final drawing will be plotted on an A-size sheet (11 × 8.5 inches) using a ¾ scale. Using the formula presented in chapter 6, the Ltscale is calculated as:

$$\text{Plot Scale} \times \text{Ltscale} = 1 \text{ inch} \times \text{conversion} \times \tfrac{3}{4}$$
$$\tfrac{3}{4} \times \text{Ltscale} = 1 \text{ inch} \times \tfrac{3}{4}$$
$$\text{Ltscale} = 1$$

Since the Ltscale is 1, which is the default value, it doesn't have to be set. Review the procedure in chapter 6, section 6.9.1, to refresh your memory on the procedure.

9.4 Octagon Plate

The octagon plate is to be drawn using the Polygon command (an octagon is an eight-sided polygon). You define a polygon's size by entering either the length of a side or the radius of a circle in which the polygon is inscribed or circumscribed about. The octagon in Figure 9.1 is to be inscribed in a 4-unit-diameter circle, with its center at coordinates 3.5,4.5:

Draw <toolbar> Polygon (Figure 9.3) <pick> Number of sides <4>: **8** <return> Edge/<center of polygon>: **3.5,4.5** <return> Inscribed in circle/Circumscribed about circle (I/C)<I>: <return> Radius of circle: **2** <return>

Draw the 1-unit-diameter circle at the center of the octagon. When asked for the center of the circle, enter **@**, which tells AutoCAD to use the last point—the center of the octagon. Then the octagon will be rotated 22.5 degrees about its center:

Modify <toolbar> Rotate <pick> Select objects: Digitize a point on the octagon. <pick> Select objects: <return> Base point: <shift>–<right> Center <pick> of Place the center object snap aperture on the circumference of the circle. <pick> <Rotation angle>/Reference: **22.5** <return>

9.4.1 Array command

The center lines crossing the octagon will be drawn with the array command. You'll use the Array command to draw a cluster of similar items. The array can be rectangular or circular. In a rectangular array, the items are repeated in rows and columns in a block or rectangular pattern, as illustrated in Figure 9.4. That array has four columns and three rows. The original item is in the lower left corner of the array. The unit cell distance between rows is a and the unit cell distance between columns is distance b. If the unit cell distances are entered as positive numbers, the array "grows" upward and to the right (positive Cartesian coordinates). To replicate the objects to the left, enter a negative unit cell distance for the columns. To replicate the objects downward, enter a negative unit cell distance for the rows.

In a circular array, the items are repeated along the circumference of a circle, as illustrated in Figure 9.5. AutoCAD will ask if the items are to be rotated as they're copied. The items in Figure 9.5a weren't rotated, whereas the items in Figure 9.5b were rotated as they were copied. If you enter a positive angle between items, AutoCAD will copy the objects by rotating about the circle center in a counterclockwise direction.

If the item to be repeated in a circular array is made up of a number of objects and the objects aren't to be rotated as they're copied, you might have to save the item as

Figure 9.3 Polygon flyout.

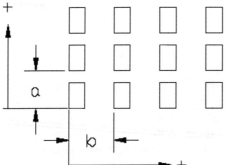

Figure 9.4 Rectangular array.

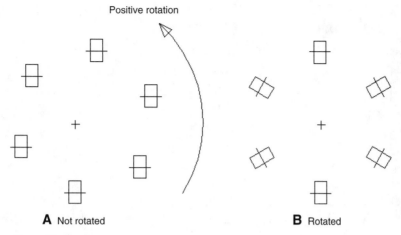

A Not rotated   **B** Rotated

Figure 9.5 Circular array.

a block (see chapter 10) before constructing the array. AutoCAD rotates each object in the item about the center point of the array, and the relative position of the objects, with respect to each other, may change. If the objects are part of a block, the item becomes a single object and the item doesn't become disjointed. This isn't a problem when items are rotated as they're copied.

To use the Array command, draw a single item first. Then invoke the Array command and select a rectangular or circular pattern. Repeat the items in the selected pattern and space them as necessary.

To begin the array, draw a horizontal line first across the center of the octagon. Then invoke the Array command to draw an array of lines around the octagon at 45-degree intervals. You'll have to rotate the lines as they're copied so each line is at a 45-degree interval from the previous line and passes through the center of the octagon:

Draw <toolbar> Line <return> From point: Using the cursor, draw a horizontal line across the center of the octagon. Ensure that the line extends slightly past the edges on each side (Figure 9.1).

Draw the polar (circular) array as follows (in DOS, select Array in the Construct menu, and then enter p (polar) when requested for Rectangular or Polar array (R/P)):

Modify <toolbar> Polar Array (see Figure 9.6) <pick> Select objects: **l** (Last) <return> Select objects: <return> Rectangular or Polar array (R/P):-p Center point of array: <shift>–<right> Center <pick> of Place the object snap aperture anywhere on the circumference of the circle. <pick> Number of items: **4** <return> Angle to fill (+=CCW,-CW)<360>: **0** (Zero is a no response forcing a request for angle between items.) <return> Angle between items (+=CCW,-CW): **45** <return> Rotate objects as they are copied <N>: **y** <return>

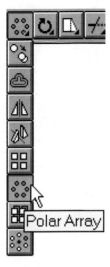

Figure 9.6 Special edit flyout.

Note the use of the Center object snap command to snap the cursor onto the center of the circle.

Draw a 2.5-unit-diameter circle. This circle will form the center line for the circles to be drawn later that are 0.5 units in diameter. Remember to use the Center object snap to pick the center of the main circle when asked for the location (of the center of the 2.5-units-diameter center) line circle.

Draw a 0.5-unit-diameter circle with its center at the intersection of the 2.5-unit-diameter center circle just drawn and the vertical line passing through the middle of the octagon. You can locate that point by using the Intersection object snap. Draw the circle with a diameter of 0.5 units. Then draw the circular array of 0.5-unit-diameter circles as follows:

Modify <toolbar> Polar array <pick> Select objects: **l** (Last) <return> Select objects: <return> Rectangular or polar array (R/P):–p Center point of array: <shift>–<right> Center <pick> of Place the object snap target on the circumference of the large circle. <pick> Number of items: <return> Angle to fill (+=CCW,-=CW)<360>: (select default 360) <return> Angle between items (+=CCW,-=CW): **45** <return> Rotate objects as they are copied <Y>: <return>

Note the two different methods used to draw an array of items. The number of items was entered for the lines, but an "angle to fill" of 0 was used. This forced AutoCAD to ask for the angles between items. Since the number of items wasn't entered for the circles, the angle to fill (360 degrees) had to be entered.

9.4.2 Change command

The lines crossing the center of the polygon and the 2.5-unit-diameter circle are to be center lines. You'll use the Ddchprop command to change the layer on which the lines and circle reside to Center, which has a center linetype (in DOS, enter **ddchprop** at the command line):

Change Properties <toolbar> Properties (Figure 9.7) <pick> Select objects: digitize each of the four lines, and the 2.5-unit-diameter circle. <pick> Select objects: <return>

The Change Properties dialog box illustrated in Figure 9.8 will be displayed. Click on the Layer... box to display a Change Layer dialog box. Click on Layer Center and then click OK. The Change Properties dialog box will be redisplayed with the Center layer, colored blue, listed.

You can enter the Linetype Scale (Celtscale) by object in the Change Properties dialog box. This linetype scale is different than the global Ltscale used in chapter 6, section 6.9.1, where Ltscale was used to set the global scale. The Celtscale can be different for each object, allowing the same linetype (center in this case) to be drawn at a different scale for different objects. You can do this by entering Celtscale at the command line prior to drawing the object, then all objects drawn use the Celtscale entered. Note, however, that the actual scale used by AutoCAD to draw the object is the product of Ltscale and Celtscale. Usually Ltscale is calculated and entered as discussed in chapter 6, section 6.9.1. If an object is drawn using a different scale, you can set the Celtscale for the object by using the Change Properties dialog box. In this case, enter a Linetype scale (Celtscale) of **0.5**. Click OK; the center lines will be changed to layer Center and their linetype scale will be 0.5×1 (the global Ltscale factor set in section 9.3).

You can also change an object's color and linetype with the Change Properties dialog box.

Figure 9.7 Properties tool.

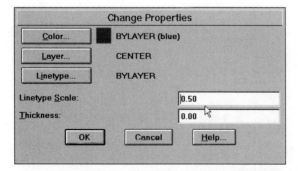

Figure 9.8 Change Properties dialog box.

9.5 Rectangular Plate

You'll be using the Rectang command in the Polygon flyout of the Draw toolbar (see sections A.3 and A.3.6 in appendix A) to draw the rectangular plate, starting with the lower left corner at coordinates 7.5,2.5 (in DOS, select Draw, then Polygon, then Rectang):

Draw <toolbar> Polygon flyout (Figure 9.3) <pick> Rectangle <pick> First cor-ner: **7.5,2.5** <return> Other corner: **@3.5,4** <return>

Draw one equilateral triangle in the upper left corner of the plate. Then use the From and Intersection object snaps to locate the cursor on the upper left corner of the rectangular plate, and use relative coordinates to locate the top left corner of the triangle from that point. Then draw the triangle:

Draw <toolbar> Line <pick> <shift>–<right> From <pick> Base point: <shift>–<right> Intersection <pick> of Place the intersection aperture on the top left corner of the rectangle. <pick> <Offset>: **@0.5,–0.5** <return> To point: **@1<0** <re-turn> To point: **@1<240** <return> To point: **c** <return>

9.5.1 Copying the triangle

The triangle is now copied to the right by a distance of 1.5 units. When asked to Se-lect objects, use a Wpolygon (window polygon) to select the triangle by enclos-ing it with a polygon window. All entities enclosed by the window polygon are selected by AutoCAD (in DOS, select Assist, then WPolygon):

Modify <toolbar> Copy <pick> Select objects: Select <toolbar> Window Poly-gon <pick> First polygon point: Digitize point a (Figure 9.9). <pick> Undo/<Endpoint of line>: Digitize point b. <pick> Undo/<Endpoint of line>: Digitize point c. <pick> Undo/<Endpoint of line>: <return> Select objects: <return> <Base point or displacement>/Multiple: Digitize a point anywhere on the monitor to act as a reference point. <pick> Second point of displacement: **@1.5<0** <return>

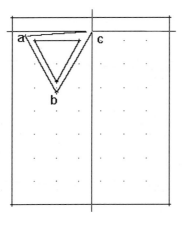

Figure 9.9 Selecting entities using WPolygon.

When AutoCAD requests <Base point or displacement>/Multiple, select a point anywhere on the screen. AutoCAD then requests Second point of displacement: and you enter a distance and angle relative to the first point. AutoCAD then copies the selected object(s) by that relative distance and angle. If M (Multiple) is entered, AutoCAD will continue to request Second point of displacement:, allowing you to create multiple copies of the object(s).

9.5.2 Drawing mirror images of triangles

You'll draw the two bottom triangles by mirroring the image of the two top triangles as follows (in DOS, select Construct, then Mirror):

Modify <toolbar> Copy flyout <Pick> Mirror <pick> Select objects: Use a window to select the two triangles by digitizing a point in space to the left and below the left triangle. <pick> Digitize the second point of the window enclosing the triangles. <pick> First point of mirror line:

The mirror line is a horizontal line crossing the midpoint of the rectangular plate. Use the Midpoint object snap to locate the midpoint of the side of the rectangle, then:

<shift>–<right> Midpoint <pick> of Place the midpoint aperture box on the vertical line defining the left side of the rectangle. <pick> Second point: <shift>–<right> Midpoint <Pick> of Place the midpoint aperture on the vertical line on the right side of the rectangle. <pick> Delete old objects? <N>: **n** <return>

Because the top two triangles aren't to be deleted, enter **n** (no) in response to the last question. Notice how the window selection option was invoked when you picked a point in space (not on an object), defining the lower left corner of the window.

9.5.3 Chamfering the rectangle

Each side of the rectangular plate is to be chamfered, as illustrated back in Figure 9.1. The chamfer is to be 0.5 units horizontally and 0.25 units vertically. You'll define the size of the chamfer first, then select the corners to be chamfered (in DOS, select Construct, then Chamfer):

Modify <toolbar> Chamfer <pick> Polyline/Distance/Angle/Trim/Method <Select first line>: **d** (distance) <return> Enter first chamfer distance <0.00>: **0.5** <return> Enter second chamfer distance <0.00>: **0.25** <return> <return> Chamfer Polyline/Distance/Angle/Trim/Method <Select first line>: Digitize the top line of the rectangle near the left side. <pick> Second line of chamfer: Digitize the left side of the triangle near the top. <pick>

AutoCAD will chamfer the left corner of the triangle, as shown back in Figure 9.1. Repeat the Chamfer command, chamfering the other corners of the triangle. Other chamfer options are:

Polyline. Chamfers an entire 2-D polyline.

Angle. Allows you to define the chamfer by entering the length of the chamfer and the angle.

Trim. If Trim is on, AutoCAD removes the original corner lines as it draws the chamfer. If Trim is off, the original corner lines aren't trimmed.

9.6 Dimensions and Text

Determine the text height and set the dimension scale. The drawing units are inches, it's to be plotted at a ¾ scale, and ⅛-inch-high text is to be used on the plotted drawing:

$$¾ × h = ⅛$$
$$h = 0.20 \text{ drawing units}$$

The dimension scale, Dimscale, is calculated using the second equation in chapter 4, as follows:

$$\text{Dimscale} × 0.18 = \text{Text Height}$$
$$\text{Dimscale} × 0.18 = 0.20, \text{ giving Dimscale} = 1.11$$

Reviewing the dimension style used in Figure 9.1, display the Dimension Style dialog box (Figure 9.10) and set the dimension variables as illustrated in the following (in DOS, select Data, then Dimension Style):

Dimensioning <toolbar> Dimension Style

Press the Parent Family button and then press the Geometry... command button to display the Geometry dialog box, illustrated in Figure 9.11. Complete the settings as shown: set the Overall Scale to the calculated Dimscale of 1.11, make the arrowheads Closed Filled, and select a None Center mark (circles already have center lines). The remaining settings are generally the default. Press OK to return to the Dimension Style dialog box.

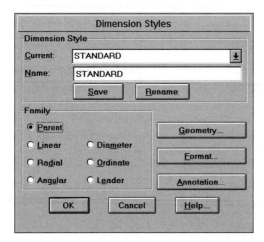

Figure 9.10 Dimension Style dialog box.

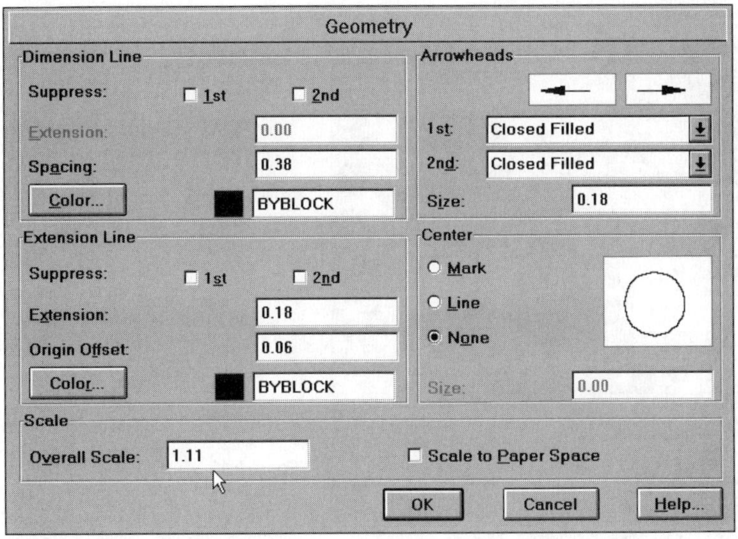

Figure 9.11 Geometry settings.

Press the Format... command button to display the Format dialog box shown in Figure 9.12. Complete the settings: Turn User Defined off to let AutoCAD choose where to place the dimension text, set Force Line Inside off to set the fit to Best Fit, turn Text Inside Horizontal and Outside Horizontal on so the dimension text will be horizontal (linear text alignment will be set later), and set both Horizontal and Vertical Justification to Centered. Press OK to exit to the Dimension Style dialog box.

Press the Annotation... command button to display the Annotation dialog box illustrated in Figure 9.13, and complete the settings shown, which are generally all the default. Press the Units... command button to display the Primary Units dialog box shown in Figure 9.14. Set the Units to Decimal, and the Dimension Precision to 0.00. Turn Zero Suppression, Leading and Trailing off so zeros are displayed to the left and right of the decimal point. Tolerance does not have to be set. Press OK to return to the Annotation dialog box, and then press OK to return to the Dimension Style dialog box.

The precision for linear dimensions is two digits to the right of the decimal, which is set for the Parent group in the preceding instructions. The precision for angular dimension, however, is zero digits to the right of the decimal, so the angular family has to be set. Press the Angular family button in the Dimension Style dialog box (Figure 9.10). AutoCAD will display a warning box asking if you want to save the changes to the current style. Answer Yes, then press the Annotation... command button to display the Annotation dialog box (Figure 9.13). Press the Units... command button to display the Primary Units dialog box (Figure 9.14). Set the Dimension Precision to 0, then press OK in both dialog boxes to return to the Dimension Style dialog box.

Also, the linear text is to be placed aligned with the dimension line (all other text is horizontal, which is the Parent setting). Press the Linear Family button and then press the Format... command button. In the Format dialog box, turn the Inside Horizontal and Outside Horizontal buttons off (they should not have a ×). Press OK to

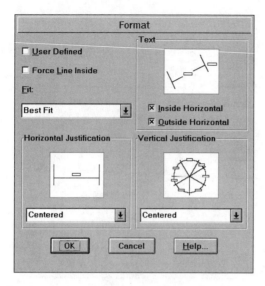

Figure 9.12 Format settings.

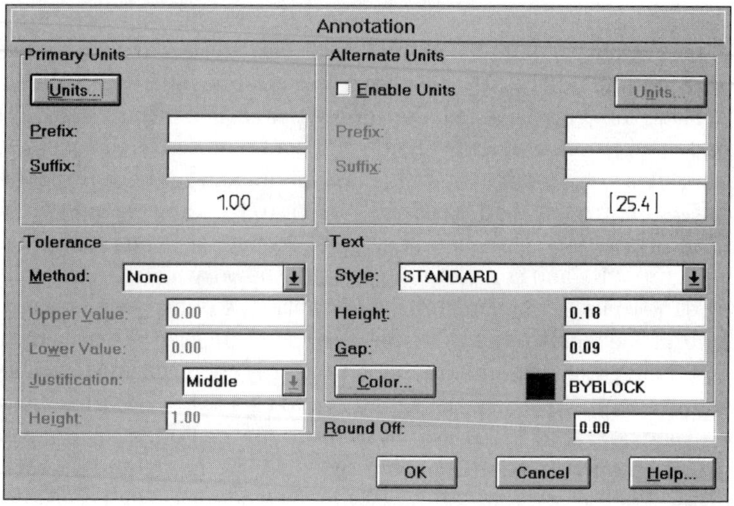

Figure 9.13 Annotation settings.

return to the Dimension Style dialog box. Press the Save command button to save the settings to the Standard dimension style, and then press OK.

Hint: If there's a particular dimension style you use on a regular basis, load the prototype drawing ACAD (English measurement system) or ACADISO (Metric measurement system). Display the Dimension Style dialog box and enter an appropriate name for the dimension style in the Name box, Mechanical, Architectural, etc. (refer back to Figure 9.10). Then set the dimension variables for that style and save the style. Create as many new styles as you want and then save the drawing. The prototype drawings are loaded each time a new drawing is started, and you can select any dimension styles available in the prototype drawing for the new drawing from the drop-down Dimension Style Current box in the Dimension Style dialog box.

9.6.1 Angular dimensioning

Set the current layer to Dimens and use the angular dimension tool to add the 45-degree dimension on the right side of the octagon plate:

Dimensioning <toolbar> Angular Dimension <pick> `Select arc, circle, line or RETURN:` <shift>–<right> Endpoint <pick> of Place the Endpoint object snap aperture on the right end of the horizontal center line (Figure 9.1). <pick> `Second line:` <shift>–<right> Endpoint <pick> of Place the Endpoint object snap aperture on the right end of the 45-degree line. <pick> `Dimension arc line location (Text/Angle):` Digitize the point where you want the dimension line to be located. <pick>

Compare this procedure, to draw an angular dimension, with that used in section 4.8 of chapter 4, where you were prompted to `Select arc, circle, line or RETURN` and then pressed the <return> key. This prompted AutoCAD to request the angle vertex. In the preceding set of commands, you selected a point on a line instead. AutoCAD then asked for a second line and used the point of intersection as the vertex for the angular dimension.

9.6.2 Diameter dimensioning

Dimension the 1-unit-diameter circle, noting that AutoCAD doesn't allow you to stretch the leader, as shown back in Figure 9.1, and also places a dimension line and arrows inside the circle. Press Undo to undo the command. Display the Dimension Style dialog box and press the Diameter family button. Then press the Format...

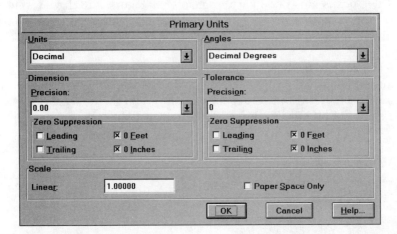

Figure 9.14 Units settings.

command button and turn the User Defined button on. Change the Fit setting to Text and Arrows so AutoCAD keeps the text and arrows together. Press OK to return to the Dimension Style dialog box, and press Save to save the setting. Then press OK. Redo the diameter dimension. This family setting could have been done earlier with the other settings.

9.6.3 Linear dimensioning

Add the remaining dimensions by using object snaps to locate the extension line points on the object. When placing the horizontal dimensions on the top left side of the plate, begin with the 0.5-unit dimension and specify the top left corner of the rectangle (using the Intersection object snap) as the first extension line origin (see Figure 9.1). The second extension line origin is then the top left corner of the triangle. AutoCAD will place the 0.5 text on the side of the second extension line. It will be moved to the other side later. Use the Baseline Dimension tool to add the 1.5-unit dimension. Then use the Left tool in the Home flyout (see Figure 9.15) of the Dimensioning tool (in DOS, select Dimensioning, then Left) to move the dimension to the left side of the dimension line (see also chapter 6, section 6.5.4).

When placing some dimensions (such as the 0.25-unit chamfer dimension), Auto-CAD might try to use a horizontal dimension when a vertical dimension is required (or vice versa). You can resolve this by responding to the dimension prompt (Text/Angle/Horizontal/Vertical/Rotated) with **v** (vertical). Then add the text to the drawing.

The grid on the screen falls within the drawing limits of 0,0 and 14,9 that were set at the beginning of the drawing. If part of your drawing falls outside the grid, reset the limits accordingly. Then save the drawing.

9.7 Plotting

Choose Plot from the Standard toolbar or from the File menu. The Plot Configuration dialog box is illustrated back in chapter 7, Figure 7.13. If you want to use a plotter other than that shown in the Device and Default Information box, select it from the drop-down Device and Default selection box, as outlined in chapter 7, section 7.2.1.

The plot scale to fit Proj-9 on an A-size sheet (11 × 8.5 inches) is ¾" = 1". Set the plot configuration as shown back in Figure 7.13 in chapter 7, using inches units and an A-size sheet. Press the Size... command button and set the sheet size to A-size (or a user size of 11 by 8.5). Black (or white), red, and blue colors appear in the draw-

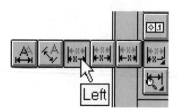

Figure 9.15 Home flyout.

ing. Press the Pen Assignments... command button and set the pens as: color 1 (red) as pen number 2, color 5 (blue) as pen number 3, and color 7 (black) as pen 1. Press OK to return to the Plot Configuration dialog box. Place a black pen in your pen holder slot 1, a red pen in pen holder slot 2, and a blue pen in pen holder slot 3. Press the Plot Preview Full button and then press the Preview... command button. If the paper orientation is incorrect, press the Rotation and Origin... command button and rotate the paper. Press OK when the settings are correct to execute the plot. Save the drawing and exit AutoCAD.

10

Blocks

Objective: Create block files to be inserted as components in another drawing; use coordinate and dynamic insertion; use blocks with layers, colors, and linetypes; write blocks to a file; modify blocks; use the Solid and Donut commands; complete an electronic circuit drawing.

Drawing: Draw an electronic circuit diagram with blocks created for each of the electrical components.

10.1 Blocks

Blocks are entities that are grouped together to form a complex object that's then defined as one object. If the block is repeated in a number of locations on the drawing, there's a considerable saving in disk space since the block objects don't have to be redefined with each use. Using blocks also speeds up the drawing process by allowing the insertion of complex block units as single objects into the drawing.

Making revisions to components on drawings is often very tedious. If a component was drawn as a block, all copies of the component will automatically be altered if you revise the original block, saving a considerable amount of time.

When you create a block, AutoCAD asks you for an insertion point for the block. You specify the point to be used for that block on any subsequent drawings, often the lower left corner of the block.

When blocks are inserted into drawings, AutoCAD asks for x and y scale factors. This lets you input multipliers of the x and y axes, modifying the x and y dimensions of the block being inserted. The program also asks for the rotation angle for the block, allowing you to draw the block at any angle. You can also use the drag mode for any of these items, which means you can visually insert the component into the drawing.

If components are to be stored in a drawing file for insertion into different drawings, or if the component might have different x-y dimensions on the drawing, a useful convention is to draw the component in a 1 × 1-unit block. When the block is inserted into the drawing, the x and y scale factors then become the actual dimensions in drawing units.

After a block is initially defined on a drawing and saved as a block, it's usually deleted from the screen by AutoCAD. If you need the initial location of the block, you can recall it as individual component (not a block) by immediately using the Oops command.

When a block is created, it's defined as a block in the current drawing file only. To create a drawing file of the block to use with other drawings, you must use the Wblock (export or write block) command. The electronic components used on this project will be stored as drawing files to be used with other drawings. If the blocks are to be stored on the data diskette in drive A, you must remember to put A: in front of the filename.

Block names can be up to 31 characters long and can contain letters, digits, and the characters -, _, and >. Filenames for blocks are subject to the same restrictions as drawing filenames (eight characters maximum). If a block is to be stored as a file, you'll usually want to use the same block name and filename, hence the more stringent restrictions of the filename are used when naming the block.

Blocks can be composed of other blocks. This is referred to as *nesting* blocks.

10.2 Block Color and Linetype

Information about the initial color and linetype of the components of a block are part of the block information stored with the block on the disk, for example:

- If the initial color and linetype of a block component are explicit, e.g., the object color is set to red, the block component will retain that color and linetype when the block is inserted.

- If the block component was initially on layer 0, with color and linetype set to BYLAYER, the component will become part of the layer that's current when the block is inserted.

- If the initial color and linetype of an object in a block are BYBLOCK, the block component will take on the current explicit color and linetype.

Boot AutoCAD (do not name the drawing) and draw a triangle. Then, following the procedures in chapter 9, section 9.4.2, choose the Change Properties tool (in DOS, enter **ddchprop**). When asked to select objects, select the right side of the triangle (marked red in Figure 10.1). AutoCAD will then display the Change Properties dialog box illustrated back in Figure 9.8 in chapter 9. Press the Color... command button and change the color to Red. Repeat the Change command and change the color of the left side of the triangle to BYBLOCK. Repeat the procedure and change the color of the bottom of the triangle to BYLAYER (the default color setting).

Now, following the procedures in chapter 6, section 6.4, create a new layer named Test, colored blue, and make Test the current layer.

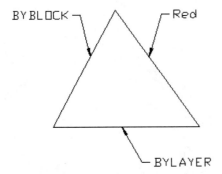

Figure 10.1 Block component's colors.

Next, press the Color Control tool in the Object Properties toolbar (in DOS, enter **ddcolor** at the command line) to display a Select Color dialog box. Select the color green, and then press OK. The Object Properties toolbar should show that the current layer is Test with a blue color, and the Color Control tool is green.

10.3 Block Command

An item block is created as follows (in DOS, select Construct, then Block):

Draw <toolbar> Block (Figure 10.2) <pick> `Block name (or ?):` **triangle** <return> `Insertion base point:` <shift>–<right> Intersection <pick> of Place the intersection aperture over the bottom left corner of the triangle. <pick> `Select objects:` Place a selection window around the triangle. <pick> `Select objects:` <return>

The triangle will be deleted from the screen and saved by AutoCAD in the current drawing file as a block named triangle.

10.4 Insert Command

Insert the Triangle block into the current drawing as follows (in DOS, select Draw, then Insert, then Block):

Draw <toolbar> Insert Block (Figure 10.3) <pick>

The Insert dialog box illustrated in Figure 10.4 will be displayed. Press the Block... command button to display a Defined Blocks list selection box. Select triangle in the list by clicking on it, and then press OK to return to the Insert dialog box. You can set the block insertion point, scale, and rotation angle parameters either in the dialog box or on the screen. Turn the Specify Parameters on Screen box on (it should have an × in it). The Explode option allows you to insert a block not as a block, but rather as a collection of individual objects (as it was originally drawn before being made

Figure 10.2 Block tool.

Figure 10.3 Insert Block tool.

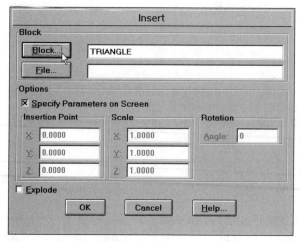

Figure 10.4 Insert dialog box.

into a block). Explode should be off (*no* × in it). When your dialog box settings match those in Figure 10.4, press OK. AutoCAD will continue with:

`Insertion point:` Drag the triangle block to a suitable point on the screen. `<pick> X scale factor <1>/Corner/XYZ:` Use the default value of 1. `<return>` `Y scale factor (default=X):` `<return> Rotation angle <0>:` `<return>`

The block will be inserted on the screen with the following colors:

- The right side in its original color, red.
- The bottom the color of the current layer, blue.
- The left side the color of the current explicit color, green.

Review these colors with respect to the discussion in section 10.2.

10.5 Electronic Schematic Drawing

AutoCAD should currently be loaded. Choose the New tool and begin a drawing named D:\DRAWINGS\PROJ-10. AutoCAD will ask if the previous drawing (of the triangle) is to be saved. Answer No. Set the drawing units to Decimal with one digit to the right of the decimal. Set the drawing limits to 0,0 and 12,9. The current layer is to be 0 and the color BYLAYER (the default settings).

Now you'll draw the electronic schematic diagram illustrated in Figure 10.5. You'll complete a block drawing file for each of the electrical components, illustrated in Figure 10.6, and then insert the blocks into the circuit drawing.

10.5.1 Drawing the resistor block

Each of the electronic components shown in Figure 10.6 is to be drawn as a block and stored as a file for later insertion into a drawing. Draw each component as a 1 × 1 block to allow you to modify the size when the block is inserted into the drawing. Select the insertion point on the left side of the component at a point where it would be connected to the electronic circuit.

The Grid command is very useful when working with blocks. You should draw the blocks in a grid that will be used in the final drawing. Points on the block entities will then coincide with the grid on the final drawing, facilitating the connection of entities on the main drawing.

Set Snap to 0.1 and Grid to 0.2, and turn both Snap and Grid on (refer to chapter 9, section 9.2). The blocks will be drawn in a 1-square-unit box starting at coordinate

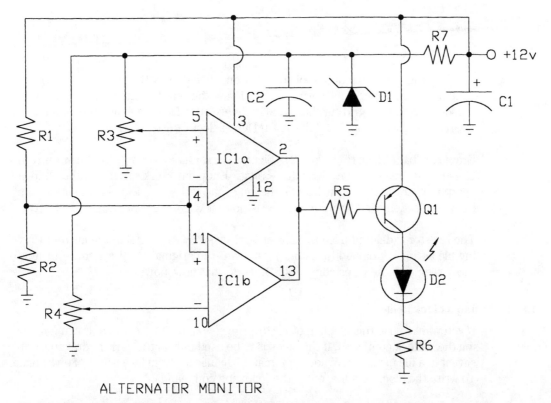

Figure 10.5 Electronics schematic drawing.

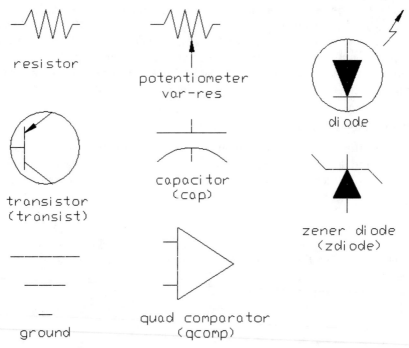

Figure 10.6 Electronic components.

1,1. Use the Zoom Window tool to zoom on a window with a lower left corner of 0.2,0.2 and an upper right corner of 2,2. Draw the resistor one unit long using the cursor snap and the grid, as illustrated in Figure 10.7. Do not include the dimensions.

Create a resistor block as follows (in DOS, select Construct, then Block):

Draw <toolbar> Block (Figure 10.2) <pick> Block name (or ?): **resistor** <return> Insertion base point: <shift>–<right> Endpoint <pick> of Place the endpoint aperture over the end of the lead on the left of the resistor. <pick> Select objects: Place a selection window around the resistor. <pick> Select objects: <return>

The resistor is deleted from the screen and saved by AutoCAD in the current drawing file as a block named Resistor. If you want the original resistor item returned to the screen, use the Oops command. Don't do that now, however.

10.5.2 Writing a block to file

If you want to use this block in other drawings, you must save it in a drawing file using the Wblock command. If the block is to be used only in the current drawing, don't save it in a file using the Wblock command because it would be a waste of disk space. To write the block to a file, enter the following commands:

Command: **wblock** <return>

The Create Drawing File dialog box illustrated in Figure 10.8 will be displayed. Following the procedures shown back in chapter 1, in Figures 1.16 and 1.17, use the slider bar to change the directory to C:/DRAWINGS. Then move the cursor to the File Name: edit box and enter the filename **resistor**. Press OK to open the file. Blocks written to files are regular AutoCAD drawings, as indicated by the file extension .DWG.

AutoCAD will now request the name of the block to save in the file Resistor.Dwg. In this case, since the same name was used for the file and the block, resistor, you can simply enter an equal sign:

```
Block: = <return>
```

If you want to clean up the drawing, use the Redraw tool.

10.5.3 Drawing the potentiometer block

You can create a potentiometer (refer back to Figure 10.6) by adding an arrow to the resistor block. Use the Insert Block tool to recall the resistor block (in DOS, select

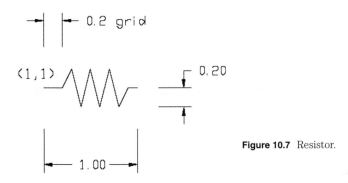

Figure 10.7 Resistor.

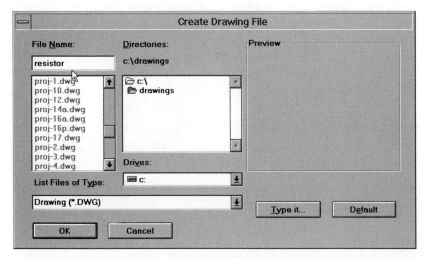

Figure 10.8 Write block to file.

Draw, then Insert, then Block):

Draw <toolbar> Insert Block (Figure 10.3) <pick>

The Insert dialog box, illustrated in Figure 10.4, will be displayed. Press the Block... command button to display the Defined Blocks selection box. Select Resistor in the list by clicking on it and then press OK to return to the Insert dialog box. Turn the Specify Parameters on Screen box off (there should not be an × in it). In the Insertion Point box, enter x as **1**, and y as **1**. Enter **1** for the x and y Scale, and enter the Rotation Angle as **0**. Explode is to be off (no × in it). When your dialog box settings match those shown back in Figure 10.4, press OK. AutoCAD will insert the resistor block using the parameters specified in the dialog box. Compare this use of the dialog box with that in section 10.4.

Create a variable resistor (potentiometer) by adding an arrow to the resistor, using the dimension Leader tool:

Dimensioning <toolbar> Leader <pick> From point: Digitize the tip of the arrow of the leader. <Pick> To point (Format/Annotation/Undo) <Annotation>: Digitize the end of the arrow. <pick> To point (Format/Annotation/Undo) <Annotation>: **a** <return> Tolerance/Copy/Block/None/<Mtext>: **n** <return>

If AutoCAD won't place an arrowhead on the leader, the leader line is too short. Use Undo to delete the leader and then draw a slightly longer one. You can use Break to later shorten the leader.

Save the block using the name Var-res, and write the block to a drawing file using the same name.

If the resistor block inserted into the drawing in the preceding instructions isn't part of the current drawing database, it won't be listed in the Blocks list box (refer back to Figure 10.4). This would happen, for instance, if you wanted to insert the resistor file in a different drawing. In that case, you can locate the file by pressing the File... command button in the Insert dialog box, which will display the Select Drawing File dialog box. Locate the file by choosing the location in the directory list box and then choosing the drawing file in the filename list box. Then press OK. Once the block is inserted in the current drawing, it becomes part of that drawing database and you can insert it later by using the Blocks list box.

10.5.4 Drawing the diode block

You'll draw the diode, as illustrated in Figure 10.9, with a grid. Draw the diode as shown, and use the Solid command to fill in the arrowhead in the block, as follows:

Draw <toolbar> Solid (Figure 10.10) <pick> First point: Place the cursor on the tip of the arrowhead in the diode. <Pick> Second point: Place the cursor on a corner of the arrowhead. <pick> Third point: Place the target on the next corner. <pick> Fourth point: <return> Third point: <return>

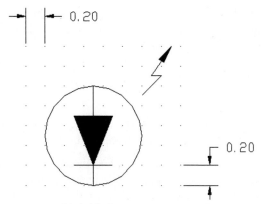

Figure 10.9 Diode block.

  Figure 10.10 Solid tool.

Since a triangular solid is being drawn, there's no fourth point to enter. AutoCAD will request a fourth point, assuming you want to continue with another adjoining solid using the previous second and third points as its first and second point. When drawing a rectangular solid, the third and fourth points must cross (like a bowtie) so the third point is on the same side as the first, and the fourth on the same side as the second.

Save the diode as a block and then write it to file using the Wblock command. The insertion point is the intersection of the line and circle at the top of the circle. Then draw the remaining blocks and write each one to file. The insertion point for each block should be a point on the block where the component connects to the electronic circuit line.

10.6 Block Modifications

Regardless of a block's complexity, it's treated as a single entity in a drawing. As such, components in the block cannot be altered. To transcribe a block and retain its separate entities, click on the Explode check box in the Insert dialog box (refer back to Figure 10.4). Normally it should be off. Once the block is exploded, it can be modified and reblocked. If the block is already inserted into the drawing, you can explode it by using the Explode tool from the Modify menu (see sections A.4 and A.4.9 in appendix A). In DOS, select Modify, then Explode.

If you attempt to make a block using the name of an existing block, AutoCAD will query A block with this name already exists in the drawing. Do you want to redefine it? (Y/N). If you're attempting to make another block out of a block that hasn't been exploded using the block's original name, enter **N**. Then explode the block. Once the block is exploded, you can save it as a block using the original name. If you try to make a block out of a block that hasn't been exploded using the block's original name, AutoCAD will display the message `Error: this block references itself.`

If a block has been exploded, you can modify and reblock it using the same name.

10.7 Circuit Drawing

Use Zoom All to zoom to the full screen limits of 0,0 and 12,9. Prior to starting the drawing, familiarize yourself with the block insert command, as follows:

Insertion point. You can enter the insertion point as a coordinate in the Insert dialog box (refer back to Figure 10.4), or by specifying the insertion point on the screen. When specifying the insertion point on the screen, you can digitize it using an object snap or enter it as a relative coordinate or distance/angle using the relative symbol @. Alternatively, you can use the From object snap to locate the insertion point from a known point.

X scale factor <1>/Corner/XYZ. You can enter the XYZ scale factors in the Insert dialog box, or specify them on the screen. Any value entered will be a multiplier of the x dimension of the resistor, and AutoCAD will then prompt for the y scale factor. To visually drag the x and y dimensions of the resistor, type **c** (corner) and press <return>. Use the cursor to drag the length and height of the resistor to what you want. Note that an invalid entry will result if you attempt to drag only one axis of the entity by moving the cursor only horizontally or only vertically, which implies that the orthogonal multiplier is 0, an impossible value. To scale the block in three dimensions, enter **XYZ**.

Rotation angle <0>. You can enter the rotation angle in the Insert dialog box, or specify it on the screen. To rotate the resistor, enter the angle desired where 0 degrees is horizontal. You can also drag the rotation angle using the cursor.

If the block to be inserted isn't part of the current drawing, press the File... command button in the Insert dialog box (refer back to Figure 10.4) to locate the block file. Following the first insertion, the block becomes part of the current drawing file.

Try the various methods of inserting the var-res block into the drawing. Then Use the Undo tool remove the var-res block, and begin the circuit drawing.

Prior to beginning the circuit drawing, you'll use the Donut command to draw a small dot that will be used for the circuit drawing connections (in DOS, select Draw, then Circle, then Donut):

Draw <toolbar> Circle <flyout> Donut `Inside diameter:` **0** <return> `Outside diameter:` **0.1** <return> `Center of doughnut:` Pick a grid point. <pick> `Center of doughnut:` <return>

Save the donut as a block named Dot. The insertion point is the grid point that's selected as the center of the donut.

Complete the circuit drawing, as illustrated back in Figure 10.5. Use the object snaps—Intersection, Endpoint, and From—as required to make the drawing production easier. Use the Copy command to copy segments of the drawing. For instance, you'll use the resistor connected to a ground twice; draw one and then copy it to the next location. Then use same procedure for the var-res, with its ground and capacitor. Occasionally, it's easier to insert the block close to where you want it and then use the Move command to move it into the desired position, making use of temporary object snap commands such as Endpoint. This is especially useful when a block is to be rotated.

Don't worry about where to start the drawing. Remember you can use the Move command at any time to move the entire drawing to a new location. If the drawing exceeds the drawing limits, change the limits.

Most items will be inserted using an x and y scale factor of 1. When inserting the Qcomp (quad comparator), use a scale factor of 2. (1.5 might appear okay, but the points on the comparator won't fall on the snap lines, making it more difficult to connect lines to those points.) Insert the ground using an x and y scale factor of 0.25. If you insert an object and want to reinsert it at a different scale, use the Undo command and then reinsert the item.

When the schematic drawing is completed, plot it onto an A4 sheet. For the plot scale, choose Scale to Fit.

10.8 Drawing Modifications

You can modify block files at any time by inserting them into the drawing exploded (press Explode on in the Insert dialog box), or by inserting the block and then exploding it. If an exploded block is modified and then reblocked using the original block name, all of its copies in the current drawing are updated by AutoCAD to comply with the revised block file.

11

Custom Menu

Objective: Customize menus to simplify drawing construction; write a pull-down menu with cascading menus, a cursor menu, and a pointing device menu; create menu macros; load menu files; load a partial menu in Windows; and use a line editor.

11.1 Menu Files

Menu customization allows you to create new AutoCAD menus or modify AutoCAD's standard menu to meet your specific requirements, increasing your productivity. An AutoCAD menu file is a text file with the extension .MNU. You can create the customized file with any text editor or word processor that allows you to save in ASCII or straight text. AutoCAD Windows also uses the concept of partial and base menus. The *base menu* is the initial menu loaded, such as the default Acad menu. A *partial menu* is another menu that can be loaded into the base menu. AutoCAD stores the name of the last menu loaded into the drawing. When the drawing is reloaded, the last menu used for the drawing is loaded. The default AutoCAD menu is Acad.mnu.

In order to write menu files, you have to be very familiar with the sequence of the AutoCAD commands to be used in the menu. Refer to either AutoCAD's Help program (see section D.5 in appendix D) or the *AutoCAD User's Guide* for a list of commands and their syntax.

11.2 Section Labels

You can write pull-down and cursor menus, screen menus, pointing device button menus, digitizing tablet menus, and image tile menus for AutoCAD. Table 11.1 lists the section labels for the different menu types in AutoCAD. This chapter will cover pull-down and cursor menus, and pointing device menus. For information on writing other menus, refer to your *AutoCAD User's Guide*.

TABLE 11.1 Menu Section Labels

Section label	Menu area
***AUXn	System pointing device button menu (where n is a number from 1 to 4)
***BUTTONSn	Pointing device menu (where n is a number from 1 to 4)
***POPn	Pull-down/cursor menu (where n is a number from 1 to 16)
***SCREEN	Screen menu
***IMAGE	Image tile menu
***TABLETn	Tablet menu (where n is a number from 1 to 4)

11.3 Writing a Menu

As mentioned at the beginning of this chapter, AutoCAD menu files have the extension .MNU and can be created with any text editor or word processor that doesn't put extra coding in the text. The program Edit that's provided with DOS is a suitable text editor, so I'll use it for instructions in this chapter. Notepad, which is available with Windows, is also suitable, but can edit only files of a limited size.

Boot AutoCAD and begin a new drawing named D:\DRAWINGS\PROJ-11 using the default units and limits. Then load Edit or Notepad. If you're using Windows, you might find it more convenient to work with Notepad, but you can also use Edit. If you're using DOS, you must use Edit. For DOS, load Edit by entering the following at the command line:

Command: **edit** <return> File to edit: **c:\drawings\border.mnu** <return>

For Windows, load Notepad as follows (See appendix H for Windows 95):

1. While holding down the <alt> key, press the <tab> key once (don't release <alt>). A box will appear in the middle of the screen. If the box displays the Program Manager, release the <alt> key. If it doesn't, press the <tab> key repeatedly until the box displays the Program Manager.

2. In the Program Manager screen, click on the Accessories Window to bring it to the front.

3. Double-click on the Notepad icon, as shown back in Figure 11.1, to load Notepad. If Notepad isn't in your Accessories window, look for it in another window.

4. Select the New command in Notepad's File menu and open a new file named C:\DRAWINGS\BORDER.MNU.

Write the menu shown in Figure 11.2. Type in each line exactly as it's shown and press <return> at the end of each line. If you make a mistake, move the cursor to the line containing the error and fix it using the <delete> and <insert> keys.

AutoCAD processes each blank space in a menu as though the <spacebar> were pressed. As is normal with AutoCAD, the <spacebar> usually functions as <return>.

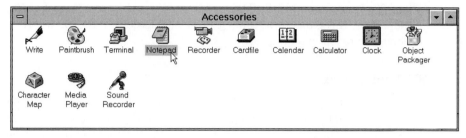

Figure 11.1 Loading Notepad.

Figure 11.2 Writing the menu.

For instance, in AutoCAD when you type Line and press the <spacebar> , the Line command is invoked. This same process happens in the menu, so each space is crucial. Adding two spaces is like typing a command and pressing the <spacebar> twice. AutoCAD also adds a space at the end of each line unless it ends with a semicolon, which is interpreted as the <return> key by AutoCAD. This menu is discussed in detail in the following sections.

11.4 Pull-Down (POPn) Menus

You can define up to 16 pull-down menus (POP1 through POP16) for AutoCAD's menu bar. The pull-down menus display as cascading menus. Pull-down menus can contain up to 999 menu items, but the maximum number of items that can be displayed is governed by the number of rows visible on the display device, which can be as low as 21. The first item in the menu in Figure 11.2 is the POP1 menu's title, Easy1. Titles in the menu can be up to 14 characters long, but many monitors allow only 80 characters, so, if all 16 POP positions are to be used, the title is limited to five characters. If the menu titles don't fit on the screen, AutoCAD will truncate them, which can result in odd titles.

11.5 POPn Menu Syntax

The item ***POP1 at the top of the menu in Figure 11.2 is the *section label* for a pull-down menu in the first position (at the left side) of the menu bar. Immediately below that, enclosed in square brackets, is the title, [Easy1], that will appear in the POP1 position of the menu bar. Figure 11.3 shows the menu as it appears in AutoCAD.

Line and Circle are standard AutoCAD commands. When chosen from the Easy1 menu in AutoCAD, they behave as they do in AutoCAD's standard menu. Text casing in the menu is insignificant; either upper- or lowercase can be used.

11.5.1 Menu item labels

[label]commands

Menu item labels are enclosed in square brackets, [ ], and appear on the screen when the menu is displayed. The remainder of the menu is invisible, as shown in Figure 11.3. AutoCAD doesn't interpret item labels. Only the data immediately following the right square bracket of the item label is interpreted by AutoCAD as a command.

In AutoCAD for Windows, each line in the menu must be preceded with a menu item label. In DOS, menu item labels are required only to improve the look of the menu on the screen. For example, in DOS, the menu item label [Line] in line 3 of the menu can be deleted. The menu displayed on the screen would then display the Line command. If, however, the menu item label [BORDER LINE] in line 5 was removed, the commands following the label would appear on the screen, pline \w 0.2;0.2, which probably isn't what you want. Since Windows requires the menu item labels for each line, they're included in the menu, making it usable in both Windows and DOS.

Line 5 in the menu is called a *macro* because it automatically performs a sequence of operations. The operation immediately following the closing bracket of the menu item label is invoked when the label is selected in the menu. AutoCAD's Pline command draws connected lines and arcs of varying width. When Pline is invoked, it asks for the Start point of line. After you enter the start point of the line, AutoCAD requests

Figure 11.3 Easyl menu.

arc/Close/Halfwidth/Length/Undo/Width/<endpoint of line> and the option w (Width) is read from the macro. AutoCAD then requests the starting line width, which is read from the macro as 0.2, and the end width, which is read from the macro as 0.2. Consequently, when you select Border from the menu, the Pline command is invoked, allowing you to draw polylines 0.2 units in width. The syntax of this macro is discussed further in following sections of this chapter.

11.5.2   Embedding keyboard input

[BORDER LINE]Pline \w 0.2;0.2

To allow keyboard input in the menu macro, place a backslash character (\) at the location where the keyboard input is required. In the previous line, AutoCAD will pause at the backslash (\), allowing you to enter the start point of the polyline. Note that no space follows the backslash.

A backslash isn't required at the end of a line since control automatically returns to the user if the command requires input and there's no additional data in the menu line.

11.5.3   Embedding the <enter> key

[Border]Pline \w 0.2;0.2
Erase W
[Erase L]erase l;;

The <return> key is embedded in a menu line when you place a semicolon (;) or a single blank space (representing the <spacebar>) at the location where the <return> key is required. AutoCAD interprets the <spacebar> as the <return> key, except when text is being entered and the <spacebar> is interpreted as a blank space in the text. There's a single space in the macro immediately following the Pline command. This is interpreted as <return> , which enters the command. There's no blank space or semicolon following the backslash (\), which embeds keyboard input in the menu. When keyboard input is required, enter the required data and press the <return> key or the <pick> button to enter the data.

In the line containing [ERASE W]erase w, the Erase command (following the right square bracket) is entered when you use a single blank space to invoke <return> following the command. The W (Window) option is then read from the menu. The remainder of the operation continues at the command line as follows:

Window First corner: Pick a corner of the window <pick> Other corner: Pick the next corner <pick> Select objects:

After the window is defined, the Erase command continues to request entities to be erased. In order to exit the command, you must press <return> .

The next line, [ERASE L]erase l;;, invokes the Erase command. AutoCAD then reads the l (last) and invokes the <return> when it reads the semicolon immediately following the l. As is normal with AutoCAD, the last entity drawn becomes dotted and AutoCAD requests `Select objects`. In this case, however, the next semicolon enters <return> and the command is exited. Consequently, the last entity drawn is immediately erased.

11.5.4 Menu separator

[--]

A menu item with two hyphens in square brackets creates a separator the width of the pull-down menu. You can also gray out menu items by placing a tilde (~) at the start of the menu item, so the following would create a grayed-out separator: [~--].

11.5.5 POPn menu syntax reference

Table 11.2 lists some of the special characters used in pull-down/cursor menu files.

11.6 AUXn/BUTTONSn Menu Syntax

The AUXn and BUTTONSn menu controls the buttons on your system pointing device. If your computer uses a system mouse (Windows), then your pointing device uses the AUXn menu. If your computer doesn't use a system mouse (DOS), your pointing device uses the BUTTONSn menu. By including both menu sections, which would be redundant, the menu is applicable to all systems.

You cannot reassign the <pick> button on your pointing device. Consequently, on a two-button mouse there's only one button left to program. You can, however, use a key-button sequence to invoke other Aux/Buttons menus. This is used in AutoCAD's standard menu, allowing you to hold down the <shift> key and press the second button on the mouse to display the floating object snap cursor menu. Table 11.3 shows the Button menus accessed with key/button sequences.

11.6.1 Adding a buttons menu

Complete the EASY1 menu exactly as shown in Figure 11.4. To add the POP0 menu section, move the cursor to the top left corner of the existing menu using the mouse and press <return> . This pushes the current top line down one line. Move the cursor up to the blank line and begin entering the new lines. Press <return> at the end of line to make space below it for the next line. If you want to delete a blank line, move the cursor to the blank line and press Delete. The new entries are discussed in the following sections.

AUX1/BUTTONS1 is the section label for the first programmable button on the pointing device. On a two-button mouse, this is the second button. The first button is reserved as the <pick> button. In this menu, the second button invokes <return> . If you have a three-button or more pointing device, you can add more lines of commands (operations) in this section.

TABLE 11.2 Menu Characters

Characters	Description
***	Section title
**	Submenu section title
[ ]	Encloses a label
;	Issues <return>
<space>	Single blank space is equivalent to <spacebar>
\	Pauses for user input
-	Translates AutoCAD commands and keywords that follow
[--]	Item label to create a separator line in the menu
->	Label prefix for a cascading menu
<-	Label prefix indicates last item in cascading menu
+	Continues menu line on the next line
$	Loads a menu
=*	Displays the current pull-down or cursor menu
*^C^C	Prefix for a repeating item
^B	Toggles snap on/off
^C	Cancel command
^D	Toggles coordinates
^E	Toggles isometric planes
^G	Toggles grid on/off
^H	Issues <backspace>
^I	Issues <tab>
^M	Issues <return>
^O	Toggles Ortho mode on/off
^P	Toggles menu echoing on/off
^Q	Echoes prompts, status listings, and input to printer
^T	Toggles tablet on/off
^V	Changes current viewport
^Z	Suppresses the <spacebar> at the end of a menu item

TABLE 11.3 Button menus

Button menu	Key/button sequence
AUX1/BUTTONS1	Simple button pick
AUX2/BUTTONS2	Shift + button
AUX3/BUTTONS3	Ctrl + button
AUX4/BUTTONS4	Ctrl + Shift + button

Figure 11.4 Extending the menu.

11.7 Floating Cursor Menu

***AUX2 (or ***BUTTONS2)
$P0=*

AUX2/BUTTONS2 is the section label for the menu section that's invoked when you hold down the <shift> key and clicking the second button on the pointing device. The line immediately following the section label is invoked. In this case, $P0 is interpreted by AutoCAD as "load menu POP0," and =* is interpreted as "display the current loaded menu," which in this case is POP0. Consequently, menu POP0 is displayed at the current location of the cursor on the monitor.

    ***POP0 is the section label for the cursor menu. The first line of the menu must be the menu title. In this case, the menu title [Osnap] is used. The title has a specific application for a pull-down menu since it's displayed in the menu bar. It's meaningless for the cursor menu because it isn't displayed, but it is a syntax requirement of AutoCAD. The menu items in the POP0 section of this menu are object snaps, but it isn't limited to being an object snap menu. It could include macros like those used in the POP1 menu. In DOS, the menu item labels in square brackets aren't required. They *are* required for Windows.

11.8 Saving the Menu

Click on Notepad's (or Edit's) File button (see Figure 11.4), to display the File menu. Choose Save from the File menu to save the file using the name entered when the file was opened, C:\DRAWINGS\BORDER.MNU.

The first time a menu is loaded, AutoCAD compiles it, creating a compiled menu. In Windows, AutoCAD creates two files: *filename*.MNC, and *filename*.MNR. In DOS, AutoCAD creates a compiled file, *filename*.MNX. This is done automatically. If the file is revised, AutoCAD compares the dates and times of the .MNU and the compiled files (.MNC and .MNR, or .MNX). Then, if the .MNU file has a later date/time, it's re-compiled and new compiled files are created. The file loaded into AutoCAD is the compiled version.

Press OK to exit the Save dialog box. Then redisplay the File menu and choose Exit.

When you exit Edit, you'll be returned to AutoCAD. If you used Windows, you'll have to toggle to AutoCAD by holding the <alt> key down and pressing <tab>. Each time you press <tab>, a box is displayed in the middle of the screen with the name of an open program. When the box displays AutoCAD - [PROJ-11.DWG], release the <alt> key to return to the AutoCAD program.

11.9 Loading a Menu

In DOS and Windows, you can load a menu in place of the base menu (ACAD.MNU). In Windows, you can load the menu as a partial menu so it's displayed with the base menu (ACAD.MNU). Both procedures will be illustrated in this chapter. If you're using Windows, you can use either.

11.9.1 Loading a base menu

You load a base menu with the Menu command. In DOS, only base menus can be loaded. In Windows, both base and partial menus can be loaded. Load the menu as follows (in DOS, select the Menu command from the Tools menu):

Command: **menu** <return>

The Select Menu File dialog box illustrated in Figure 11.5 will be displayed. Set the directory to C:\DRAWINGS, as shown, and choose the Border file. Note that the List Files of Type box is set to *.MNU files. Press OK to load the Border.mnu file. Auto-CAD will indicate at the command window that it's compiling the file, and it will then load the file. Note if any errors are indicated. If there are, you'll have to reload the file in Edit or Notepad and correct the errors.

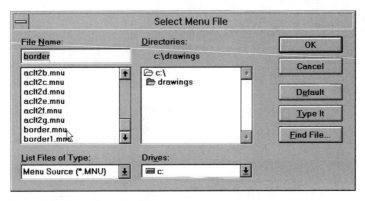

Figure 11.5 Select Menu File dialog box.

11.9.2 Loading a partial menu

A partial menu is loaded into the base menu. Partial menus cannot be loaded in DOS. Select Customize Menus... in the Tools menu, as illustrated in Figure 11.6.

The Menu Customization dialog box illustrated in Figure 11.7 will be displayed. Press the Browse... command button to display the Select Menu File dialog box, illustrated in Figure 11.5. Set the directory to C:\Drawings, as shown, and choose the Border file. Note that the List Files of Type box is set to *.MNU files. Press OK to choose the Border.mnu file.

The Menu Customization dialog will be redisplayed with the C:\DRAWINGS\BORDER.MNU file listed in the File Name box. Press the Load... command button to load the file into the Menu Groups box. Select C:\DRAWINGS\BORDER.MNU in the Menu Groups box by clicking on it, as shown in Figure 11.7. Then press the Menu Bar tab on the top right-hand side of the box to display the Menu Bar window, illustrated in Figure 11.8. Display the drop-down Menu Group box and select the Border.mnu file.

The Menus list box (on the left side of the dialog box) will now show Easy1 as an available menu. Highlight Easy1 in the Menu list box, and then press the Insert >> button to move the Easy1 menu listing into the Menu Bar box on the right side of the dialog box, as shown in Figure 11.9. Menus in this box are displayed in AutoCAD's menu bar. Press the Close button to exit the dialog box.

11.10 Using the Border Menu

Try your Easy1 menu. Select the Line command and draw a triangle using your floating cursor menu (holding down Shift and press the second button on your mouse) to snap the last line onto the start of the first. If your menu does not work correctly you will have to correct it in Notepad or in Edit. You will have a chance to do that in the following.

11.11 Cascading Menu

Load Notepad or Edit and edit the file C:\DRAWINGS\BORDER.MNU, as outlined in section 11.3. Click on File in Notepad's menu bar (refer back to Figure 11.2) and then click Open... to display the Open file dialog box, illustrated in Figure 11.10. Set the Directories to c:\drawings. Then move the cursor into the File Name edit box, change *.txt to *.mnu, and press <return>. The menu files in directory c:\drawings will be listed in the file list box. Double-click border.mnu to load it. A similar process is used to locate a file in Edit.

Add the POP2 menu section to your menu, shown in Figure 11.11, between Quit and ***AUX1 (the other sections of the menu completed earlier aren't shown).

The POP2 menu section is not complete because no operations follow the menu item labels [A-Size] and [B-Size]. The operations (commands) to follow these item labels will be written in chapter 12. I've added the menu item labels here to illustrate cascading menus. The menu is shown in Figure 11.12 as it will appear in AutoCAD when Metric is selected in the Title Blk menu.

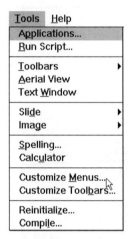

Figure 11.6   Tools menu.

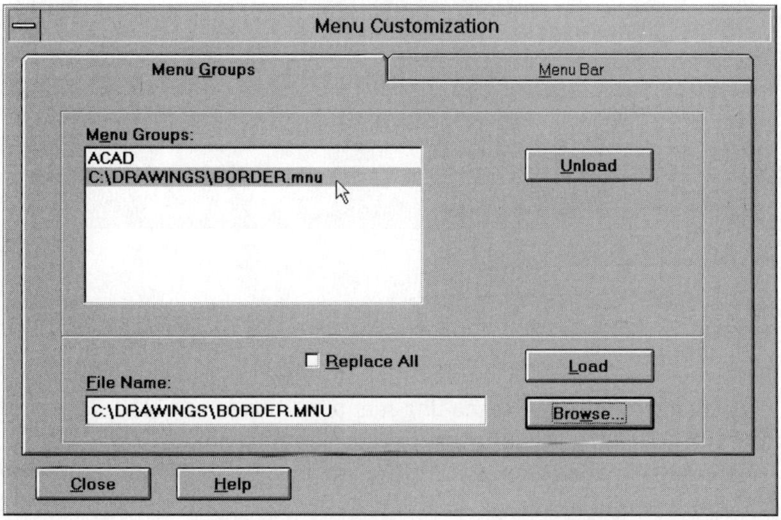

Figure 11.7   Menu Customization dialog box.

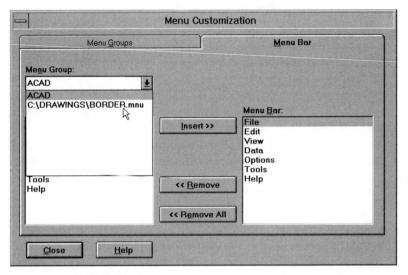

Figure 11.8 Menu Bar customization.

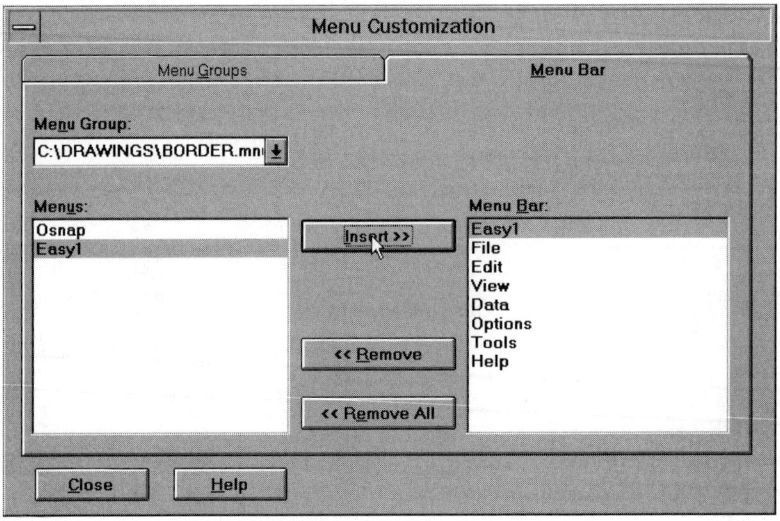

Figure 11.9 Inserting a partial menu.

In the menu (Figure 11.11) the -> in [->Metric] is a label prefix indicating the start of a cascading menu. The cascading menu continues until the label prefix <- is encountered, indicating the last item in the cascading menu.

Each cascading menu starts with the label prefix ->. If more than one menu cascades from a parent menu, the last item in the last cascading menu must have one <- symbol for each cascading menu, e.g.:

[->Metric]
[-> Landscape]
[A Size]
[<-<-B Size]

Save the menu using the filename c:\drawings\border.mnu, and exit Edit or Notepad. If you're using Edit, you'll be returned to AutoCAD. If you're using Notepad with Windows, hold down the <alt> key and press <tab> to toggle back to AutoCAD.

11.12   Reloading a Modified Menu

You must now load the modified menu into AutoCAD. If you're using DOS (or didn't load the previous menu as a partial menu in Windows), enter the Menu command as outlined in section 11.9.1 and the modified menu will be loaded.

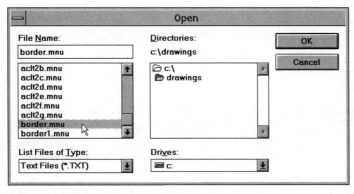

Figure 11.10   Open the menu file.

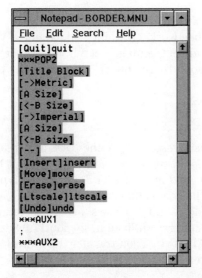

Figure 11.11   Adding POP2.

If you loaded the previous menu into Windows as a partial menu, you have to follow the same procedure outlined in section 11.9.2, *Loading a partial menu*. The steps are as follows:

1. Choose Customize Menus... in the Tools menu to display the Menu Customization dialog box illustrated back in Figure 11.7.

2. Choose C:\DRAWINGS\BORDER.MNU in the Menu Groups dialog box, and then press the Unload command button to unload the previous menu.

3. Press the Browse... button to display the Select Menu File dialog box (refer back to Figure 11.5), select the c:\drawings directory, then select the border menu file, and press OK.

4. The Menu Customization dialog box is redisplayed with C:\DRAWINGS\BORDER.MNU listed in the File Name box. Press the Load command button to load it into the Menu Groups list box. AutoCAD might display an alert box stating: "Loading of a template menu file (MNU file) overwrites and redefines the menu source file (MNS file), which results in the loss of any toolbar customization changes that have been made." You haven't made any changes to the toolbar, so press OK.

5. Choose C:\DRAWINGS\BORDER.MNU in the Menu Groups list box, and then press the Menu Bar tab to display the Menu Bar dialog box (refer back to Figure 11.8).

The new menus in the Border menu will be listed in the Menus list, as shown back in Figure 11.12. Highlight Easy1 in the Menus list box, as shown, and press Insert >>. The Easy1 menu will be added to AutoCAD's menu bar.

Highlight File in the Menu Bar list box by clicking on it, and then click on Title Block in the Menus list box, as shown in Figure 11.13. Press Insert >> to insert Title Block between the Easy1 and File menu of the menu bar. Press Close to exit.

11.12.1 Testing the menu

The menu is illustrated in Figure 11.14 with the Metric cascading item. Try the menu. Check that your cascading menus work. (Nothing will happen if you select A-Size or B-Size there are no commands in the menu yet.) If you still have errors, edit the menu, fix the errors, and reload the menu as outlined in the preceding sections.

11.13 Loading the Acad Menu

If you lose your Acad menu, you can easily restore it in either DOS or Windows. Load the full menu by entering the **Menu** command at the command prompt to display the Select Menu File dialog box, illustrated in Figure 11.5. Press the Type It command button, and then enter **acad** at the command line.

If you're using a partial menu in Windows and you lose some of the standard Acad menus in the menu bar, follow the procedures outlined in section 11.9.2 to load the menu C:\ACAD13\WIN\SUPPORT\ACAD.MNU. Then transfer the individual menus from the Menus list to the menu bar (refer back to Figure 11.12).

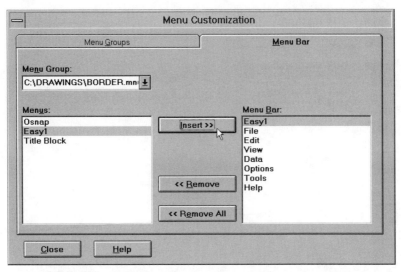

Figure 11.12 Inserting the Easyl menu.

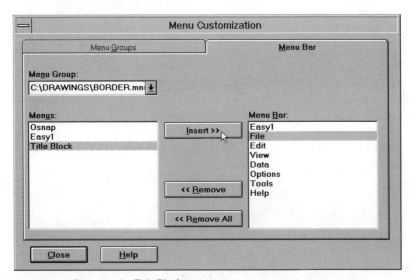

Figure 11.13 Inserting the Title Block menu.

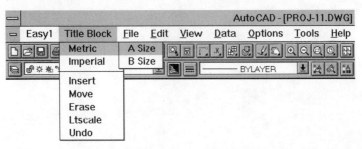

Figure 11.14 Cascading menu.

12

Attributes

Objective: Use blocks with attributes, construct a custom menu to draw borders and title blocks for drawings, insert drawings to scale into a border and title block drawing, edit attribute definitions, edit attributes, and plot drawings with borders and title blocks.

12.1 Attributes

Attributes are used to tag information to graphical drawing elements that are stored as blocks. The information can be constants, such as heat loss coefficients tagged with window blocks, or variable information that AutoCAD requests as the block is being inserted into the drawing.

Attribute information can be displayed on the drawing with the graphic block, or it can be collected on a disk for later processing to create, for instance, a bill of material. Such information can then be collected from the disk by database or word processing software. The procedure for using attributes is as follows: Create an attribute definition using the Attdef command, then create a block that includes the desired graphical information and the Attribute Definition.

The block, including the attribute definition, can be part of the current drawing only, or you can save it as a separate file by using the Wblock command and inserting it into another drawing. A block can have more than one attribute associated with it. AutoCAD will prompt you for the value of each Attribute when the block is inserted.

12.2 Attdef Command

The attribute definition is created with the Attdef command. When you enter **Attdef**, the following settings are available:

Invisible. When the Invisible mode is turned on, information relevant to that attribute isn't displayed on the drawing. For instance, if you want to tag building window blocks with heat loss factors, you might not want that information to be displayed on the drawing. The information is stored in the drawing file, however, and can be retrieved by another program that might perform heat loss calculations. When the invisible mode is off, attribute information tagged to a block is displayed on the drawing with the block.

Constant. When the Constant mode is off, the attribute tagged to the block is variable, and AutoCAD requests when the block is inserted. If the Constant mode is on, the attribute information tagged with the block is entered during the creation of the block, and isn't requested by AutoCAD when the block with the attribute is inserted into a drawing.

Verify. If Verify is on, any variable information you enter when the block is inserted will be redisplayed and you'll be allowed to modify the entry. If verify is off, the information will be accepted immediately as it's entered, and you won't be given the opportunity to modify the entry.

Attribute tag. The Attribute tag is any name you want to use to identify the attribute. This tag name must not include blank spaces and must not be a null value. It's printed on the drawing when the attribute is created, but it isn't printed on the drawing with the block it's associated with when the block is inserted. The attribute tag should be a short identifier name.

Attribute prompt. You enter a prompt line that's to be displayed on the command line when the block containing this attribute is inserted into a drawing. The prompt isn't displayed on the block during the creation of the attribute. The prompt is any text you want to use to prompt the user to input the attribute value when the block containing the attribute is inserted into a drawing. If you specified a Constant mode for the attribute, a prompt isn't required.

Attribute value. If Constant and Preset are off, this is the default value that will be displayed with the Attribute prompt. Default values are displayed in angle brackets (<>). If Constant or Preset are on, this is the constant that will be inserted with the attribute, and you won't be prompted for input.

Insertion point. You can enter the attribute location directly into the dialog box or from the command line.

Text options. This defines the attribute text that's inserted when the attribute is invoked. You can set the text justification and style from drop-down boxes, and either enter the text height and rotation in the dialog box or select it on the screen.

12.3 Border/Title Block with Attributes

A standard border and title block will be constructed for an A-size drawing (8.5 × 11 inches or 215 × 280 mm) and stored as a block. You'll use attributes to attach information to the title block when the block is inserted into a drawing.

12.3.1 Border and title block construction

In this example, we'll use metric units on an A-size sheet, so the screen limits will be set at 280 mm × 215 mm. A 20-mm border will be provided on the top, long side of

Figure 12.1 Polyline tool.

the page, and 15-mm border provided on the other sides. The drawing border line will be started at coordinates 0,15 (for a Hewlett Packard HP 7470A graphics plotter), so the sides will be 250 mm × 175 mm long.

The border dimensions and the start point are dependent on the plotter you're using. You can determine the proper values for your plotter by drawing the border, as outlined in the following section, but use the Line command rather than the Pline (polyline) command. Then plot the display. If any of the border lines aren't plotted, use the plot sheet to estimate where the line should be and move the line on the screen using the Move command. Plot the display again, and relocate lines if necessary. You might also have to move the entire border so it fits properly on the sheet. When your border is plotting properly, use the Pline command and the Intersection object snap to draw polylines over the lines.

12.3.2 Polyline command

Boot AutoCAD. This drawing won't be saved in the normal way, so you won't use the New command to name it. Set the drawing units to Decimal with two digits to the right of the decimal. Set the drawing limits at –5,–5 and 280,215 (the size of the sheet of paper, allowing a 5-mm space along the bottom and left side). Use Zoom All to zoom the screen to the specified limits.

The border is to be drawn on a new layer named Border. That layer name should be reserved for the border and not used for any other entities on your drawing. Using the Layer Control dialog box to create the Border layer, colored blue. Make Border the current layer.

The border lines are to be drawn using the Pline (polyline) command with a polyline 0.2 millimeters wide:

Draw <toolbar> Polyline (Figure 12.1) <pick> From point: **0,15** <return> Current line width is 0.00. Arc/Close/Halfwidth/Length/Undo/Width/ <Endpoint of line>: **w** (width) <return> Starting width <0.00>: **0.2** <return> Ending width <0.20>: <return> Arc/Close/Halfwidth/Length/Undo/ Width/<Endpoint of line>: **@250<0** <return> Arc/Close/Halfwidth/ Length/Undo/Width/<Endpoint of line>: **@175<90** <return>Arc/Close/ Halfwidth/Length/Undo/Width/<Endpoint of line>: **@250<180** <return> Arc/Close/Halfwidth/Length/Undo/Width/<Endpoint of line>: **c** (close) <return>

Use the Pline command to draw the 125 mm × 30 mm title block shown in Figure 12.2. Use 0.2-mm-wide lines and start at coordinate 125,15, as shown. Don't add the text or dimensions. The Polyline command has the following options:

Arc. Changes to arc mode in which you can continue the polyline as an arc.

Close. Closes the polyline sequence on the starting point.

Halfwidth. Specifies the start and end width of the polyline from its center to one of its edges.

Length. Draws a polyline segment of a specified length at the same angle as the previous segment.

Undo. Removes the most previous line segment.

Width. Specifies the start and end width of the next line segment.

12.3.3 Title block headings

When entering headings in the title block, you must be very specific where the text is to be located. The Dtext (dynamic text) command allows you to enter text dynamically on the screen. When you press <return> after typing in the text, the cursor drops down to the next line so you can continue the text directly below the previous text. This is what you want in the title block, but you want the spacing between the text to meet your own requirements. I also assume you want the same text height and justification, so you'll use the Text command. The text style name Romanc is set for the title block headings:

Data <pick> Text Style <pick> `Text style name (or ?) <Standard>:` **title** `<return> New Style`

The Select Font File dialog box illustrated in Figure 5.22 will be displayed. Choose the Romanc font and press OK. AutoCAD will continue with:

`Select romanc.shx New style. Height <0.00>: <return> Width factor <1.00>: <return> Obliquing factor <0>: <return> Backwards? <N>: <return> Upside-down? <N>: <return> Vertical? <N>: <return> Title is the current text style.`

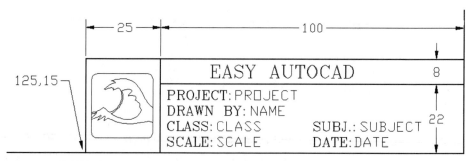

Figure 12.2 Title block.

Enter the title block headings (shown in Romanc font in Figure 12.2) as follows (don't add the text shown in regular type):

Draw <toolbar> Single-Line Text <pick> Justify/Style/<Start point>: **j** (justify) <return> Align/Fit/Center/Middle/Right: **c** (center) <return> Center point: **200,39** Use the cursor to verify this on the monitor. <return> Height <0.20>: **4** <return> Rotation angle <0>: <return> Text: **EASY AUTOCAD** <return> <return> Text Justify/Style/<Start point>: **152,32** <return> Height <4>: **3** <return> Rotation angle <0:>: <return> Text: **Project** <return>

Then add the remaining heading (shown in Romanc style in Figure 12.2) using a spacing of two units between the text, and a text height of three units.

You can draw the logo as a block and insert it. If you want to reuse your logo in other drawings, use the Wblock command to save it to file. You can also import the logo as a Windows metafile from other application files. If you want to do that, refer to chapter 20, section 20.6.

12.3.4   Create attributes

In AutoCAD for Windows, the attribute tools are in the Attribute toolbar, which you load by choosing it from the Tool flyout, as shown in Figure 12.3. The Attribute toolbar illustrated in Figure 12.4 is then displayed on the screen. Drag the toolbar to a suitable location on your screen.

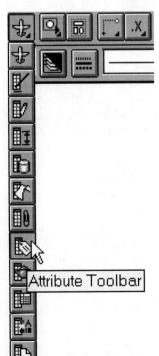

Figure 12.3 Loading the Attribute toolbar.

Figure 12.4 Attribute toolbar.

The system variable Attdia determines if AutoCAD uses command-line dialog or dialog boxes for attributes. By default Attdia is set to 1, so AutoCAD uses dialog boxes. Check that it's 1 by entering the following at the command line:

Command: **attdia** <return> New value for ATTDIA <0>: **1** <return>

Attributes are used to put variable text into the title block. As they're created, Auto-CAD puts the attribute tag in the location where the text is to go. The attribute tags are shown in standard text back in Figure 12.2. When the attributes are invoked later, you're asked to provide the actual text to go into each title block. Create the attributes as follows (in DOS, select Construct, then Attribute):

Attribute <toolbar> Define Attributes <pick>

The Attribute Definition dialog box (Figure 12.5) will be displayed. The options are discussed at the beginning of this chapter. Enter the tag and prompt, as shown, and set the text style to Standard. Enter the text height as 3 units (mm), and set the justification to Left so the text insertion point is the start point in the title block. Enter **175** for X and **32** for Y. If you want to select the points on the screen, press the Pick Point < command button. Turn the Verify check box on (so it has × in it). Press OK to exit the dialog box.

AutoCAD will enter the attribute tag PROJECT beside the heading PROJECT: in the title block, as shown back in Figure 12.2. This is where the attribute text (the project name) will eventually be placed by AutoCAD when the attributes are invoked. If the tag isn't in the correct location, use the Move command to move it.

Before entering the remaining attributes, zoom on the title block and determine the start point for each attribute tag. Use the cursor to estimate the location, reading the coordinates from the coordinate display window in the button bar (press <F6> or <ctrl>–D if the coordinates aren't calculated as the cursor is moved). Then calculate the value using a text height of three and the spacing between text lines as two units.

Display the Attribute Definition dialog box and enter the next attribute. There are six attributes to enter, so you must repeat the process six times. When entering the attribute for Scale, use a default scale of NTS (not to scale). You can enter default values in the Value edit box (see Figure 12.5). Figure 12.2 shows the title block with the attribute tags I used.

12.3.5 Editing attribute definitions

You can edit the attribute definition as follows:

Modify <toolbar> Special edit <flyout> Edit Text (Figure 12.6) <pick> <Select a TEXT or ATTDEF object>/Undo: Click on the attribute tag PROJECT. <pick>

The Edit Attribute Definition edit box in Figure 12.7 will be displayed. Move the cursor into the Prompt edit box and type **Name**, as shown. Press OK and then:

<Select a TEXT or ATTDEF object>/Undo: <return>

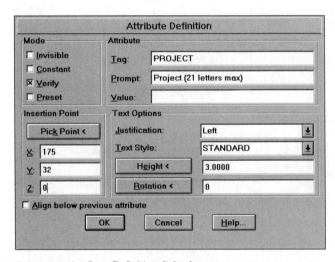

Figure 12.5 Attribute Definition dialog box.

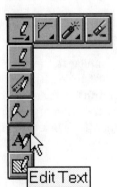

Figure 12.6 Special Edit flyout.

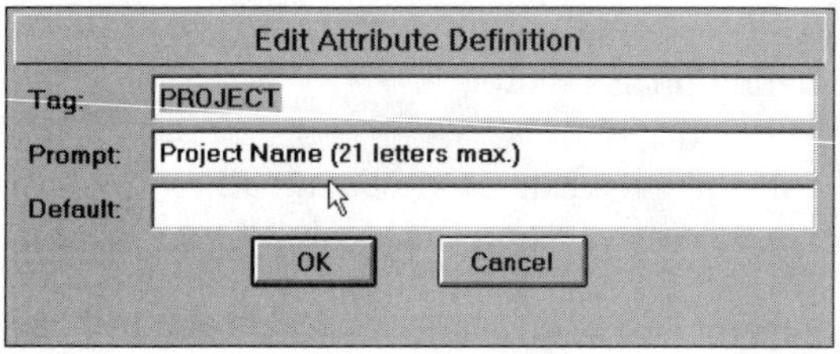

Figure 12.7 Editing an attribute definition.

If you want to change the location of the attribute, you can move it with the Move command. You can also change the attribute location, height, layer, etc. by choosing the Properties tool (in DOS, select Modify, then Change Properties...) to display the Change Properties dialog box, illustrated in Figure 12.8. Refer back to Figure 9.8 in chapter 9, noting that the dialog box that's displayed depends on the object selected to be changed.

12.3.6 Create the block

The entire drawing is to be saved as a block for insertion into other drawings. The block name will be Am-hbdr (A-size drawing, metric, horizontal border):

Draw <toolbar> Block <pick> Block name: **am-hbdr** <return> Insertion base point: **0,0** <pick> Select objects: Use a Windows selection box to place a window around the border and title block. <Pick> Select objects: <return>

AutoCAD will remove the entire block from the screen. If a portion of the drawing remains on the screen, you didn't select everything in the selection window. Press Undo and redo the block. Write the block to a drawing file using a filename the same as the block name:

Command: **wblock** <return>

The Create Drawing File dialog box that's displayed is similar to the one shown back in Figure 10.8 in chapter 10. Change the directory to C:/DRAWINGS and then move the cursor to the File Name: edit box and enter **am-hbdr.dwg**. Press OK to open the file. AutoCAD will now request, at the command line, the name of the block to save in the file named Am-Hbdr.dwg. Enter **=**, indicating that the block name is the same as the opened filename (am-hbdr):

Block name: = <return>

12.3.7 Test Am-hbdr

You'll use the Am-hbdr block to draw a border and title block. You'll be prompted to insert the following into the title block:

Draw <toolbar> Insert Block (see Figure 10.3) <Pick>

An Insert dialog box similar to the one shown in Figure 10.4 is now displayed. The block to be inserted is in the current drawing database. Press the Block... command button to display the Blocks list box. Click on AM-HBDR in the list, which moves its name into the Selection box, then press OK. The Insert dialog box will show the block name AM-HBDR in the Block name box. Click the Specify Parameters on Screen box to off (there should *not* be an × in it). Then enter the insertion point values of **0** for X and **0** for Y. Enter an X and Y Scale of **1.0**, and a scale and rotation angle of **0**. Press OK to exit the dialog box.

AutoCAD will prompt you to enter data for each attribute variable, using the prompts entered when the attribute was defined (the order might be different than that shown):

Proj. name (21 letters max): **Testing** <return> Your name: **J.D. Smith** <return> Class: **CVTY 11** <return> Scale <NTS>: <return> Subject #: **CAD 1000-3** <return> Date: **1995-05-03**

Because you turned the Verify mode on when defining the attributes, the prompts will be redisplayed showing the variable data entered. You might want to change the data or simply press <return> for each one.

The drawing border and title block are drawn by AutoCAD, with the text information inserted into the title block.

If your attributes didn't work properly, exit the current drawing without saving it. Then edit the drawing c:\drawings\am-hbdr and make the appropriate corrections to the attribute. Exit the drawing and save it using the name c:\drawings\am-hbdr. Start another blank drawing, set the limits to –5,–5 and 280,215, and zoom all. Then try inserting the c:\drawings\am-hbdr block.

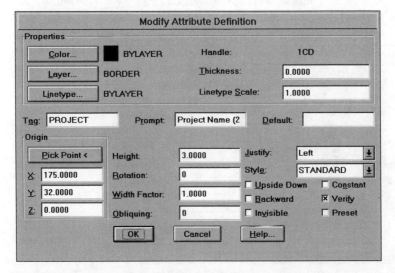

Figure 12.8 Change properties of attribute definitions.

Do not exit the current drawing with the inserted am-hbdr block and attributes. It will be used to demonstrate editing attributes.

12.4 Editing Attributes

After attributes have been invoked (after the block containing the attributes is inserted), you can edit them as follows (in DOS, select Modify, then Attribute, then Edit):

Attribute <toolbar> Edit Attributes <pick> Select block: Pick a point anywhere on the block inserted. <pick>

The Edit Attributes dialog box in Figure 12.9 will be displayed. Change the scale from NTS to ½, as shown, then select OK to exit. Exit AutoCAD without saving the current drawing.

12.5 Creating a Special Border Menu

When you tested the Am-hbdr.dwg file, you were required to set limits and use the Insert command. You'll now create a special menu to create drawings with borders and title blocks.

You'll use the Border menu to set up a plot drawing. A *plot drawing* is limited to the size of the sheet on which the drawing is plotted. The drawing Am-hbdr.dwg is inserted into the plot drawing, invoking the attributes, and drawings to be plotted are then inserted to scale as blocks into the plot drawing. You can insert a number of drawing files onto a plot drawing, each at a different scale.

The procedure is illustrated in Figure 12.10, where the Border menu is loaded into a new drawing. The Am-hbdr drawing is then inserted into the drawing, providing a border and title block (with attribute data). Then a drawing named Proj-5 is inserted into the drawing using an appropriate scale. The drawing is then saved with a new name (Plot-5). You can plot Plot-5 using a 1:1 scale to provide a hardcopy drawing.

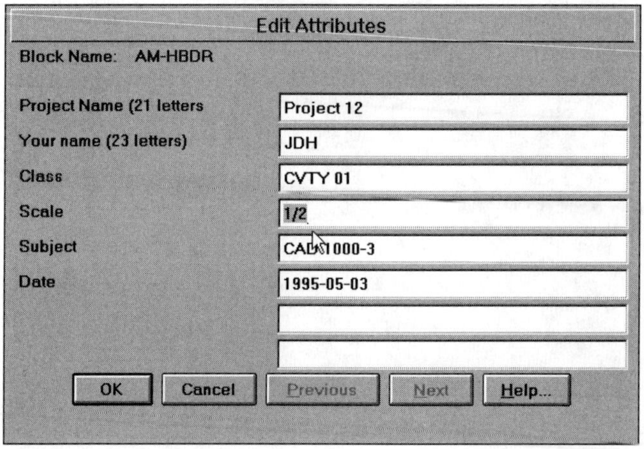

Figure 12.9 Editing Attributes.

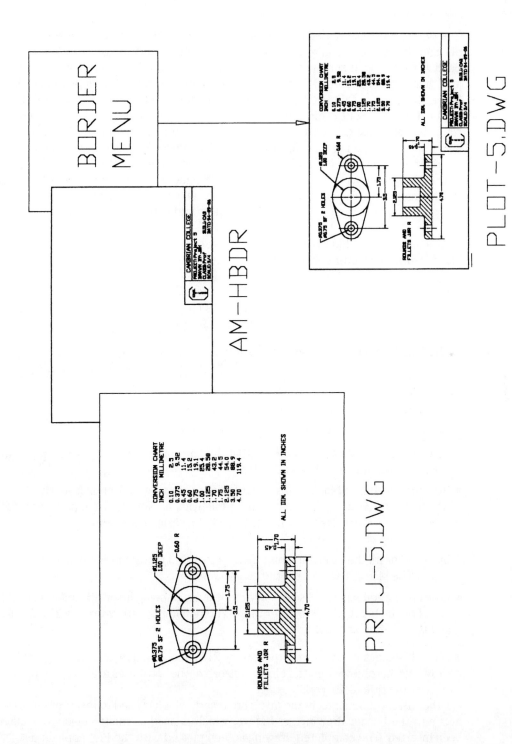

Figure 12.10 Plot-drawing construction sequence.

12.5.1 Creating the menu

The Border.mnu file created in chapter 11 will be modified and used to insert the border and title block. If you're using Windows, the Program Manager should currently be displayed on your screen. Click on the Accessories window to bring it to the front, and then click on Notepad. With DOS, enter **Edit** at the DOS prompt to load Edit. When Notepad (or Edit) is loaded, choose File and then Open. The Open dialog box will be displayed. Set the directory to C:\DRAWINGS, then move the cursor to the File Name box and change *.txt to *.mnu and press <return>. The menu files in c:\drawings will be displayed in the Files list box. Click on BORDER.MNU and then press OK.

Edit the Border.mnu file, adding the commands in Figure 12.11 to the POP2 section of the menu. Commands in other sections of the menu are not changed. When your Border.mnu menu is exactly the same as the one shown, choose Save in the File menu to save the file and then choose Exit. The macro added to the menu is:

[A-Size]limits –5,–5 280,215 zoom a +
insert c:/drawings/am-hbdr;0,0 1 1 0

When Border.mnu is loaded into AutoCAD, the pull-down menu appears as shown back in Figure 11.14 in chapter 11. If A-Size is chosen from the menu, the following sequence of operations is invoked (refer to Figure 12.11):

- The Limits command is loaded and entered by the single blank space following it.
- The lower left corner limits are read from the menu as –5,–5 and entered by the space following the coordinates.
- The upper right corner limits are read as 280,215 and entered.
- The Zoom command and the All option are entered.
- The plus sign indicates to AutoCAD that the line continues to the next line, where the Insert command is read and entered.
- Insert requests the block to insert and read c:/drawings/am-hbdr from the menu, which is entered with the semicolon (;) following it. Note that file paths are indicated by a forward slash in a menu file. The backslash is reserved for user input (see chapter 11, section 11.5.2).
- Insert requests the insertion point for the block and reads coordinates 0,0 from the menu. The blank space enters the coordinates.
- Insert next requests the X scale factor for the block being inserted, and reads 1 followed by the blank space to enter the 1. The remaining entries are the Y scale of 1, and the rotation angle of 0.

The line [A-Size] sets the screen to a 280 by 215 sheet of paper, and inserts the block c:\drawings\am-hbdr. When the block is inserted, the attributes are invoked and you can enter the title block variables.

Other useful commands in the menu are Insert, which is used to Insert other drawings into the border drawing, and Move, which is used to move objects that have been inserted. The completed drawing is then plotted with the Plot command.

TABLE 12.1 Plot-Drawing Scale Factors

Drawing units	Scale	X-scale factor
feet (architect)	⅛" = 1'0"	0.0104167[1]
feet (architect)	¼" = 1'0"	0.0208333[1]
inches (decimal)	¾"	0.75
feet (engineer)	1" = 50'0"	0.0016667[2]
meters (decimal)	1:100	10[3]
millimeters (decimal)	1:100	0.01

NOTE: See appendix B for a complete listing of plot-drawing scale factors.

[1]When using AutoCAD's architectural units, the drawing units are always inches, even though the coordinates are displayed on the monitor in feet and inches. The scale factor is then $1/(N \times 12)$. For ⅛" = 1', the scale factor is $1/(8 \times 12) = 0.0104167$.

[2]AutoCAD's engineering units are in inches, even though the monitor displays feet and inches. The scale factor is then $1/(N \times 12)$. For 1" = 50', the scale factor is $1/(50 \times 12) = 0.0016667$.

[3]The units used to draw the border are millimeters, and the units used for the drawing are meters. The scale 1:100 means that 1 mm = 100 mm or 1 mm = 0.1 m. The scale factor is then $1/0.1 = 10$.

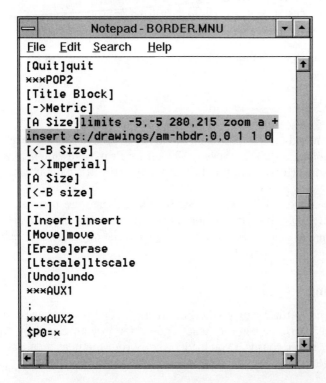

Figure 12.11 Adding commands to POP2.

The menu is currently only for drawing limits set to 280 by 215, which is a sheet of A-size paper (11 × 8.5 inches). When drawings are inserted, you'll be required to enter the insertion point. Enter **0,0** and then use Move to relocate the inserted object if necessary. Then you'll be asked to enter an X-scale factor. If you had both an Imperial unit border and a Metric border, you'd enter the scale factors listed in Table 12.1 and appendix B. Imperial unit borders will be drawn later.

12.6 Plot Drawing Example

Boot AutoCAD and begin a new drawing named C:\DRAWINGS\PLOT-5. Load the Border.mnu menu following the procedures outlined in section 11.9 of chapter 11 to load either a base or partial menu (also refer to section 11.12 when loading a partial menu).

Click on Title Blk in the menu bar, then click on Metric and A Size. AutoCAD will insert am-hbdr.dwg and invoke the attributes. Enter the requested data, using a project name Proj-5. When prompted for the scale enter ¾, assuming Proj-5 is being plotted on an A-size sheet.

Project-5 is to be plotted on an A-size (Imperial) sheet using a ¾ scale. When inserting the Proj-5.dwg drawing into the Plot-5.dwg, you must take into account that Plot-5 was drawn using millimeter units (refer to Figure 12.11) so the insertion scale becomes ¾ × 25.4 = 19.05. Select Insert from the Title Block menu:

Insert <pick> Block name: **c:\drawings\proj-5** <return> Insertion point: **0,0** <return> X-Scale factor <1>: **19.05** <return> Y-Scale factor <19.05>: <return> Rotation angle <0>: <return>

You can call the File dialog when AutoCAD requests the block name by entering a tilde (~), as follows:

Insert <pick> Block name: **~** <return>

Use the Move command in the Title Block menu (or the Move tool) to locate the entity into a better location on the drawing. The entire Proj-5 drawing is now a single entity since it was inserted as a block. To move it with the Move command, use:

Title Block <pick> Move <pick> Select objects: **l** (Last) <return> Base point or displacement: Digitize a convenient point on the Proj-5 block to act as a first point during the move. <pick> Second point: Drag the object to the desired location. <pick>

12.7 Plotting a Plot-Drawing

If you don't have the AutoCAD menu on the screen (if you loaded your Border menu as a base menu in DOS), choose the Acad-Mnu option in your Easy1 menu to load the Acad.mnu file. Don't do this if you loaded the Border menu as a partial menu (if you're using Windows).

Use the Print tool or the Print... command in the File menu to plot the drawing. The scale is 1:1 because the drawing was scaled when inserted into the border, which was drawn to fit onto an A-size sheet (280×250 mm).

A Plot configuration dialog box similar to the one shown back in Figure 7.1 in chapter 7 is displayed. Set the appropriate settings as outlined in section 7.3, and set a user paper size of 280×215, which is an A-size sheet converted to millimeters. The scale is 1=1. Complete the other settings and preview the plot. If the preview is proper, press OK to complete the plot.

Save the drawing using the filename c:\drawings\plot-5. Do *not* save the drawing as Proj-5 or you'll write the block over your original drawing, thereby losing both. If you're warned that the drawing already exists, look carefully at the filename.

The drawing cannot be modified on the plot drawing because it was inserted onto that drawing as a block. If you want to modify it, load the original drawing, e.g., C\DRAWINGS\PLOT-5.DWG, and make the changes. Then save the drawing and re-load the plot drawing, C:\DRAWINGS\PLOT-5.DWG. The block definition on the plot drawing is updated as follows:

```
Command: Insert <return> Block name: proj-5=c:\drawings\proj-5 <return>
Insertion point: Press <esc> or <ctrl>–C.
```

AutoCAD will load the revised version of c:\drawings\proj-5, replacing the version stored in the current drawing file.

12.8 Plot Proj-6 Drawing

Use a similar procedure to plot Proj-6.dwg. That drawing was done in meters and will be inserted into a plot drawing using a scale of 1 mm = 300 mm. The x and y insertion scale factor will be $\frac{1}{300} \times 1000 = 3.33$ (since the drawing was drawn in meters and the border is drawn in millimeters, the 1000 multiplier converts the drawing units from meters to millimeters).

12.8.1 Linetype scale

When a block is inserted into a drawing, it uses the linetype scale (Ltscale) of the current drawing. After Proj-6 is inserted into the plot drawing, you can set the linetype scale by using the Ltscale command in the Title Block menu, or select Options from the Acad menu, then Linetypes, then Global Linetype Scale. The linetype scale used in chapter 6, section 6.9.1 was 5.7. This value must be multiplied by the x,y insertion scale factor of 3.33, giving a Linetype scale of 19:

```
Options <pick> Linetypes <pick> Global Linetype Scale <pick> New scale fac-
tor <1>: 19 <return>
```

The drawing is then regenerated with the new linetype scale. Plot the drawing. Referring to Figure 7.1 back in chapter 7, set the size units to MM and the Paper Size to 280×215. The plot scale is 1=1. Save the drawing as C:\DRAWINGS\PLOT-6.DWG.

12.9 Assignment

Boot AutoCAD and edit the c:\drawings\am-hbdr drawing. Then invoke the Block command and make a block of the title block. Select the insertion point of the block from the screen as the lower right corner of the border, using an Intersection object snap. Select the block using a selection window, enclosing the title block. Although the selection window crosses the two border lines, they aren't included in the block. Name the block Title, and then write it to file (Wblock) using the filename c:\drawings\title.dwg. Exit the drawing without saving the changes.

You're to create an Imperial A-size border (8.5 × 11 inches), an Imperial B-size border (17 × 11 inches), and a metric B-size border (430 × 280 mm), each with a title block, following the procedures outlined in this chapter. Each is to be saved in the c:\drawings directory under an original name. The actual border frame size is to be less than the sheet sizes, and can be governed by your plotter's limitations. The procedure to draw each of the borders is as follows:

- Draw the borders using lines instead of polylines. Do not draw a title block.

- Plot the border to see how it fits the sheet. Edit the border as required.

- Use the Pline command to draw a solid polyline over the border lines, snapping onto the intersections. Use a polyline width of 0.2 mm with a metric border and width of 0.01 inches for the Imperial borders.

- Insert the title block you created and wrote to a file named c:\drawings\title.dwg. The insertion point is picked from the screen as the lower right corner of the border. Use the Intersection object snap to select the insertion point. The x and y scale factors are each 1 when inserting a title block into a metric drawing (since title was drawn in millimeters). When inserting into an Imperial-unit drawing, the x and y scale factors are 0.0394 ($\frac{1}{25.4}$) to convert the title block from millimeters to inches. Click on the Explode check box to turn it on, so the attributes aren't invoked when the title.dwg block is inserted.

- Save the border to a file in c:\drawings using an original name.

When you've written all the blocks to disk, edit the customized c:\drawings\aclt2 .mnu menu and add the appropriate macros to the lines in the POP2 section, following the same procedures used for the metric A-size item.

13

Working Spaces
and External References

Objectives: Use paper space to arrange and plot drawings, use and scale in viewports, set linetype scale in paper space, use external references, stretch associative dimensions, and stretch associative hatching.

Drawing: Edit drawing Proj-6.

13.1 Working Space

AutoCAD has two working space areas: model space and paper space. *Model space* is where you do most of your drafting (all the drawings in previous chapters were done in model space). *Paper space* is where you create the image, usually within a border, that's sent to the printer/plotter to be transferred onto paper. The application of paper space is similar to that of the border drawing introduced in chapter 12, where you arranged and scaled views to plot. In chapter 12, however, the border was also done in model space.

Boot AutoCAD and open drawing C:\DRAWINGS\PROJ-6.DWG, which was completed in chapter 6. The coordinate system icon illustrated in Figure 13.1 is displayed in the lower left corner of the screen when you're working in model space. If the icon isn't displayed, choose the menu items shown in Figure 13.2 and choose Icon and Icon Origin to display the icon at coordinates 0,0,0 (the origin). Note the word MODEL in the status bar, indicating that the current working space is model space.

You'll use paper space to place a border around drawing Proj-6 and plot the drawing using a scale of 1:300. To turn paper space on, turn off the Tilemode system variable by setting it to 0. Tilemode is discussed more in later chapters. Set Paper Space on as follows (see Figure 13.3):

View <pick> Paper Space <pick> AutoCAD will put a check mark in front of Paper Space, indicating paper space is on (Tilemode is off).

AutoCAD will show the following at the command line:

```
New value for TILEMODE <1>: 0 Entering Paper Space.
Use MVIEW to insert Model space viewports.
```

The working mode is now paper space. The model space icon in the bottom-left corner is replaced by the paper space icon (Figure 13.4). If there's no paper space icon on your screen, follow the commands at the start of this chapter to turn the UCS (user coordinate system) icon on. When paper space is on, PAPER is listed in the status bar (replacing MODEL).

Your Proj-6 drawing has also disappeared. It's not really gone; it's just in model space. In order to see it, you have to open a viewport in paper space or return to model space.

Move the cursor around the screen, noting that drawing limits have changed to 0,0 and about 420,297. These are the default limits of paper space in the Metric measurement settings, which was set for Proj-6 (see chapter 6). In the English measurement settings, the limits are 12,9.

Figure 13.1 Model space icon.

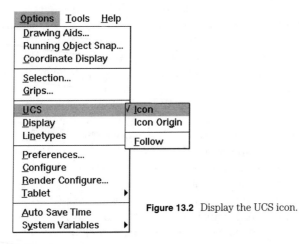

Figure 13.2 Display the UCS icon.

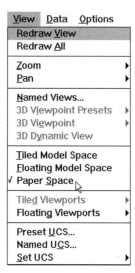

Figure 13.3 Choosing paper space.

Figure 13.4 Paper space icon.

13.1.1 Adding a border in paper space

You're now ready to draw a border, using the Border menu created in chapter 12. Follow the procedures outlined in chapter 11, section 11.9, to load either a base or partial menu, and load the file c:\drawings\border.mnu.

The customized Border menu is now loaded into AutoCAD. Click on Title Block in the menu bar, then click on Metric and A Size. The macro will set the screen limits to –5,–5 and 280,215 and invokes Zoom and All. The c:\drawings\am-hbdr.dwg drawing will be inserted and the attributes invoked. Enter the requested data. When prompted for the scale, enter **1:300**.

If you loaded the Border menu as a base menu (in DOS), the AutoCAD menu won't be visible, so you'll have to load it. To do so, select Easy1, then ACAD-MNU. If you loaded the Border menu as a partial menu, the Acad menu items will be visible, and you can use the current menu.

13.1.2 Opening a viewport

Prior to opening a viewport to see the Proj-6 drawing, you need to create a layer for the viewport to reside on. Create a new layer name VIEWLYR1 (view layer 1) and set its color to green. Make Viewlyr1 the current layer.

Then use the Mview command to open a viewport and view model space items in paper space (refer back to Figure 13.3). Choose Floating Model Space in the View menu to issue the Mview command and switch to model space:

View <pick> Floating Model Space: <pick> ON/OFF/Hideplot/Fit/2/3/4/ Restore/<First point>: <shift>–<right> Intersection <pick> Place the intersection target on the lower left corner of the border. <pick> Second point: <shift>–<right> Intersection <pick> Place the intersection target on the upper right corner of the border. <pick>

The two points you selected will open a viewport the size of the border. You could also have used the Fit option to open a viewport the size of the graphics screen. The other options to Mview will be discussed in later chapters.

Proj-6 is now visible on the screen, and a green line bounds the border. The green line is the viewport boundary, which is opened with the Mview command. It's green because it resides on layer Viewlyr1, which was the current layer when the viewport was created. Note that the cursor appears as crosshairs in open viewport and an arrow outside of the current viewport. If the model space icon isn't visible, turn it on with the Options menu, as illustrated back in Figure 13.2.

AutoCAD scaled Proj-6 to fit the viewport opened with the MView command. As specified in chapter 6, the drawing scale is to be 1:300. Because the border limits are in millimeters and Proj-6 is drawn in meters, the scale should be 1/0.3 or 3.33, as discussed in chapter 12, section 12.8. The XP option to the Zoom command allows you to scale the model space "times paper space." Since the Proj-6 lot plan drawing resides in model space, you must be in model space before you can zoom the lot plan. The icon should currently indicate you're in model space (see MODEL in the status bar). The scale is 1/0.3, but AutoCAD might not accept the 0.3 in that format and you might have to enter the division as 10/3 or 3.333. Enter the Zoom command as follows (in DOS, select View, then Zoom):

Standard <toolbar> Zoom Scale (Figure 13.5) <pick> All/Center/Dynamic/Extents/Left/Previous/Window/<Scale<X/XP): **10/3xp** <return>

The model is scaled 10/3 in the viewport by AutoCAD. Use the Pan command to pan the object in the viewport so it's located properly within the border (in DOS, select View, then Pan, then Point):

Standard <toolbar> Pan Point (Figure 13.6) <pick> Displacement: Pick a point on the object to be panned. <pick> Second point: Drag the object to the desired location. <pick>

The green line around the perimeter of the screen is the viewport boundary. You can use the List command to list its data, but the viewport boundary line resides in paper space, so you'll have to return to paper space before you can select it. Do this by either double-clicking on MODEL in the status bar or selecting View, then Paper Space in the menu bar.

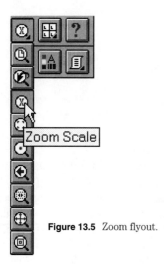

Figure 13.5 Zoom flyout.

Figure 13.6 Pan Point tool.

When Tilemode is set to 1 and a viewport has been opened, you can toggle between paper and model space using the MODEL/PAPER button in the status bar. Then invoke the List as follows (in DOS, select Assist, then Inquiry, then List):

Object Properties <toolbar> List (Figure 13.7) <pick> `Select objects:` Digitize a point on the green viewport boundary. <pick> `Select objects:` <return>

AutoCAD will display a text window that reports the following on the viewport:

```
VIEWPORT   Layer: VIEWLAYER1
           Space: Paper space
     Handle = D51
           Status: On and Active
           Scale relative to Paper space:    3.3333xp
 center point, X= 124.900 Y= 102.600 Z=0.000
  width   250.000
 height   175.000
```

Press <F2> (or <F1> with DOS) to exit the text window.

Noting that the Viewport green boundary line is on layer Viewlyr1, use the Layer Control box to set layer Text as current and freeze layer Viewlyr1. The green boundary line will disappear. If at any time your drawing disappears, use the Regen command to regenerate the screen.

Use Zoom Window to zoom on a small area of the drawing. Try erasing something in the Proj-6 lot plan drawing. You can't do it because the current working space is

Figure 13.7 List tool.

paper space. You can't edit items in model space when you're in paper space. Use Zoom Previous to return to the previous zoom view.

Change to model space by clicking on either PAPER in the status bar or Floating Model Space in the View menu. Now use Zoom Window. What happened? In model space, items in paper space aren't accessible, so the border in paper space won't zoom. Use Zoom Previous to return to the original zoom, or reenter Zoom Scale as 10/3xp. If you set Tilemode to 1 by selecting View, then Tiled Model Space, the working space will be changed to model space and anything drawn in paper space will be deleted from the screen. Reset Tilemode to 0 by selecting View and then Floating Model Space (to return to model space in a viewport), or View and then Paper Space to return the paper space entities to the screen.

13.1.3 Scaling linetypes in paper space

In chapter 6, section 6.9.1, the global linetype scale (Ltscale) for Proj-6 was set to 5.7. In paper space, you can scale linetypes based on paper space drawing units, or model space drawing units using the Psltscale command. If Psltscale is 1, linetypes are scaled based on paper space drawing units. If Psltscale is 0, linetypes are scaled based on model space drawing units. You'll usually want your linetype scale based on model space drawing units. Psltscale must be set in model space. Set the current working space to MODEL, and then set Psltscale by choosing the following from the menu bar:

Options <pick> Linetypes <pick> Paper Space Linetype Scale

Then set Psltscale to 0 based on the following:

- If there's a tick mark in front of Paper Space Linetype Scale, then Psltscale is set to 1 (linetype scale is based on paper space).
- If there's no tick mark in front of Paper Space Linetype Scale, then Psltscale is set to 0 (linetype scale is based on model space).

Enter **regen** at the command line to regenerate the drawing and view the results.

13.1.4 Plotting paper-space drawings

Set the working space to paper space before continuing. Because the border is drawn to suit a sheet of paper 280×215 mm, which is the size of the paper you're going to plot on, the plot scale is 1=1. Plot the drawing following the procedures outlined in section 7.3 in chapter 7, but use a plot scale of 1=1.

After the plot is complete, set the working space to model space and try plotting again using a scale of 1=1. Notice how small the plot is. That's because in model space the screen limits are those set for Proj-6, which are 0,0 and 70,50 (see chapter 6) and the drawing units are meters. If you plot using a scale of 1=1, then 1 millimeter of the plot equals 1 meter of the drawing, and the drawing fits in an area of about 70×50 mm. If you plot from model space, you have to consider the 1:300 scale of the drawing, which for plotting is interpreted as 1 millimeter of the plot equalling 0.3 meters of the drawing, giving a plot scale of 1=0.3. Also notice that the border, which is in paper space, isn't plotted when you plot from model space.

You should usually plot from paper space using a scale of 1=1. Change the drawing back to paper space so it's ready if you want to plot it again. Then save the drawing.

13.2 External References

AutoCAD's external reference is similar to the concept used in chapter 12 to insert drawings as blocks into a plot drawing. Although the concept is similar, attaching an external reference, Xref, is different from inserting a block file into a drawing in a number of ways.

Unlike a block, an Xref's definition is not saved with the drawing. It's reloaded each time the drawing is edited so, if the referenced drawing is updated, its latest version will be read into the parent drawing the next time it's edited. Because the referenced drawing data isn't read into the drawing file, using Xref also reduces the size of drawing files. The only reference to the referenced drawing in the master drawing file is the referenced drawing's name, path, and insertion scale and location.

You can attach any drawing or Wblock file to a master drawing as an external reference.

You can nest Xrefs so one loads another, which loads another, etc. A change in a lower-level Xref would then change all the Xrefs above it.

13.2.1 The drawing

Now you'll draw a border using the Border menu from chapter 12, and link the lot plan in chapter 6 to the border drawing as an external reference.

Begin a new drawing named C:\DRAWINGS\PROJ-6X.DWG. Load the Border.mnu menu file as either a base or a partial menu (see chapter 11, sections 11.9 and 11.12). Select Title Block, then Metric, and A Size. Then enter the attribute data requested, entering the scale as 1:300 and the project name as Proj-6x.

When the border and title block are complete, if AutoCAD's menu isn't loaded (if you loaded the Border menu as a base menu), then load AutoCAD's menu by selecting Easy1, then Acad Mnu.

13.2.2 Xref command

In Windows, load the External Reference toolbar by clicking on it in the Tool Windows flyout, as illustrated in Figure 13.8. Then move the External Reference toolbar (Figure 13.9) to the right side of your screen.

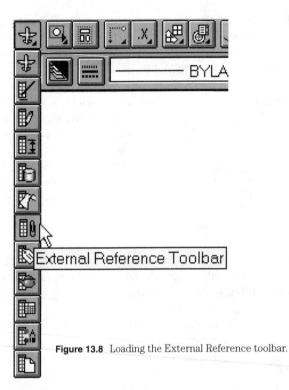

Figure 13.8 Loading the External Reference toolbar.

Figure 13.9 External reference toolbar.

You'll add external references to a drawing by using the Xref command. The Proj-6.Dwg file is to be attached to this drawing with a scale of 10/3 (see chapter 12, section 12.8) as follows. In DOS, select File, then External Reference, then enter Attach from the options `?/Bind/Detach/Path/reload<Attach>`:

External Reference <toolbar> Attach <pick>

The Select file to attach dialog box illustrated in Figure 13.10 should be displayed. If it isn't, enter ~ in response to ?/Bind/Detach/Path/Reload<Attach>: attach Xref to Attach:). Set the path and file as shown and press OK. AutoCAD will continue with:

PROJ-6 loaded. Insertion point: **0,0** <return> X scale factor <1>/ Corner/XYZ: **10/3** <return> Y scale factor (default=X): <return> Rotation angle <0>: <return>

The Proj-6 drawing is now attached and displayed. Notice that the border added to the Proj-6 drawing in section 13.1 and drawn in paper space isn't displayed. When reading entities from the attached drawing, AutoCAD copies only entities created in model space. This is useful because you wouldn't want the border copied into the current drawing.

Use the Move command to relocate the lot plan better within the border. Note how the entire lot plan is treated as a single entity when it's moved.

The property boundary center line type appears at an incorrect scale, and might even appear to be a continuous line. When a referenced drawing is loaded, it uses the linetype scale of the master drawing. Change the Ltscale setting to 19, as calculated in chapter 12.

13.2.3 Reporting Xref partnerships

The ? option to the Xref command lists a report of the external references. Choose the following (in DOS, select File, then External Reference, then enter ? from the options ?/Bind/Detach/Path/reload<Attach>):

External References <toolbar> List <pick> Xref(s) to list<*>: <return>

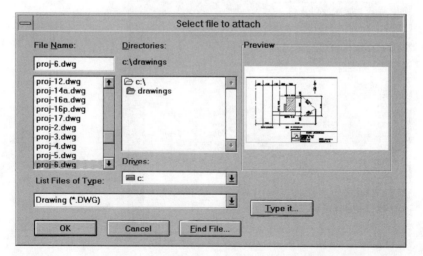

Figure 13.10 Attaching an Xref.

AutoCAD will report:

```
Xref Name        Path          Xref type
------------     -----------   -----------
PROJ-6           PROJ-6        Attach
TOTAL Xref(s): 1
```

XRefs are also reported in response to the ? option to the Block command. Press <F2> (Windows) or <F1> (DOS) to return to the graphics screen, and enter the following (in DOS, select Construc, then Block):

Draw <toolbar> Block: <pick> Block name (or ?): **?** <return> Block(s) to list <*>: <return>

A report similar to that shown in Figure 13.11 will be displayed. Depending on the blocks in your Proj-6 drawing, you might have fewer defined blocks than those shown. The Xref: resolved statement to the right of PROJ-6 indicates that AutoCAD had no problem attaching the Xref, and that object name conflicts were successfully managed (see the next section). The Xdep: PROJ-6 statements in the next several lines indicate that those blocks are named objects in the referenced drawing Proj-6. The WMF 2 item is the Window metafile block I used as a logo in the title block (refer to chapter 20). In Windows, press the bar in the Control Menu box (the dash in the top left corner of the text window) and either hide the text window or press <F2>. In DOS, press F1 to exit the text screen.

13.2.4 External references and named objects

Certain objects associated with a drawing are referred to as *named objects*: blocks, dimension styles, layers, linetypes, text styles, and items to be discussed in later

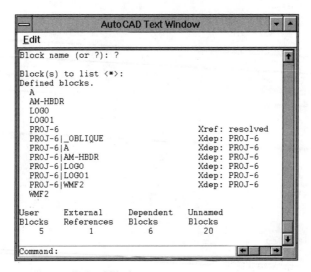

Figure 13.11 Defined Blocks.

chapters, such as named user coordinate systems, named views, and named viewport configurations.

You can rename named objects with the Rename command, and purge them from the drawing with the Purge command. When AutoCAD prompts you for a named object, you can also use wildcard characters, such as * and ?. Refer to your *AutoCAD Reference Manual* for more information on named objects.

When a drawing is attached to another as an external reference, its definition is reloaded from the reference file each time the master drawing is loaded. The named objects in the attached drawing are referred to as *dependent symbols* and are temporarily renamed by AutoCAD so they don't conflict with similarly named objects in the master drawing. Dependent symbol names are formed as a combination of the referenced drawing's name and the named object's name separated by a vertical bar (|). For example, the report by the ? option to the Block command in Figure 13.11 shows blocks A, AM-HBDR, and LOGO from the referenced drawing, Proj-6, to be temporarily renamed as PROJ-6|A, PROJ-6|AM-HBDR, and PROJ-6|LOGO.

Layer name objects are also temporarily renamed and can be displayed in the Layer Control dialog box (in DOS, select Data, then Layers):

Object Properties <toolbar> Layers <pick>

The layers in the Proj-6 drawing have been temporarily renamed, as illustrated in Figure 13.12. For example, layer Center, which has a Center linetype (see chapter 6, section 6.4), has been temporarily renamed to layer PROJ-6|CENTER and its linetype renamed to PROJ-6|CENTER. This allows you to have a layer named Center in blue on the master drawing, and another layer named Center in a different color on the referenced drawing, since the referenced drawing layer is temporarily renamed PROJ-6|CENTER. (You might have fewer layers than those shown.)

Layers 0 and DEFPOINTS (see the following section) and the linetype CONTINUOUS aren't renamed when the referenced drawing is loaded. The master drawing overrides those named objects so, if layer 0 is red on the master drawing and green on the referenced drawing, objects on layer 0 in the referenced drawing will appear as red. Because layer DEFPOINTS resides on the master drawing, Proj-6X, and also on the referenced drawing, Proj-6, AutoCAD reports that the duplicate DEFPOINTS layer definition is ignored when this drawing is reloaded (see chapter 13, section 13.2.6).

You can change the visibility, color, and linetype of dependent layers on the master drawing, but changes normally apply only to the current drawing session and aren't saved with the drawing. If, however, the system variable Visretain is set to 1, changes will be stored with the drawing and will appear the next time the drawing is loaded (by default, Visretain is set to 0). Save the drawing as C:\DRAWINGS\PROJ-6X.DWG. Do not exit AutoCAD.

13.2.5 Stretching associative dimensions

Edit an existing drawing, C:\DRAWINGS\PROJ-6.DWG. If the drawing is in paper space (refer to the icon or the status bar), double-click on PAPER in the status bar

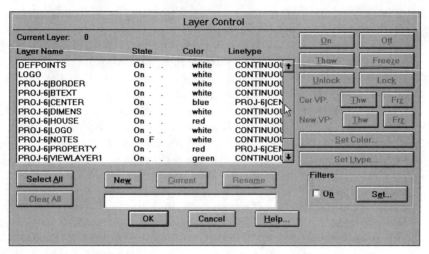

Figure 13.12 Dependent symbols.

to change to model space (MODEL). Then stretch the house width from 7.200 meters to 8.000 meters, as follows:

Modify <toolbar> Stretch: (Figure 13.13) <pick> `Select objects to stretch by crossing CWindow or CPolygon...` `Select objects:` Invoke a crossing window by digitizing the top right corner of the window (Figure 13.14). <pick> `Other corner:` Select the lower left corner of the window. <pick> `Select objects:`

The Stretch command requires you to use a crossing window or polygon. To use a crossing polygon, enter **CP**. The crossing window (or polygon) selects objects enclosed within or crossed by the window boundaries. In this case, you must ensure that entities affected by the change in width of the house from 7.200 to 8.000 are crossed or enclosed in the crossing window. The hatching must also be crossed by the window so it's also stretched. If you miss objects, you can still select them individually. Once the required entities are selected, press <return> to exit the selection:

`Select objects:` <return> `Base point or displacement:` Select any point as a reference. <pick> `Second point of displacement:` **@0.8<0** <return> `Analyzing associative hatch`

Notice that the house width increased by 0.8 meters, the dimension along the top of the house increased from 7.200 to 8.000 meters, and the hatching in the house stretched to suit the revised house size.

The dimension stretched because associative dimensioning (see chapter 6, section 6.12.2) was used to dimension the house. Associative dimensions have a definition point at the selection points for the first and second extension lines. When a definition point is moved, for instance by the Stretch command, AutoCAD automatically modifies the dimension to suit the relocation of the definition point. The hatching was also made associative in chapter 6, section 6.8, and consequently was re-drawn by AutoCAD to suit the stretched hatch boundaries.

The associative dimension definition points might occasionally be visible on the screen, but they won't be visible on the plot since AutoCAD puts them on a layer named Defpoints, which isn't plotted by AutoCAD. Set the working space to paper space. Then save the drawing.

13.2.6 Reloading the master drawing

Edit an existing drawing, C:\DRAWINGS\PROJ-6X.DWG. AutoCAD will load Proj-6X, and if it has no problems attaching the Proj-6 Xref it will report the following:

```
Resolved Xref PROJ-6: PROJ-6.DWG
PROJ-6 loaded. Regenerating drawing.
```

If AutoCAD is unable to locate the Xref file (Proj-6.dwg) in the original path used when you attached it to Proj-6X, it will report the following error:

```
"c:\drawings\proj-6.dwg" Can't open file.
error resolving Xref PROJ-6.
```

If this happens, check that the Proj-6.dwg file is where it should be and invoke the Reload or Path option to the Xref command (see chapter 13, section 13.2.7). Notice that the latest version of the reference file with the house width modified from 7.200 to 8.000 is loaded.

Figure 13.13 Stretch tool.

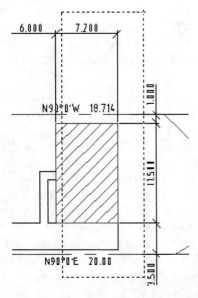

Figure 13.14 Stretch crossing window.

13.2.7 Other Xref commands

The Xref command has the following options:

```
?/Bind/Detach/Path/Reload/Overlay/Xbind<Attach>
```

The Attach and List (?) options have been discussed. The rest of the options are as follows:

Bind. Allows you to permanently attach an external reference to your drawing. You might want to use this command to send a master drawing to someone if you don't want to send the Xref drawings. Also, when archiving drawings, if you don't want to archive the Xref drawings with the master drawing, you must use the Bind command to permanently attach the Xreferences to the master drawing.

Detach. Allows you to remove unnecessary external references from your drawing. Xrefs loaded but not inserted are purged by AutoCAD when the master drawing is exited.

Path. Allows you to edit the filename or path AutoCAD uses when loading an external reference. This is useful if the path to an external reference is changed, for instance if you move the referenced file from a floppy diskette to the hard drive.

Reload. This option allows you to reload an external reference without exiting and reentering the master drawing. This might be useful if, for instance, a colleague has modified the referenced drawing and you want to reload the new edition.

Overlay. Allows you to have Xrefs that are attached to and visible in your drawing, but not visible in another drawing that calls yours as an Xref.

Xbind. Lets you add a selected subset of an external reference's dependent symbols to your master drawing permanently. For instance, PROJ-6|CENTER linetype can't be accessed. Try it. Pull down the Layer Control dialog box and try to change the linetype for layer House to PROJ-6|CENTER. AutoCAD will report that you can't make an externally referenced linetype current. Use the Xbind command to load the PROJ-6|CENTER linetype into the master drawing as follows:

Command: **xbind** <return> Block/Dimstyle/LAyer/LType/Style: **LT** (Ltype) <return> Linetype name: **Proj-6|Center** <return> (Note the | separator)

Now pull down the Layer Control dialog box. Note that the PROJ-6|CENTER linetype has been renamed to PROJ-6$0$CENTER (it might not be completely visible in the list window). The vertical bar, |, is replaced with 0.

Change the linetype for layer House to PROJ-6$0$CENTER. Note the change in the linetype for the house. Save the drawing and then open drawing C:\DRAWINGS\PROJ-6X.DWG for editing. Notice that the house layer linetype is plotted as a continuous linetype. The house layer linetype was temporarily changed to PROJ-6$0$CENTER in the master drawing, but AutoCAD reloads the reference drawing file each time the master drawing is loaded. Plot the drawing on an A-size sheet using millimeter units and a scale of 1=1.

13.2.8 Assignment

Using Notepad or Edit, modify the customized menu file C:\DRAWINGS\BOR-DER.MNU, adding a POP3 Attach menu section with cascading menus, as illustrated in Figure 13.15. Attach is to have three options—Xref, Block, and Edit—each with cascading menus, as shown in an expanded Border menu listed in appendix E.

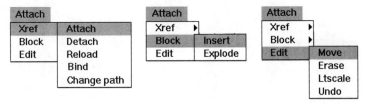

Figure 13.15 POP3 Attach menu.

14

Multiscale Drawings

Objective: Write a menu to facilitate full-size drawing on a sheet containing a border and title block; write a pull-down menu with submenus; load a partial menu in Windows; create a multiscale drawing with a building floor plan drawn to one scale and, on the same sheet, a detail drawing drawn to a different scale, maintaining uniform text and dimension variable sizes; use the View and Multiline commands.

Drawing: The final plotted drawing is shown in Figure 14.1. The steps required to complete the drawing are outlined in this chapter. Make sure to set AutoCAD's measurement to English before naming your drawing.

14.1 Scaling Drawings

When drawing with AutoCAD, items are drawn full scale, and scaling takes place either during the plotting of the drawing or on a plot drawing, as outlined in chapter 12. To create a multiscale drawing, each of the items is draw full size on a separate drawing, and each is then inserted into a final plot drawing using the scale desired for that item.

The procedure is illustrated in Figure 14.1, where the plan view and the wall elevation are to reside on the same final drawing, but each is drawn using a different scale. The plan view and wall elevation are first drawn full scale as separate drawing files. In the final hard copy drawing, The plan view is to be drawn at a scale of ¼ inch = 1 foot, and the wall elevation is to be drawn at a scale of ½ inch = 1 foot. You do this by loading the customized Border.Mnu menu file into a plot drawing and inserting the plan view using an x and y factor of 0.020833, or 1 / (4 × 12), and the wall elevation using an x and y factor of 0.0416667, or 1 / (2 × 12), into the plot drawing. The drawing is then plotted using a scale of 1=1. The scale factors are illustrated in Table 12.1 back in chapter 12 and appendix B.

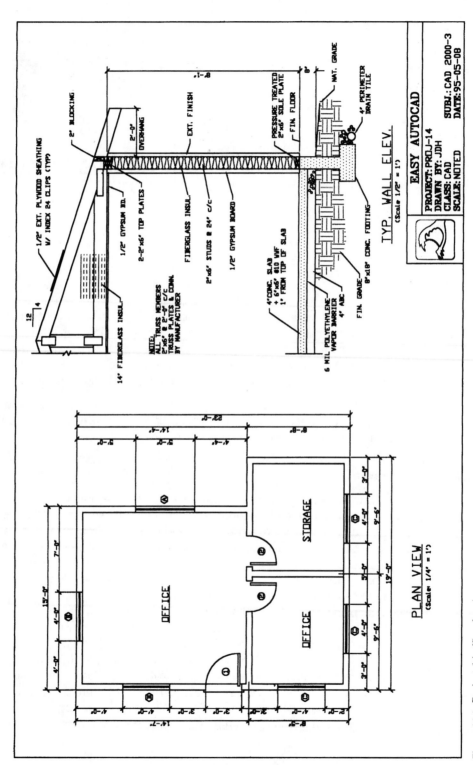

Figure 14.1 Project 14 office drawing.

You also have to ensure that the text height, dimension variables, and hatch scale factors are set for each full-scale drawing to provide a consistent size on the composite plot drawing. If the text height desired on the plot drawing is ³⁄₃₂ inch, the text height on the plan view drawing, which is to be plotted at a scale of ¼ inch = 1 foot, will have to be 4.5 inch, or $1 / (4 \times 12) \times H = ³⁄₃₂$. The text height on the wall elevation drawing, which is to be plotted at a scale of ½ inch = 1 foot, will have to be 2.25 inches, or $1 / (2 \times 12) \times H = ³⁄₃₂$. This same ratio must be used for the dimension variables and the hatch scale (also see Table C.1B in appendix C).

14.2 Custom Full Size Menu

The purpose of the Full Size menu is to provide a drawing sheet with a border and title block on which you can draw full-size drawings. You can plot the completed drawing to scale as a final drawing with a border and title block, or insert it to scale into a plot drawing that's plotted with a scale of 1=1.

This project will be drawn on a B-size sheet (17 × 11 inches) with a drawing sheet frame size of 15 × 9.5 inches, allowing for borders. I calculated the limits by multiplying the sheet frame size by the inverse of the scale. For instance, if the drawing is to be drawn on the plot drawing using an architectural scale of ¼ inch = 1 foot, or ¹⁄₄₈, the limits are set at 0,0 and 720,456 (15 × 48 = 720, and 9.5 × 48 = 456).

14.2.1 Creating the title.dwg block

The title block drawing will be adopted from the title block created in Proj. 12. Boot AutoCAD and open drawing C:\DRAWINGS\AM-HBDR.DWG for editing. Then create a new layer named **Border1**, and change the layer of the title block to layer Border1 (in DOS enter ddchprop at the command line):

Change Properties <toolbar> Properties <pick> Select objects: Digitize the lower left corner of a window to enclose the title block. <pick> Second point: Digitize the other corner of the window enclosing only the title block. Your window will cross the drawing border lines. <pick> Select objects:

The title block and text in it should be dotted, indicating they're in the selection set. The drawing borders should not be dotted. If parts of the title block aren't dotted, digitize them. If parts of the border are dotted, enter **r** (remove) and select the items to be removed from the selection set. To return to the Add mode, enter **a**. Press <return> when the selection is complete.

The Change Properties dialog box (refer back to Figure 9.8 in chapter 9) will be displayed. Click on Layer... to display a Layer selection dialog box. Click Border1 and press OK. Border1 will appear beside the Layer... box in the Change Properties dialog box. Press OK to change the selected entities (the title block) to the layer Border1. Use the Wblock command to create a drawing named C:\DRAWING\TITLE1.DWG:

Command: **wblock** <return>

The Create Drawing File dialog box, similar to the one shown back in chapter 10 in Figure 10.8, will be displayed. Set the directory to c:\drawings, and then enter a file-name as **title1**. Press OK to exit the dialog box. AutoCAD will continue with:

```
Block name: <return> Insertion base point: <shift>-<right> Intersection:
<pick> of Place the intersection aperture on the lower right corner of the border.
<pick> Select objects: Place a selection window around the title block. <pick>
Select objects:
```

The title block and text in it should be dotted, indicating they're in the selection set. The drawing borders should not be dotted. If parts of the title block aren't dotted, digitize them. If parts of the border are dotted, enter **r** (remove) and select the items to be removed from the selection set. To return to the Add mode, enter **a**. Press <return> when the selection is complete. The title block should disappear, indicating it's saved as a drawing (wblock) file. Enter Undo to bring the title block objects back to the current drawing.

14.2.2 Adding the Full Size menu

Load Notepad or Edit and open the menu file C:\DRAWINGS\BORDER.MNU that was created in chapter 12, section 12.5.1. Sections of the menu are shown in previous chapters, in Figures 11.4, 11.11 and 12.11. If you didn't create the POP3 menu at the end of chapter 12, add the following POP3 section:

**POP3
[Attach]

The completed menu (with the full POP3 section) is listed in appendix E. Edit the menu, inserting the POP4 section shown in Figure 14.2 for Windows and Figure 14.3 for DOS. In the figure, POP4 is completed only for Imperial units with a B-size sheet, and AutoCAD's architectural units. Other sections are to be completed later.

In Windows, add the Menugroup label at the top of the menu, as shown in Figure 14.4. The ***POP4 section of the menu has the heading Full Size and is used to draw a border and title block on a sheet scaled *up* so the drawing can be drawn full scale, such as the plan view or wall elevation in Figure 14.1.

When you pull down the menu in AutoCAD and select Imperial, the cascaded menu will appear, as shown in Figure 14.5 (as a partial menu in Windows). When you choose B Size, the following sequence of commands is initiated (refer to the menu listing in Figures 14.2 and 14.3):

Layer. The Layer command is read and entered with a single blank space following it.

Make. The Make option to Layer creates a new layer and makes it the current working layer. AutoCAD's response is to request the new layer's name.

Border1;;. The new layer's name is read as Border1. It's entered with the first semicolon. The Layer command is still in effect. The next semicolon invokes <return> to exit Layer.

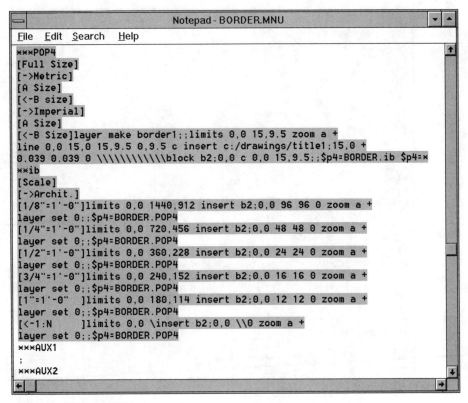

Figure 14.2 Windows POP4 menu section.

Limits 0,0 15,9.5. The Limits command is entered and the limits of 0,0 and 15,9.5 are read and entered from the menu.

Zoom a. Zoom and All zoom on the new limits.

+. This specifies that the macro continues on the next line.

Line 0,0 15,0 15,9.5 0,9.5 c. Draws a border around the drawing with its lower left corner at 0,0 and the upper right at 15,9.5.

Insert c:/drawings/title1;15,0 +. The Insert command is invoked and the drawing to be inserted is c:\drawing\title1. Note that the usual path symbol, a backslash (\), must be entered as a forward slash (/) in a menu since the backslash is reserved for user input in AutoCAD menus. The semicolon enters the drawing name and the insertion point is read from the menu as 15,0. The plus sign (+) indicates that the menu macro continues onto the next line.

0.039 0.039 0. Continuing the Insert command, AutoCAD requests the x scale factor, which is read as 0.039. Since the title block was drawn in millimeter units and this border is to be inch units, the scale factor is 1 / 25.4 = 0.039, converting millimeters to inches. The next value is the y scale factor of 0.039 and the insertion angle of 0 degrees.

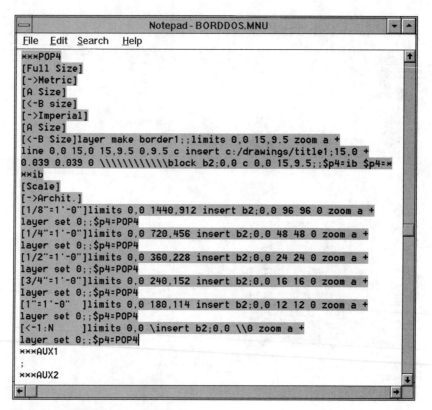

Figure 14.3 DOS POP4 menu section.

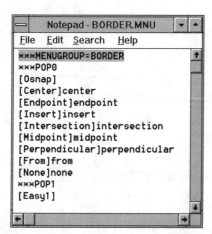

Figure 14.4 Windows Menugroup label.

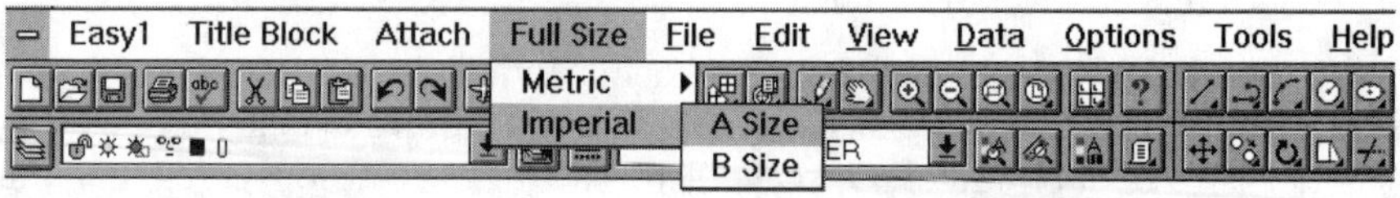

Figure 14.5 Full Size menu.

\\\\\\\\\\\\. The 12 backslashes are necessary to cause AutoCAD to pause for six attribute entries by the user in the title block, plus six verifications of those entries. There's no space following the last backslash.

Block b2;0,0 c 0,0 15,9.5;;. The Block command is invoked, and the name of the block is read as B2 from the menu and entered with the semicolon. A blank space can't be used for <return> following text data. AutoCAD requests the block's insertion point, which is read as 0,0. AutoCAD then expects the object to be selected. C enters the crossing window option, so entities crossing or enclosed by a crossing window are included in the selection set. The corners of the crossing window are read as 0,0 and 15,9.5, so the entire border and title block are included in the selection set. AutoCAD is still expecting the selection of objects, so the last semicolon invokes <return> to exit the command. The entire drawing is blocked with the name B2 and removed from the screen.

$p4=BORDER.ib (Windows) or $p4=ib (DOS). This loads the submenu named ib into the POP4 position. In Windows, the ***MENUGROUP=BORDER label at the top of the menu (see Figure 14.4) defines the menu group name for menu tag definitions. Consequently, $p4=BORDER.ib loads the submenu ib from the menu group BORDER. The menu group definition, BORDER in this case, is a string of up to 32 alphanumeric characters (spaces and punctuation marks are not allowed). The ***MENU-GROUP= label must proceed all menu section definitions.

$p4=*. This displays the loaded menu in the POP4 position.

14.2.3 Submenu **ib

A submenu label item begins with two asterisks (**) followed by the submenu name. The submenu items follow the submenu label up to the next section label (e.g., ***AUX1) or another submenu label. When $p4=BORDER.ib $p4=* is invoked, the submenu ib is loaded in the POP4 position and then displayed. The submenu with its Archit. menu cascaded is shown in Figure 14.6. Refer back to Figures 14.2 and 14.3 for the menu listing. The lines in the menu are as follows:

[¼"=1'–0"]limits 0,0 720,456. When ¼"=1'0" is selected in the menu, the Limits command is entered and the limits are read from the menu as 0,0 and 720,456. In AutoCAD's architectural units, the scale ¼"=1'0" is interpreted as ¼ = 12, or $\frac{1}{48}$. Consequently the drawing is to be enlarged to 48/1 in order to draw full size on the sheet. The limits are based on a B-size sheet with a drawing area of 15×9.5 inches, each multiplied by 48, giving 720×456 inches.

insert b2;0,0,48,48 0. The block b2 created earlier in the menu is the border and title block. It's inserted at coordinates 0,0 with an x scale of 48, a y scale of 48, and a rotation angle of 0.

zoom a +. Enters Zoom and All to zoom on the new limits. The + continues the macro onto the next line.

layer set 0;;. Sets layer 0 as the current layer. The first semicolon enters the layer name of 0, and the next semicolon exits the Layer command.

$p4=BORDER.POP4 (Windows) or $p4=POP4 (DOS). Loads the POP4 menu back in the POP4 position, in place of the **ib submenu loaded earlier. The POP4 menu isn't displayed because there's no $p4=* command.

Complete the POP4 menu and the ib submenu (for Windows, see Figures 14.2 and 14.4; for DOS, see Figure 14.3) exactly as shown. When completed, use the Save... command in the Notepad or Edit File menu to save the file under its original name, c:\drawings\border.mnu. Exit Notepad or Edit, returning to AutoCAD.

14.3 Drawing a Full-Size Border

Start a new drawing named C:\DRAWINGS\PROJ-14A.DWG. Because the current drawing is C:\DRAWINGS\AM-HBDR.DWG, AutoCAD might ask if the changes made to the drawing are to be saved. Answer No.

When the drawing editor is loaded, load the Border menu as a base menu (DOS) by entering **menu** at the command line (see chapter 11, section 11.9.9). In Windows, you can load the menu as either a base menu or a partial menu (see chapter 11, section 11.9.2). The procedure to load a partial menu is:

1. Select Customize Menus... in the Tools menu to load the Menu Customization dialog box.

2. Press Browse, choose c:\drawings\border.mnu, and press OK.

3. Press Load... to load c:\drawings\border.mnu into the Menu Groups box.

4. Click on C:\DRAWINGS\BORDER.MNU in the Menu Groups box, and then press the Menu Bar tab to display the menu bar illustrated in Figure 14.7.

5. Move the Easy1, Title Block, Attach, and Full Size menus from the Menus box to the Menu Bar box, as shown in Figure 14.7. Note that it's important for Full Size to be the 4th item in the list, as shown. (Do not load the Scale menu.)

6. Press Close.

The partial menu as it appears in AutoCAD's menu bar is illustrated back in Figure 14.5. If AutoCAD indicates there's an error in your menu, fix the menu with Notepad. Then Unload the previous version of the menu in the Menu Customization box and repeat the previous steps to load the corrected menu.

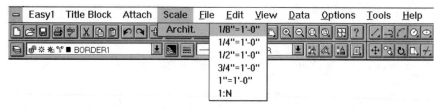

Figure 14.6 Architec. submenu.

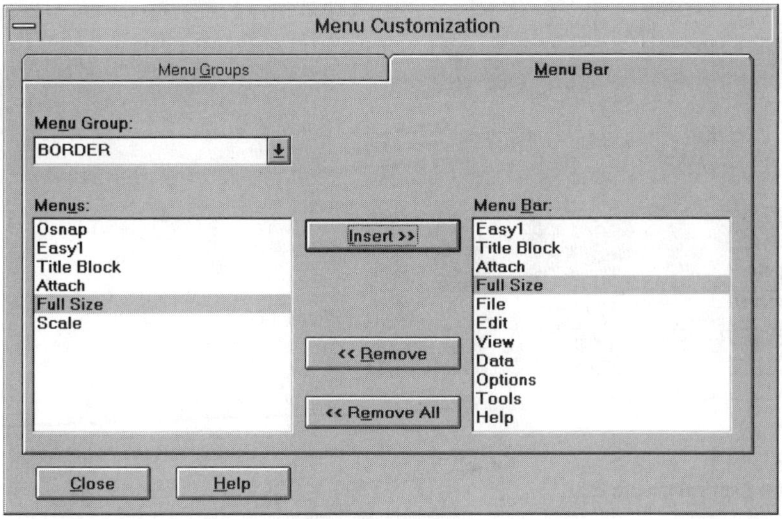

Figure 14.7 Loading the menu.

Choose Full Size in the pull-down menu to display the menu shown in Figure 14.5. Choose Imperial and then B-Size. The macro in the menu will be invoked, drawing the border and inserting the title block. Enter the data requested by the attributes, and specify the drawing scale as ¼"=1'. When the attributes are complete, the block b2 (refer to section 14.2.3) is created and the border and title block are removed from the screen. The Scale submenu is loaded into the POP4 position by the submenu call, and the Scale menu is pulled down. Choose ¼"=1'–0". The block b2 will be inserted into the drawing at a scale of 48 and the layer set to 0. You can now draw full size on the screen and plot the drawing on a B-size sheet using a scale of ¼ inch = 1 foot. If you loaded the menu as a base menu (with DOS), you'll have to load AutoCAD's menu. If you loaded the menu as a partial menu (with Windows), AutoCAD's menu is currently loaded.

14.4 Floor-Plan Drawing

The drawing limits were set by the Full Size menu to suit a plot scale of ¼ inch = 1 foot. The drawing units are to be set to architectural. Display the Units Control dialog box and set the units to architectural with a precision of ³⁄₃₂ inch, as shown in Figure 14.8. Although the precision of the drawing is to the nearest inch, it's necessary to set the units to ³⁄₃₂ inch to facilitate setting the dimension variables, which appear as 0 inch in the dialog box when no fractional decimal is used for the units setting, requiring that you set each one individually. Dimension precision will be set to 0 in section 14.4.1.

Use the Drawing Aids dialog box to set a grid of 12 (inches) × 12 (inches) and set snap to 2 (inches). Turn Snap and Grid on. Exit the dialog box and then press <ctrl>–D or <F6> to turn the coordinate display on. Use the Layer Control dialog box to create the layers listed in Table 14.1, and set the current layer as Plan.

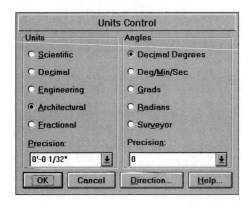

Figure 14.8 Architectural units.

TABLE 14.1 Layers Created with the Layer Control Dialog Box

Item	Name	Color	Linetype
Object lines	Plan	White	Continuous
Dimensions	Dim	Red	Continuous
Text	Text	Red	Continuous
Doors and windows	Details	Blue	Continuous

Two additional layers will be available; layer 0 is created automatically and layer Border1 was created when the border and title block were inserted.

Draw the walls of the house, as illustrated in Figure 14.9 (the current layer should be Plan). Use the grid and cursor snap and also observe the line lengths and angles in the coordinate display box. When entering distances in the architectural (and engineering) units mode, you can enter distances in inches with no units symbol, e.g., 228, or in feet with the foot symbol, e.g., 19'6 (you don't have to include the inch symbol). Then draw the walls using the multiline (Mline) command:

Draw <toolbar> Multiline <pick> `Justification/Scale/STyle/`
`<From point>:` **s** (Scale) <return> set Mline scale `<1.00>:` **6** <return> `Justification/Scale/STyle/<From point>:` **j** (Justification) <return> `Top/Zero/Bottom <Zero>:` **b** (Bottom) <return> `Justification/Scale/STyle/<From point>:` Digitize the location of the outside lower left corner of the building. <pick> `Close/Undo/<To point>:` **@19'<0** <return> `Close/Undo/<To point>:` **@8'8<90** <return> etc.

Note that the scale of the multiline is the width of the wall to be drawn, and the justification determines how the multiline is drawn. For this building, the dimensions of the house are based on the outside dimensions of the wall, and bottom justification is used.

14.4.1 Text and dimension scales

The floor plan is to be plotted using a scale of ¼ inch = 1 foot (¼ inch = 12 inch). For the plotted text to be ³⁄₃₂ inch high, the text height on the monitor is calculated as follows:

$$1 / (4 \times 12) \times H = \text{³⁄₃₂ inch}$$
$$H = 4.5$$

The text height is made relatively small since the mechanically made letters will be quite readable and the smaller dimension text will fit more easily into the space between the extension lines. The dimension scale, Dimscale, is calculated as follows:

$$\text{Dimscale} \times 0.18 = H$$
$$\text{Dimscale} \times 0.18 = 4.5$$
$$\text{Dimscale} = 25$$

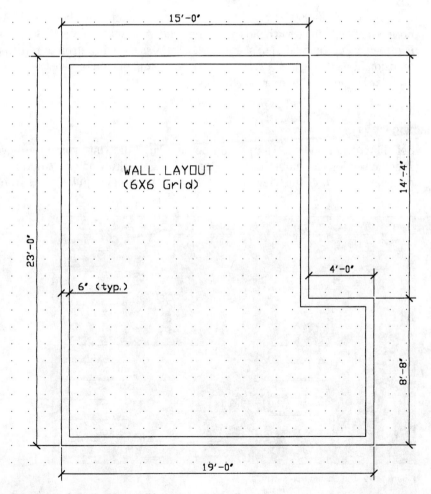

Figure 14.9 Office building wall layout.

14.4.2 Setting dimension variables

Display the Dimension Style dialog box, and press the Annotation... command button to display the Annotation dialog box, illustrated in Figure 14.10. Then press the Units... button to display the Primary Units dialog box, shown in Figure 14.11. Set the Units to Architectural, Precision to 0'–0", and Zero suppression, as shown. Dimensions won't display zero feet, for example 0'–6" will appear as 6" but will display zero inches: 8'–0". Press the OK button to return to the Annotation dialog box and make the Text settings as shown in Figure 14.10. Press OK to return to the Dimension Style dialog box.

Press the Format... command button and set the dimensioning format as shown in Figure 14.12 with Vertical Justification set to Above, placing the text on top (above) the dimension line. Also set Inside Horizontal and Outside Horizontal off so the text is aligned with the dimension line. Press OK to return to the Dimension Style dialog box.

Click on Geometry... and set the dimension geometry as shown in Figure 14.13, noting that Oblique arrowheads are to be used. Also set the Overall Scale to 25.0, the Dimscale value calculated in section 14.4.1. Press the OK button to return to the Dimension Style dialog box. Press the Save command button to save the settings to the Standard style, and then press OK.

14.4.3 Naming views

Set the current layer to Dim. When doing a large drawing, you often have to view specific sections a number of times throughout the drawing construction. The View command lets you name views and later recall those views quickly. The front wall will

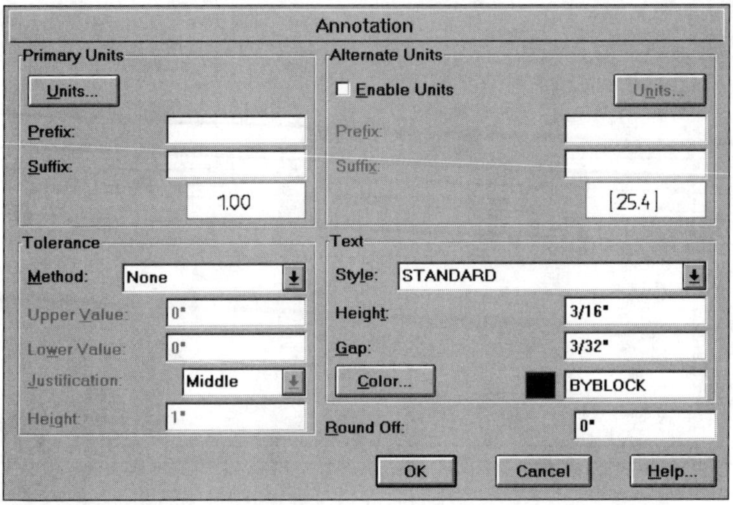

Figure 14.10 Dimension text settings.

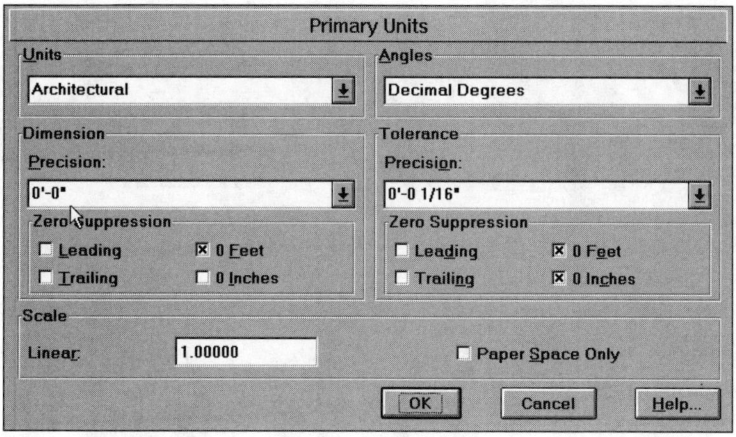

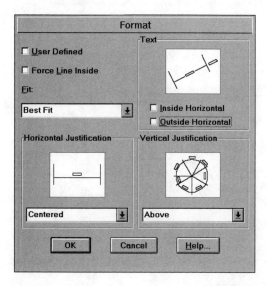

Figure 14.11 Dimension units settings.

Figure 14.12 Dimension format.

be named Front, the back wall, Back, the right wall, Right, and the left wall, Left. Choose the following (in DOS, select View, then Named Views):

Standard <toolbar> View (Figure 14.14) <pick>

The View Control dialog box illustrated in Figure 14.15 will be displayed (the only view is *CURRENT*). Press the New... command button to display the Define New View dialog box, shown in Figure 14.16. Enter a new view name, Front. Then press

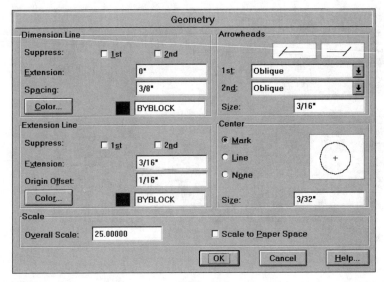

Figure 14.13 Dimension geometry and scale settings.

    Figure 14.14 View tool.

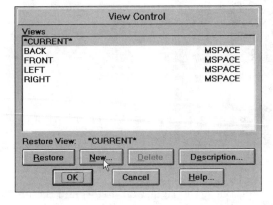

Figure 14.15 View Control dialog box.

the Define Window button and press Window < to define the view using a window. The drawing screen will be displayed as follows:

`First corner:` Pick the first corner of a window selection box to enclose the front wall of the building, allowing sufficient room for the dimensions required along the front wall of the building. The objective is to obtain a larger view of the front wall, making it easier to do the dimensioning along that wall. <pick> `Other corner:` Digitize the other corner of the window. <pick>

The Define New View dialog box will be redisplaycd. Press the Save View button. Repeat the process, naming a view of the back wall, the right wall, and the left wall. When all walls are named, highlight Front in the Views box of the View Control dialog box and then press Restore to restore the front wall view onto the screen. The front wall is enlarged on the screen based on the selection window used. (The side walls will also be visible.)

14.4.4 Dimensioning the drawing

You'll need to add dimensions to the building before drawing doors and windows. This way, you can locate the doors and windows by their dimensions and easily insert them as blocks. It will be easier to do the dimensioning if snap is set as large as possible. The smallest dimensional unit along the front wall is 6 inches. Using the Drawing Aides dialog box, set snap to 6, and turn snap on. Then enter the dimensions as follows:

Dimensioning <toolbar> Linear Dimensions <pick> `First extension line origin or RETURN to select:` <shift>–<right> Intersection <pick> of Place the target on the lower left corner of the building. <pick> `Second extension line origin:` Digitize a 3-foot 0-inch distance horizontally on the grid using the 6-inch snap (Figure 14.17). <pick> `Dimension line location:` Digitize a 3 snap point (1 foot 6 inches) in front of the wall. <pick> `Dimension text <3'-0">:` <return> Continue Dimension <pick> `Second extension line or RETURN to select:` Digitize a 4-foot 0-inch distance horizontally on the grid using the 6-inch snap. <pick> etc.

When all dimensions are added to the front wall, use the View command to view the left wall (view name is Left) for dimensioning along that wall.

Complete the dimensions illustrated in Figure 14.17. Remember to adjust snap as required to make the locating of points easier. Also use the object snaps where possible.

14.4.5 Window and door blocks

Set the current drawing layer to Details. Use the Zoom command to enlarge an area about 6 feet × 6 feet, and draw the windows and doors as illustrated in Figure 14.18.

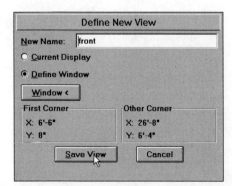

Figure 14.16 Defining a new view.

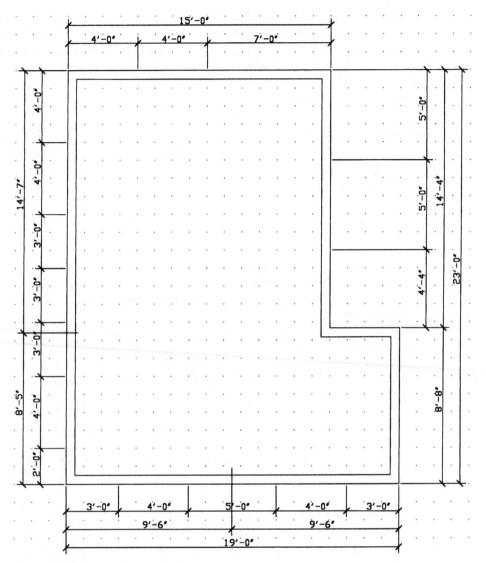

Figure 14.17 Exterior wall dimensions.

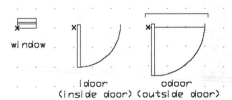

window

idoor
(inside door)

odoor
(outside door)

Figure 14.18 Windows and door blocks.

As each is drawn, use the Block command to save it as a block and, if desired, use the Wblock to save the block to file for use in other drawings. Use the block names illustrated in Figure 14.18. Insertion points are marked x (do not include the block name and x with the block diagram). The Attdef command will *not* be used to tag attribute information to the windows and doors, but consider the possibilities: you could create a program to read the door files and then create a door schedule. When drawing the doors and windows, use the Snap command to alternate snap as required to facilitate the drawing.

14.4.6 Editing multilines

Set the current layer as Plan. When the blocks are inserted, they'll retain their identity on layer Details (which they were drawn on), and won't reside on layer Plan, even though that's the current drawing layer. If the blocks had been drawn on layer 0, they'd reside on the current layer Plan when inserted.

Prior to inserting the blocks, draw the internal 6-inch partition walls using the Mline (multiline) command. Press ORTHO in the status bar (or <ctrl>–O) to turn the orthogonal mode on, facilitating the drawing of the horizontal and vertical wall lines. Use the multiline command with center justification to draw the walls illustrated in Figure 14.19 (don't provide door openings yet).

You'll make the opening of the wall at the intersection of the interior and exterior walls, and openings for the doors and windows, with the Mledit (multiline edit) command. Before continuing, however, save your drawing. I had problems with an early release of Release 13, which crashed when editing multilines. Edit the multilines as follows (in DOS, select Modify, then Edit Multiline):

Modify <toolbar> Multiline Edit (Figure 14.20) <pick>

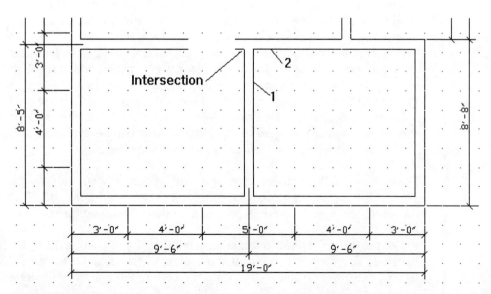

Figure 14.19 Interior walls.

Figure 14.20 Multiline Edit tool.

The Multiline Edit Tools dialog box is illustrated in Figure 14.21. Choose the Merged Tee box, as shown, and then press OK. AutoCAD will continue with:

`Select first mline:` Select the mline to trim or extend (line 1 in Figure 14.19). `<pick> Select second mline:` Select the intersecting mline (line 2). `<pick> Select first mline (or Undo):` Continue with the remaining intersection walls.

Entering U in response to the last request undoes the edit. Because of problems in earlier releases, you might have problems editing multilines. If AutoCAD crashes when you're using the merged tee, use the Explode command to convert the multilines to lines and then use the Trim and Break commands to open the wall intersections. In that case, you'll also have to open the wall for windows and doors with the Break command.

Make openings for windows and doors in the multiline wall by using the Cut All option in the Multiline edit Tools:

Modify <toolbar> Multiline Edit <pick> Choose the Cut All option <pick> `Select mline:` <shift>–<right> From <pick> `from Base point:` <shift>–<right> Intersection <pick> of Place the aperture on the intersection (Figure 14.19) <Pick> <Offset>: **@6<180** <return> `Select second point:` **@2'6<180** <return>

Complete the remaining openings with a procedure similar to that used previously to locate the openings. Then insert the doors and windows using the Endpoint object snap to locate the insertion points. Because the window block was drawn 1 unit in length, you'll use the length of the window for the x scale when inserting the window. Therefore, the front wall windows will have an x scale of 4 (feet). The y scale is 1 since the width of the window in the block was 6 inches, which is the width of the wall. To insert a mirror image of the door block (see doors referenced as 2 back in Figure 14.1), use a negative value for the x scale factor when inserting the block.

Insert the door reference symbol by creating a block drawing of a hexagon, with the reference symbol tagged to the block as an attribute. Set the current layer as Text. Then zoom on a 4 × 4 foot area and draw the block:

Draw <toolbar> Polygon <pick> `Number of sides <4>:` **6** <return> `Edge/<Center of polygon>:` **e** (Edge) <return> `First Endpoint of Edge:` Pick a point on the screen. <pick> `Second point of edge:` **@4<0** <return>

Following the procedures outlined in section 12.3.4 in chapter 12 and referring to Figure 12.5, create one visible attribute using the tag A and the prompt "Enter the letter." For the insertion point, locate the bottom left corner of the letter A inside the polygon. The height of the attribute text is 4 units, and the rotation angle is 0 degrees.

Create a block named Hex made up of the polygon (hexagon) and the attribute. The insertion point of the block is the midpoint of the bottom line of the hexagon.

Following the same procedures, create the door reference symbol using a circle 5 units in diameter with an attribute in it. Save it as a block and insert the window and door reference blocks into the drawing. Set the current layer to Text and add the text to the drawing using the Dtext command.

14.4.7 Test-plotting a drawing and saving the file

Check that the floor plan is located on the drawing where you want it to be located on the final plot. If not, use the Move command to relocate the floor. Then plot the drawing to visually ensure that the floor plan is complete. The drawing is to be plotted on a B-size sheet (17×11 inches, giving a plot area of 15×9.5 inches), using a scale of ¼ inch = 1 foot.

When the drawing is complete, set the current layer to Plan and turn the Border1 layer off. Save the file as C:\DRAWINGS\PROJ-14A.DWG.

14.5 Wall Detail Drawing

Start a new drawing named C:\DRAWINGS\PROJ-14B.DWG. When the drawing editor is loaded, load the Border menu as a base menu (DOS) by entering **menu** at the command line (see chapter 11, section 11.9.9). In Windows, load the menu as either a base menu or a partial menu (chapter 11, section 11.9.2). Also refer to section 14.3 earlier in this chapter.

Following the procedures used for the floor plan, use the Full Size menu to draw the border and title block for a scale of ½" = 1' – 0". If you loaded the menu as a base menu (with DOS), you'll have to load AutoCAD's menu. If you loaded the menu as a partial menu (with Windows), AutoCAD's menu is currently loaded.

Once the AutoCAD menu is loaded, use the Layer command to set the layers shown in Table 14.2, set Elev1 as the current drawing layer, select architectural units with ¹⁄₃₂ inch as the smallest fraction, and set Grid to 12 and Snap to 6.

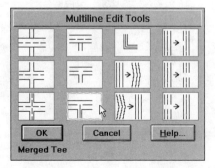

Figure 14.21 Multiline Edit Tools.

TABLE 14.2 Layers Set with the Layer Command

Object	Name	Color	Linetype
Wall	elev1	white	continuous
Text	text	red	continuous
Dimensions	dim	red	continuous
Details	details	blue	continuous
Hatching	hatch	yellow	continuous
Construction lines	const	white	continuous

14.5.1 Text and dimension scale

You need to plot the floor plan previously drawn using a scale of ¼ inch = 1 foot. In section 14.4.1, the text height was calculated as 4.5 inches to give a plotted text of ³⁄₃₂. Since the wall detail is to be plotted using a scale of ½ inch = 1 foot and since the two plots are to reside on the same drawing, calculate the text height for the detail drawing as follows:

$$1 / (2 \times 12) \times H = \tfrac{3}{32} \text{ inch}$$
$$H = 2.25$$

Dimscale was set as 25 for the floor plan. For the wall, calculate Dimscale as follows:

$$\text{Dimscale} \times 0.18 = H$$
$$\text{Dimscale} \times 0.18 = 2.25$$
$$\text{Dimscale} = 12.5$$

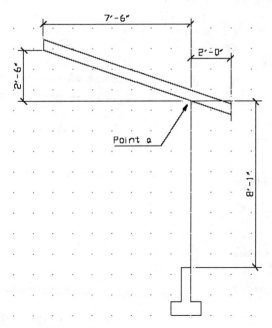

Figure 14.22 Wall construction lines.

Set the dimension variables for the wall elevation drawing the same as those set for the floor plan (see the following section), but set the overall (dimension) scale to 12.5, as shown back in Figure 14.13. Also, although dimension arrowheads are to be oblique, you want to use dimension leaders in the wall elevation (refer back to Figure 14.1), and they should have standard arrowheads rather than ticks. After making the Parent dimension settings, press the Leader Family button and then press the Geometry command button. Set the arrowheads for leaders to Closed Filled. Then return to the Dimension Style dialog and save the settings to Standard.

14.4.2 Wall

The current layer should be Elev1. Draw the wall footing on the right side of the drawing area using the grid. The footing wall was drawn 18 inches high. This is unsatisfactory in northern climates, but this is a CAD exercise, not an actual building. Use break lines in the footing if you want.

Set the current layer to Const. Draw construction lines representing the face of the wall, the 2-foot roof overhang, and the bottom of the roof beam (see Figure 14.22):

Draw <toolbar> Line <pick> From point: <shift>–<right> Intersection <pick> of Place the target on the top right corner of the footing wall. <pick> To point: **@8'1<90** <return> To point: <return> <return> Line From point: **@2'<0** <return>To point: **@1'<270** <return> To point: <return>

The roof slope is 4/12, which means a 4-inch rise for every 12 inches (1 foot) of run. For the 15-foot-wide section of the building, the rise will be $4 \times 15 / 2 = 30$ inches (2 feet 6 inches). Draw the construction line for the bottom of the roof as follows (see Figure 14.22):

Draw <toolbar> Line <pick> From point: <shift>–<right> From <pick> from Base point: <shift>–<right> Intersection <pick> of Place the aperture on the top of the wall construction line, point a in Figure 14.22. <pick> <Offset>: **@–7'6,2'6** (7 feet 6 inches to the left of a, and 2 feet 6 inches above a) <return> To point: <shift>–<right> Endpoint <pick> of Place the target on the top of the wall construction line, point a. <Pick> To point: <return>

Modify <toolbar> Extend <pick> Select boundary edge(s) ... Select objects: Digitize the vertical line 2 feet to the right of the wall. <pick> <return> Select object to extend: Pick the roof line. <pick> Select objects: <return>

Now rotate the grid (by rotating snap) so it aligns with the roof slope. In order to do this, enter **snap** at the command line rather than using the Drawing Aids dialog box, which doesn't allow you to select rotation angles on the screen:

Command: **snap** <return> Snap spacing or ON/OFF/Aspect/Rotate/ Style<>: **r** (Rotate) <return> Base point: <shift>–<right> Intersection <pick>

of Place aperture on the intersection point of the roof and the wall. <pick> `Rota-tion Angle:` <shift>–<right> Endpoint <pick> of Place the target on the left end of the roof line. <return>

Offset a copy of the previous line 6 inches above it:

Modify <toolbar> Offset (Figure 3.4) <pick> `Offset distance or Through:` **6** <return> `Select object to offset:` Digitize a point on the current roof line. <pick> `Side to offset:` Digitize a point above the roof line. <pick>

Return the snap plane to 0 degrees with a base point of 0,0. Then set snap to 2 inches and turn ORTHO mode on. Complete the roof member by drawing a vertical line 90 degrees from the lower roof line, to act as the top end of the room member. Then use the Trim and Extend commands to complete the sloping roof member. Use the Change command to transfer the roof beam and wall line to the Elev1 layer.

Turn the Const layer off and set Elev1 as the current layer. Draw the remaining roof and wall objects. Do not draw the 2-inch × 6-inch members individually; draw one as a block and then use the Insert command to insert the object where required.

14.5.3 Complex linetypes

You can draw the wall insulation in an imaginary 1-foot-high by 6-inch-wide rectangle and save it as a block (see Figure 14.23). Insert one block at the base of the wall and then use the Array command to repeat the entity seven times. You'll have to edit the last insulation unit, erasing parts that run into other members, so it must be exploded so it's no longer a block. Invoke the explode command as follows:

Modify <toolbar> Explode <pick> `Select objects:` Choose the top wall insulation block. <pick> `Select objects:` <return>

Alternatively, AutoCAD provides a *complex linetype*, which can be used for the insulation. To load the linetype, display the Layer Control dialog box and create a new layer name Insul, colored green. Then press the Set Ltype... command button to display the Select Linetype dialog box. Press the Load... command button to display the Load or Reload Linetypes dialog box. Press File... and locate the file c:\acadr13\common\support\ell\tpeshp.lin, as illustrated in Figure 14.24.

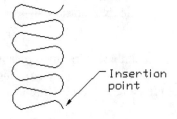

INSUL
(INSULATION BLOCK)

Figure 14.23 Wall insulation block.

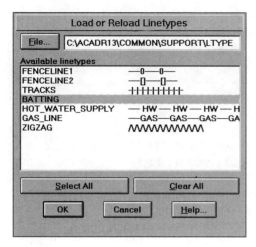

Figure 14.24 Complex linetypes.

Select the Batting linetype, as shown, and press OK. Then set layer Insul as the current layer. Draw a line centered in the wall where the insulation is to be located. The linetype scale will be incorrect and the line might initially appear as a straight line. Experiment with the scale using the Properties tool (refer to sections A.2 and A.2.6 in appendix A), and in DOS select Modify, then Properties to display the Modify Line dialog box shown in Figure 14.25. Try a linetype scale, and AutoCAD will update the scale of the line to suit. I used 6, the width of the insulation, which appeared to be okay. If the scale isn't suitable, try another.

This linetype scale is set by object (Celtscale), and is different than that used in chapter 6, section 6.9.1, where a global linetype scale (Ltscale) was set. Remember, however, that the actual scale of a linetype is the product of Ltscale and the object's Celtscale. If you change Ltscale, the scale of all lines will change accordingly. You can also create your own complex linetypes. For more information, refer to your *Auto-CAD User's Guide*.

14.5.4 Hatching

Calculate the hatch scale using the following equation (the wall is to be at a scale of ½ inch = 1 foot, or ½ = 12, or ¹⁄₂₄):

$$\text{Plot Scale} \times \text{Hatch} = 1 \text{ inch} \times \text{conversion}$$
$$\tfrac{1}{24} \times \text{Hatch} = 1 \times 1$$
$$\text{Hatch} = 24$$

Set the current layer to Hatch. Using the Bhatch command, hatch the footing and floor separately using the Dots hatch style, as outlined in chapter 7, section 7.4.1. Select the boundaries by using Pick Points < (refer to Figure 6.21 in chapter 6) and picking a point within the enclosed area to be hatched.

The Earth hatch doesn't have a boundary area, and Hatch will be used instead of Bhatch (which requires a boundary). Enter Hatch at the command prompt:

Command: **hatch** <return> Pattern (? or name/U.style) <current>: **earth** <return> Scale for pattern <1>: **24** <return> Angle for pattern <0>: <return> Select objects: <return> Retain polyline? <N>: <return> From point: Pick one point for the hatch boundary. <pick> Arc/Close/Length/Undo/ <Next point>: Continue to pick points (or enter one of the options, e.g., Arc) <pick> Arc/Close/Length/Undo/<Next point>: <return> From point or RETURN to apply hatch: <return>

Notice that you must press <return> when AutoCAD requests Select objects, forcing AutoCAD to request points defining a boundary. At the last request, From point or RETURN to apply hatch: , you can continue to pick points or press <return>, which causes AutoCAD to create the hatch. When using AutoCAD hatches, you might have to vary the hatch scale to get a suitable effect.

14.5.5 Text and dimensions

Set the current layer to Dim and add the dimensions. Then set the current layer to Text and add the text to the drawing using the Dtext (dynamic text) command.

14.5.6 Test plotting and saving the file

Test plot the drawing on a B-size sheet using a scale of ½ inch = 1 foot. The plot units are inches. Make necessary corrections to the drawing and then freeze layer Border1. Save the drawing under the filename C:\DRAWINGS\PROJ-14B.DWG.

14.6 Creating a Multiscale Drawing

Begin a new drawing named C:\DRAWINGS\PROJ-14.DWG, then load your Border menu as a full or partial menu. Choose Title Block from the menu (do *not* choose Full

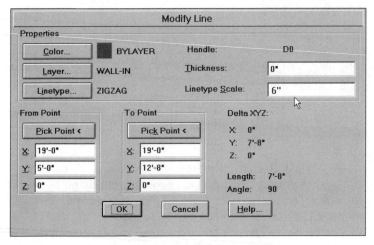

Figure 14.25 Modifying lines.

Size). Select Imperial and then B Size. (If you didn't do the assignment in chapter 12, section 12.9, you won't have a BI-Hbdr drawing and this menu item won't work. In that case, refer to section 14.6.1). AutoCAD will draw the border and the title block, and prompt you for the variable attribute information. When the scale is requested, enter **NOTED**. The border will remain on the screen, and the limits are based on a B-size sheet of paper.

Use the Xref command (added to the Border menu from the assignment at the end of chapter 13) to attach the Proj-14a drawing to the current drawing (if you didn't do that exercise, enter the command):

Attach <pick> Xref <pick> Attach <pick>

The Select file to attach dialog box (Figure 13.11) will be displayed. Set the path to C:\DRAWINGS, and choose the drawing PROJ-14A.DWG. AutoCAD will continue with (the insertion scale is 1 / (4 × 12), which is 0.0208):

Insertion point: **0,0** <return> X scale factor (1): **0.0208** <return> Y-Scale factor (default=X): <return> Rotation angle <0>: <return>

Then AutoCAD will attach Proj-14a. Repeat the process for Proj-14b using a scale of 1 / (2 × 12), or 0.0417. Use the Move command to locate the objects correctly on the drawing. The wall insulation might not appear correct. I set a linetype scale (chapter 6, section 6.9.1) of 0.0417 (the same as the insertion scale) and the insulation appeared okay. Save the drawing, and then plot it using the following data:

Units	Inches
Width	17"
Height	11"
Scale	1=1

14.6.1 Setup command

If you didn't do the BI-HBDR drawing, you can use AutoCAD's SETUP command, which lets you draw a border and title block. You might want to consider the following procedure to insert a border for a multiscale drawing:

Begin a new drawing (C:\PROJ-14.DWG) and select the following in the Acad menu:

View <pick> Paper Space <pick> View <pick> Floating Viewports <pick> MV Setup <pick> Align/Create/Scale viewports/Options/Title Block/Undo: **t** <return>

AutoCAD will display the title block options illustrated in Figure 14.26. Enter **8**, as shown. AutoCAD will continue with:

Create a drawing named ansi-b.dwg?<Y>: N <return> Align/Create/Scale viewports/Options/Title Block/Undo: Press <esc> or <ctrl>–C to cancel.

AutoCAD will draw a rectangle defining the sheet boundary, and a border and title block (without attributes). Use the Xref command to attach your drawings, as outlined in section 14.5. MVSetup, as outlined previously, works in paper space and can be used to create a border for a drawing, as outlined in chapter 13, section 13.1.

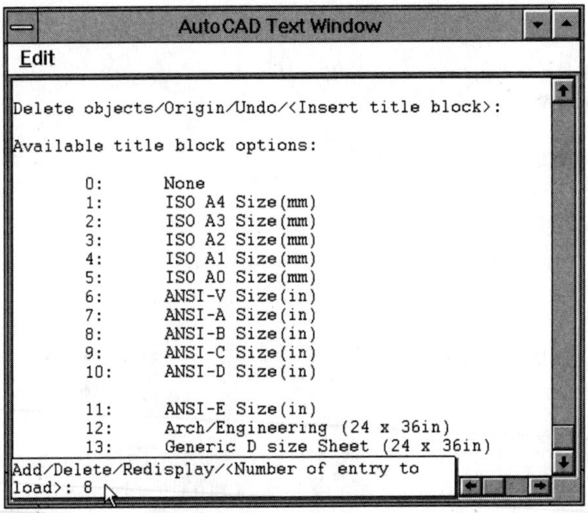

```
─                    AutoCAD Text Window              ▼  ▲
 Edit

Delete objects/Origin/Undo/<Insert title block>:         ↑

Available title block options:

        0:      None
        1:      ISO A4 Size(mm)
        2:      ISO A3 Size(mm)
        3:      ISO A2 Size(mm)
        4:      ISO A1 Size(mm)
        5:      ISO A0 Size(mm)
        6:      ANSI-V Size(in)
        7:      ANSI-A Size(in)
        8:      ANSI-B Size(in)
        9:      ANSI-C Size(in)
       10:      ANSI-D Size(in)

       11:      ANSI-E Size(in)
       12:      Arch/Engineering (24 x 36in)
       13:      Generic D size Sheet (24 x 36in)
Add/Delete/Redisplay/<Number of entry to                 ↓
load>: 8
```

Figure 14.26 Title block options.

Chapter 15

3-D Drawing

Objective: To introduce the concepts of three-dimensional drafting, elevation and thickness, viewing objects in three dimensions, 3-D faces, 3-D polygon meshes, dynamic 3-D views, perspective views, clipping views, editing polylines, and manipulating user coordinate systems.

15.1 Thickness and Elevation

To construct three-dimensional (3-D) objects, you must define entity positions using 3-D x, y, and z coordinates. The Elev command lets you set a default z value and extrusion thickness for subsequent objects that you draw. You can convert two-dimensional (2-D) objects to 3-D by changing their elevation and thickness.

15.2 Converting Proj-4 Drawing to 3-D

Boot up AutoCAD and open an existing drawing, C:\DRAWINGS\PROJ-4.DWG. When Proj-4 was drawn, all of the entities were on layer 0. You'll use the Change command to change the layer on which the object resides to a new layer, Object. You'll leave the dimensions and text on layer 0, which will then be frozen. When a layer is frozen, it's turned off and the items on that layer are ignored by AutoCAD when the drawing is regenerated. If the layer is quite complex and it won't be displayed, freezing it speeds up the regeneration process considerably. To turn a frozen layer on, use the Thaw option of the Layer command.

Using the Layer Control dialog box, make a new layer named Object and set Object as the current layer. Change the figure in Proj-4 to layer Object as follows (in DOS, enter **ddchprop** at the command line). You'll use a selection fence by entering **f** when requested to select objects:

Object Properties <toolbar> (section A.2 in appendix A) Properties <pick> Select objects: **f** <return> Undo/<Endpoint of line>: Run a selection fence through each of the object line, including the circle (Figure 15.1). Don't cross any of the text or dimension lines. <pick> Undo/<Endpoint of line>: <return> Select objects: <return>

The Change Properties dialog box, shown back in Figure 9.8 in chapter 9, will be displayed. Press the Layer... command button and change the layer to Object. Then, using the Layer Control box (refer back to Figure 6.19 in chapter 6), freeze layer 0. The dimensions on layer 0 will be removed from the screen, leaving only the object visible.

15.2.1 Adding a third dimension to 2-D objects

Two-dimensional objects are drawn on a flat plane using an x,y axis. For an object to be a three-dimensional extruded plane, it must have thickness along the z axis. If an object was initially drawn with 2-D entities, you can use the Change command to specify depth in the z axis, making the entity 3-D. For this drawing, the base of the object will be set as elevation 0 (which is the default elevation), and the thickness of the object is 6 units.

You'll also give the circle (hole) in the object a base elevation of 4 units and a thickness of 2 units. This will place the top of the hole at the top of the object (at elevation 6) and it will extend 2 units into the object. You could obtain a similar effect by setting the elevation of the object and circle as 0 and then defining the thickness of the object as –6 units and the thickness of the circle as –2 units.

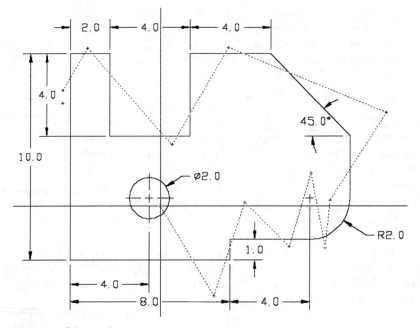

Figure 15.1 Selection fence.

Object Properties <toolbar> Properties <pick> Select objects: Place a selection window around the entire object. <return> Select objects: **r** (Remove) <return> Remove objects: Digitize the circumference of the circle <pick> Undo/<Endpoint of line>: <return> Remove objects: <return>

The Change Properties dialog box illustrated in Figure 9.8 will be displayed. Enter a thickness of **6** and press OK. Change the circle elevation to 3 and its thickness to 3 using the Change command (in DOS, enter **Change** at the command prompt):

Modify <toolbar> Point <pick> Select objects: Digitize the circle. <pick> Select objects: <return> Property/<Change point>: **p** (Property) <return> Change what property (Color/Elev/LAyer/LType/+Scale/Thickness)?: **e** (Elev) <return> New Elevation <0.0>: **4** <return> Change what property (Color/Elev/LAyer/LType/+Scale/Thickness)?: t (Thickness) <return> New thickness <0.0>: **2** <return> Change what property (Color/Elev/LAyer/LType/+Scale/Thickness)?: <return>

15.2.2 Drawing a three-dimensional extruded object

Prior to drawing a new 3-D extruded object, you must set the elevation and thickness for the object. Set the elevation to 0 (the current default value) and the thickness to 6 units. Then draw a new hole in the object as follows:

Data <pick> Object Creation... <pick>

The Object Creation dialog box illustrated in Figure 15.2 is displayed. Set the Elevation to **0.0** and the Thickness to **6.0**. Press OK to exit. Now draw a circle with its center point at coordinates **10,5**, and with a **1.5** units radius. When the object is viewed from a 3-D viewpoint it will be seen that the circle has a base elevation of 0 and a thickness of 6 units.

You can use the Object Creation dialog box to set the layer, line type, and text style. You can also change the color by entity, block, or layer. By block means that entities are colored white until collected into a block. When the block is inserted, they adopt the current color setting. By layer is what is used throughout this book. Colors set by entity means that an entity can be on a blue layer but have its color set to red, which is often confusing. Note that you can also set the Celtscale (linetype scale by object) in this dialog box.

If other objects are to be drawn with the same current elevation and thickness, you can draw them without resetting the elevation and thickness. If you need a different elevation or thickness for an entity, use the Object Creation Modes dialog box to set the current elevation and thickness prior to drawing the entity (unless you use the Change command later to modify the elevation and/or thickness of an entity).

15.3 Viewing the Z Plane of Three-Dimensional Objects

You must use the Vpoint command to view the z axis of the screen. You cannot, however, view one object on the screen in three dimensions and leave other objects on

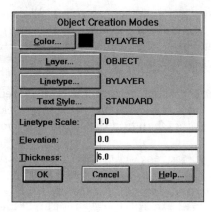

Figure 15.2 Object Creation Modes dialog box.

the same screen in two dimensions. In order to plot an x, y, z view of an object within a border and title block in the x-y axis, you have to plot the border and title block separately from the 3-D view, on the same sheet. (You can create multiview drawings by defining user coordinate system (UCS) views, which are Wblocked and inserted into the drawing. See chapter 16.)

Before I discuss the Vpoint command options, let's use the command to view the z-axis of the object (see Figure 15.3):

View <pick> 3D Viewpoint <pick> Vector <pick> vpoint Rotate/<View point> (0.0,0.0,1.0): **–1,–3,3.5** <return>

You should now have a wireframe 3-D view of the object on your monitor, similar to Figure 15.4.

When the Vpoint command is executed, the current viewpoint is displayed in angle brackets. If you enter a new x, y, z viewpoint (as in the preceding commands), AutoCAD will regenerate the drawing and display the new view. If you enter a null response or select the Tripod option (refer back to Figure 15.3), a compass and tripod will be displayed, as illustrated in Figure 15.5.

View <pick> 3D Viewpoint <pick> Tripod <pick>

The upper right corner of the monitor should now display a 2-D representation of globe. AutoCAD refers to the center point of the globe as the north pole (0,0,1), the inner ring as the equator (n,n,0), and the outer ring as the south pole (0,0,–1). A small crosshair indicates the viewpoint looking toward the coordinate origin (0,0,0). An axis tripod in the center of the monitor illustrates the view position. As the cursor is moved, the crosshair moves in the globe and the axis tripod rotates, indicating the view obtained if you select the position by pressing <pick>. In either case, you're specifying only the view direction. It isn't possible to specify a view distance.

You can also select viewpoints from presets, as illustrated in Figure 15.6. Table 15.1 illustrates the Vpoint vectors to enter and presets to obtain standard views. Try a number of viewpoints using the compass and tripod, and the presets.

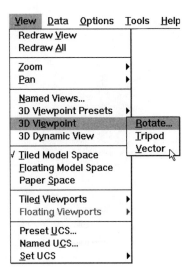

Figure 15.3 3-D Viewpoint options.

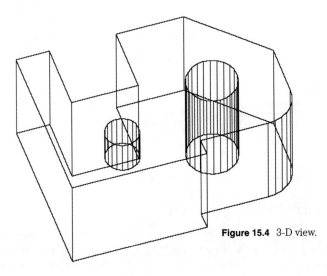

Figure 15.4 3-D view.

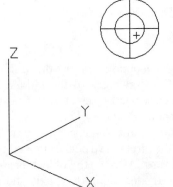

Figure 15.5 Tripod.

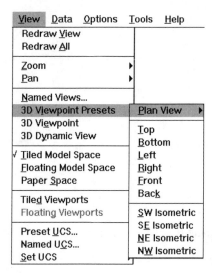

Figure 15.6 Preset viewpoints

TABLE 15.1 Vpoint Vectors

Vector	View	3-D viewpoint presets
0,0,1	Plan view	Top
0,0,–1	Plan view from south pole	Bottom
–1,0,0	Left view	Left
1,0,0	Right view	Right
0,–1,0	Front view	Front
0,1,0	View from back	Back

15.4 Suppressing Hidden Lines

The Vpoint command draws a wireframe display of the object. In a wireframe display, all the lines are present, including those that would be hidden by other parts of the object. In Windows, the Hide command is in the Render toolbar, which isn't currently displayed. Rather than display the toolbar for one command, you can enter the command at the command prompt (in DOS, select Tools, then Hide):

Command: **Hide** <enter>

The screen will go blank for a period of time (depending on the drawing's complexity) as AutoCAD proceeds to regenerate the drawing with the hidden lines suppressed (see Figure 15.7). The wireframe view will be restored the next time the drawing is regenerated with, for instance, Zoom, Regen, or Pan.

As illustrated back in Figure 15.2, the Hide command doesn't necessarily hide the lines you want. In the drawing, the sides of the circle have been removed only where they're covered by the sides of the object. AutoCAD sees the object as a room with the roof removed because the lines were extruded along the z axis and there's no surface on the top or bottom of the object.

To plot a 3-D view of the object with hidden lines removed, you don't have to generate the view on the monitor with hidden lines removed. In the Plot Configuration dialog box, an option in the Additional Parameters box is Hide Lines. If Hide Lines is turned on, AutoCAD will process the vectors with hidden lines removed and plot the drawing.

Generate a 3-D view of the object and then Plot the view with hidden lines removed. A scale of 1 = 3 should fit an 11 × 8.5-inch sheet of paper.

15.5 Topographic Map Drawing

A topographic map shows, by contour lines, the spatial configuration of the earth's surface. A contour line is an imaginary line of constant elevation on the ground surface. An example of a contour line is the shoreline of a still lake.

In this project, you'll draw a topographic map of a 40 × 40-meter lot. The ground elevations have been determined by a field survey and are illustrated at grid points in Figure 15.8. The grid spacings are 10 meters c/c vertically and horizontally.

To draw the topographical map, you must locate points of equal elevation on the drawing. The line joining those points is called a *contour line*. Successive contour lines will be drawn at a fixed contour interval of one meter. The drawing will then illustrate the spatial "flow of the land." Where contour lines are closely spaced, the change in elevation is steep. Where contour lines are spaced far apart, the change in elevation is gradual. The final topographical map is illustrated in Figure 15.9.

15.5.1 Calculation of even contour elevations

Even-contour elevation locations are determined by interpolating elevations between the grid lines. A sample calculation is illustrated in the following, where the 47-meter elevation location is interpolated between the 0- and 10-meter grid point on the horizontal (the x axis in Figure 15.8):

Distance = (47.0 − 46.0) / (47.2 − 46.0) × 10 m = 8.33 m

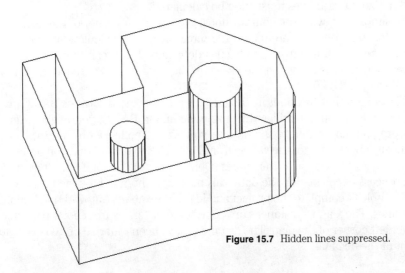

Figure 15.7 Hidden lines suppressed.

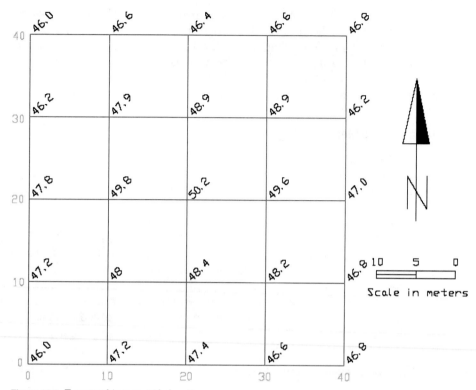

Figure 15.8 Topographic map grid elevations.

Notice that the only 46-meter elevation points are at the lower left and upper right corners of the plan. The required even elevations, therefore, fall in the range of 47 meters to 50 meters. The locations where each of those elevations cross the vertical and horizontal grid lines must then be calculated.

To simplify drawing the contour lines, the lower left corner of the grid is assumed to be located at coordinate 0,0 on the monitor. As you calculate each contour location, its total distance from point 0,0 is determined. You can then use those coordinates to locate the points on the drawing. The coordinates of the 47-meter elevation then become 8.33,0.

The contour line locations in Table 15.2 were calculated with the BASIC program in appendix F. If you're familiar with programming in BASIC, you might want to enter the program and generate the data. If you aren't familiar with the BASIC language, manually check a few of the values from Table 15.2 to ensure that you understand the concept used to calculate the values. Don't worry too much if you don't understand the process of calculating the data; this book isn't intended to teach surveying. You'll still be able to complete the project and learn more about AutoCAD's 3-D abilities and polylines. The x and y distances are coordinate distances from point 0,0, which is the lower left corner of the plan. The distances have been rounded off to two digits to the right of the decimal.

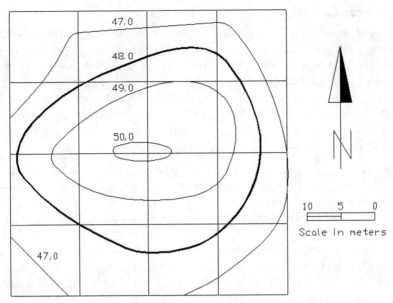

Figure 15.9 Topographic map contours.

TABLE 15.2 Contour Lines

Elevation	x dist.	y dist.	Elevation	x dist.	y dist.
46	0	0	48	36.15	20
47	8.33	0	49	32.31	20
47	25	0	47	0	25
47	0	8.33	48	10	29.47
48	20	6.00	49	10	24.21
47	30	2.50	49	20	29.33
48	30	8.75	50	20	21.54
48	10	10	49	30	28.57
47	38.57	10	47	4.71	30
48	31.43	10	48	11.00	30
49	10	15.56	47	37.04	30
49	20	13.33	48	33.33	30
50	20	18.89	47	10	36.62
49	30	15.71	47	20	37.60
48	1.00	20	48	20	33.60
49	6.00	20	47	30	38.26
50	15	20	48	30	33.91
50	23.33	20	46	0	40
47	40	20			

15.5.2 Drawing the contour lines

Boot up AutoCAD and begin a new drawing named C:\DRAWINGS\PROJ-15.DWG. The even contour distances listed in Table 15.2 are located from the lower left corner of the grid, which will be given the coordinates of 0.0 to simplify the drawing process. The grid is 40 × 40. Screen limits should allow some space around the grid (5 units), plus additional space on the east side for the north arrow and some text. Set the screen limits to –5,–5 and 65,45. Set the units as decimal (meters), with two digits to the right of the decimal. Create the layers (continuous linetype for All) listed in Table 15.3, and set Grid as the current layer.

Setting the elevation. Because you'll be using the 3-D function of AutoCAD, you must define an elevation for each entity. Usually all text, dimensions, grid lines, etc. are placed on elevation 0 (z coordinate = 0), but the lowest grid elevation is 47 meters (there's no contour for elevation 46), so all text and the grid lines will be placed on elevation 47 (z coordinate = 47). This way, if the text or dimension layers are on when the drawing is viewed in three dimensions, the text and dimensions will appear on the same elevation as the lowest contour in the view. Because each contour line represents a single elevation, the contour lines will have elevation, but a thickness of 0 units. Use the Object Creation Modes dialog box (refer back to Figure 15.2) to set the current Elevation to 47 and the Thickness to 0.

Drawing the grid. You'll draw one grid line and use the Array command to replicate it:

Draw <toolbar> Line <pick> From point: **0,0** <return> To point: **@40<90** <return> Modify <toolbar> Rectangular Array <pick> Select objects: **l** (last) <return> Select object: <return> Rectangular or Polar array (R/P): rectangular Number of rows (---) <1>: <return> Number of columns (lll) <1>: **5** <return> Distance between columns (lll): **10** <return>

Then use the same procedure to draw the horizontal grid lines.

Adding grid elevations and coordinates. The text scale will be based on the drawing being plotted on a 280 × 215-mm (11 × 8.5-inch) sheet using a scale of 1:300. The text height on the plotted drawing is to be 3 mm. Then the drawing text height is calculated as follows:

$$\tfrac{1}{300} \times H = 3 \text{ mm}$$
$$H = 900 \text{ mm}$$
$$H = 0.9 \text{ m (drawing units)}$$

Add the horizontal and vertical coordinate text (0, 10, 20, etc.) to the drawing (refer back to Figure 15.8). Place the north arrow and the text below it on the drawing. The grid elevations shouldn't be displayed on the final drawing. They're added so a plot of the grid displaying the grid elevations can be generated, then the layer they reside on is turned off. They're therefore placed on a separate layer named Gridel.

Set Gridel as the current layer. Rather than entering each of the grid point elevations individually, enter the lower left corner elevation and use the Rectangular Ar-

TABLE 15.3 Layers to Create

Item	Layer	Color
Contour lines	contour	white
Text	text	white
Grid lines	grid	red
Grid-point elevations	gridel	yellow
Coordinate values	coord	green

ray command to replicate that value across the grid. Then use the Change command to change each of the grid elevations to its proper value. This method is easier than specifying each individual text location, and also gives a more uniform drawing.

Draw <pick> Single Line Text <pick> `Justify/Style` `<Start point>`: Digitize the start point for the grid elevation near 0,0. <pick> `Height`: **0.9** <return> `Rotation angle <0>`: **45** <return> `Text`: **46.0** <return>

Modify <toolbar> Rectangular Array: <pick> `Select objects`: **l** (last) <return> `Select objects`: <return> `Rectangular or Polar Array (R/P):-r` Number of rows (---): **5** <return> `Number of columns (lll)`: **5** <return> Unit cell or distance between rows (---): **10** <return> `Distance between columns (lll)`: **10** <return>

AutoCAD will array the 46.0 elevation text to each of the grid points. The grid elevation values at points other than 0,0 are now to be changed to their proper value. When the Change command is invoked, each grid elevation to be changed is digitized, indicating the items to be changed. When AutoCAD requests `Properties/<Change point>`:, press <return>. This informs the program that you want to change the text value and not its location. For all the remaining input, the default values are selected, except for the text itself, which is to be changed. Enter Change at the command line to bypass the dialing box:

`Command`: **change** <return> `Select objects`: Digitize each of the grid elevations except for the text at 0,0. <return>

Assuming the first two digitized texts were at grid coordinates 10,0 and 20,0, the entries should be as given follows (watch the monitor and you'll notice a line connecting the cursor and each text item as its turn to be changed comes up):

`Properties/<Change point>`: <return> `Enter text insertion point`: <return> `Text style: STANDARD New style or RETURN for no change`: <return> `New height <0.9>`: <return> `New rotation angle <45>`: <return> `New text <46.0>`: **47.2** <return> `Enter text insertion point`: <return> `Text style: STANDARD New style or RETURN for no change`: <return> New

height <0.9>: <return> New rotation angle: <45>: <return> New text
<46.0>: **47.4** <return>

AutoCAD will continue with each text, in the order it was digitized. Plot the grid elevations and grid using a scale of 1:300 on a 280-mm × 215-mm sheet. The scale entered would be 1 = 0.3.

15.5.3 Using polylines

Set Contour as the current layer and turn layer Gridel off. The contour lines will be drawn using the Pline (polyline) command rather than the Line command. Polylines have specific properties that lines don't have (refer to the discussion on polylines in your AutoCAD manual). In this project you want to edit a polyline and create a smooth curve, fitting the vertices of the original straight-line segments. This will create a better contour line because real contour lines are seldom made up of straight-line segments, unless the ground elevations have been modified by machinery.

Because you'll be viewing the contour drawing later in three dimensions, you have to set the elevation of each contour line. The first contour to be drawn, however, is at elevation 47, which was previously set. Read the polyline coordinates from Table 15.2. The first coordinate selected for the 47-meter elevation is 8.33,0.

Draw <toolbar> Polyline (Figure 15.10) <pick> From point: **8.33,0** <return>

The coordinate 8.33,0 is listed as the first in the list for elevation 47 in Table 15.2 (the second row of the table). The next point to be used is 0,8.33 (the fourth row of the table). A line is then to be drawn from point 8.33,0 to 0,8.33.

The Pline command causes AutoCAD to respond with the following options rather than the familiar "to point" of the Line command. Refer to the *AutoCAD Command Reference* manual for a complete discussion of the options. The entry will be the second coordinate of the line, as follows:

Current line-width is 0.00
Arc/Close/Halfwidth/Length/Undo/Width/<Endpoint of line>: **0,8.33**
<return>

You can select the second coordinate, 0,8.33, only by reviewing all the coordinates for elevation 47 in Table 15.2 and considering the possibilities for the next coordinates. If you look at the previous coordinate, 8.33,0, and the grid back in Figure 15.8, you'll see that the next coordinate must be either on the column line where x = 10 and y falls between 0 and 10, the column where x = 0 and y falls between 0 and 10, or the row line where x falls between 0 and 10 and y = 10. Remember that x is hori-

Figure 15.10 Polyline tool.

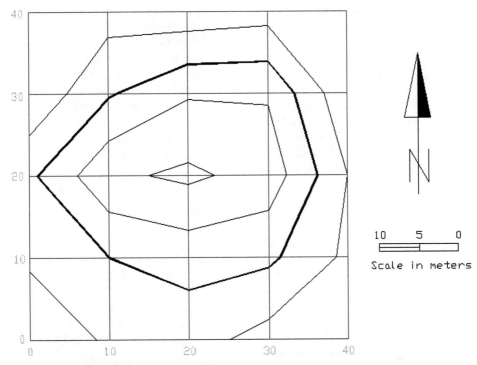

Figure 15.11 Topographic map contour polylines.

zontal (row) and y is vertical (column). As you use an elevation in Table 15.2, tick it off so you need not consider it again.

AutoCAD will again respond with the list of options. The next point must fall on either column x = 10 with y from 0 to 10, or row x = 0 to 10 and y = 10. None exist in the list, so this contour is discontinuous (see Figure 15.11). Recall the Pline command by pressing <return>. The points to enter and the reasoning are listed in Table 15.4.

TABLE 15.4 Coordinate Points to Enter

Coordinate	Reasoning
25,0	Next 47 elevation in list.
30,2.50	x = 30–40; y = 0–10
38.57,10	x = 30–40; y = 0–10
40,20	x = 30–40; y = 10–20
37.04,30	x = 30–40; y = 20–30
30,38.26	x = 30–40; y = 30–40
20,37.6	x = 20–30; y = 30–40
10,36.92	x = 10–20; y = 30–40
4.71,30	x = 0–10; y = 30–40
0,25	x = 0–10; y = 20–30

Since there are no more than 47 elevations and the contour line isn't in the proximity to close on the first point at 25,0, the contour is discontinuous. Press <return> to exit the Pline command. Now you have to draw the 48-meter-elevation contour lines. Prior to drawing any lines, however, you must set the elevation to 48 using the Object Creation Modes dialog box. Then set the Thickness to 0.

When drawing contour lines, it's customary to draw every fifth contour line heavier. For this drawing, the 48-meter-elevation contour line will be made heavier to demonstrate the procedure to be used with polylines. Assuming that the width of the line on the plotted drawing is 0.5 mm and the plot will be done using a scale of 1:300, the width of the polyline in meters (the drawing units) will be:

$$\tfrac{1}{300} \times W = 0.5 \text{ mm}$$
$$W = 150 \text{ mm}$$
$$W = 0.15 \text{ m}$$

You'll draw the polyline starting with the first 48 elevation coordinates in the list in Table 15.2. Prior to entering the endpoint, however, you have to select the Width option for polylines in order to enter a polyline width of 0.15 units.

Draw <toolbar> Polyline <pick> From point: **20,6** <return> Current line width is 0.00 Arc/Close/Halfwidth/length/Undo/Width/<Endpoint of Line>:**w** (width) <return> Starting width <0.00>: **0.15** <return> Ending width <0.15>: <return>

Table 15.5 shows the next To point: values entered and their reasoning. Notice that the possible coordinates for the last point are the same as those for the first point, so the Close command is used. Complete the topographical drawing. Remember to begin by setting the contour elevation, then to change the polyline width back to 0,00 since only the 48-meter elevation is to be heavier. Figure 15.10 illustrates the plan with all the contour lines drawn.

15.5.4 Editing polylines for curve fitting

The Pedit (edit polyline) command lets you edit polylines in a number of different ways. Refer to the *AutoCAD Command Reference* manual for a complete discussion. In this project, you'll use the "fit curve" option to create a smooth curve fitting all of the vertices of the polyline for each contour:

Modify <toolbar> Edit Polyline (Figure 15.12) <pick> Select polyline: Digitize a point on the 47-meter elevation polyline, on the east side of the plan. <return> Close/Join/Width/Edit vertex/Fit/Spline/Decurve/Ltype gen/Undo/exit <X>: **f** (fit) <return>

The 47-meter elevation contour is then redrawn by AutoCAD as a smooth curve. Continue the process for each of the contours. The final contour plan is shown back in Figure 15.9.

TABLE 15.5 To Point: Values

Coordinate	Reasoning
30,8.75	x = 20–30; y = 0–10
31.43,10	x = 30–40; y = 0–10
36.15,20	x = 30–40; y = 10–20
33.33,30	x = 30–40; y = 20–30
30,33.91	x = 30–40; y = 30–40
20,33.60	x = 20–30; y = 30–40
11,30	x = 10–20; y = 30–40
10,29.47	x = 10–20; y = 20–30
1,20	x = 0–10; y = 20–30
10,10	x = 0–10; y = 10–20
c (close)	x = 10–20; y = 0–10

To complete the drawing, set the current layer to Text and the Elevation to 47. Then add the contour elevations and save the file. Plot the drawing using a scale of 1:300 on an A4-size sheet. The scale specified when plotting is 1 = 0.3 since the drawing is in meter units and the plot sheet size is in millimeters.

15.6 Three-Dimensional View of Topographical Drawing

If your monitor doesn't have good resolution, you might want to turn the Grid layer off prior to using the Vpoint (3D Viewpoint) command since some views will look quite cluttered. Try the Vpoint command with layer Grid on and also with layer Grid off to see the difference.

Try a number of viewpoints. When you get a good viewpoint (see Figure 15.13), plot it. If you want to save a view, see the discussion in the following section on naming views, prior to creating another 3-D viewpoint. The Hide command doesn't change the views since none of the entities were given a thickness. Therefore, no lines are hidden behind any other entity.

15.7 Naming (Saving) Views

Often you'll want to return to a view many times. This is especially true in large drawings when you work with specific zones in a drawing and want to move quickly from zone (view) to zone (view). In 3-D drawings, you might also want to save specific viewpoints for later use or reference. You'll use the View command to name views.

Figure 15.12 Edit Polyline tool.

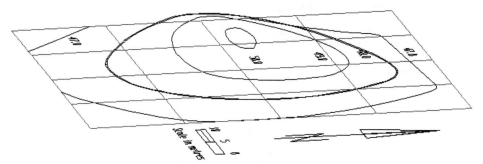

Figure 15.13 Three-dimensional view of contours.

When a view is named, you can quickly recall it using the View command. Prior to using the View command, however, you must use the 3D Viewpoint command to get a 3-D view of the topographical drawing you want to refer to at a later time. The commands to name the view are:

View <pick> Named Views... <pick>

AutoCAD will now display the View Control dialog box illustrated in Figure 15.14. Press the New... command button to display the Define New View dialog box illustrated in Figure 15.15. Notice that you can name the current display (which should be turned on) or use a define window to select the view. Name the view and press Save View. The Description command button in the View Control dialog box provides descriptions of named views. Then press OK to exit.

Use the Plan command, as shown in Figure 15.16, to return to the plan view of the Current viewport. You can plot a view by pressing the View... button in the Plot Configuration dialog box, which displays the View Names list box, from which you can select a named view to plot. Plot the saved view named 3DVIEW. The plot scale is 1:300, which translates to 1 mm = 300, but the drawing units are meters, so the plot scale translated into drawing units is 1 mm = 0.3 m, giving a plot scale of 1 = 0.3.

15.8 Lines and Plates in Space

You can draw objects in 3-D space by entering their x, y, z coordinates when points are requested by AutoCAD. The Polyline command, however, is used to draw only 2-D polylines. You draw 3-D polylines using the 3Dpoly command (3D Polyline in the polyline flyout, as shown in sections A.3 and A.3.2 in appendix A), which creates 3-D polylines consisting entirely of straight-line segments. You can edit 3-D polylines with the Edit Polyline command.

15.9 Three-Dimensional Storage Bin

The storage bin illustrated in Figure 15.17 is to be drawn in 3-D space to illustrate the 3Dface command. Begin a new drawing named C:\DRAWINGS\BIN.DWG, and set the drawing units to architectural with the denomination of thc smallest unit as ¼ inch. Set the drawing limits to –4',–4' and 16',12', and Zoom All to zoom the screen to the limits. Make a new layer named SS (structural steel) and set it as the current working layer.

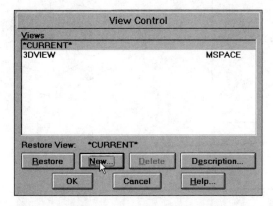

Figure 15.14 Saving a view.

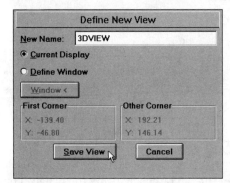

Figure 15.15 Naming a view.

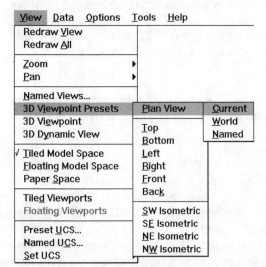

Figure 15.16 Getting a plan view.

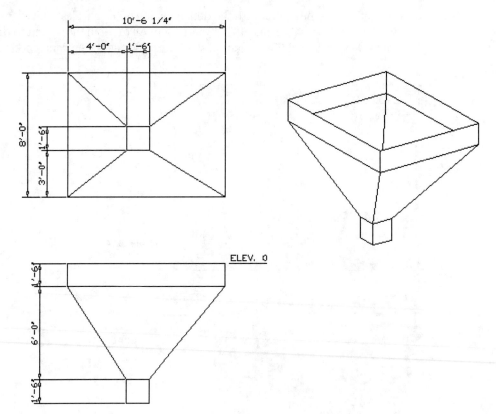

Figure 15.17 Storage Bin.

You can draw the top lip plates of the bin either by using the 3Dface command or as extruded lines. It's easiest to draw them as extruded lines, so draw the top plates as extruded lines with a thickness (height) of 1 foot 6 inches. Using the Object Creation Modes dialog box (refer back to Figure 15.2), set the current elevation as 0 and the thickness as –1'6. As the top section is drawn, the lines will have a thickness of 1 foot 6 inches:

Draw <toolbar> Line <pick> From point: **0,0** <return> To point: **@10'6–1/4<0** <return> To point: **@8'<90** <return> To point: **@10'6–1/4<180** <return> To point: **C** <return>

Draw the bottom opening plates by setting the elevation to –7'6 (negative because it's below elevation zero, in the negative z direction), and the thickness to –1'6 (negative because the thickness is in the negative z direction). Then draw the opening with the Line command, starting at coordinate 4',3'. After you've completed the bottom opening, set the elevation to 0 and the thickness to 0.

You'll use the Rotate... option in the 3D Viewpoint menu to view the storage bin from a point above the right corner, which is an isometric view from the southeast:

View <pick> 3D Viewpoint <pick> Rotate... <pick>

The Viewpoint Presets dialog box illustrated in Figure 15.18 will be displayed. Enter the x rotation as 330 degrees and the y rotation as 30 degrees. Notice that you can select the x and y rotations in the figure boxes in the dialog box. Press OK. Save the view using the name 3D so you can easily restore it later (refer to section 15.7).

15.10 Drawing Coordinate Systems

AutoCAD uses a fixed *world coordinate system* (WCS) and an arbitrary *user coordinate system* (UCS). WCS is a fixed Cartesian coordinate system, and is illustrated in Figure 15.19. All drawings completed in earlier chapters of this book are done in WCS.

Positive rotational angles about an axis are based on the right-hand rule. For example, positive rotation about the z axis is determined by pointing the thumb of your right hand in the positive direction of the axis (out of the screen) and curling your fingers. The direction in which the tips of your fingers point is the direction of positive rotation about the z axis (see Figure 15.19).

AutoCAD displays a coordinate system icon (Figure 15.20) to show the positive direction of the x and y axes, along with other relevant information about WCS.

If the WCS icon isn't displayed on the screen, select Options, then UCS (Figure 15.21). The icon is on when there's a tick in front of Icon, and it's displayed at its origin (point 0,0,0) when there's a tick in front of Icon Origin. If the icon is in the lower left corner of the screen, use the Pan command to pan the bin into the middle of the screen. If there's insufficient room for the icon to be placed at its origin, AutoCAD will place it in the lower left corner of the screen. The icon should appear as shown in Figure 15.22.

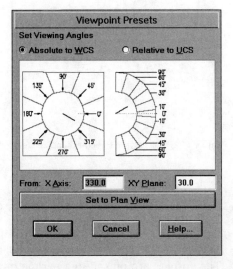

Figure 15.18 View rotate dialog.

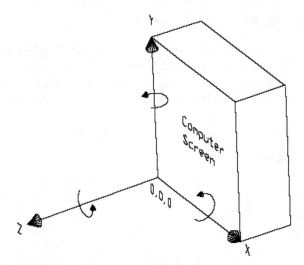

Figure 15.19   Cartesian Coordinate System.

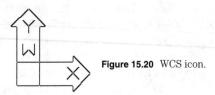

Figure 15.20   WCS icon.

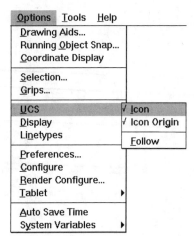

Figure 15.21   Displaying the coordinate system icon.

15.10.1 Plates (faces) in space

The current elevation should be 0, and the thickness should be 0. You define a 3-D face in space with three or four corner points using the 3Dface command. Each corner has an x, y, and z coordinate. The corners are picked in a perimeter sequence (unlike the Solid command). You can draw a continuous series of sides, with the fourth and third points of the previous plate becoming the first and second points of the next face. To draw the sides of the bin in a series, set the Intersection running object snap, allowing snapping onto the corners of the extruded lines, defining the plates at the top and bottom openings of the bin:

Standard <toolbar> Running Object Snap (Figure 5.2) <pick>

Choose the Intersection object snap in the Running Object Snap dialog box. The 3Dface command is in the Surfaces toolbar (Figure 15.23). Load the toolbar, then using the 3D Face tool draw the front face of the bin (side abcd back in Figure 15.22) as follows (in DOS, select Draw, then Surfaces, then 3D Face):

Surfaces <toolbar> 3D Face <pick> First point: Place the running intersection aperture on point a (Figure 15.22). <pick> Second point: Place the intersection aperture on b. <return> Third point: Place the intersection aperture on c. <pick> Fourth point: Point d <pick> Third point:

AutoCAD will draw face abcd and then request the third point of the next face, assuming c and d are the first and second points of the face. Continue the right-side plate cdef as follows:

Third point: Point e. <pick> Fourth point: Point f <return> Third point:

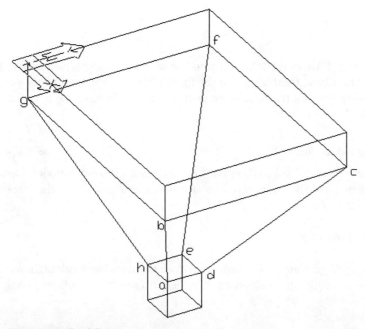

Figure 15.22 Bin 3-D faces.

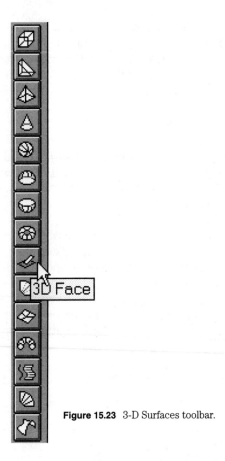

Figure 15.23 3-D Surfaces toolbar.

AutoCAD will draw face cdef. Continue the sequence by entering points g and h to finish the third face, then complete the fourth face by selecting points a and b. Then press <return> to exit the 3dface command. The bin should appear as shown back in Figure 15.17.

15.10.2 Suppressing hidden lines

The 3-D view that's displayed on your monitor is a wireframe model. Lines that are behind faces might be suppressed by the Hide command. View the bin in three dimensions and then enter:

Command: **hide** <return>

The screen will go blank while AutoCAD does the necessary calculations and regenerates the drawing with hidden lines removed (see the 3-D figure back in Figure 15.17).

15.11 Dynamic View

The 3D Dynamic View option (Dview command) in the View menu allows you to view models three dimensionally, and dynamically control all aspects of the view. The location of the viewer's eye is called the *camera* and the focus point is the *target*. The line between these two points is the line of site. You can adjust the line of site by moving the camera and/or the target. You can zoom on the object by using a slider bar, and you can pan and twist the object around the line of site. Finally, you can create a perspective view where the focal lines converge on a distant point, giving a look of depth.

15.11.1 Setting the camera and target

The camera option allows you to specify the camera position along the line of site:

View <pick> 3D Dynamic View <pick> Select objects: Place a selection window around the entire storage bin. <pick> Select objects: <return> Camera/TArget/Distance/POints/PAn/Zoom/TWist/CLip/Hide/Off/Undo/<eXit>:

Controlling the 3-D view is based on the WCS (even if you're working in a defined user coordinate system, UCS). If the view is too large on your screen, enter the Z (Zoom) option and enter a zoom factor to reduce the object size. For example, 0.5 would reduce the object to half its size. Then set the camera position by entering:

ca <return> Toggle angle in/Enter angle from XY plane <35.26>:

The first angle requested is the vertical rotation of the camera. A 0 angle points the camera parallel to the XY plane. Move the cursor up (positive) and you'll look down on the XY plane (into the bin). Move the cursor down (negative) and you'll look up from below the XY plane (below the bin). The angles are displayed dynamically in the coordinate display window so you can visually rotate the object. Enter a value of **15**. AutoCAD will continue with:

Toggle angle in/Enter angle in XY plane from X axis <-45.00>:

The next angle requested is the horizontal rotation of the camera. A 0 angle places the camera looking directly into the X axis (icon). Moving the cursor to the right (positive) walks the camera to the right (counterclockwise) around the object. Moving the camera to the left (negative) walks it to the left (clockwise) around the object. Enter a value of **–60**, and AutoCAD will continue with:

CAmera/TArget/Distance/POints/PAn/Zoom/TWist/CLip/Hide/Off/Undo/<eXit>: **ta** <return> Toggle angle in/Enter angle from XY plane <15>:

Entering **ta** (target) allows you to move the target around the camera, which remains stationary. The first angle requested is the vertical rotation of the target. Moving the cursor up (positive) rotates the target (object) above the camera, and the line of site is toward bottom of the bin. Moving the cursor down (negative) is like rotating the target (object) below the camera, and the line of site is into the bin. Enter a value of **–20**. AutoCAD will continue with:

```
Toggle angle in/Enter angle in XY plane from X axis <120>:
```

The next angle requested is the horizontal rotation of the target. A 0 angle places the target looking directly along the x axis (icon). Moving the cursor to the right (positive) walks the target (object) to the right (counterclockwise) around the camera. Moving the target to the left (negative) walks it to the left (clockwise) around the camera. Enter a value of **150**. The current view on the screen is shown in Figure 15.24. An easier way to set the camera and target is using the POints option:

```
CAmera/TArget/Distance/POints/PAn/Zoom/TWist/CLip/Hide/Off/Undo
/<eXit>:
```
po <return> Enter target point <9'-3 ³/₄",9'-0 ¹/₄",-2'-1">:
<shift>–<right> Intersection <pick> of Click the Intersection object snap aperture box on the front corner of the bin (Figure 15.24). <pick> Enter camera point <10'6",8'4",1'7">: Digitize a point in front of the bin (Figure 15.24). <pick>

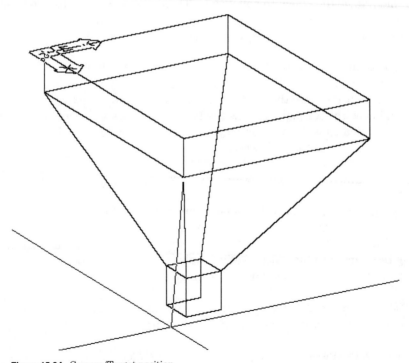

Figure 15.24 Camera/Target position.

The Zoom option allows you to zoom on an object:

```
CAmera/TArget/Distance/POints/PAn/Zoom/TWist/CLip/Hide/Off/Undo
/<eXit>: Z <return> Adjust zoom scale factor:
```

AutoCAD will display a slider bar across the top of the screen, ranging from 0x to 16x. The zoom scale is also displayed in the coordinate display box. Moving the cursor towards 0x reduces the size of the object, and moving toward 16x enlarges the size. Use the coordinate display box to choose a zoom of about 0.66.

15.11.2 Three-dimensional perspective view

You can create a perspective view with lines converging on a distant point using the Distance option:

```
CAmera/TArget/Distance/POints/PAn/Zoom/TWist/CLip/Hide/Off/Undo
/<eXit>: d <return> New camera/target distance <43'8">:
```

A slider bar along the top allows you to move the camera a distance from the target. Select a distance of about 30 feet. The drawing will be regenerated as a perspective view, indicated by the perspective icon in the lower left corner of the screen, illustrated in Figure 15.25. The convergence of the lines depends on the length of the object in comparison to the camera/target distance.

15.11.3 Clipping parts of an object

You can cut off the front or back of an object by using clipping planes. A clipping plane is perpendicular to your line of site, and a specified distance from the target. Positive distances are in front of the target, and negative distances are behind the target. Enter the following:

```
CAmera/TArget/Distance/POints/PAn/Zoom/TWist/CLip/Hide/Off/Undo
/<eXit>: cl <return> Back/Front/<off>: f<return> Eye/<Distance from
target><27'-9">:
```

A slider bar will be displayed across the top of the screen. Move along the slider bar and select a distance of about –2'–4", reading the value in the coordinate display window. Then enter Hide:

```
Camera/TArget/Distance/POints/PAn/Zoom/TWist/CLip/Hide/Off/Undo
/<eXit>: h <return>
```

The clipped view with hidden lines suppressed is shown in Figure 15.26. Try clipping the back of the object. The Off option turns front and back clipping off. The eXit (x) option exits the 3D Dynamic View (Dview) command and regenerates the drawing using the last view established. Exit the Dynamic View command and plot your drawing. Turn the Hide Lines button on in the Plot Configuration dialog box.

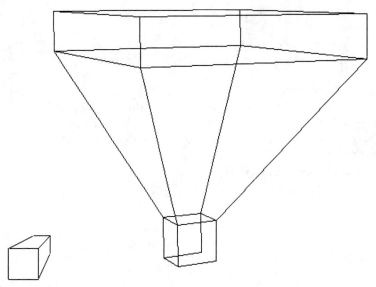

Figure 15.25 Perspective view.

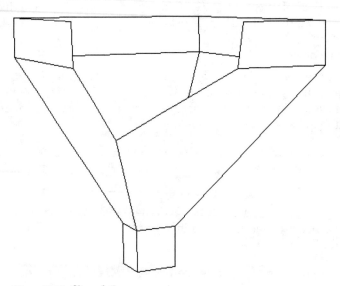

Figure 15.26 Clipped view.

If you press <return> instead of selecting an object when the 3D Dynamic View option is initially selected, AutoCAD will display a small house for you to use to set the view you want. When the command is exited, your model replaces the house using the last established view. In a complex drawing, it's often easier and faster to establish a view this way.

15.12 Three-Dimensional Polygon Meshes

A 3-D polygon mesh is composed of a multiple of faces that form a flat surface in space or approximate a curved surface in space. AutoCAD commands that generate polygon meshes are shown in Figure 15.27.

A 3-D polygon mesh generated by AutoCAD is a single entity. It's constructed as a grid with M columns and N rows. AutoCAD allows you to control the resolution of the mesh by defining the relative spacing between the rows and columns.

The 3Dmesh and Pface commands allow you to construct a 3-D polygon mesh by entering the mesh (grid) vertices, coordinate by coordinate. The process is time-consuming since you must enter each grid coordinate of the mesh. The remaining 3-D polygon mesh commands generate mesh vertices automatically once the mesh structure has been defined. For example, you can create a 3-D goblet with the Revsurf command to rotate the goblet's profile about an axis of revolution to form the surface mesh structure of the goblet (see the following section).

15.12.1 Three-dimensional goblet

The goblet illustrated in Figure 15.28 is to be drawn using the Revsurf command to generate a 3-D polygon mesh. Begin a new drawing named C:\DRAWINGS\GOB-LET.DWG. Set the drawing units to decimal with one unit to the right of the decimal. The default screen limits of 12,9 are to be used for this drawing.

Set the snap to 0.1 units and the grid to 0.5 units. Create a layer named Goblet, colored red, and a layer named Construc, colored yellow. Set Construc as the current layer. If the model space icon (refer back to Figure 15.20) isn't displayed in the lower left corner of the screen, use the Options menu (refer back to Figure 15.21) to turn it on, and place it at the origin.

The goblet is to be viewed as a 3-D object in space. Set the viewpoint so you're viewing the x,y axis from a point above the front right side corner of the grid, as follows:

View <pick> 3D Viewpoint <pick> Vector <pick> Rotate/<view point>: **1,–1,1** <return>

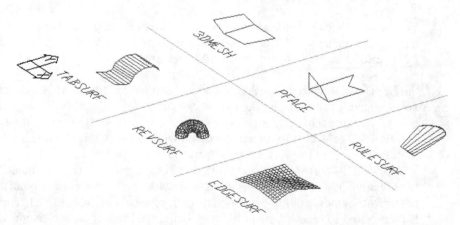

Figure 15.27 3-D Polygon Meshes.

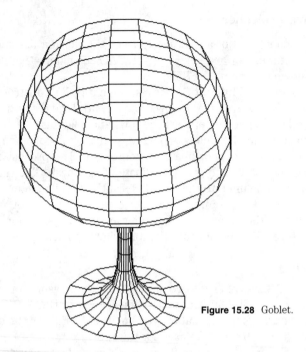

Figure 15.28 Goblet.

The grid and model space icon should now appear as illustrated in Figure 15.29. AutoCAD generates 3-D polygon meshes along the x,y plane. In order to visualize the goblet in space, you'll use the grid on the screen as a surface, such as a table top, that the goblet is to sit on. Do this by rotating the coordinate system icon 90 degrees about its x axis so the y axis projects up from the grid surface, as shown in Figure 15.30. This modified coordinate system is a UCS (see section 15.10). User coordinate systems are discussed in more detail in chapter 16. The procedure to create a UCS is as follows:

View <pick> Set UCS <pick> X Axis Rotate <pick> Origin/ZAxis/3point/Entity/oBject/View/X/Y/Z/Prev/Restore/Save/Del/?/<World>: x Rotation angle about X axis <0>: **90** <return>

Surfaces created with the Revsurf command involve rotating a profile, or path curve, about an axis of revolution. The axis of revolution for the goblet is a vertical line located approximately in the middle of the screen. Press ORTHO on in the status bar (or <ctrl>–O or <F8>) to turn the orthogonal mode on, and use the Line command to draw the axis of revolution line, illustrated in Figure 15.31.

Turn ORTHO (orthogonal mode) off, then set the current layer to Goblet. The profile or path curve of the goblet is initially drawn as a polyline composed of a number of straight segments defined by points 1 to 9, as shown in Figure 15.31. The polyline is then edited to create a smooth curve. Using the Pline (polyline) command, draw the continuous polyline illustrated in Figure 15.31 by selecting vertex points 1 to 9.

You created the curved contour lines of the topographic map back in Figure 15.9 by editing polylines composed of straight-line segments and using the fit curve option of the Pedit (Polyline Edit) command. The fit curve option constructs pairs of arcs that pass through every vertex of the original polyline.

Figure 15.29 Three-dimensional viewpoint.

Figure 15.30 User coordinate system.

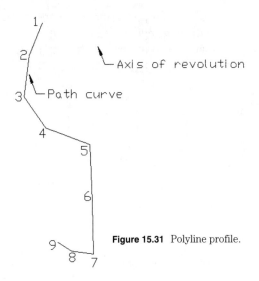

Figure 15.31 Polyline profile.

The spline curve option to the Pedit command creates curves that are very different from those produced by the fit curve option. On a contour map, the contour lines must pass through the original vertex control points, hence the fit curve option should be selected. On a goblet, however, the original straight-line segments of the polyline define the form of the goblet, and the objective is to smooth out the segments, created a pleasing curve, as illustrated in Figure 15.32. The spline curve option creates a smooth curve that follows the shape of the polyline segments and doesn't necessarily pass through the vertex points. You can select the Edit Polyline, or Polyedit, command from the pull-down Modify menu or from the screen menu, as follows:

Modify <toolbar> Edit Polyline <pick> Select polyline: Pick a point on the polyline. <pick> Close/Join/Width/Edit vertex/Fit/Spline/Decurve/ Ltype gen/Undo/eXit: **s** (Spline) <return> Close/Join/Width/edit vertex/Fit/Spline/decurve/Ltype gen/Undo/eXit: <return>

The resolution, or density, of a 3-D polygon mesh surface is controlled by the Surftab1 and Surftab2 system variables. Ruled and tabulated surfaces use Surftab1 to define the rule or tabulation intervals. Revolved surfaces use Surftab1 to define tabulation intervals in the direction of revolution, and Surftab2 to define the tabulation intervals in the other direction. A setting of 20 for Surftab1 and Surftab2 should produce a well-defined mesh surface for the goblet:

Command: **surftab1** <return> New value for Surftab1 <6>: **20** <return>
Command: **surftab2** <return> New value for Surftab2 <6>: **20** <return>

You can now create the surface of the goblet by using the Revsurf command, as follows (in DOS, select Draw, then Surfaces, then Revolved Surface):

Surfaces <toolbar> Revolved Surface (Figure 15.33) <pick> Select path curve:
Select the curved polyline defining the path curve of the goblet. <pick> Select
axis of revolution: Pick the straight line defining the axis of revolution. <pick>
Start angle <0>: <return> Included angle (+=ccw,-=cw) <full cir-
cle>: <return>

Notice that you can define the start angle for the surface and the included angle. A
positive included angle denotes a counterclockwise rotation and a negative one a
clockwise rotation.

　　Use Zoom Extents to display the view within the screen. Turn the Construc layer
off so the axis of revolution line isn't displayed on the screen. The goblet displayed
on the screen is a wireframe model. The Hide command will generate a solid model
view, as follows:

Command: **hide** <return>

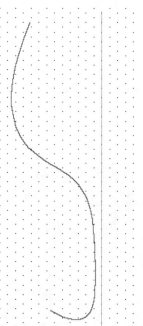

Figure 15.32 Splined polyline profile.

Figure 15.33 Revolved Surface tool.

The screen will go blank and AutoCAD will perform the necessary calculations to generate a solid model view of the goblet. Plot the goblet using the Fit option to scale the goblet to the plot sheet size. Although a solid model view of the goblet is displayed on the screen, AutoCAD will plot the wireframe model unless you turn on the Hide Lines box in the Plot Configuration dialog box.

15.12.2 Other polygon mesh commands

The Rulesurf command creates a polygon mesh as a ruled surface between two curves. The curves can be lines, points, arcs, circles, 2-D polylines, or 3-D polylines.

The Tabsurf command creates a polygon mesh defined by a path curve and a direction vector. The path curve defines the shape of the surface, and the direction vector defines the length and path along which the path curve is to be extruded as a polygon mesh. The direction vector can be a line or an open polyline.

The Edgesurf command creates a polygon mesh defined by four adjoining "path curves." The four adjoining path curves, or edges, that define the surface can be lines, arcs, or open polylines. The edges must touch at their endpoints to define a topologically rectangular closed path.

16

Multiview Drawings

Objective: Complete a three-dimensional multiview drawing of an industrial building using a user coordinate system (UCS), create viewports in model and paper space, layer visibility in viewports, scale objects and linetypes, and dimension paper space viewports.

Drawing: This drawing is to be done in SI (metric) units. Boot AutoCAD and set the measurement system to Metric, as outlined in chapter 6, section 6.1. Then begin a new drawing named C:\DRAWINGS\PROJ-16.DWG. Set the units to decimal (mm), with zero digits to the right of the decimal. The screen limits are based on floor plan dimensions of 18000 mm × 22000 mm. To allow room for dimensions, set the screen limits as 0,0 and 28000,32000. The completed drawing is illustrated in Figure 16.1.

16.1 Drawing Coordinate Systems

AutoCAD uses a fixed world coordinate system (WCS), as described in the previous chapter, section 15.10, and an arbitrary user coordinate system (UCS). UCS is a Cartesian coordinate system, which can be defined in any plane of the drawing to facilitate drawing entities on that plane, for instance, on the sloping roof of a house. Any number of UCSs can be defined. You specify the location of the UCS origin when defining the plane.

AutoCAD displays a coordinate system icon to show the positive direction of the x and y axes, along with other relevant information about the UCS. If the current UCS is the world coordinate system, a W will appear in the Y arm of the icon, as illustrated in Figure 16.2A. If the icon is located at the UCS origin, a plus sign is displayed in the base of the icon, as shown in Figures 16.2A and B. If the UCS is viewed from above, a box is formed at the base of the icon (Figures 16.2A, B, and C). If viewed from below, the box is missing (Figure 16.2D). If either the x or y axis of the UCS is within one degree of being perpendicular to the screen, the icon displayed is a broken pen-

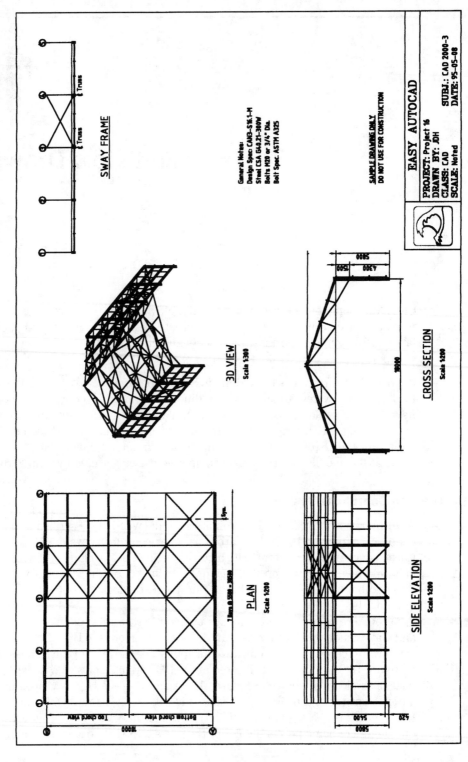

Figure 16.1 Industrial Building.

cil to indicate that UCS is being viewed on edge. Therefore, pointing to locations on the screen might be meaningless (see Figure 16.2E).

16.1.2 Viewports in model space

The computer drawing screen can be divided into several viewports. Each viewport can contain a different view of the drawing and can be zoomed or panned independently. If you modify the drawing or add entities to one viewport, the changes are reflected in each of the other viewports. Because a viewport has a smaller screen area than the full screen, drawing with viewports is advantageous only when the extra views of the entity assist in visualizing and drawing the entity. For instance, because you can select points for an entity in any viewport, it's easy to envision how the additional views can simplify the drawing of some 3-D objects.

Although you can display several viewports, only one viewport is current. When the cursor is moved into the current viewport, the familiar crosshairs are displayed. If the cursor is moved out of the current viewport into an adjacent one, the crosshairs change to a small arrow pointing in a northwest direction. You can change the current viewport by pointing to the desired viewport and pressing the <pick> button on the mouse. You can use the keyboard cursor control keys only to move the cursor within the current viewport, not to select a new viewport.

16.2 Industrial Building

You can draw a 3-D view of the industrial building to fit within a box 18,000 mm wide, 22,200 mm long, and 5,800 mm high (at the eave). Prior to drawing the structure, the outline of this box must be drawn on a construction layer. Make a new layer named Constr. If you have a color monitor, set the color of Constr as yellow so the construction lines will stand out from the object lines. If you don't have a color monitor, set the line type as Dot. Set Constr as the current layer.

The drawing is to be plotted on a B-size page (430 × 280 mm) using the Border menu created in chapters 11 and 12, and a scale of 1:200. (In SI units, you should use an A3 sheet (297 × 420 mm, but you didn't create an A3 border in the Border menu. Create one if you do a lot of SI drawings.) Then calculate Ltscale using the following equation (also see appendix C, Table C.2):

$$\text{Plot Scale} \times \text{Ltscale} = 1 \text{ in} \times \text{conversion} \times \tfrac{3}{4}$$
$$\tfrac{1}{200} \times \text{Ltscale} = 1 \times 25.4 \, / \, 1000 \times \tfrac{3}{4}$$
$$\text{Ltscale} = 3810$$

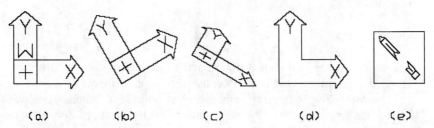

(a)   (b)   (c)   (d)   (e)

Figure 16.2 UCS Icons.

Set the Ltscale as outlined in chapter 6, section 6.9.1. Draw the front side of the box as follows:

Draw <toolbar> Line <pick> From point: **5000,5000** <return> To point: **@22000<0** <return> To point: **@0,0,5800** <return> To point: **@22000<180** <return> To point: **c** <return>

Notice that the third point entered is 5800 mm along the z axis (perpendicular to the screen). You'll use the Copy command to draw the back side:

Modity <toolbar> Copy <pick> Select objects: Place a selection window around the front wall. <pick> Select objects: <return> <Base point or displacement>/Multiple: **0,18000** <return> Second point of displacement: <return>

The end walls are easier to draw on a 3-D view of the structure. Use the Vpoint command to view the structure from a point 330 degrees in front of the plan (–30 degrees below the x axis), and 30 degrees above the plan (positive is counterclockwise from the x-y plane) as follows:

View <pick> 3D Viewpoint <pick> Rotate <pick>

The viewpoint's Presets dialog box illustrated in Figure 15.18 will be displayed. Enter an x-axis rotation of 330, and a y-axis rotation of 30. Press OK.
    Complete the box by adding the top and bottom lines on each end wall by using the Line command and the Intersection object snap. Use Named Views... in the View menu to save the three-dimensional view with the name 3D (refer to chapter 15, section 15.17, and Figure 15.14). This view will be used throughout the drawing as a reference view illustrating the entire building.

16.2.1 Coordinate system icon location

The default location of the UCS icon (see Figure 16.2) is in the lower left corner of the monitor or viewport. When defining a UCS, it's easier to visualize what's being done if the icon is located at the origin of the UCS (point 0,0,0). If the origin is off the screen or too close to the edge of the screen, the icon will be displayed in the lower left corner of the screen. Choose the following in the menu bar (refer to Figure 15.21 in chapter 15):

Options <pick> UCS <pick>

If Icon isn't turned on (if it doesn't have a tick in front of it), turn it on by picking Icon. Also turn Icon Origin on. Because the display currently fills the viewport, the UCS origin is close to the screen edge and, although the Origin option was turned on, the icon is displayed in the lower left corner of the viewport. Zoom the view to make it smaller:

View <pick> Zoom <pick> Scale <pick> `All/Center/Dynamic/Extents/Left/ Previous/ Vmax/Window/<Scale (X/XP)>:` **.9x** <return>

The current UCS is the WCS, so the icon is displayed at point 0,0,0, based on the screen limits set, which is still the lower left corner of the screen. The zoom value of 0.9x was entered to zoom .9 times the current screen.

16.2.2 Defining user coordinate systems

User coordinate systems should be defined on the top, front side, right side, and sloping roof planes of the building. The origin of the UCS on the top of the box should be at the lower left corner on the top of the box, and is created as follows (see Figure 16.3):

View <pick> Set UCS: <pick> Origin <pick> `Origin/ZAxis/3Point/object/ View/X/Y/Z/ Prev/Restore/Save/Del/?/<World>:` **o** `Origin point <0, 0,0>:` <shift>–<right> Intersection <pick> of Place the object snap box on the far left corner of the top of the box. <return>

The UCS icon will move to the top of the box in the left corner, as illustrated in Figure 16.4. Save the coordinate system using the name Roofplan, as follows:

View <pick> Named UCS... <pick>

The UCS Control dialog box illustrated in Figure 16.5 will be displayed. In the list box, *WORLD* is the world UCS, which has its origin at the 0,0,0 limits defined at the opening of the drawing. *PREVIOUS* is the previous UCS, which also happens to be the

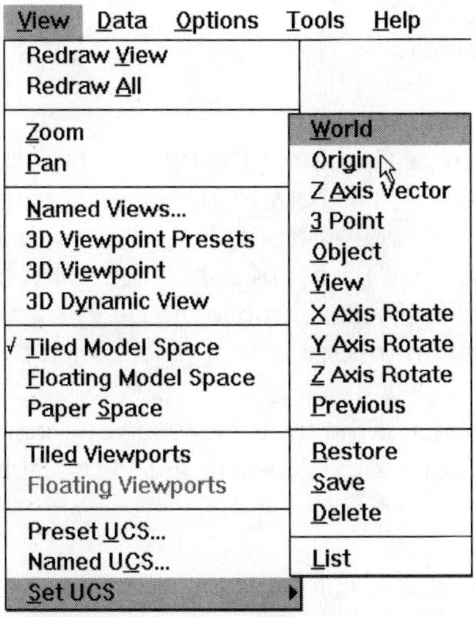

Figure 16.3 Set UCS menu.

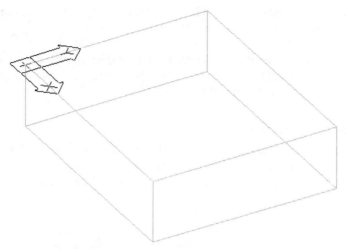

Figure 16.4 UCS Roofplan.

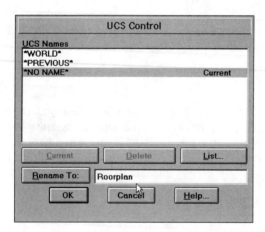

Figure 16.5 Naming a UCS.

WCS. *NO NAME* is the current UCS (note Current to the right of the name in the list box), which hasn't yet been named. Choose *NO NAME* by clicking on it. Then move the cursor into the Rename To: edit box and enter **Roofplan**. Then press Rename To: to rename the *NO NAME* UCS to Roofplan. Press OK to exit the dialog box.

Now following the procedure outlined previously, move the UCS origin to the front view, as illustrated in Figure 16.6, using the Intersection object snap to ensure the UCS is on the intersection point.

The relocated UCS is to be on the plane of the front view, so you must rotate it by 90 degrees in a positive direction about its x axis (based on the right-hand rule) to appear as shown in Figure 16.6:

View <pick> Set UCS <pick> X Axis Rotate <pick> Rotation angle about X
axis <0.0>: **90** <return>

Display the UCS Control box. The current UCS is named *NO NAME*. Rename it Front. Define a UCS on the right end of the box by moving the UCS origin to the bottom right corner of the front view of the box. Then rotate the UCS 90 degrees about the y axis. The view should appear as shown in Figure 16.7. Save the UCS with the name Rightside. The UCS in the plane of the sloping roof is created after the roof trusses have been drawn.

It's important to understand the relationship between a view and a user coordinate system, UCS. In Figure 16.7, a three-dimensional view (named 3D) of the box is displayed. The current UCS, however, is Rightside, which has its origin in the lower left corner of the right side of the box, where the UCS icon is displayed. Figure 16.6 also displays the view named 3D, but the UCS has a different origin.

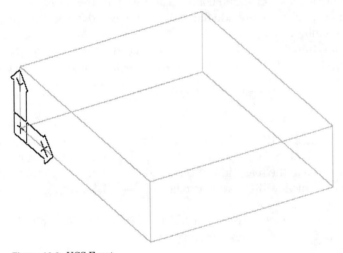

Figure 16.6 UCS Front.

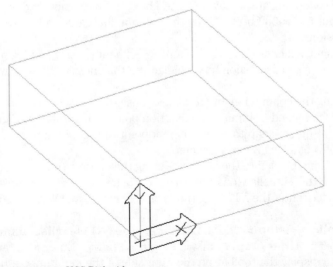

Figure 16.7 UCS Rightside.

You can use the View command to view an object from any direction, regardless of the current UCS. The UCS defines the x,y coordinate system, showing the axis and the coordinate system origin graphically.

When you invoke an AutoCAD command to create an entity, such as a line, you define its position by entering its x,y,z coordinates. The coordinates are interpreted by AutoCAD with respect to the current UCS.

16.3 Columns and Roof Trusses

Building columns are vertical primary structural members that support the building and rest on the footings. Roof trusses are horizontal primary structural members that, in this building, span between columns and support the roof loads. A roof truss is composed of a number of individual members connected in a geometric pattern to form a single member.

The structural framework is to be drawn on a layer named SS (structural steel). Use the Layer Control dialog box to make the new layer and set it as the current layer.

16.3.1 Columns

You can add columns to the structure by creating a block and inserting it into the drawing with the Minsert (multiple insert) command. You want to draw the column block on elevation 0 in the plan view of the building, which is on the WCS. The WCS is recalled and a plan view displayed, as follows:

View <pick> Set UCS <pick> World <pick> View <Pick> 3D Viewpoint Presets (Figure 15.6) <pick> Plan View <pick> World <pick>

A plan view of the world coordinate system is displayed. The current layer should be SS (verify this by looking at the Layer Control box). Using Zoom Window, zoom on a window of about 500 × 500 units. Draw the column illustrated in Figure 16.8A, excluding dimensions.

The total height (thickness) of the column is 6025 mm. Using the Properties tool and the Change Properties dialog box, change the thickness of the column to 6025 units.

After changing the column height (thickness), use the Block command to save the column as a block named Column. The insertion point is illustrated in Figure 16.8A; use the Midpoint object snap to select the midpoint of the 250-mm web. Return to the previous view by using Zoom Previous.

Insert the Column block into the structure using the Minsert (multiple insert) command located in the Miscellaneous toolbar (see Figure 16.9). If your Miscellaneous toolbar isn't loaded, enter the following (not available in the Tool Windows flyout):

Command: **toolbar** <return> Toolbar name (or All): **miscellaneous** <return> Hide/Left/Right/Top/Bottom/Float <Show>: Enter a suitable option such as Right to display the toolbar on the right side of the monitor. <return>

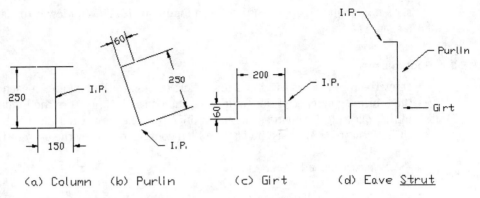

Figure 16.8 Structural components.

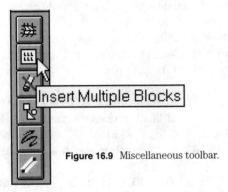

Figure 16.9 Miscellaneous toolbar.

Invoke the Minsert command as follows (in DOS, select Draw, then Insert, then Multiple Blocks):

Miscellaneous <toolbar> Insert Multiple Blocks <pick> Block name (or ?): **column** <return> Insertion point: <shift>–<right> Intersection <pick> of Place the object snap target over the lower left corner of the structure. <pick> X scale factor <1>/Corner/XYZ: <return> Y scale factor (default=X): <return> Rotation angle <0>: <return> Number of rows (---)<1>: **2** <return> Number of columns (┆┆┆)<1>: **5** <return> Unit cell or distance between rows (---): **18000** <return> Distance between columns (┆┆┆): **5500** <return>

In order to see if the columns were inserted properly, recall the 3-D view created earlier:

View <pick> Named Views <pick>

The View Control dialog box will be displayed. Click on 3D, then press the Restore command button, and then press OK to restore the 3-D view saved earlier. The screen view should appear as shown in Figure 16.10. If your view is too large, enter a zoom of 0.9x.

16.3.2 Roof trusses

Draw the roof trusses as a block and insert them into the building in each bay using the Minsert command. Prior to drawing the truss block, restore the Rightside UCS. In the following command sequence, notice that the view is not displayed when the UCS is restored; you must invoke the Plan command to view the current UCS:

View <pick> Named UCS... <pick>

The UCS Control dialog box (Figure 16.5) will be displayed. Choose RIGHTSIDE in the list box and then click on Current to make Rightside the current UCS. Click OK to close the dialog box. Choose the following to get a plan view of the current UCS:

View <pick> 3D Viewpoint Presets <pick> Plan View <pick> Current <pick> View <Pick> Zoom <pick> Scale <pick> All/Center/Dynamic/Extents/Left/Previous/Vmax/Window/<Scale(X/XP): **0.9x** <return>

The Rightside UCS origin (coordinate 0,0) is at the center of the base of the left column. The roof truss's top and bottom chord lines intersect at the center line of the left column 5,800 mm above its base. The truss width is 18,000 mm and its peak height is 3,050 mm. Draw the truss top and bottom chords as follows:

Draw <toolbar> Line <pick> From point: **0,5800** <return> To point: **@18000<0** <return> To point: **@-9000,3050** <return> To point: **c** <return>

The truss web members intersect the top chord at its quarter points. You can locate those points with AutoCAD's Divide command, which divides a line into equal-length

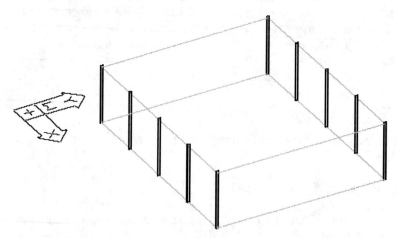

Figure 16.10   3-D view with columns inserted.

segments, placing node points at the end of each segment (the line isn't divided into separate entities). The nodes can be snapped onto with the Node object snap. Node points and points placed with the Point command are defined by the Pdmode system variable. By default, the node points are dots (pdmode = 0), which aren't visible when placed on an object line. Use Pdmode to change the point mode from a dot to a small cross (pdmode = 2):

Option <pick> Display <pick> Point Style... <pick>

Choose the cross for the pdmode, as shown in Figure 16.11, and press OK to exit. Then invoke the Divide command as follows (in DOS, select Draw, then Point, then Divide):

Point <toolbar> Divide (Figure 16.12) <pick> Select object to divide: Digitize the top chord on the left side of the truss. <pick> <Number of segments>/ Block: **4** <return>

The truss web members, shown in Figure 16.13, are to be drawn next. Since the members are perpendicular to the top chord of the truss, rotate the snap parallel to the chord:

Command: **snap** <return> Snap spacing or ON/OFF/Aspect/Rotate/Style <1>: **r** (Rotate) <return> Base point <0,0>: <shift>–<right> Endpoint <pick> of Place the endpoint aperture lower end of the left top chord. <pick> Rotation angle <0>: <shift>–<right> Endpoint <pick> of Place the target near the higher end of the top chord of the truss.<pick>

Turn the ORTHO button on (or press <ctrl>–O or <F8>). You'll draw the truss web members using the Line command, and select the start point by snapping onto the node points created by the Divide command. Since snap is set to the angle of the top chord and orthogonal mode is on, the lines will be perpendicular to the chord. Draw the lines past the bottom chord; you can trim them later. The procedure to draw the lines is as follows:

Draw <toolbar> Line <pick> From point: <shift>–<right> Node <pick> of Place the object snap target on a node point on the top chord. <pick> To point: Extend the line past the bottom chord of the truss, and trim them later. <pick> To point: <return> <return> Line From point: Repeat the process and draw the remaining three perpendicular chord members.

The points created by the Divide command are stored in the previous selection set. Erase them by entering the following (also refer to appendix D, section D.1, hint number 46):

Modify <toolbar> Erase <pick> Select objects: **p** (previous) <return> 3 found Select objects: <return>

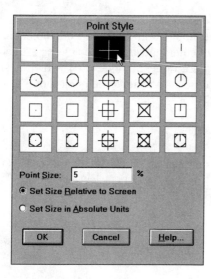

Figure 16.11 Point Styles.

Figure 16.12 Divide tool.

Next, rotate the snap to the angle of the top chord on the right side of the truss, and draw the web members perpendicular to that chord following procedures similar to those used for the left side. After you've completed those members, rotate the snap back to the 0,0 origin with an angle of 0. Remember to remove the nodes from the selection set.

Turn ORTHO (orthogonal mode) off. Draw the remaining web members of the truss, as illustrated in Figure 16.13, using the Intersection object snap. The web member at the center of the truss extends from the intersection point at the top of the truss to the midpoint of the bottom chord. The knee brace on the left side extends from coordinate 0,4300 to the intersection of the truss members. Complete the truss by trimming the web members as follows:

Modify <toolbar> Trim <pick> `Select cutting edge(s)... Select objects:` Digitize the bottom chord of the truss. <pick> `Select objects:` <return> `<Select objects to trim>/Project/Edge/Undo:` Digitize the end of each line to be trimmed. <return>

Restore the view 3D. The roof truss is to be saved as a block and inserted into the structure with the multipe insert (Minsert) command. Before creating the block, however, you must determine the current UCS when the block is inserted. If the UCS that's current when the block is created doesn't match the UCS that's current when the block is inserted, the block won't be aligned properly. Minsert inserts a block as an array along the x or y axis. The truss needs to be inserted along the length of the building, spanning between columns. Consequently, the x and y axes must fall along the roof plan when the truss is inserted, which is the Roofplan UCS. Restore the UCS Roofplan. If the View is too large, use zoom 0.9x to fit it into the screen better. You should have a 3-D view of the building with the UCS located as shown back in Figure 16.4, which is the origin (0,0,0) of the Roofplan UCS. Do *not* continue until you have the correct UCS. Make sure to freeze the Constr layer before continuing.

Save the roof truss and knee brace as a block named Truss. Use a window to select the truss and knee braces individually. Entities selected will be drawn dotted by AutoCAD. If you accidentally select any of the building columns, enter **r** (remove) in response to Select objects:, and select the dotted columns to remove them from the selection set. If you make a mistake, use the U (Undo) command to undo the commands, and then try again. The block insertion point is at the intersection of the top and bottom chords on the left side of the truss (don't include the column in the intersection aperture box).

Insert the Truss block into the structure using the Minsert (multiple insert) command. Prior to inserting the Truss block, use the Zoom command and enter a magnification of **0.8**. This is necessary since the Truss block is complex and, if part of the truss is off the screen when it's being inserted, your system might be slowed considerably when you enter the block.

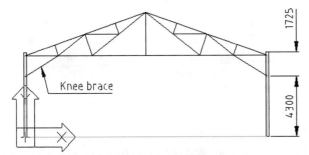

Figure 16.13   Roof truss and knee braces.

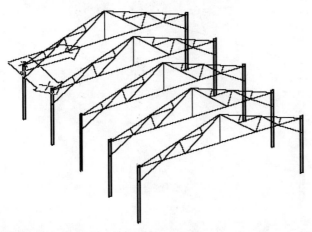

Figure 16.14   Structure with trusses inserted.

Use the Minsert command to insert the block named Truss. The insertion point is the origin of the Roofplan UCS, point 0,0. There's to be 1 row and 5 columns, and the spacing of the columns should be 5500 mm. If the trusses aren't inserted properly, use the U (undo) command and try again. Your drawing should appear as shown in Figure 16.14.

16.4   Defining the Topchord UCS

A UCS is required on the plane of the top chord of the truss to facilitate drawing entities on that plane. Because there are two sides to the truss, you need to define two topchord planes, with the names Topchordl (left) and Topchordr (right), as viewed from the right side of the building.

The current UCS origin is the top of the building's front left column, as illustrated in Figure 16.14. Define the Topchordl UCS by rotating the UCS origin so it lies in the plane of the truss's top chord.

To facilitate the selection of points, use the Zoom and Window commands to enlarge a view that includes the current UCS icon and the left half of the roof truss, located at the left end of the building (see Figure 16.15). After enlarging the view, define the new UCS by using the 3point option, as follows:

View <pick> Set UCS <pick> 3 Point <Pick> Origin   point   <0,0,0>: <shift>–<right> Endpoint <pick> of Place the target on the left side of the top chord of the back end truss. <Pick> Point on positive portion of the X axis <default>: The x axis is not being changed, so accept the default. <return> Point of positive-Y portion of the UCS X-Y plane: <shift>–<right> Endpoint <pick> of Place the target on the top chord of the truss near the peak of the truss.

The UCS icon should be displayed at the left end of the truss with its x,y axis on the plane of the truss top chord, as illustrated in Figure 16.15. If your UCS icon is located in the lower left corner of the screen, your view might be too close to the edge of the

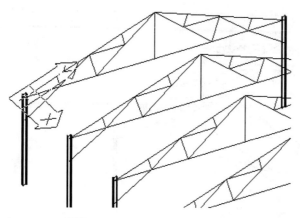

Figure 16.15 UCS Topchordl.

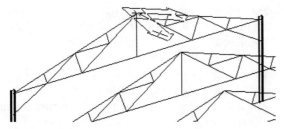

Figure 16.16 UCS Topchordr.

screen. Try panning the view slightly to the right. If you have other problems, enter U (Undo) and retry the commands, being more careful when selecting points. Save the UCS using the name Topchordl:

View <pick> Named UCS... <pick>

The UCS Control dialog box illustrated in Figure 16.5 will be displayed. Click on *NO NAME* and then enter the name TOPCHORDL in the Rename To box. Then press Rename To to rename the UCS, then press OK.

Use similar procedures to define a UCS named Topchordr (right). Its origin is the peak of the truss, and the x,y axis is to lie on the plane of the top chord on the right side of the truss, with the y axis pointing to the intersection of the top and bottom chord at the right side of the truss (see Figure 16.16). Name the UCS.

16.5 Roof Purlins

Roof purlins are members on the roof of a structure, spanning between roof trusses, and support the roof sheeting. The purlins are to be drawn on the Rightside UCS in the right end bay of the front of the building. Restore the UCS named Rightside as the current UCS, and then display the plan view of the current UCS.

After the plan view of the Rightside UCS is displayed, use Zoom Window commands to enlarge a view of the left half of the truss. The drawing plane is then rotated parallel to the top chord of the truss, as follows:

```
Command: snap <return> Snap spacing or ON/OFF/Aspect/Rotate/Style
<1>: r (Rotate) <return> Base point <0,0>: <shift>-<right> Endpoint <pick>
of Place the target near the left end of the top or bottom chord of the truss. <pick>
Rotation angle: <shift>-<right> Endpoint <pick> of Place the target on the top
chord near the peak of the truss. <pick>
```

The truss members are currently drawn as single lines, which represent the centroid of the truss members. The roof purlins, however, sit on the top chord of the truss, and should be drawn 40 mm above the truss top chord line to account for the actual thickness of the truss member above its centroid.

Create a new layer named Ssline, colored green, and make it the current layer. Draw a line representing the outside edge of the truss top chord 40 mm above the top chord on layer Ssline, as follows:

Draw <toolbar> Line <pick> From point: <shift>–<right> Endpoint <pick> of Place the aperture on the truss top chord near the left end. <pick> To point: <shift>–<right> Endpoint <pick> of Place the aperture on the truss top chord near the peak. <pick> To point: <return>

16.5.1 Selection by cycling

Use the Offset command to offset the green line 40 mm above the top chord of the truss. In order to select the last line, use the cycle mode to cycle through objects by pressing the <ctrl> button while selecting objects. Each time you <ctrl> <pick>, AutoCAD cycles through objects under the pick button:

Modify <toolbar> Offset (Figure 3.4) <pick> Offset distance or Through <Through>: **40** <return> Select objects to offset: Place the cursor on the green line and hold down the <ctrl> button while pressing <pick> <Cycle on> Either the green line or the truss is drawn dotted by AutoCAD. If the green line is dotted, it was selected by AutoCAD. If the truss is dotted, select the line again using <ctrl> and <pick> Select objects to offset: If the green line is dotted, press <return>. <Cycle off> Side to offset: Digitize a point above the top chord. <pick> <return>

Notice how you use <ctrl> and <pick> to cycle through overlapping objects. You should now have a green line offset 40 mm above the top chord of the left side of the truss and a green line along the top chord.

Use Zoom and Window to zoom on a box containing a piece of the truss top chord and sufficient space above the chord in which to draw the purlin illustrated back in Figure 16.8B. Then use the Erase command to erase the green line overlapping the top chord line of the truss (do not erase the offset line). Select by cycling to choose the green line. Use the Redraw tool to restore the truss top chord line.

Make two new layers SSTCL (SS top chord left), colored blue, and SSTCR (SS top chord right), colored red. Set the current layer to SSTCL and press ORTHO (orthogonal mode) on.

Zoom on a window containing a section of the top chord of the truss and sufficient room above it to draw the purlin shown back in Figure 16.8B. Use the Change Properties dialog box to change the thickness of the purlin to –5500 mm (the c/c spacing of trusses, negative because it's into the z axis). Save the purlin as a block using the name Purlinl (purlin left). The insertion point is also illustrated in Figure 16.8B.

Insert the roof purlin at the quarter points along the green line. Zoom all and then use the Divide command to divide the line into four segments, and insert the Purlinl block at the ¼, ½, and ¾ node points along the line, using the Node object snap. Don't insert the purlin at the truss peak. After the purlins are inserted, erase the node points using the Erase and Previous commands.

To facilitate its connection to the roof truss, locate the purlin at the truss peak 80 mm below the peak along the green line. Then use the Measure command to divide a line into equal-length segments of a specified length, and to locate node points 80 mm apart on the green line. Zoom on the peak of the truss to enlarge the area where the purlin is to be inserted, and measure the 80-mm segments as follows (in DOS, select Draw, then Point, then Measure):

Draw <toolbar> Measure (Figure 16.17) <pick> `Select object to measure:` Digitize the green line. <pick> `<Segment length>/Block:` **80** <return>

Insert the Purlinl block at the first 80-mm node on the green line at the peak end of the truss. Use Erase Previous to remove the node points from the selection set.

Set the current layer as SSTCR (SS top chord right), and draw the purlins (use the name Purlinr) on the right side of the truss. Don't be tempted to mirror the trusses from the left side, because they're blocks on layer SSTCL, and you can't change the layer on which basic elements of a block are drawn. When you've completed the right side of the truss, restore the view named 3D. The completed structure should appear as illustrated in Figure 16.18.

Set the current layer as SS and turn the SSLINE layer off. Set the Pdmode back to 0 (points). It's good practice when drawing to return items such as points to their default values. If a drawing with points were inserted into this drawing where Pdmode

Figure 16.17 Measure tool.

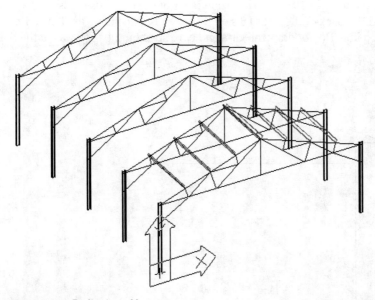

Figure 16.18 Purlins in end bay.

is 2 (cross), any points on the inserted drawing would revert to crosses and items that were invisible because they fell on objects might suddenly be quite visible.

16.6 Wall Girts and Eave Strut

Girts are members on the exterior walls of a structure, spanning between columns and supporting the wall sheeting. Girts should be initially drawn on the Rightside UCS, which should be the current UCS. Display the plan view of the current UCS. Enter the Snap command and rotate snap to 0 degree (origin is 0,0).

Set the current layer to SS, pan the structure to the right, and then enlarge a view of the left column using Zoom Window. In an open space, draw the Girt block illustrated back in Figure 16.8C. The thickness is –5500 mm, and the insertion point is noted.

The Rightside UCS origin is at the center of the base of the left column. The first girt is to be inserted 400 mm above the column base on the outside face of the 250-mm wide column, so the insertion point is –125,400, which you can enter as x and y insertion points in the Insert dialog box, turning the Specify Parameters on Screen box off. The other two girts are spaced 1800 mm and 3600 mm *above* the first girt, respectively. Insert the three girts on the left column. Do not insert the girts on the right-side column yet.

The eave strut is a member at the eave of the structure, spanning between columns, and supports the roof sheeting and the wall siding. Enlarge a view, as illustrated in Figure 16.19, and draw a construction line parallel to the top chord by first rotating the snap parallel to the top chord and then turning the orthogonal mode on. Use an object snap to snap onto the roof purlin. Rotate the snap back to 0.

Draw the eave strut block shown back in Figure 16.8D. It has a thickness of –5500 mm and an insertion point as Noted. Insert the strut at the eave of the building, as shown in Figure 16.19, so the insertion point of the eave strut falls on the construction line and the back of the strut falls on the face of the column, as shown. Erase the construction line. Do *not* draw the girts and eave strut on the back wall of the building yet.

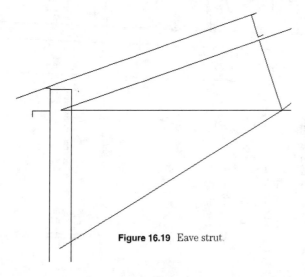

Figure 16.19 Eave strut.

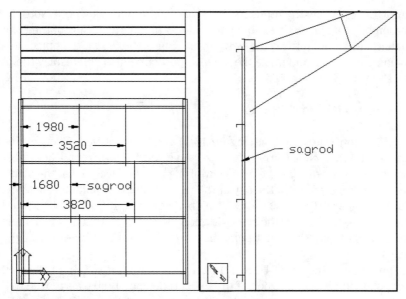

Figure 16.20 Wall sagrod viewports.

16.7 Sagrods

Girts and purlins are constructed from members that are deep and narrow (refer back to Figure 16.8). As a result, they tend to sag about their weak axis and must be supported by sagrods, as illustrated in Figure 16.20.

16.7.1 Viewports

The wall sagrods are easiest to draw if you can concurrently select points from both the front and rightside views. Those two views are displayed in viewports as follows:

View <Pick> Tiled Viewports <pick> 2 Viewports <pick> Horizontal/<Vertical>: **v** (Vertical) <return>

AutoCAD divides the screen into two equal-size viewports, with the current screen displayed in each. The viewport enclosed by the heavier border is the current viewport. Move the cursor in that viewport and the familiar horizontal and vertical cursor lines will be displayed. Move the cursor into the other viewport and the cursor will be changed to a small arrow pointing in the northwest direction. To make that viewport the current one, press the <pick> button on the mouse.

   Make the viewport on the right side of the screen the current one by moving the cursor into it and pressing <pick>. The current UCS should be Rightside. Enter the following to display the plan view of the current UCS in the right viewport:

View <pick> 3D viewpoint Presets <pick> Plan View <pick> Current <pick>

AutoCAD will draw the Rightside UCS plan in the right viewport. Note that the view is zoomed to its limit. Use Zoom and Window to enlarge a view of the column similar to that illustrated in the right viewport in Figure 16.20. Pan the object to display the column, as shown, and make the left viewport current. Then display the plan view of the Front UCS in that viewport:

View <pick> Named UCS <Pick>

The UCS control dialog box (Figure 16.5) will be displayed. Choose FRONT in the list box and then click Current to make the Front UCS current. Click OK to close the dialog box. Then display the plan view of the current UCS. When the plan view is displayed, enlarge a view of the bay at the right end of the building similar to that illustrated in Figure 16.20 (sagrods haven't been drawn yet). When the Front UCS is the current one, the icon in the right viewport becomes a broken pencil, indicating that the UCS is on edge and that pointing to locations on that viewport might be meaningless.

The origin of the Front UCS is shown back in Figure 16.13. It will be easier to select points in the left viewport if the UCS origin (point 0,0,0) is moved to the bottom of the left column in the viewport. That column is three bays to the right of the current UCS origin, and the column spacing is 5500 mm, so the origin is to be moved 16500 mm (3×5500) along the x axis. Do this as follows:

View <pick> Set UCS <pick> Origin <pick> Origin point <0,0,0>: **16500,0,0** <return>

If the icon isn't at its origin (the center of the base of the column), pan the object as required to allow room for the icon at the origin. The x distances to the sagrods on the front wall are shown in the left viewport in Figure 16.20. (The locations are 150 mm left or right of the one-third points along the girts to facilitate the connection of the sagrod to the girt.) The z position of the sagrods is at the center of the girts, as shown in the right viewport in Figure 16.20. When drawing the sagrods, you must select the x,y coordinate in the left viewport, and the z coordinate in the right viewport. Click ORTHO on. Then draw the top row of sagrods as follows:

Draw <pick> Line <pick> From point: <shift>–<right> .XY <pick>

The .XY filter allows you to enter the x,y coordinates separately from the z coordinate. The x coordinate is 1980 mm (from Figure 16.20), and the y coordinate is determined by moving the cursor to a point slightly above the eave strut and reading the y coordinate from the monitor (press <ctrl>–D if the cursor coordinates aren't updated as the cursor is moved). I read the y coordinate as 5850. The entries continue as follows:

1980,5850 <return> (need Z): Move the cursor to the right viewport. <pick> Pick a point at the middle of the girt web. <pick> To point: Move the cursor to the left viewport. <pick> Digitize a point below the middle girt (Figure 16.20). <pick> To point: <return>

Recall the Line command by pressing <return>, and draw the next sagrod in the top row. The x coordinate is 3520 and the y coordinate is 5850. Use an .XY filter. Pick the z coordinate in the right viewport and draw the remaining sagrods shown in Figure 16.20. Don't add the dimensions to your drawing.

16.7.2 Back-wall girts and sagrods

The girts, eave strut, and sagrods on the front wall are copied to the back wall of the structure with the Mirror command. The mirror line is a vertical line through the center of the truss in the right-side view, and must be in the plane of the x,y axis. Use the Named UCS... command to make the Rightside UCS current. Then make the right viewport current and enter Zoom All to display a full view of the truss in the right viewport, then zoom 0.9x. If orthogonal mode isn't on, turn it on.

Use the Mirror command to mirror the girts, sagrods, and eave strut. When selecting the objects, select them in the left viewport using a crossing window. Use the right viewport and the MIDpoint object snap to select the mirror line at the center point of the truss bottom chord.

Restore the 3-D view in the right viewport to visually ensure that all the purlins, sagrods, and the eave strut were mirrored correctly (zoom as required). If necessary, use the U (Undo) command to undo enough commands to retry the Mirror command.

16.7.3 Roof sagrods

To draw the roof sagrods on the left side of the roof, you must display the plan view of the Topchordl UCS in the left viewport, and the plan view of the Rightside UCS in the right viewport. Zoom on the views as shown in Figure 16.21. (The left viewport illustrates the front half of the roof in the right-end bay of the building.) The current UCS is Rightside.

Set the current layer as SSTCL (SS top chord left), colored blue. Move the cursor into the right viewport and press <pick>, making that viewport current (displaying the Topchord UCS). Draw the horizontal sagrod connecting the two purlins at the roof peak as follows:

ORTHO <Orthogonal on> Draw <toolbar> Line <pick> From point: <shift>–<right> .XY <pick> of Digitize point a. <pick> (need Z): **–2900** <return> To point: <shift>–<right> .XY <pick> of Digitize point b. <pick> (need Z): **–2900** <return> To point: <return> ORTHO (orthogonal off)

The left viewport isn't used to select points. It acts as a visual reference so you can see that the sagrods are being installed correctly. Prior to drawing the sagrods along the sloping right side of the truss, rotate Snap parallel to the roof slope. Then turn the orthogonal mode on. Draw the sagrods by selecting the x,y coordinate from the right viewport and enter the z coordinate from the keyboard. The z coordinate is

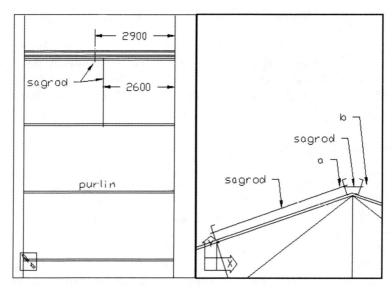

Figure 16.21 Roof sagrod viewports.

–2600 or –2900, as illustrated in Figure 16.21, to stagger the sagrods and allow room for their connections to the purlins. In order to draw the sagrods further down the slope of the roof, you have to pan the view in the right viewport to display the purlins that the sagrod spans between. Don't forget to draw the last sagrod connecting the eave strut and the lower purlin.

Set the current layer as SSTCR (SS top chord right), colored red. Draw the sagrods on the right side of the truss by displaying the plan view of the Topchordr UCS in the left viewport, and the plan view of the Rightside UCS in the right viewport. The current UCS should be Rightside. Zoom on the views similar to those shown in Figure 16.21. Turn the orthogonal mode off and rotate Snap parallel to the right side of the truss. Then turn the orthogonal mode on and draw the sagrods following the same procedure used for the other side of the roof.

Restore the 3-D view and ensure that everything drawn is correct before continuing. Leave the 3-D view on the screen. Rotate snap to a base of 0,0 and an angle of 0. Set the current layer as SS.

16.8 PGS (Purlins/Girts/Sagrods) Block

The girts, purlins, sagrods, and eave struts in the end bay are to be blocked and inserted into the bays of the building. In order to do so, you need a number of views of the structure. Use the Vport command to create four viewports:

View <pick> Tiled Viewports <pick> 1 Viewport <Pick> View <pick> Tiled Viewports <pick> 4 Viewports <pick>

Display the following in each viewport:

Upper left viewport. Roofplan UCS plan.

Lower left viewport. Front UCS plan. Zoom on the right-end bay to enlarge a view containing the end bay, including wall girts, purlins, wall and purlin sagrods, and the eave strut.

Upper right viewport. 3-D view. Zoom Extents, and then zoom magnification 0.9x.

Lower right viewport. Right-side UCS plan.

Before continuing, restore the Front UCS as the current UCS. Then create a block composed of the purlins, girts, sagrods, and eave struts in the end bay. The block insertion point is the lower left corner of the panel, which is a point 16,500 mm along the x axis. When asked to select the objects, use the Crossing option. The Crossing option is similar to the Window option, but it selects all objects within or crossing the window boundary. The commands are:

Draw <toolbar> Block <pick> Block name: **PGS** <return> Insertion base point: **16500,0,0** <return> Select objects: Make the lower left viewport current. Then pick a crossing window (pick left corner first) so the window sides cross the girts, eave strut, and purlins, and all wall sagrods are enclosed within the window. <pick> Select objects: Crossing <pick> 37 found Select objects: <return>.

If all of the girts, purlins, sagrods, and eave struts don't disappear from the screen, use U (Undo) to undo the Block command, and then retry the block entries.

Use the Minsert (Insert Multiple Blocks) command to insert the PGS block into the four bays of the structure. The insertion point is the Frontview UCS origin, point 0,0,0. The multiple insert is for one row and four columns spaced 5500 mm apart. The Front UCS was set as current before the PGS block was created. The block was then inserted, with Minsert, along the length of the building, which is the x axis of the Front UCS.

16.9 Bracing

Bracing is used in a structure to prevent the building from collapsing under horizontally applied loads, such as wind. It also prevents twisting and racking of the building, and must be installed on all planes of the structure.

Create the two viewports illustrated in Figure 16.22, then freeze layers SSTCL and SSTCR to provide a clear view of the bottom chord of the truss. Create two new layers named SSBCL (SS bottom chord left), colored blue, and SSBCR (SS bottom chord right), colored red. Draw the bottom chord bracing, shown in Figure 16.22. Bracing on the truss bottom chord along the front of the building is to be on layer SSBCL, and bracing along the back of the building is to be on layer SSBCR. Use the Zoom command in the View menu or XYZ filters to pick difficult points on the screen. Draw one panel of bracing, save it as a block, and use the Minsert command to insert it into the structure. Do the front and back bracing separately since they're to reside on different layers.

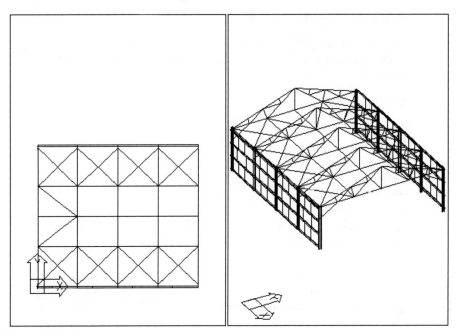

Figure 16.22 Bottom chord bracing.

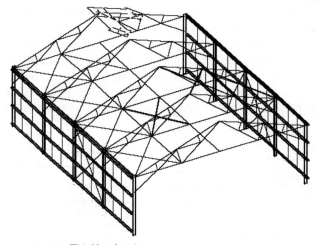

Figure 16.23 Third bay bracing.

The third bay of the building is to act as a rigid braced frame. Display the view named 3D in a single viewport, as illustrated in Figure 16.23, and add the side wall and truss top- and bottom-chord X bracing to the third bay of the structure. The bracing along the top and bottom chords of the truss extends across the full width of the building. In Figure 16.23, the SSTCL, SSTCR, and SSBCR layers are turned off for clarity. You must draw bracing on both sides of the bay. Table 16.1 lists the UCS to use when drawing the bracing, and the layer the bracing is to reside on.

TABLE 16.1 Third-bay Bracing

UCS	Layer	Comments
Front	SS	Front wall (use x, y filter, z = 0)
Rightside	SS	Back wall (mirror front bracing)
Roofplan	SSBCL	Truss bottom chord, left side
Roofplan	SSBCR	Truss bottom chord, right side
Topchordl	SSTCL	Truss top chord, left side (thaw layer SSTCL and turn layers SSBCL and SSBCR off to clear the clutter)
Topchordr	SSTCR	Truss top chord, right side (thaw layer SSTCR and turn layers SSBCL and SSBCR off to clear the clutter)

Complete the structure by adding the vertical sway frame to layer SS, connecting the third and fourth trusses. In order to draw the sway frame, move the Front UCS to point 11000,5800,–9000, creating the UCS shown in Figure 16.24. Draw the x-brace lines by entering x, y, z coordinates from the keyboard (the UCS origin is always point 0,0,0).

16.10 Multiview Drawing Using Viewports in Paper Space

Viewports in paper space behave very different from the viewports in model space used earlier in this chapter. The viewport feature allows you to create a multiview drawing by opening viewports in paper space and displaying different views in each viewport. This offers several advantages:

- The object is drawn full size in model space.
- You can create the drawing border and title block is in paper space for the plot sheet size without exiting the drawing.
- Each viewport opened in paper space can display a different view of the object.
- You can create a multiscale drawing by scaling the objects individually in each viewport.
- Viewports in paper space can overlap and can be edited with commands such as Move, Stretch, Erase, and Scale.
- A layer can be frozen in one viewport and visible in others.
- You can turn viewports off to plot a subset of viewports in a drawing.

16.10.1 Initial setup

Prior to entering paper space, make sure you're working with the following settings: You should currently be working in model space, indicated by the model space icon displayed on the screen, and you should have a single viewport open on the screen with the view named 3D displayed, as illustrated in Figure 16.24.

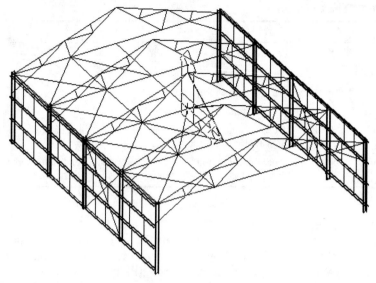

Figure 16.24 UCS Swayframe.

Use the UCS control box to restore the user coordinate system name FRONT. Turn on all of the working layers—SS, SSTCL, SSTCR, SSBCL, and SSBCR—and set layer SS as current.

16.10.2 Drawing the border in paper space

Enter paper space as follows:

View <pick> Paper Space <pick>

The paper space icon will be displayed in the lower left corner of the screen and the PAPER button will be turned on (displayed in bold text) in the status bar. The 3-D view displayed in model space is no longer on the screen. In order to see the view, you have to open a viewport.

If at any time you change the Tilemode system variable back to 1 by selecting View <pick> Tiled Model Space <pick>, the model space screen will return and the border, or any other items drawn in paper space, will no longer be displayed on the screen.

If you added the metric B-size (430 × 280 mm) or A3-size border option to your Border menu file in chapter 12, section 12.9, it will now be used to draw a border. (If you didn't create the B-size metric border, set the screen limits to 430 × 280 and draw one now.) Load the Border.mnu file as a base menu (for DOS, see chapter 11, section 11.9.1), or a partial menu (for Windows, see chapter 11, section 11.9.2). To load the Border menu as a partial menu, use the Customize Menu... option in the Tools menu to display the Menu Customization dialog box. Click the Browse command button and the Load command button to load C:\DRAWINGS\BORDER.MNU. Then highlight the BORDER.MNU file in the Menu Groups box and press the Menu

Bar tab to display the Menu Customization, Menu Bar dialog box. Highlight Easy1 in the Menus box, and then press Insert >> to transfer EASY1 to the Menu Bar box (and the menu bar). Then highlight File in the Menu Bar box and Title Block in the Menus box, and press Insert>> to transfer Title Block to the menu bar. Attach, Full Size, and Scale don't have to be transferred to the menu bar. Press the Close command button to exit the dialog box.

Click on Title Blk in the toolbar, then click on Metric and B Size. AutoCAD will insert the bm-hbdr.dwg file and invoke the attributes. Enter the requested data. The scale is to be entered as Noted.

If you loaded the Border menu as a full menu (in DOS), load AutoCAD's menu by choosing Acad-Mnu in your Easy1 menu. This isn't necessary if you loaded Border as a partial menu.

16.10.3 Viewports in paper space

In model space (Tilemode = 1), viewports function as outlined earlier in this chapter, by filling the graphics screen and lying side by side like tiles on a floor, so they're referred to as *tiled viewports*.

In paper space (Tilemode = 0), viewports behave quite different from those in model space. They might overlap and can be editing with commands such as Move, Stretch, Erase, and Scale. Because they don't have to lie side by side, they are referred to as *nontiled viewports*.

Tilemode is currently set to 0, making the working space paper space. Prior to opening a viewport, create a new layer named VIEWLYR1 (view layer 1) for the viewport to reside on. Set the color of VIEWLYR1 as magenta, and make VIEWLYR1 the current layer. The Layer Control box should show the current layer is VIEWLYR1.

A viewport is to be opened in the top left quadrant of the drawing to display the plan view of the building, as illustrated in Figure 16.25. When the viewport is initially opened, the 3-D view that was on the screen in model space is visible:

View <pick> Floating Viewports (Figure 16.26: note that Tiled Viewport, Model space option, is grayed out) <pick> 1 Viewport <pick> ON/OFF/Hideplot/Fit/2/ 3/ 4/Restore <First point>: <shift>–<right> Intersection <pick> of Place the intersection object snap on the top left corner of the drawing border. <pick> Other corner: Pick a point in approximately the middle of the screen so the viewport takes up about one quarter the screen space. The size isn't crucial as it can be modified as required. <pick>

16.10.4 Scaling the model

The roof plan of the building is to be displayed in the open viewport at a scale of 1:200. To change the UCS to ROOFPLAN and scale the model (object) in the viewport, you must set the working space to model space. Click on PAPER, changing it to MODEL in the status bar, or select Floating Model Space in the View menu. The model space icon is now at its origin in the viewport, indicating that the current working space is model space. Move the cursor on the screen, observing that the standard cursor is displayed within the viewport and the cursor becomes an arrow

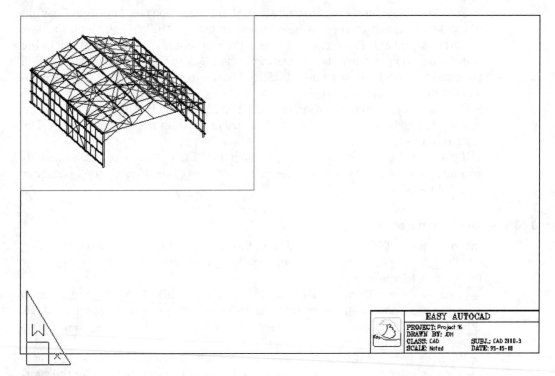

Figure 16.25   Viewport 1.

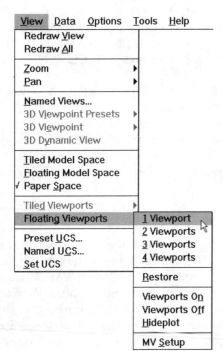

Figure 16.26   Opening a viewport in paper space.

when moved outside of the viewport. Also note that the drawing limits apply only within the viewport, which is the current working screen.

Set the current UCS to Roofplan, and display a plan view of the current UCS, Roofplan. The model space plan view is to be drawn to a scale of 1:200. Since the units of paper space and model space are both millimeters, enter the scale as ½₀₀x paper spaces:

View <pick> Zoom <pick> Scale <pick> All/Center/Dynamic/Extents/
Left/Previous/Vmax/Window/<Scale (x/xp)>: **1/200xp** <return>

The plan view of the structure in the viewport is now complete in the open viewport.

16.10.5 Copying a viewport

Now you need to create a viewport to display the front view of the building. To open or edit a viewport, the working space must be paper space, so change the working space to paper space. Don't continue until the paper space icon is displayed in the lower left corner of the screen.

Instead of opening another viewport, copy the current viewport to the desired location (although either procedure is acceptable). You can select the Copy command from the screen menu or the pull-down menu. Copy the viewport using the pull-down menu as follows (or use Edit from the screen menu):

Modify <toolbar> Copy Object <pick> Select objects: Pick a point on the magenta-colored viewport window. The viewport window should become dotted. <pick> Select objects: <return> <Base point or displacement>/Multiple: <shift>–<right> Intersection <pick> of Place the object snap selection box on the lower left corner of the viewport window. <pick> Second point of displacement: <shift>–<right> Intersection <pick> of Select the lower left corner of the drawing border. <pick>

The drawing should appear as shown in Figure 16.27. Notice that the viewports overlap, hence the paper space viewports are referred to as *nontiled*.

The new viewport currently displays the plan view of the Roofplan UCS. In order to modify the model to display the plan view of the Front UCS in the new viewport, the working space must be model space, so change the working space to model space. The model space icon must be displayed in each viewport before you continue.

Pick a point in the bottom left viewport to make it current. When the cursor is located in the lower left viewport, the standard crosshair cursor will be displayed. Move the cursor outside the current viewport and it will become an arrow, indicating you're outside of the current model space viewport.

Set the current UCS to Front, then display the plan view of the Front UCS in the current viewport. Following the procedure outlined in section 16.10.4, scale the model to ½₀₀x paper space.

16.10.6 Stretching a viewport

The lower left viewport displays the plan view of the Front UCS. The viewport is larger than it need be, so you can stretch it to a more appropriate size. Since view-

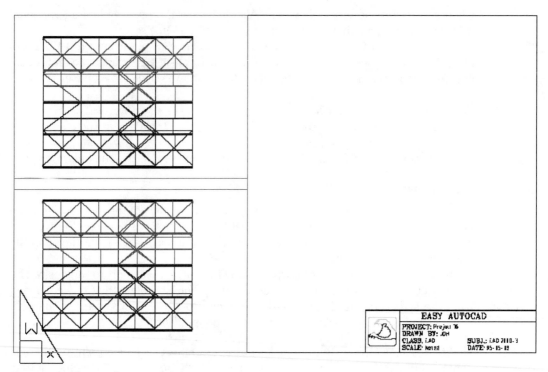

Figure 16.27 Viewport 2.

ports reside in paper space, you must change working space to paper space before editing the viewport.

The stretch command requires you to select the objects to be stretched, with a crossing window or polygon. When selecting a viewport, you must include both a horizontal and vertical viewport window line in the crossing window:

Modify <toolbar> Stretch <pick> Select object to stretch by crossing window or polygon...Select objects: Select a point so the crossing window crosses only the top and right-side lines of the lower left viewport window, picking the left point of the window first to invoke a crossing window. <pick> Other corner: Select the other corner of the crossing window. The viewport window should become dotted. <pick> Select object:

If the viewport window for the top viewport is dotted, or if the drawing border is dotted, select the Remove command and then pick a point on those lines to remove them from the selection set. To return to the Add mode, enter **a**. Complete the selection as follows:

Select objects: <return> Base point or displacement: Pick a point on the top line of the window for the front view viewport. <pick> Second point of displacement: Pick a point where you want the top line of the viewport to be relocated (Figure 16.28). <pick>

If you want to retry the Stretch command, enter **U** to undo the last command and then reenter the Stretch command. Then copy the lower left viewport to the right side of the border. Display the plan view of the Rightside UCS in the viewport and scale it to a scale of 1:200. The viewport should appear similar to the one illustrated in Figure 16.28 (minus the alignment line, and your working space is still model space).

16.10.7 Aligning models in viewports

Set the working space to paper space before continuing (also, see hint 36 in appendix D). You'll be aligning the top and front, and the front and right-side views of the building following orthographic projection standards in drafting. Create a new layer, Align, set its color as green, and make it the current layer.

Draw the alignment line along the left side and across the bottom of the drawing, as shown in Figure 16.28. Align the front view in the lower left viewport by moving the viewport so point 1 in Figure 16.29 is located at the intersection of the alignment lines at point 2. Zoom on a window encompassing the alignment lines, the bottom line of the viewport window, and the lower left corner of the front view of the build-

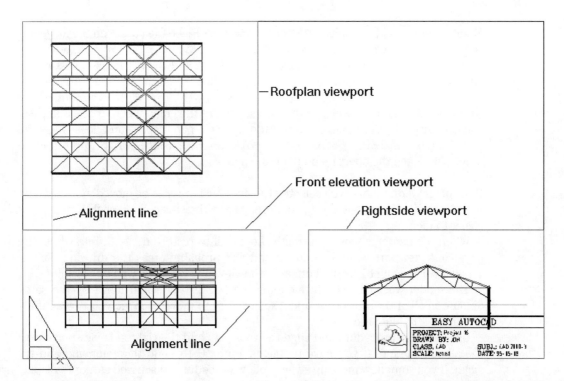

Figure 16.28 Viewports.

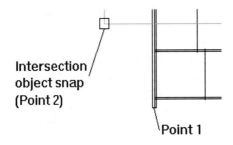

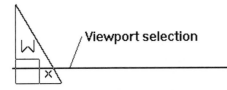

Viewport selection

Figure 16.29 Alignment of front view.

ing, illustrated in Figure 16.29. The window should be tight enough so you'll have no difficulty placing the cursor on point 1, which is the center of the column base, and point 2 at the corner of the green lines. If the bottom of the viewport window isn't displayed, use the Pan command to pan the view up slightly. Then move the viewport as follows:

Modify <toolbar> Move <pick> Select objects: Place the cursor on the magenta-colored viewport window and press <ctrl> and <pick>. <Cycle on> Select objects: If the magenta line isn't dotted, you've selected the border, so press <ctrl> and <pick>. Select objects: If the magenta line is dotted, press <return>. <Cycle off> Select objects: <return> Base point or displacement: Very carefully select point 1, which is the intersection of the column center line and base. You can't use an object snap because AutoCAD is in paper space and doesn't see the model. <pick> Second point of displacement: <shift>-<right> Intersection <pick> of Place the aperture on point 2. <pick>

If the object didn't move, you selected the drawing border to be moved, not the viewport. Enter **U** (Undo) and try again. Perhaps pan the viewport up slightly, making it easier to pick.

When the model is moved correctly, Zoom All to restore the entire drawing. The lower left viewport will have moved and will probably cross the drawing border. When layer Viewlyr1 is turned off later, the viewport windows won't be visible.

The model wasn't moved in model space because it would move by the same amount in all of the viewports, and it's necessary to move each viewport by a different amount to align the models.

Use a similar procedure and align the roof plan and the right-side viewports with the alignment line. If you have problems, enter **U** to undo the command and try again. If you somehow mess up a view, follow procedures discussed earlier to display the proper plan view and scale the view with respect to paper space. Once the viewports are aligned, if you must move one, move the adjacent one concurrently to maintain the alignment.

Set the current layer to Viewlyr1 and freeze the Align layer. The current working space is to be paper space. The drawing should appear as illustrated in Figure 16.30 (minus the 3D and sway frame viewport).

Once the viewports are aligned, save each view so you can restore it if it gets out of alignment. Set model space on and click in the roofplan viewport, making it current. Then save the view following the procedures outlined in chapter 14, section 14.15. Follow the same procedure to name the Front and Rightside views. You can restore a named view at any time using the Restore option.

Use Floating Viewports in the View menu to open 1 Viewport for the 3-D view by selecting the viewport window boundaries to match those in Figure 16.30. Use the Named View... option in the View menu to display the 3-D view. The scale for the 3-D view is to be 1:300. Pan the view in the viewport and/or stretch the viewport as required to display the entire 3-D view.

Open a viewport in the top right corner of the border to display a side view of the roof in the Front UCS, as illustrated in Figure 16.30. The scale is 1:200. Stretch the viewport (in paper space) so the sway frame bracing fits within the viewport, as shown. If you zoom on the viewport to stretch it, you'll have to include enough of the viewport to be able to select it with the Stretch command's crossing window. You can edit viewports at any time, as required. In paper space, Zoom All to view the entire drawing in the border.

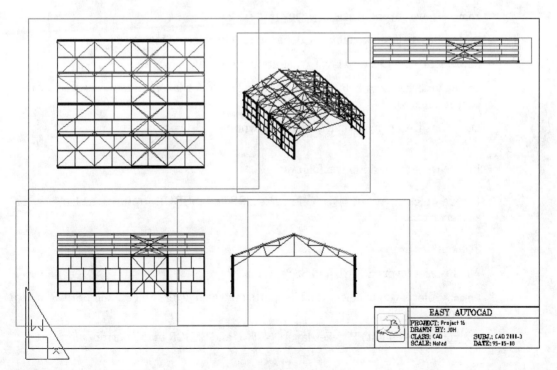

Figure 16.30 Final viewports.

16.10.8 Controlling layer visibility in viewports

The On/Off and Freeze/Thaw options of the Layer command set the visibility of layers globally, in all viewports. The Vplayer command allows you to set layer visibility by viewport, so a layer can be off in one viewport and on in other viewports.

The Plan view of the building (refer back to Figure 16.1) should display bracing and purlins in the top half of the plan (on the top chord of the truss) and bracing in the bottom half of the plan (on the bottom chord of the truss). You can do this by using the VPlayer command to turn layers SSBCR and SSTCL off in the viewport displaying the Plan view. These layers should be turned off in the Side Elevation and 3D View, as well. In the Cross Section, layers SSBCR and SSTCL should be turned on.

Using the Layer Control box in the Object Properties toolbar, turn layers SS, SSTCL, SSBCL, SSTCR, and SSBCR on. You can invoke the VPlayer command in either model or paper space. If the current working space is model space, AutoCAD will switch to paper space when VPlayer is invoked, and return to model space after the command is exited. Enter the Vplayer command as follows:

Data <pick> Viewport Layer Controls <pick>

Options for the Vplayer command are:

Freeze. Freezes layers in selected viewports.

Thaw. Thaws layers in selected viewports.

Reset. Resets layer visibility to global setting in selected viewports.

New Freeze. Creates new layers that are frozen in all viewports.

Default Visibility. Sets default frozen thawed state for layers in new viewports when they're created.

List. Lists frozen layers in a selected viewport.

Invoke the Freeze option as follows:

Freeze <pick> `Layer(s) to Freeze:` **SSTCL,SSBCR** <return> `All/Select/` `<Current>:`

The options are:

All. Freezes layers SSTCL and SSBCR in all viewports.

Select. Allows you to select the viewports on which layers SSTCL and SSBCR are to be frozen.

Current. (the default) Freezes layers SSTCL and SSBCR in the current viewport.

Enter Select to select viewports in which layers SSTCL and SSBCR are to be frozen:

s (Select) <return> `Select objects:` Pick each of the following viewport windows in which layer SSTCL is to be frozen (see view titles in Figure 16.1: Plan, Side Elevation, 3D View, Sway Frame). <pick> `Select object:` <return> `?/Freeze/` `Thaw/Reset/Newfrz/Vpvisdfit:`

Freeze layers SSTCR and SSBCL in the viewport containing the Sway Frame view. Press <return> to exit the command. The viewports should appear as shown back in Figure 16.1.

16.10.9 Dimensioning in viewports

As discussed in chapter 4, section 4.4, the dimension variable Dimscale (overall scale) is a global factor applied to all numeric dimension variables. If Dimscale is set to 0.0, AutoCAD will compute a reasonable value for Dimscale for each viewport, based on the scaling between the current model space viewport and paper space. The height of dimension text, for instance, will be 2.5 mm (the default value for the dimension text height when the metric measurement system is set; see chapter 6, section 6.12) in the *plotted* drawing, regardless of the zoom scale used for the model in the viewport. If you set Scale to Paper Space on, the Overall Scale option in the Geometry dialog box won't be available and, for dimensions done in paper space, AutoCAD will calculate the numeric dimension variables as though Dimscale were 1.0.

The drawing unit precision was set to 0 at the start of the drawing, but some of the dimension variable values are set one digit to the right of the decimal and will be confusing in the dimension dialog boxes if the drawing units aren't set to 0.0. Display the Units Control dialog box and set Units Precision to 0.0.

Display the Dimension Style dialog box, illustrated in Figure 16.31, and make the settings that are shown. Then press the Geometry... command button to display the geometry dialog box, illustrated in Figure 16.32. Press the Scale to Paper Space button on. When Scale to Paper Space is on, the overall scale (Dimscale) is set to 0 by AutoCAD and can't be modified. Set the color of dimension lines and extension lines to BYBLOCK. When set to bylock, the block (dimension object) is the color that's current when the block (dimension object) is inserted. Complete the settings as shown and press OK to return to the Dimension Style dialog box.

Press the Format... command button to display the Format dialog box shown in Figure 16.33. Make the settings shown and then press OK to return to the Dimension Style dialog box.

Press the Annotation... command button to display the Annotation dialog box illustrated in Figure 16.34. Make the settings shown, noting that the text color is BYBLOCK. Press the Units... command button to display the Primary Units dialog box shown in Figure 16.35. Set the Units to Decimal and the Dimension Precision to 0. In the Scale box, you can set a linear scale so all dimensions read by AutCAD are multiplied by that value. If the Paper Space Only button is on, AutoCAD will apply the Linear scale factor to dimensions done in paper space, hence you could dimension model space objects in paper space by setting an appropriate linear scale factor. Exit both dialog boxes, returning to the Dimension Style dialog box.

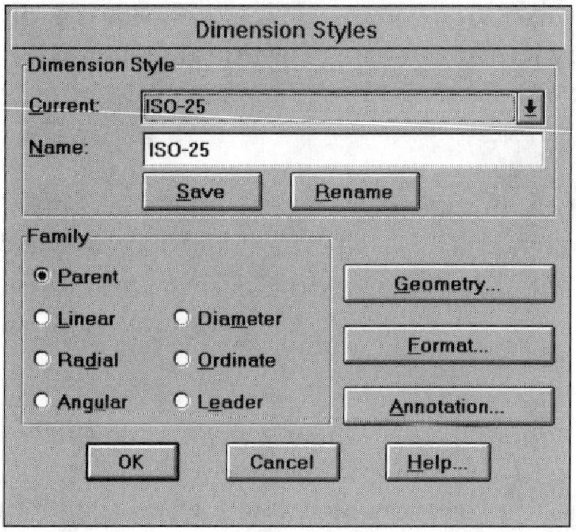

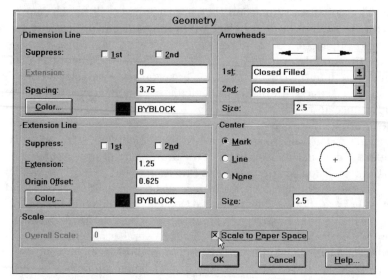

Figure 16.31 Dimension style settings.

Figure 16.32 Scaling dimension objects to paper space scale.

Press the Save command button (Figure 16.31) to save the dimension settings to the ISO-25 style. Then press OK.

16.10.10 Creating viewport dimensioning layers

It isn't usually desirable to have dimensions that were drawn on a specific view show up on other views. You can use the Vplayer command's Newfrz (new freeze) option to create new layers frozen in all viewports. You can then thaw the layers in specific viewports as required.

Create dimension layers for each view using the following layer names: DimT (top view), DimF (front view), DimRS (right side) and DimSF (sway frame). Freeze the layers on all layers, then thaw layer Dimt for the Roof Plan (top view) as follows:

Data <pick> Viewport Layer Controls <pick> New Freeze <pick> `?/Freeze/Thaw/`
`Reset/Newfrz/Vpvisdfit: _n New Viewport frozen layer name(s):`
dimt,dimf,dimrs,dimsf <return> `?/Freeze/Thaw/Reset/Newfrz/Vpvisdfit:` **t** (Thaw)
<return> `Layer(s) to Thaw:` **dimt** <return> `All/Select/<Current>:` **s** (Se-
lect) <return> `Select objects:` Pick a point on the viewport window for the roof
plan. <pick> `Select  objects:` <return> `?/Freeze/Thaw/Reset/Newfrz/`
`Vpvisdfit:` <return>

Use the Layer Control dialog box to set the color of layers Dimt, Dimf, Dimrs, and
Dimsw to black (or white). Set Dimt as the current layer.

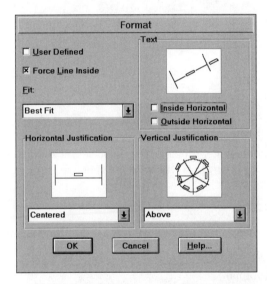

Figure 16.33 Format settings.

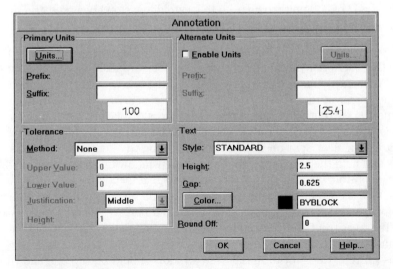

Figure 16.34 Annotation settings.

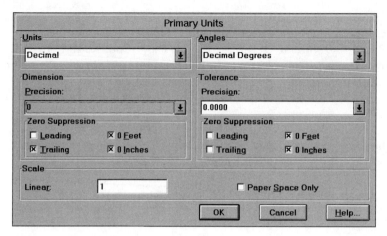

Figure 16.35 Primary dimension units settings.

16.10.11 Dimensioning the roof plan

Dimt should be displayed in the Object Properties toolbar as the current layer. In order to dimension the roof plan, it will have to be zoomed on the screen. If you use the zoom command while in model space, the selected area will be zoomed only in its viewport. In order to zoom on the viewport, the working space must be paper space. Do the following:

1. Change the working space to paper space.
2. Zoom on the Roof Plan viewport window, allowing space for dimensioning.
3. Change the working space to model space.
4. Set the current UCS to Roofplan.
5. Set a grid of 300 units to be used to locate dimension lines. The grid might not be visible until you zoom in on a smaller area.

Now you have to add the horizontal dimension 7 Bays @ 5500 = 38500 to the roof plan. Use the Aerial View window to assist in selecting the first point of the extension line. First, check that the current viewport is the one with the roof plan in it by moving the cursor in that viewport. If the cursor is an arrow, click in the viewport. The viewport is current when the standard cursor is displayed. Next, if the aerial viewport isn't displayed, click on its icon in the standard toolbar. Move the Aerial View window to a clear spot on the screen by placing the cursor into its title box; then press and hold the pick button and move the window by sliding the cursor. Release the pick button when the window is in the correct location.

In DOS, there's no Aerial View window, so you have to use Zoom Window, Zoom Previous, and Pan to locate points. If Zoom and Pan are selected in the View menu, they're transparent and you can invoke them from inside another command without causing AutoCAD to cancel the command.

The current view in the Aerial View window should be the one shown in Figure 16.36 (minus the Zoom window). Now start the dimensioning:

Dimensioning <toolbar> Linear Dimensions <pick> `First extension line ori-gin or RETURN to select:`

Move the cursor into the Aerial View window and place a window around the lower left column, as shown by the dotted rectangle in Figure 16.36. When the second corner of the Zoom window is picked, the windowed area is displayed (enlarged) on the drawing screen. Move the cursor back onto the drawing screen, press <pick>, and continue:

`First extension line origin or RETURN to select:` Digitize a point in line with the column center line in front of the column (Figure 16.1). <pick> `Second extension line origin:`

Move the cursor into the Aerial View window and place a window around the front part of the plan, as shown in Figure 16.37. When the second corner of the Zoom window is picked, the windowed area is displayed on the drawing screen. Continue the dimension:

`Second extension line origin:` Pick a point to the right of the roof plan (Figure 16.1). <pick> `Dimension line location (Text/Angle/Horizontal/Vertical/Rotated):` **t** (text) <return>

The Edit Mtext dialog box, illustrated in Figure 16.38, will be displayed. (You might get a Select Font dialog box first. If you do, select a font, such as Aerial, from the

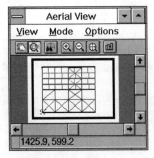

Figure 16.36 Zoom in—aerial view.

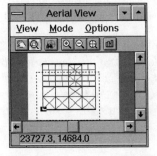

Figure 16.37 Zoom out—aerial view.

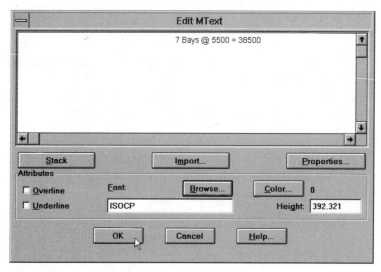

Figure 16.38 Mtext dialog box.

drop-down box and press OK.) In DOS, you'll enter the text at the command line. Enter the text **7 Bays @ 5500 = 38500**, as shown. Make sure the angle brackets, <>, are not included in the text or AutoCAD will insert the dimension read at the location of the brackets. Press OK. AutoCAD will continue with:

```
Dimension  line  location  (Text/Angle/Horizontal/Vertical/  Ro-
tated): Pick the dimension line location using grid points (2 or 3 grid units).
<pick>
```

The completed dimension will have an extension line on the right-hand side, which isn't correct. Remove it as follows (in DOS, select Data, then Object Creation):

Object Properties <toolbar> Properties <pick> `Select objects:` Pick a point on the last dimension. <pick> `Select objects:` <return>

The Modify Dimension dialog box, illustrated in Figure 16.39, will be displayed. Press the Geometry... command button to display the dimension Geometry dialog box. In the Extension Line box, press the Suppress 2nd box on, as shown in Figure 16.40. Press OK to exit both dialog boxes. The dimension will be regenerated without the second extension line.

Add the remaining dimensions to the roof plan. You can locate dimension extension line points by using the Aerial View window or transparent zooms, or entering real or relative coordinates. Don't add the view's title and scale yet. You can add the column row numbers (in circles) in paper space later. Add the center line (see Figure 16.1), then set the linetype scale to paper space and the scale value to 10:

Options <pick> Linetypes <pick>

If Paper Space Linetype Scale doesn't have a check mark beside it, click on it and then redisplay the Linetypes menu. The menu will return with a tick beside Paper Space Linetype Scale, as shown in Figure 16.41, indicating that scaling of linetypes is to be based on the paper space scale and will appear the same in all viewports regardless of the model scale in the viewport. Click on Global Linetype Scale to set the overall scale. AutoCAD will continue with (the 10 is determined by trial):

```
New scale factor <1>: 10 <return>
```

When the dimensions are complete on the roof plan, view Roofplan with the Named Views dialog box to ensure it's realigned with the other views. Then dimension the other views, as shown in Figure 16.1. Prior to dimensioning in a new viewport, complete the following sequence:

1. Set the working space to paper space.
2. Zoom on the desired viewport(s) (you might want to include part of an adjacent viewport to ensure the dimension lines are in line in each view).
3. Set the working space to model space.
4. Set the viewport as current by picking a point in it.
5. Set the appropriate UCS.
6. Set the dimension layer visibility (see the following).
7. Set the dimension layer as current.
8. Set a grid (300) to use for locating dimension lines.

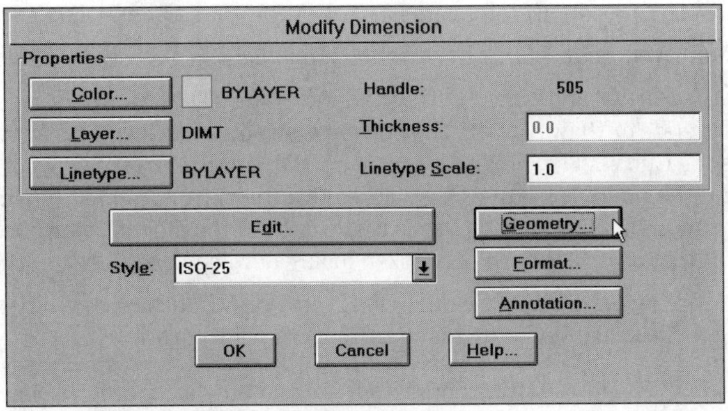

Figure 16.39 Editing dimension objects.

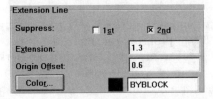

Figure 16.40 Suppressing an extension line.

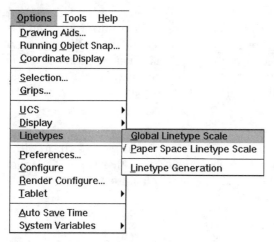

Figure 16.41 Setting the linetype scale factor in paper space.

Prior to dimensioning the Side Elevation (front UCS), set it as the current viewport. Then thaw layer DIMF (dimension front view) for the current viewport and set it as the current layer. All other layers should be frozen in the current viewport.

You can set the viewport layer visibility using either the Vplayer command, as illustrated in section 16.10.10, or the Layer Control dialog box. Set the layer visibility for the current viewport with the Layer Control dialog box, as follows:

1. Display the Layer Control dialog box, illustrated in Figure 16.42. Using the slider bar, display the listings for layers DIMF, DIMRS, DIMSF, and DIMT in the list box.

2. Click on layer name DIMF in the list box, highlighting its row.

3. Note the Cur VP and New VP Thw and Frz boxes. They allow you to set the visibility (freeze or thaw) of both the current viewport and viewports not yet created. Press the Cur VP Thw box, thawing layer DIMF in the current viewport (the front view of the building). AutoCAD will remove the C from the list box in the DIMF layer row, indicating that the layer isn't frozen in the current viewport. The N indicates that layer DIMF will be frozen in any new viewports created.

4. Make sure layers DIMRS, DIMSF, DIMT, and CENTER have the letter C in their listing, indicating they're frozen in the current viewport.

Note that the C and N settings apply only to the current viewport. These settings might change as different viewports are selected as current, and will probably be different in paper space. You can also set viewport layer visibility in Windows' Layer Control box.

In model space it's often difficult to zoom on a desired view, particularly when dimensioning. If you're confronted with that problem, set the working space to paper space, zoom tightly on the largest view you want, and then return the working space to model space. When dimensioning, use the Aerial View window and/or transparent zooms as required to select points, and use Zoom Previous to return to the original display. After dimensioning a viewport, restore the named view to return the original (aligned) view.

When dimensioning is complete, change the working space to paper space. Enter Zoom All to zoom on the entire drawing. Don't add the text to the drawing yet, since text is usually added in paper space.

Freeze layer Viewlyr1 to make the viewport windows invisible, turn the grid off in model space, set the current working space to paper space, and add text to the drawing in paper space on a layer named Txt. In paper space, the screen limits are the plot sheet size and the text height is the actual text height for the plot, which is 2.5 mm. Titles should be 4 mm in height. Create a block with attributes for the column row marks, and plot the drawing in paper space on a B-size (or A3) sheet using a scale of 1=1.

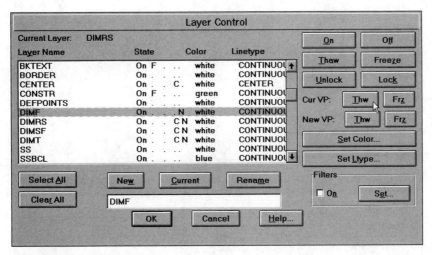

Figure 16.42 Setting viewport layer visibility.

17

Solid Three-Dimensional Modeling

Objective: Create a solid, three-dimensional model using AutoCAD's solid modeling commands, render the solid model, create a cross section of the model, complete an orthographic projection drawing of the three-dimensional model, plot to a DXB file, and use apparent intersection object snaps.

Drawing: Boot AutoCAD. In the Preference dialog box, set the measurement to English and the drawing type to Standard Imperial. Begin a new drawing named C:\DRAWINGS\PROJ-17. You'll be drawing a solid, 3-D model of the control block from chapter 5 (refer to Figure 5.1), with some minor modifications.

17.1 Solid Modeling

Solid 3-D models are constructed with the building-block approach. You create a basic solid primitive, such as a box, cube, cylinder, sphere, torus, cone, wedge, or a solid, by sweeping a polyline about an axis. Then you add (union) or subtract solid objects, creating a complex 3-D solid model. AutoCAD solids are represented by boundaries and edges, so a hole in the solid isn't seen by AutoCAD as a hole, but something defined by a boundary. Consequently, while you can edit an object in the solid using most standard AutoCAD commands, such as Move, Copy, Mirror, Rotate, Fillet, Trim, and Extend, you can't stretch it. If you want to change the dimensions of a solid object, e.g., a hole in a solid object, you must erase the hole and redraw it.

The solid model is initially displayed as a wireframe model. It can be meshed so the surfaces appear as a series of planar faces, and you can remove hidden lines with the Hide command.

You can also create cross sections and slice the solid. AutoCAD doesn't have a command to create a profile (2-D geometric shapes from the 3-D model), but a procedure will be illustrated to construct the orthographic projection engineering drawing (see Figure 17.1).

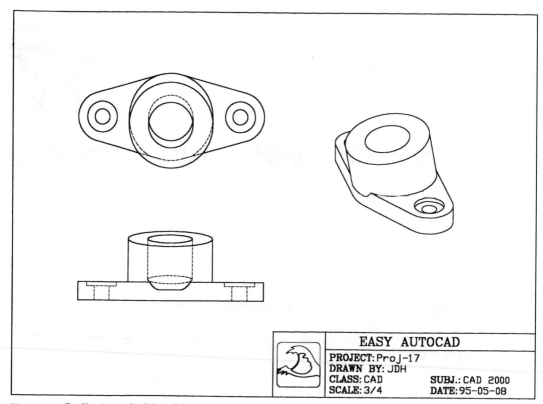

Figure 17.1 Profile views of solid model.

17.2 Creating an Extruded Solid Primitive

You'll be drawing the 3-D model of the control block shown back in chapter 5 in Figure 5.1, with some alterations. Set the drawing limits at 0,0 and 11,8 and the drawing units as decimal with three digits to the right of the decimal. The current working space is to be model space. Create a new layer named Object and make it the current layer.

Begin drawing the base of the control block by drawing a 2.125-unit-diameter circle with its center at coordinates 4,6. Then draw a 0.6-unit-radius circle with its center at coordinates 2.25,6. Use the Line command and the Tangent object snap to draw a line tangent to the top of both circles, and another line tangent to the bottom of both circles.

Use the Mirror command and the Center object snap, with ORTHO on, to mirror the small circle, plus the tangency lines, about the center of the large circle. Using the Trim command, trim the arcs to create the base shape illustrated in Figure 17.2. To convert the base into a solid, you'll have to change it into a polyline:

Modify <toolbar> Edit Polyline <pick> Select polyline: **w** (Window) <return> First point: Pick a corner of a window enclosing the shape. <pick> Second point: Pick the other corner of the window. <pick> Object selected is not a

```
polyline. Do you want to turn it into one?<Y>: <return> Close/
Join/Width/Edit vertex/Fit/Spline/Decurve/Ltype gen/Undo/eXit<X>:
```
j (Join) <return> Select each of the entities making up the shape, following a clockwise order around the shape. <pick> <return>
```
7 segments added to polyline: Open/Join/Width/Edit vertex/Fit/
Spline/Decurve/Ltype gen/Undo/eXit <X>: <return>
```

In Windows, load the Solids menu shown in Figure 17.3. The Isolines system variable defines the number of tessellation lines AutoCAD uses to visualize curved portions of solids. A reasonable value for Isolines is 12:

```
Command: Isolines <return> New value for ISOLINES <4>: 12 <return>
```

You use the Extrude command to create a unique solid object by extruding two-dimensional objects (closed polygons, circles, ellipses, closed splines, donuts, and regions) along a specified path. You can't extrude objects contained within a block

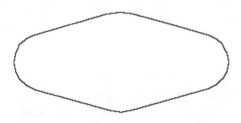

Figure 17.2 Initial base shape.

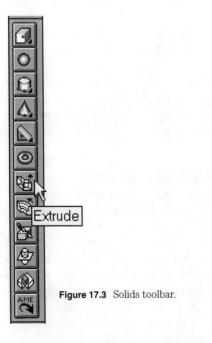

Figure 17.3 Solids toolbar.

and polylines that have crossings or self-intersecting segments. You can enter the height of the extrusion or point to an object, such as a line, circle, arc, ellipse, polyline, or spline, defining the path for the extrusion. If you specify the extrusion as a height, you can taper the sides of the extrusion.

The base of the control block is to be 0.45 units in height. Invoke the Extrude command (Figure 17.3) as follows (in DOS, select Draw, then Solids, then Extrude):

Solids <toolbar> Extrude <pick> Select objects: Select a point on the polyline. <pick> 1 found, Select objects: <return> Path/<Height of extrusion>: **0.45** <return> Extrusion taper angle <0>: <return>

Then change the viewing angle to obtain a 3-D view of the solid model as follows:

View <pick> 3D View Point <pick> Rotate <pick>

The Viewpoint Presets dialog box will be displayed. Set the x axis to 330 and the xy plane to 30. Press OK to exit the dialog box. Then use the View Control dialog box to name the view 3D so you can restore it at any time.

17.3 Creating a Cylinder

You can produce a solid cylinder by extruding a circle with the Extrude command, or more directly by using the Cylinder command to draw a solid cylinder with either a circular or elliptical base. When drawing the cylinder, you can enter the center of the base and the center of the other end, thereby specifying the orientation of the cylinder.

Construct a 2.125-unit-diameter, 1.25-unit- high cylinder on the base with the Cylinder command, as follows (in DOS, select Draw, then Solids, then Cylinder):

Solids <toolbar>Center (cylinder, Figure 17.4) <pick> Center/Elliptical/ <Center point><0,0,0>: <shift>–<right> Center <pick> of Place the center object snap target on the 2.125-unit-diameter arc on the *top* surface of the base. <pick> Diameter/<Radius>: **d** <return> Diameter: **2.125** <return> Center of other end <Height>: **1.25** <return>

Holes are initially created as solids, which are later subtracted from the solid model. Draw the 0.75-unit-diameter × 0.1-unit-deep cylinder for the surface flush hole in the base as follows (make sure to enter the thickness as a negative value):

Solids <toolbar>Center (cylinder) <pick> Center/Elliptical/<Center point><0,0,0>: <shift>–<right> Center <pick> of Place the Center object snap target on the arc on the surface of the base at the right-hand side of the base. <pick> Diameter/<Radius>: **d** <return> Diameter: **0.75** <return> Center of other end <Height>: **–0.1** <return>

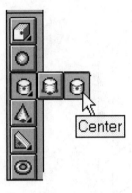

Figure 17.4 Cylinder flyout.

Use the Cylinder command to add the 0.375-unit-diameter × 0.35-unit-deep cylinder representing the hole extending from the bottom of the last cylinder to the bottom of the base. Then, using the Copy command, copy the two cylinders from the right side of the base 3.5 units to the left side of the base to complete the cylinders shown in Figure 17.5.

Add the 1.125-unit-diameter × 1.00-unit-deep cylinder representing the hole in the center cylinder of the model.

17.4 Repositioning Solid Objects

You can use most of the AutoCAD repositioning commands, such as Copy, Mirror, Move, and Rotate, to modify the solid. For example, you need to rotate the cylinder on the top of the base ten degrees from the vertical, as shown in Figure 17.6. Prior to modifying the model, create a UCS named Center, with its origin on the top surface of the base, at the center of the 2.125-unit-diameter cylinder, as follows:

View <pick> Set UCS <pick> Origin <pick> Origin/ZAxis/3point/Object/View/ X/Y/Z/Prev/Restore/Save/Del/?/<World>:_o Origin point <0,0,0>: <shift>–<right> Center <pick> of Place the Center object snap aperture on the circumference of the 2.125-unit-diameter cylinder at the elevation of the surface of the base unit. <pick> View <pick> Named UCS... <pick>

The Named UCS Control dialog box will be displayed. Name the current UCS Center. The Center UCS is to act as a reference origin and you can restore it any time in the UCS Control dialog box (Figure 16.5) by choosing Named UCS... and Current. Remember to press the Rename To button before exiting the dialog box (review chapter 16, section 16.2.2). If the UCS icon doesn't move to its origin, enter the following commands:

Options <pick> UCS <pick> Icon Origin <pick>

The cylinder is rotated 10 degrees toward the front of the control block, as illustrated in Figure 17.6. The rotation point is on the surface of the base at the point where the

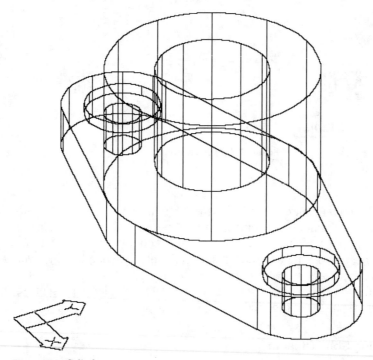

Figure 17.5 Cylinders.

center line of the 2.125-unit-diameter cylinder crosses its circumference at the back of the base. This point is the location of the UCS, illustrated in Figure 17.6.

Create a new UCS with its origin at the origin point for the movement (rotation). The rotation point origin is 1.063 units (2.125 / 2) along a line 90 degrees from the Center UCS origin. The UCS will also have to be rotated. Save the new UCS with the name Rotate and construct it as follows:

View <pick> Set UCS <pick> Origin <pick> Origin/ZAxis/3point/OBject/View/ X/Y/Z/Prev/Restore/Save/Del/?/<World>:_o Origin point <0,0,0>: **1.063<90** <return> View <pick> Set UCS <pick> X Axis Rotate <pick> Origin/ZAxis/3point/OBject/View/X/Y/Z/Prev/Restore/Save/Del/?/<World>:_x Rotation angle about X axis <0>: **90** <return> View <pick> Set UCS <pick> Y Axis Rotate <pick> Origin/ZAxis/3point/OBject/View/X/Y/Z/Prev/Restore/Save/Del/?/<World>:_y Rotation angle about Y axis <0>: **90** <return> View <pick> Named UCS... <pick>

The Named UCS Control dialog box will be displayed. Name the current UCS as Rotate. Then use the Rotate command to rotate the cylinders as follows:

Modify <toolbar> Rotate <pick> Select objects: Select a point on the 2.125-unit-diameter cylinder. <pick> Select objects: Pick a point on the "hole" in the cylinder. <pick> `Select objects:` <return> `Base point:` **0,0,0** <return> <Rotation angle>/Reference: **10** <return>

The cylinder and "hole" are now rotated 10 degrees in a positive direction (positive angles are measured in a counterclockwise direction) from the x axis, as shown in Figure 17-6.

17.5 Creating the Composite Solid

Composite solids are created by combining primitive solids. You can add solids to create a union, subtract them to form a composite solid, or combine them to define the new solid. The process of adding solids (Union command), subtracting solids (Subtract command), and finding the overlapping volume of solid objects (Intersect command) is a *Boolean* operation in which you form a new composite solid. You can undo Boolean operations with the Solsep command. Boolean operations create the composite solid on the current layer even if the primitives involved are on different layers.

The solid primitives for the control block have been located properly and are ready to be combined. First, add the base and cylinder of the control block to form a union, and subtract cylinders representing holes from the composite solid to form holes in the new composite solid. Then invoke the Union command (Figure 17.7) to add the base and the cylinder as follows (in DOS, select Construct, then Union):

Modify <toolbar> Union <pick> `Select objects:` Select the shaft. <pick> `Select objects:` Select the base. <pick> `Select objects:` <return>

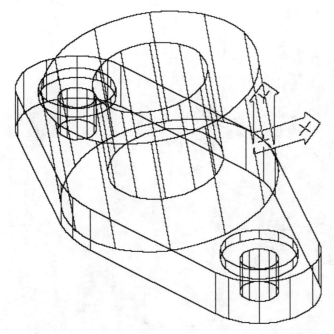

Figure 17.6 Rotation of cylinder.

Subtract the holes using the Subtract command as follows:

Modify <toolbar> Subtract <pick> Solids and regions to subtract from...
Select objects: Pick a point on the base or shaft (which is one unit). <pick> 1
found, Select objects: <return> Select solids or regions to subtract... Select objects: Carefully digitize the five holes. <pick> <return>

When the Boolean operations are completed, regenerate the model on the screen, as
illustrated in Figure 17.8.

Figure 17.7 Union tool.

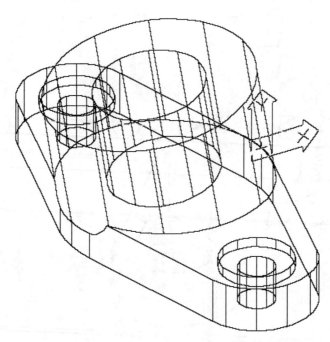

Figure 17.8 Composite solid.

17.6 Rendering the Solid Model

The solid model is currently represented as a wireframe model. Although you can invoke the Hide command, the hidden line view is composed of a number of 3-D faces that might not produce the desired effect. If the Render toolbar (Figure 17.9) isn't visible on the screen, display it by using the Tool Windows tool in the standard toolbar (refer to section A.1 in appendix A). Invoke the Hide command using the Hide tool, as shown in Figure 17.9 (in DOS, select Tools, then Hide).

You can shade the solid using the Shade command, which will produce a more realistic image of the object. Shade simulates a light source directly in front of the screen. It's affected by the angle (view) of the object on the screen, and the setting of the Shadedif and Shadedge system variables. The higher the value of Shadedif, the greater the contrast between light and dark on the image. The following values apply to Shadedge:

Shadedge	Effect
0	No edge highlighting.
1	Edges highlighted in the background color.
2	Colors surfaces of polygons in background color and visible edges in object's color.
3	Colors surfaces in original color and edges in background color; no lighting effect.

Enter the following commands (in DOS, select Tools, then Shade):

Command: **Shadedif** <return> New value for SHADEDIF: **100** <return>
Command: **Shadedge** <return> New value for SHADEDGE: **1** <return>
Render <toolbar> Shade <pick>

The shaded drawing is illustrated in Figure 17.10. Try other values for Shadedge and Shadedif (Figure 17.11). With DOS, select Tools and Hide, then choose 256Color, Color Edge Highlight, 16 Color Hidden Line, or 16 Color Filled.

You can't print the shaded drawing, but you can make a slide of it with the Mslide command. In Windows, you can also copy the image to the Clipboard (refer to chapter 19).

The Render command allows you to develop a presentation-quality drawing by defining the location and type of lighting sources, color, and reflective qualities of materials, and merging an AutoCAD rendered image with imported background images such as a landscape. Rendering is beyond the scope of this book, however, so I'll only introduce the topic. For more information, refer to your *AutoCAD User's Guide*. Enter the following (in DOS, select Tools, then Render):

Render <toolbar> Render <pick>

AutoCAD will display the Render dialog box, illustrated in Figure 17.12. Set the values as shown and then press More Options... to display the AutoCAD Render Op-

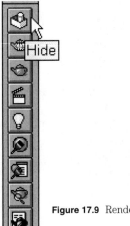

Figure 17.9 Render toolbar.

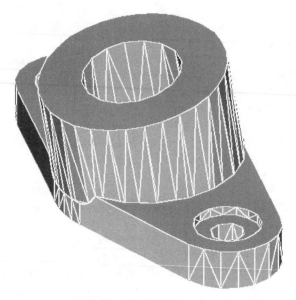

Figure 17.10 Shadedif = 100, Shadedge = 1.

tions dialog box, shown in Figure 17.13. Set the values as shown. Then press OK to return to the Render dialog box, and press the Render Objects < command button. AutoCAD will continue with:

Using current view. Default scene selected. Select objects: Digitize a point on the object. <pick> Select objects: <return>

The rendered object is illustrated in Figure 17.14.

17.6.1 Printing a rendered image

In Windows, you can print the rendered image. Make sure you've configured Windows for your Windows printer (refer to chapter 7, section 7.3).

Use the Pan command to locate the object near the center of your screen, and invoke the Render command to display the Render dialog box (refer back to Figure 17.12). Choose Render Window from the drop-down box in the Destination box, as shown in Figure 17.15. Press the Render Objects < command button and select the

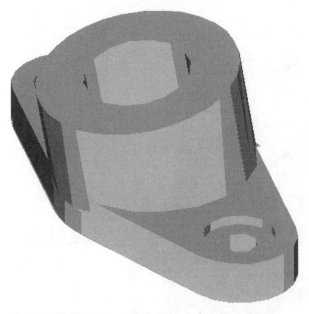

Figure 17.11 Shadedif = 100, Shadedge = 0.

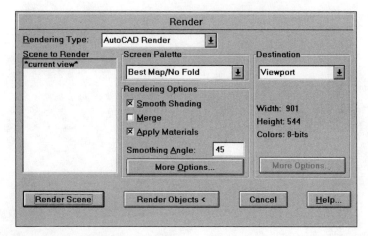

Figure 17.12 Render dialog box.

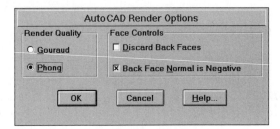

Figure 17.13 Render setting options.

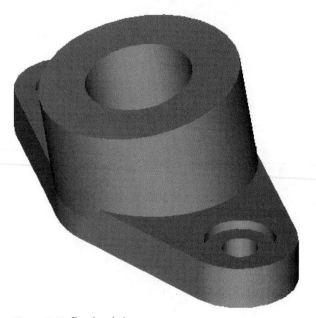

Figure 17.14 Rendered view.

Figure 17.15 Render destination.

object to be rendered. AutoCAD will display the rendered object in the Render window. Choose the Print tool to display the Print dialog box, shown in Figure 17.16. The large rectangular box around the object is the paper size. The box with the red squares in its corners is the current display, and the red squares are the resize handles. You can alter the image to be printed as follows:

1. Click and hold the button down inside the image area and drag the image to the desired location on the paper.

2. Click on a resize handle and hold the button down, dragging the image to the desired size.

3. Use the Tiled Pages, Across, and Down slider bars to tile the image across several pages, allowing you to print large poster-size images.

Locate the image as desired in the Print dialog box, and press OK to send the image to the printer.

17.7 Modifying the Size of Objects

Restore the meshed view by typing **regen** and pressing <return>. If you want to make a hole in the object larger, add a larger cylinder using the procedure outlined in section 17.3. Then use the Subtract command to "remove" the larger cylinder from the object. If you want to make a hole smaller, you must "plug" the existing hole by adding a cylinder of equal or larger size to replace the current hole in the object. Then you can create a new cylinder and subtract it from the object.

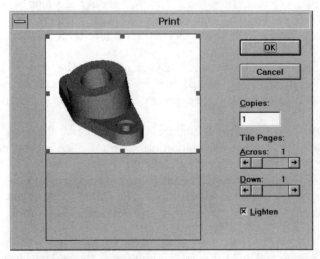

Figure 17.16 Render Print dialog box.

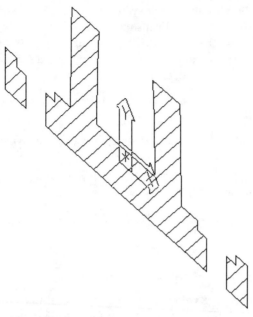

Figure 17.17 Cross section.

17.8 Creating a Cross Section

Create a new layer named Section, colored red, and set Section as the current layer. Restore the UCS name Center. Then rotate the UCS about the x axis by 90 degrees (see Figure 17.17). Save the UCS using the name Vertical, then enter the following to create a cross section (in DOS, select Draw, then Solids, then Section):

Solids <toolbar> Section <pick> Select object: Digitize the object. <pick> Select objects: <return> Section plane by object/Zaxis/View/XY/YZ/ZX/<3Points>: **XY** <return> Point on XY plane <0,0,0>: <return>

Hatch the cross section. Display the Boundary Hatch dialog box illustrated in Figure 6.22. Press the Select Objects < command button and digitize a point on the red cross-section line. The hatched cross section is illustrated in Figure 17.17 with the Object layer turned off. You can save the hatch layer as a block and insert it elsewhere in the drawing, or move it to another location outside of the object.

17.9 Slicing a Solid

Turn the Object layer on and make it current, then freeze the Section layer. The current UCS is named Vertical, set for the cross section in section 17.8. The current layer is Object. Enter the following:

Solids <toolbar> Slice <pick> `Select object:` Digitize the object. <pick> `Select objects:` <return> `Slicing plane by object/Zaxis/View/XY/YZ/ZX/<3Points>:` **xy** <return> `Point on XY plane <0,0,0>:` <return> `Both sides/<Point on desired side of the plane:` <shift>–<right> Endpoint <pick> `of` Place the endpoint aperture on a line on the back of the object. <pick>

Render the object. The rendered view is illustrated in Figure 17.18. Save the sliced object as C:\DRAWINGS\SLICE17.DWG using Save As... in the File menu.

Undo the drawing to return to the solid object. Undo won't undo the saved Sliced17 drawing. Use Save As... to save the current drawing as C:\DRAWINGS\PROJ-17.DWG. Do *not* use Save because AutoCAD will save the drawing using the last filename, which is Slice17, and you'll lose the original drawing. By using Save As, you're restoring the default filename to Proj-17.

17.10 Creating Profile Views

AutoCAD 13 doesn't allow you to generate profile images of solid models, but you can create a profile image in Windows by exporting the image to the Windows metafile (WMF) format, which saves the object as a two-dimensional image. You can then import the file back into AutoCAD and modify it as necessary to represent the desired profile image.

In DOS, you can plot the desired 3-D view to the DXF (drawing interchange file) format, where the drawing is also saved as two-dimensional image. Then simply import the DXF plot file back into AutoCAD and modify it to represent the desired profile image. Save the current drawing as C:\DRAWINGS\PROJ-17.DWG.

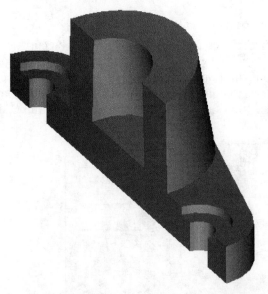

Figure 17.18 Rendered view of sliced model.

17.10.1 Creating profile images in Windows

The UCS named Vertical (see Figure 17.17) should be current. Display a plan view of the current UCS, which will display a front view of the solid object.

A Windows metafile (WMF) contains screen vector graphic information. If the object is exported to a WMF, the file will contain only the 2-D view of the object. But you can then import the object back into AutoCAD and modify it to display a correct profile view. Create a WMF as follows:

File <pick> Export... <pick>

The Export Data dialog box illustrated in Figure 17.19 will be displayed. Set the file-name as C:\DRAWINGS\FRONT17.WMF and press OK. AutoCAD will continue with:

`Select object:` Place a selection window around the object. <pick> `Select objects:` <return>

Then import the object into AutoCAD as follows:

File <pick> Import... <pick>

An Import File dialog box will be displayed. Select the C:\DRAWINGS\FRONT17 .WMF file and press OK, and the drawing will be imported into AutoCAD. Move the view into a clear location on the screen and explode the imported object using the Explode tool (see section A.4 and A.4.9 in appendix A).

17.10.2 Creating profile images in DOS (or Windows)

The UCS named Vertical (refer back to Figure 17.17) should be current. Display a plan view of the current UCS, which will display a front view of the solid object.

Display the AutoCAD Configuration menu by following the procedures outlined in chapter 7, section 7.1. Choose item number 5, Configure Plotter, to display the Plot Configuration menu. Choose Item 1, Add a Plotter Configuration. AutoCAD will dis-

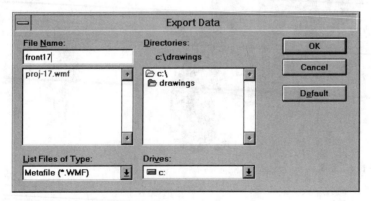

Figure 17.19 Exporting a file.

play a list of available plotters. To plot to a file, select the AutoCAD File Output Formats (pre-4.1) by Autodesk device driver. AutoCAD will display a list of file formats; choose the AutoCAD.DXB file. AutoCAD will prompt for information. Select the defaults. When asked to enter a description of the plotter, enter DXBfile. Save the configuration changes and return to the AutoCAD drawing screen.

Enter the Plot command to display the Plot Configuration dialog box, and press the Device and Default Selection... button. Choose the DXFfile device in the Device and Selection dialog box, and press the OK button to return to the Plot Configuration dialog box. Press the Window... command button to display the Window selection dialog box, and press the Pick < command button and place a window around the solid object. Then press the File Name... box to display the Create Plot File dialog box. Set the filename to C:\DRAWINGS\FRONT17.DXB and press OK. Set the paper size to inches and the scale to 1 = 1. Press OK to plot to the file, which you can import to AutoCAD as follows:

Command: **dxbin** <return>

The Select DXB File dialog box will be displayed. Select the file C:\DRAWINGS\ FRONT17.DXB and press OK. The drawing will be imported into AutoCAD. Move the view into a clear location on the screen.

17.10.3 Completing the profile

Using the Change tool (in DOS, enter **ddchprop**), change the color of the imported object to BYLAYER and the layer to Object. Create a new layer named Hide, colored green, and with a hidden linetype. Carefully erase lines you don't want in your profile image, and use Redraw to redraw the image after a line is erased. You'll have to erase some lines twice since they fall on the back and front of the object. Use the r (restore) and a (add) options of the Erase command, as required, when selecting objects. You might have to redraw some items. Also use Trim, Extend, Break, and Undo as required. It might help to thaw the Section layer so you can see where the sides of the holes in the object are. Change lines that should be hidden onto the Hide layer. The hidden lines should be colored green. Set the Ltscale to about 0.2.

The ellipse is a curved polyline and the hidden lines might not appear as a continuous pattern; some sections will appear as a dashed hidden line, and others as a continuous line. You can force AutoCAD, however, to generate the polyline as a continuous pattern by setting Ltype gen on:

Modify <pick> Edit Polyline (pedit) <pick> Select polyline: Digitize a curved hidden line. <pick> Close/Join/Width/edit vertex/Fit/Spline/Decurve/ Ltype gen/Udo/eXit (X): L (Ltype gen) <return> Full PLINE linetype ON/ OFF <off>: **on** <return>

Repeat these commands for each hidden polyline. WBlock the view using the filename C:\DRAWINGS\FRONT17.DWG. When AutoCAD asks for the block name, hit <return>. Use a suitable insertion point on the object. Then remove the view from the screen and save it to a file.

Set the current UCS to Center, and display a plan view of the current UCS. Following the previous procedure, create a DXB or WMF file Plan17. Import the file and modify the profile view, as described in the previous section. Create a layer name Hide, colored green, with a Hidden linetype. Change the color of the imported object to BYLAYER and the layer to Object.

To change part of a curved line to the Hide layer (see Figure 17.1), you must break the curved line into appropriate pieces. If the intersection point where the break is to occur is an apparent intersection, e.g., the intersection lines aren't on the same elevation, you must use the Apparent Intersection object snap to locate the intersection. The break is done as follows:

Modify <pick> Break <flyout> 1 Point Select <Pick> `Select object:` Pick a point on the curved line. <pick> `_f Enter first point:` <shift>–<right> Apparent Intersection <Pick> Place the apparent intersection aperture on the intersection where the lines are to be broken. <pick> `Second point:`

The curved line is now broken at the apparent intersection, and you can use the Change tool to change the layer of the appropriate new piece of the curve. Set the Ltype gen on for the hidden polylines. When the view is completed, Wblock the profile view as a file named C:\DRAWINGS\PLAN17.DWG.

17.10.4 Creating a 3-D profile

Use Named View... in the View menu to restore the view named 3D, then do the following:

View <Pick> Set UCS <pick> View <pick>

Following the previous procedure, create a DXB or WMF file Plan17. Import the file and modify the profile view as outlined. Wblock the revised view to a file named C:\DRAWINGS\3D17.DWG.

17.11 Create the Profile Drawing

Begin a new drawing name C:\DRAWINGS\PLOT17.DWG. Draw the border using your Border menu. Load your menu as a full or partial menu. If a partial menu, you'll require only the Easy1, Title Block, and Attach menu items to be loaded. When the menu is loaded, select Title Block, then Imperial, then A-size (if you didn't do an Imperial A-size, then use Metric A-size). When requested by the attributes, enter the drawing scale as 3/4. Next, select Attach, then Xref, then Attach (or return to AutoCAD's menu and use the Xref command). Attach each of the profile drawings using a scale of 0.75 (in metric, use 19.05) and complete the drawing as illustrated back in Figure 17.1. Set the Ltscale to 0.2 and plot the drawing on an A-size sheet using a scale of 1=1.

Chapter 18

Slide Show

Objective: Use AutoCAD's slide-show facility to display the sequence of operation for a construction or production operation, create a script file to automatically invoke commands, and demonstrate further applications of the View command.

Drawing: Produce a series of slides (drawings) that outline the erection sequence for a precast concrete bridge. You'll then use a script file to display the slides in sequence, demonstrating the bridge erection procedure.

Boot AutoCAD and begin a new drawing named C:\DRAWINGS\PROJ-18.DWG. Set the limits at 0,0 and 110,70, and invoke Zoom All. The drawing is to be done in decimal (foot) units. Set the units to decimal with 1 digit to the right of the decimal. Set angle units to decimal degrees with 0 fractional places for the display of angles.

For drawings of this type, it's best to have a color monitor. The purpose of the slide show is to illustrate the location of various components during the erection of a bridge girder. A color monitor lets you separate components in the drawing by color. If you have a color monitor, you should use a new layer for each color. The layers to use are specified in the following sections. If you don't have a color monitor, you could draw all items on one layer unless you intend to plot the views and use a different pen for each component. Create the layers listed in Table 18.1.

TABLE 18.1 Slide-show Layers

Item	Name	Color	Linetype
Miscellaneous	Construc	White	Continuous
Bridge piers	Pier	White	Continuous
Overhead gantry	Gantry	Blue	Continuous
Bridge girders	Girder	Red	Continuous
Gantry supports	Support	Green	Continuous

18.1 Bridge Component Blocks

The overhead gantry (see Figure 18.1) is a box truss arrangement that supports the moving hoists for the bridge. The gantry itself is a movable system that "creeps" along the bridge as the bridge girders are erected between piers.

18.1.1 Gantry

The total length of the gantry is to be 60 feet. Initially, a 15-foot-long section will be drawn and stored as a block. You'll then use the Array command to replicate the block four times, creating the 60-foot gantry.

Set Gantry as the current layer. Zoom on an area about 20×10 units, and draw the outside rectangular of the gantry 15×2.6 units, as illustrated in Figure 18.1. Do not dimension the gantry.

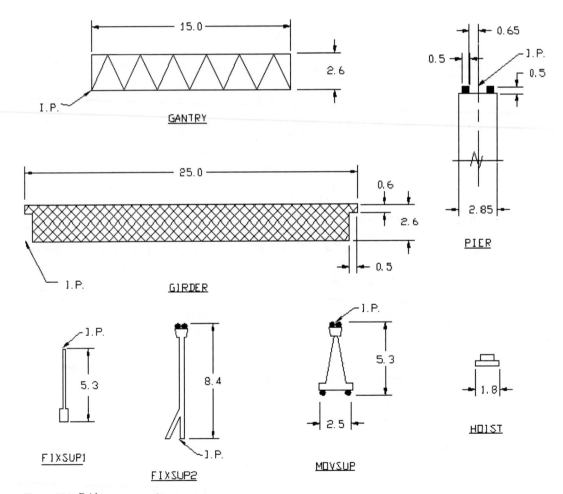

Figure 18.1 Bridge components.

Because the web members divide the gantry length into 12 sections, the horizontal distance for each diagonal is 1.25 ($^{15}/_{12}$) units. The depth of the gantry truss is 2.6 units. The commands to draw the web members are:

Draw <toolbar> Line <pick> From point: <shift>–<right> Intersection <pick> of Place the aperture over the lower left corner of the gantry. <pick> To point: **@1.25,2.6** <return> To point: **@1.25,–2.6** <return> etc.

Save the gantry as a block named Gantry. Designate the lower left corner as the insertion point, using the Intersection object snap to locate the point.

18.1.2 Girder

Girders are the bridge members that span from pier to pier and support the roadway. The slide show you create in this chapter will illustrate the procedure for erecting a precast concrete bridge girder.

Set the current layer as Girder. Zoom on an area that's approximately 30 × 15 units. Draw the outline of the girder, as illustrated in Figure 18.1. Do not dimension the girder. Rather than selecting an AutoCAD pattern for hatching, you'll define a new pattern at an angle of 45 degrees, spaced 0.5 units, and double hatched. The commands are:

Draw <toolbar> Hatch <pick>

The Boundary Hatch dialog box will be displayed. In the drop-down Pattern Type box, select User Defined. Then enter the angle as 45 and the spacing as 0.5, and turn the Double box on (there should be an × in it). Press the Pick Points < command button, and digitize a point inside the girder boundary. Press the Preview Hatch < command button, and modify the hatch if it doesn't appear correct. When the hatch is satisfactory, press the Apply command button to hatch the girder.

Save the girder as a block named Girder. Select the lower left corner as the insertion point (indicated as I.P. in Figure 18.1). Be sure that the cursor is exactly on the imaginary lower left corner when selecting the insertion point.

18.1.3 Pier

Piers support the girders of the bridge, as illustrated in Figure 18.2, and transfer the load to the ground. Set the current layer as Pier and draw the pier, as illustrated back in Figure 18.1.

Bearing pads are the solid squares on the top of the pier. To draw the pads, first draw one using the Rectang command. Then use the Solid command to solid fill the pad. Solids are filled only if the Fillmode system variable is on (the default value):

Command: **fillmode** <return> New value for FILEMODE <OFF>: **on** <return> Draw <toolbar> Solid <pick> First point: Digitize the upper left corner of the pad. <pick> Second point: Digitize the upper right corner of the pad. <pick> Third point: Digitize the lower left corner of the pad. <pick> Fourth point: Digitize the lower right corner of the pad. <pick> Fifth point: <return>

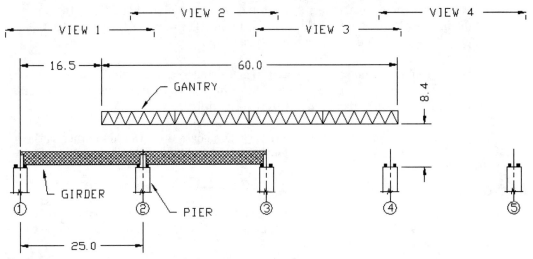

Figure 18.2 Initial position of gantry, and view locations.

Draw the second support pad by using the Copy command to make a copy of the first support. Save the pier as a block with the name Pier. The insertion point is the middle point of the top line of the pier, as illustrated back in Figure 18.1.

18.1.4 Gantry supports

The gantry has three supports: Fixsup1, the far left support; Fixsup2, the far right support; and Movsup, the middle support (see Figure 18.3). Set the current layer as Sups. Prior to drawing the gantry supports, create a roller and store it as a block. You can then insert the roller onto the supports as required:

Draw <toolbar> Circle <flyout> Donut <pick> Inside diameter: **0** <return> Outside diameter: **0.4** <return> Center of doughnut: Digitize a point in a clear space on the monitor. <pick> Center of doughnut: <return>

Save the donut as a block with the name Roller. Select the bottom of the circle as the insertion point, then draw the gantry supports and save each as a block. The crucial dimension is the overall height of each, which is illustrated back in Figure 18.1. The other dimensions can be estimated. Draw the hoist block, illustrated in Figure 18.1, on the Construct layer.

18.2 AutoCAD Slides

An AutoCAD slide is a file containing a "snapshot" of a screen. You start by creating a drawing with ordinary AutoCAD commands. When the screen shows everything you want on the slide, use the Mslide command to create the snapshot slide file. Slide filenames have the extension .SLD.

A Initial positon of gantry on bridge

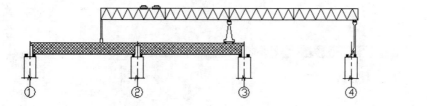

B Move new girder into bays 2 and 3 (zoomed view)

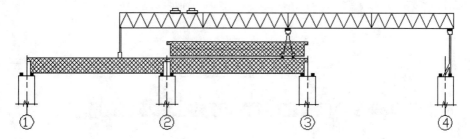

C Raise left fixed support and move gantry 15 feet to the right

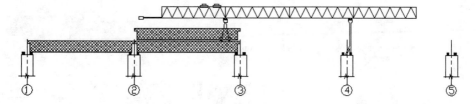

D Using hoists, move girder into position between bays 3-4

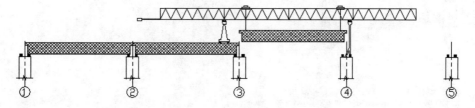

E Lower girder into place

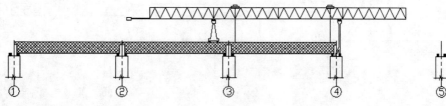

Figure 18.3   (a to i) Slide show views.

F Release hosit cables and move gantry 10 feet to the right

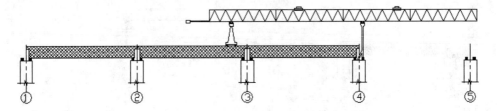

G Zoomed view of bays 2-5. Lower left fixed support and move middle support to the right

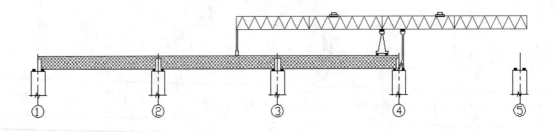

H Move right side support from pier 4 to pier 5. Zoomed view

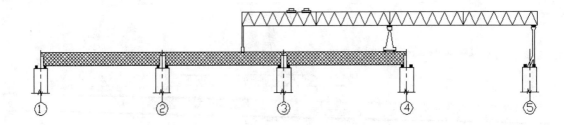

I Final positon of sequence. Start postion of next sequence

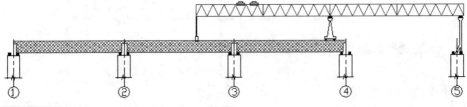

Figure 18.3 Continued.

Slide files contain only information describing the saved snapshot, and cannot be altered. Don't try to alter a slide. If a slide is loaded and you attempt to alter it, the alterations will appear on the drawing that was on the screen prior to the slide file that's displayed. The only way to change a slide file is to redraw the original picture and use the Mslide command to save the new picture under the same slide filename.

To view a slide, use the Vslide command. You can produce a slide show by creating a script file (see section 18.8), which contains a sequence of Vslide commands loading sequential files. AutoCAD's script facility allows a sequence of commands to be read from a text file.

18.3   Slide Dwg-1

Dwg-1 shows the initial position of the gantry on the bridge, as illustrated in Figure 18.3A. The relative dimensions for the items in the initial position are illustrated back in Figure 18.2.

Set the current drawing layer as Construc. Use Zoom All to zoom to the initial limits set for the screen (0,0 and 110,70). Press <ctrl>–D or <F6> to display the cursor coordinates.

You'll use the coordinates 6,20 for the insertion point of the first pier. Because there are five piers to be inserted at a spacing of 25 units center to center, use the Minsert (multiple insert) command to insert an array as follows (in DOS, select Draw, then Insert, then Multiple Blocks):

Miscellaneous <toolbar> Insert Multiple Blocks <pick> Block name: **pier** <return> Insert point: **6,20** <return> X scale factor <1>/Corner/X/Y/Z: <return> Y scale factor (default = X): <return> Rotation angle <0>: <return> Number of rows (–) <1>: <return> Number of columns (⦙⦙⦙) <1>: **5** <return> Distance between columns (⦙⦙⦙): **25** <return>

Insert the two girders with the Minsert command. The insertion point is the same as for pier 1 (6,20) and the spacing of the girders is 25 units. You can also insert the 60-meter gantry with the Minsert command. The insertion point is 22.5,27.9, where x = 6 + 16.5 and y = 20 + (8.4 – 0.5). Refer back to Figures 18.1 and 18.2 to understand the calculations in determining the coordinates. A single gantry section is 15 units long, so there will be four columns in the array.

18.3.1 Designate views

When continuing the drawing, you'll often have to zoom on a section of the bridge to locate points more accurately. To speed up the drawing process, enlarge each of the bays with the Zoom command, and name the view with the View command. Once a view is named, you can quickly restore it. Following the procedures outlined in chapter 14, section 14.4.3, name each of the views illustrated back in Figure 18.2 (in DOS, select View, then Named Views):

Standard <toolbar> Named Views <pick>

The View Control dialog box will be displayed. Press the New... command button to display the New View dialog box. Enter a new view name View1, press the Define Window button, and then press the Window < command button. Then:

`First corner`: Place a window around the bridge area enclosing piers 1 and 2 (see view 1 in Figure 18.2). <pick>

The Define New View dialog box will be redisplayed. Press the Save View command button, then repeat the process and save each of the views shown in Figure 18.2. To display View1, use the Restore command (in DOS, select View, then Named Views):

Standard <toolbar> Named Views <pick>

The View Control dialog box will be displayed. Click on View1 in the Views list box, then press the Restore command button. Insert Fixsup1 at the lower left corner of the gantry, and use the Intersect object snap to digitize the point of insertion. Restore View2 and insert Movsup 30 units to the right of the left end of the gantry. Because the last point was the left end of the gantry, enter the insertion point relative to that point: **@30<0**.

Insert the first hoist on top of the gantry at coordinates 32.5,30.4 and the second hoist at coordinates 35.5,30.4. Restore View3, and insert Fixsup2 using an insertion point at the left side of the right support pad on pier 4 (see Figure 18.3A).

18.3.2 Use attributes to draw pier column numbers

The pier mark numbers will be enclosed in a 2.5-unit-diameter circle, which will allow room for a 1.5-unit-high number inside the circle. Draw a 2.5-unit circle on the screen outside of the current drawing. Attributes will allow each pier column number block to be inserted with a different number. Use the Attribute Definition dialog box to attach an attribute inside the circle. Use the attribute tag T, and make the height of the attribute 1.5 units.

The attribute tag T will be displayed inside the 2.5-unit circle. Use the Move command to locate it properly in the circle (unless it's already centered). Save the block. The insertion point should be the top of the circle. Restore View1 and insert the pier column number at the bottom center line of the pier, as shown back in Figure 18.2. Add the pier column numbers to each of the other piers.

18.3.3 Adding Text

Use Zoom All to obtain a view of the entire bridge. The start location for the text are coordinates 6,50. Select the text height as 1.5 units to adequately allow the text to be read when the views are displayed. Using the Dtext command add the text INITIAL POSITION OF GANTRY ON BRIDGE to the drawing.

18.3.4 Saving the Slide

Make sure the drawing includes all the items illustrated in Figure 18.3A. This drawing will be the first slide to be named Dwg-1. Select the following in the menu bar:

Tools <pick> Slide <pick> Save <pick>

The Create Slide file dialog box will be displayed. Set the Directory to c:\drawings and enter the filename **Dwg-1**. Note that the List Files of Type is .SLD. Press OK to save the slide file. This screen is now saved as a slide file with the name Dwg-1.sld. The file size is small because only the location of vectors on the screen are saved.

You might now want to save a drawing file of this screen. Remember that slides can't be altered; if you later want to change the slide and you've saved the screen in a drawing file, you can load the drawing file, change the drawing, and then resave the slide. The only problem in saving the drawing file is that it will contain all the information about the drawing and hence use up disk space. If you do want to save the screen, use the Save As command and use an original name such as c:\drawings\ dwg-1. You can do this for each slide (using consecutive names such as dwg-2 and dwg-3). When the project is complete and the slides have been finalized, you can erase the drawing files to conserve disk space.

18.4 Slide Dwg-2

Dwg-2 illustrates the positioning of a new girder in preparation for being lifted into bays 3 and 4 (see Figure 18.3B). This girder is located 25 units to the right and 3 units (girder depth plus 0.4 units for rollers) above the insertion point of the first pier. The cursor's last position should be the insertion point of the first pier, and you can then insert the new girder @25,3 units relative to that position. Usually you'd use the From object snap to specify the last point while inserting the block. but AutoCAD doesn't allow you to use From while dragging a block into place. Set the last point before inserting the block, as follows (in DOS, select Assist, then Inquiry, then Point):

Object Properties <toolbar> Locate Point (Figure 18.4) <pick> id Point: <shift>–<right> Insertion <pick> of Place the aperture on the first pier. <pick>

AutoCAD will locate the insertion point of the first pier and report its coordinates. That point is now the last point. Insert the girder as follows:

Draw <toolbar> Insert Block <pick>

The Insert dialog box will be displayed. Press the Block... command button and select Girder from the Defined Blocks dialog box. Turn on the Specify Parameters on Screen box, then press OK. AutoCAD will continue with:

Insertion point: **@25,3** <return>, etc.

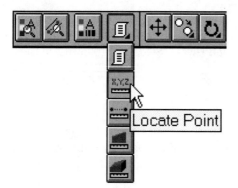

Figure 18.4 Locate Point tool.

Use the Zoom command to enlarge a view of the bridge from piers 1 to 4. At coordinates 31,50, add the text MOVE NEW GIRDER INTO BAYS 2 & 3. Use the Mslide command to save this screen, using the filename c:\drawings\dwg-2.sld. Also save the drawing as a drawing file if you've decided to follow that process.

18.5   Slide Dwg-3

In Dwg-3, raise Fixsup1 and move the gantry 15 units to the right. Use the View command to restore View2 (bays 2 and 3). To raise Fixsup1, use the Rotate command, as follows:

Modify <toolbar> Rotate <pick> Select objects: Digitize Fixsup1 <pick> Select objects: <return> Base point: <shift>–<right> Insertion <pick> of Place the aperture on Fixsup1. <pick> <Rotation angle>/reference: **–90** <return>

Move the gantry, hoists, and Fixsup1 15 units to the right, as illustrated in Figure 18.3C.

Modify <toolbar> Move <pick> Select objects: Place a selection window (pick left corner first) to enclose the gantry, hoists, and Fixsup1. <pick> Select objects: <return> Base point or displacement: Pick a point on the screen <pick> Second point of displacement: **@15<0** <return>

Use Zoom All to view the entire bridge. At coordinates 6.50, add the text RAISE LEFT FIXED SUPPORT &, and on the line below add MOVE GANTRY 15 FEET TO THE RIGHT. Save the slide using the name c:\drawings\dwg-3.sld.

18.6   Slides Dwg-4, Dwg-5, and Dwg-6

In Dwg-4, pick the girder up with the hoists and move it into position over and between piers 3 to 4. Use the Move command to move the girder 25 units to the right. To select the object to be moved, digitize a point on the girder. Enter the second point of displacement as **@25<0**. Then move the left hoist 10 units to the right (@10<0), and the right hoist 29 units to the right.

Use the View command to view bays 3 and 4 (View1), and then use the Line command to add cables connecting the hoists to the girder, as illustrated back in Figure 18.3D. Enter Zoom All, and then add the text USING HOISTS, MOVE GIRDER INTO POSITION BETWEEN BAYS 3–4. Save the slide as c:\drawings\dwg-4.sld.

In Dwg-5, lower (move) the girder into position (@3<270). Add the text shown back in Figure 18.3E, and save the slide as c:\drawings\dwg-5.sld. In Dwg-6, erase the hoist cables and move the gantry, including the hoists and left gantry support, 10 units to the right. Add the text back in Figure 18.3F, and save the slide as c:\drawings\dwg-6.sld.

18.7 Slides Dwg-7, Dwg-8 and Dwg-9

Both Dwg-7 and Dwg-8 are zoomed views of the bridge from bays 2 to 5. Remember to use View1 to View4 to provide enlarged views of the bridge bays when drawing.

In Dwg-7, rotate Fixsup1 90 degrees, as illustrated back in Figure 18.3G. Move Movsup 25 units (@25<0) to the right. Add the text to the drawing at coordinates 31,50, and save the slide using the name c:\drawings\dwg-7.sld.

In Dwg-8, move Fixsup2 from pier 4 to pier 5 by 25 units (@25<0). Then move the hoists back to the left end of the gantry in preparation for the next girder to be installed. Move them back by the amount they were moved forward in Dwg-4, i.e., @-10<0 for the left hoist and @-29<0 for the right hoist. Add the text back in Figure 18.3H and save the slide as c:\drawings\dwg-8.sld. Dwg-9 is a Zoom All view of Dwg-8, with the text in Figure 18.3I added.

18.8 Writing the Script

A script file is a text file with the extension .SCR, which contains a list of AutoCAD commands incorporating a sequence of drawing operations that can be read by AutoCAD.

You can write a script filein Windows' Notepad program (see chapter 11, section 11.3). The syntax for writing script files is different in many ways from that for writing menu files. In both, a space invokes the <return> key, but the semicolon (;) doesn't invoke a <return> in script files. Other menu file commands, such as \ and +, don't apply to script files. Lines that begin with a semicolon are considered comment lines by AutoCAD.

The script file for the slide show is shown after this paragraph, followed by a discussion of the file. Read the discussion before writing the file. Load Edit (DOS) or Notepad (Windows), as outlined in chapter 11, section 11.3. The filename is to be c:\drawings\bridge.scr. Note that script files have the file extension .SCR. Enter the following in the file (don't include the number and colon at the start of each line):

```
1: layer make construc
2:
3: limits 0,0 110,70 zoom all
4: rectang 10,10 100,60
5: text c 55,40 2 0
6: PRECAST CONCRETE BRIDGE CONSTRUCTION
7:   BY
8:   EASY CONSTRUCTION INC.
```

```
 9: vslide *c:\drawings\dwg-1
10: delay 2000
11: vslide
12: vslide *c:\drawings\dwg-2
13: delay 4000
14: vslide
15: vslide *c:\drawings\dwg-3
16: delay 4000
17: vslide
18: vslide *c:\drawings\dwg-4
19: delay 4000
20: vslide
21: vslide *c:\drawings\dwg-5
22: delay 4000
23: vslide
24: vslide *c:\drawings\dwg-6
25: delay 4000
26: vslide
27: vslide *c:\drawings\dwg-7
28: delay 4000
29: vslide
30: vslide *c:\drawings\dwg-8
31: delay 4000
32: vslide
33: vslide *c:\drawings\dwg-9
34: delay 4000
35: vslide
36: delay 6000
37: rscript
```

Make sure the file you've written is exactly the same as that illustrated (without the number and colon at the start of each line). Then save the file as c:\drawings\bridge .scr, exit the word processor, and return to AutoCAD. A discussion of the script file follows:

Line 1. Calls the Layer command, creates a new layer called Construc, and sets the current layer as Construc. You don't have to create the other layers used in the script drawings; this is done automatically when the entities on them are inserted into the drawing. Making the current layer Construc eliminates the possible problems resulting if layer 0, which wasn't used in the slide drawings, was turned off when creating the slides. The space between commands invokes the <return> key required to call a command.

Line 2. This is a blank line to invoke the <return> key required to exit the Layer command. When writing script files, you must be very familiar with the syntax of Auto-CAD commands. Refer to Section D.5 in appendix D, which gives information on AutoCAD command syntax and using Help.

Line 3. Sets the drawing limits and zooms.

Line 4. Draws a rectangle on the screen with a 10-unit border.

Line 5. Invokes the Text command with the c (center) option. The center point is then specified as coordinates 55,40, the text height is 2 units, and the rotation angle is 0 degrees.

Line 6. This is the text to be printed on the screen.

Lines 7 and 8. These lines begin with two blank spaces, which invoke the <return> key to recall the previous Text command. When Text is recalled, it uses the same height and angle as used for the previous text and, if <return> is pressed again, the text is placed directly below the previous line. In this case it's centered because the previous text was centered. The text is then read from the script and printed on the screen by AutoCAD.

Line 9. The Vslide command calls a slide. In this case, the slide filename is preceded with an asterisk (*), indicating that the slide file is to be loaded but not shown. It will be shown when Vslide is next encountered. If the filename isn't preceded with an asterisk, the fill is loaded and shown immediately. The procedure that's used preloads the slide, thereby eliminating the delay caused by AutoCAD having to read the file from the disk when it's to be shown.

Line 10. The Delay command delays the slide show, allowing you to see the current screen before viewing the next screen. The current screen contains the rectangle that encloses the text of lines 6, 7, and 8. A delay of 1000 takes about one second, so a delay of about two seconds is invoked.

Line 11. This Vslide command causes AutoCAD to display the slide c:\drawings\dwg-1 that was preloaded in line 9.

Line 12. Preloads c:\drawings\dwg-2.

Line 13. Delays AutoCAD operation for about four seconds to display the current slide c:\drawings\dwg-3.

Lines 14 to 34. This is a continuous sequence of displaying a preloaded file, preloading the next, and delaying the AutoCAD sequence for about four seconds.

Line 36. Delays the AutoCAD operation for about six seconds to display the last slide in the slide show.

Line 37. Enters the Rscript command, which repeats the script.

18.8.1 Invoking the script

This script is designed to be invoked from the AutoCAD drawing editor with the Script command. Boot up AutoCAD and begin a new drawing named c:\drawings\bridge.dwg. Load the script file by selecting the following in the menu bar:

Tools <pick> Run Script... <pick>

The Select Script File dialog box, illustrated in Figure 18.5, will be displayed. Set the directory as c:\drawings, the pattern as *.scr, and the file as bridge.

When you press OK, AutoCAD loads the script file and the slide show begins. If the show is interrupted because of an error in the script file, exit AutoCAD and correct the error in the script file using Notepad or Edit. If you want to see the remainder of the file prior to making the corrections, enter the Resume command. You can interrupt a slide show at any time by pressing <esc>, <ctrl>–C, or <backspace> key. To continue the show, enter **Resume**.

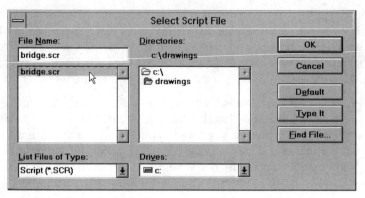

Figure 18.5 Loading a script file.

19

Introduction to AutoLISP

Objective: Provide an introduction to the capabilities of AutoLISP through writing, loading, and running an AutoLISP program incorporating the following functions: setq, prompt, defun, setvar, getdist, list, and command.

Drawing: The function draws the plan view of the three-dimensional house illustrated in Figure 19.1.

19.1 Introduction to AutoLISP

LISP is an acronym for *LIST processing*. It was initially developed for programming artificial intelligence, and has numerous dialects. AutoLISP is one of them. Programs written in AutoLISP let you write functions that allow for interaction between user and program, and automate drawing sequences. All LISP instructions are evaluated as mathematical functions that take values, operate on them, and return a value. The function and its values are enclosed in parentheses, ( ). The function name immediately follows the left parenthesis, and it's in turn followed by the values to be operated on. A right parenthesis marks the end of the function. Boot AutoCAD and enter the following LISP functions at the command prompt:

LISP function	Answer
(+ 5 3)	8
(– 8 2)	6
(* 6 5)	30
(/ 18 6)	3
(+ 12 23.0)	35.0
(/ 9 2)	4
(/ 9 2.0)	4.5

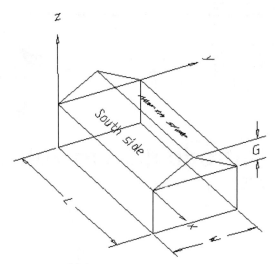

Figure 19.1 3-D house.

You should now understand how to use AutoLISP functions to add, subtract, multiply, and divide. Each expression is enclosed in parentheses, and the first item is the function to be invoked. The +, –, *, and / are AutoLISP's defined functions, which are referred to as *primitives*.

Press the <F2> key to display AutoCAD's text window. Note the difference in answers obtained for the last two expressions. The former expression uses integer data and returns an integer. The latter uses one real number and returns a real number. If the output returned is to be a real number, ensure that one of the pieces of data in the expression is a real number.

Enter **(* 3 (/ 12 4))** and AutoLISP will return a 9. Now enter **(/ 24 (* 2 3)**, but don't add the missing right parenthesis. AutoLISP will return a **1>**. Enter **)** and Auto-LISP will return the result of the expression, 4. Notice how you were prompted for the missing right parenthesis.

19.2 User-Defined Functions

In the preceding section you used some of AutoLISP's predefined functions. You can also define your own functions and incorporate AutoLISP's functions with functions you've written. This is the secret of LISP; you can write large functions by incorporating a number of smaller functions. For clarity's sake, I'll refer to AutoCAD's predefined functions as *primitives* and user-defined functions as *functions*.

You'll be writing a program to draw a 3-D house. It will be made up of a main program that invokes a number of user-defined functions. As such, it can be written and tested in stages. The program incorporates the following:

- Setting AutoCAD units to Architecture, with ¼-inch precision.
- Getting input of the building width, length, eave height, and gable end height.

- Setting the drawing limits (screen width 1.5 × building length, screen height 1.5 × building height).
- Drawing the house.

19.3 House Function

Begin a new drawing named c:\drawings\house.dwg. Following the procedures in chapter 11, section 11.3, load Edit (DOS) or Notepad (Windows) to edit a file named c:\drawings\house.lsp. All AutoLISP files must end with the extension .LSP. The following function contains the basic steps needed to draw the house, as outlined in the previous section. Notice that each of the lines inside the function (enclosed within the opening and closing parentheses) is indented. The number of spaces isn't important, but the indent shows the structure of the program. Enter the following (do *not* include the line numbers and colon at the start of each line, which are included in the text to facilitate the discussion of the function by line number):

```
 1:   ; This program draws a 3D house.
 2:   (defun house ()
 3:      ;    ** set system variables **
 4:      (setvar "lunits" 4)   ;Architectural units
 5:      (setvar "luprec" 2)   ;1/4 inch precision
 6:      ;    ** PROGRAM **
 7:      ; (input)             ;Call INPUT function
 8:      ; (drawlim)           ;Call DRAWing LIMits function
 9:      ; (housedrw)          ;Call HOUSE DRaW function
10:   )
11:   ;-------------------------------------------------
```

The lines preceded with a semicolon, ;, are comment lines and are ignored by the LISP evaluator. They're generally used to document the program.

The semicolon preceding line 1 makes it a comment line. It has no effect on the program.

Line 2 uses the AutoLISP Defun primitive to define a function named House (this name doesn't have to be the same as the lisp filename). The function begins with a left parenthesis on line 2 and ends with a right parenthesis on line 10. All data between those parentheses is part of the function. The right and left parentheses following the function name are necessary. Their function is beyond the scope of this book.

Line 4 uses the AutoLISP's Setvar primitive to set an AutoCAD system variable. The variable set is *lunits*, which defines the linear units in which AutoCAD will be working (1 = scientific, 2 = decimal, 3 = engineering, 4 = architectural).

In line 5, the Setvar primitive is used to set Luprec, the system variable containing the linear unit number of decimal places or denominator. For decimal units, the value assigned to Luprec is the number of digits to the right of the decimal. For architectural and engineering units, the following values are used: 0 = no fraction, 1 = ½, 2 = ¼, 3 = ⅛, 4 = 1/16, 5 = 1/32, and 6 = 1/64.

Lines 7, 8, and 9 are currently comment lines because they're preceded by a semicolon. These are actually function calls that you'll invoke by deleting the semicolon when the program is completed.

Line 10 ends the function with a closing parenthesis. Note how the entire function is enclosed in parentheses, as are individual expressions within the function.

19.4 Input Function

A user-defined function named Input is to be invoked in line 7 of the House function (when the semicolon is removed). Add the following function to the end of the House.lsp file:

```
12: ;
13: (defun input ()
14:     (prompt "\nEnter dimensions in ft. & in. (ex 6'3-1/4)")
15:     (setq W (getdist "\n\tHouse width: ")
16:           L (getdist "\n\tHouse length: ")
17:           V (getdist "\n\tHouse eave height: ")
18:           G (getdist "\n\tHouse gable height: ")))
19: )
20: ;-----------------------------------------------------
```

Lines 12 and 20 are comment lines that make the program listing clearer.

The Defun primitive is used in line 13 to define a function named Input. The function is enclosed between an opening parenthesis in line 13 and a closing parenthesis in line 19.

The Prompt primitive in line 14 prints a literal string in AutoCAD's prompt area of the monitor. The literal string is enclosed in quotation marks. The \n in the literal string is a control code recognized by the interpreter as a line feed, and *must* be lowercase.

Line 15 uses two primitives, Setq and Getdist. Setq binds data to a symbol. For example, (setq a 2) binds the integer 2 to the symbol a, and (setq b 3) binds the integer 3 to the symbol b. The expression (+ a b) will return the value 5.

The Getdist function pauses for input of a distance. In line 15, (getdist "\n\tHouse width: ") prints the string House width: on a new line, controlled by the code \n and indented to the right by one indent, which is controlled by the code \t. Both control codes, \n and \t, must be in lowercase. The value entered in response to the Getdist primitive is bound to the symbol W by the Setq primitive.

You can make multiple assignments with the Setq function. For instance, (setq a 2 b 3) will bind 2 to a and 3 to b. Multiple assignments are often written on more than one line to improve the clarity of the program, as follows:

```
(setq a 2
      b 3)
```

This is used in lines 15, 16, 17, and 18 to assign the house width to W, length to L, eave height to V, and gable height to G. Each of those values is obtained by a Getdist function. As required for all LISP functions, each Getdist function is enclosed inside left and right parentheses, as is the Setq function, which begins with an opening parenthesis in line 15 and ends with a closing parentheses at the end of line 18. That is how the AutoLISP evaluator keeps track of things.

19.5 Testing the Program

Before continuing, you must test the program. Save the file as c:\drawings\house.lsp and then exit Edit (DOS) or, in Windows, press <alt> and <tab> together to toggle back to the AutoCAD window. Then load the House.lsp file from within AutoCAD by selecting the following in the menu bar:

Tools <pick> Applications... <pick>

The Load AutoLISP, ADX, and ARX Files dialog box illustrated in Figure 19.2 will be displayed. Press the Files... command button and select the file path c:\drawings, select the lisp file House.lsp, and press OK. Then press the Load command box to load the file. If your file has errors, AutoCAD will indicate that at the command line. If necessary, toggle back to Notepad (Windows) or reload Edit (DOS) and compare your file to that in the text and make the corrections. Save the file, return to Auto-CAD, and reload the House.lsp file. To run the House function, enter:

Command: **(house)** <return>

AutoCAD will respond with 2, which is the value assigned to Luprec in line 5. All the remaining lines in the House function are preceded by a semicolon and are comment lines. Run the INPUT function by entering:

Command: **(input)** <return>

If you're prompted to enter the house dimensions, then everything is okay and you should enter some values. The last operation in the function, the binding of the value

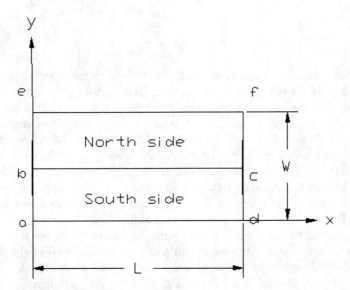

Figure 19.2 Roof plan of a house.

you entered for the house gable height in line 18 to the symbol G, is returned in inch units because AutoCAD works internally in inches. So if you entered the gable height as 4 (feet), AutoCAD would return 48 (inches). If you have an error in your function, return to the House.lsp file and make the corrections. Then save the file and reload it in AutoCAD. Retry the function. Don't continue until it's correct.

To review the bindings to variables in the Input function, enter the following at the command line:

Command: **!w** <return>

AutoCAD should return the value you entered for the house width, in inches. You can retrieve data bound to a symbol while in the AutoCAD editor by preceding the symbol name with !. Get the data bound to L, V, and E. If the data is incorrect or if you have other problems, edit the House.lsp file and compare it to the text. Then save it, load it, and run it again. Don't continue until you get correct responses.

19.6 Drawing Limits Function

Toggle to Notepad (Windows) or load Edit (DOS) and add the following to the House.lsp file (be very careful with spaces; there's no space immediately following a starting parenthesis, and there's at least one space between every piece of data within the parentheses):

```
21: ;
22: (defun drawlim ()
23:     (setq min (list (* -1 (/ L 4.0)) (* -1 (/ W 4.0)))
24:           max (list (+ L (/ L 4.0)) (+ W (/ W 4.0))))
25:     (setvar "limmin" min)
26:     (setvar "limmax" max)
27:     (command "zoom" "all")
28: )
29: ;-------------------------------------------------------
```

Line 22 defines a function named Drawlim that starts with the opening parenthesis on line 22 and ends with the closing parenthesis on line 28.

The List primitive is used in line 23. An example of a list primitive is (list 2 3), which returns the list (2 3). In line 23, List defines a 2-D point, specifying the lower left corner of the screen. The lower left corner of the plan view of the house is to be 0,0. The x coordinate of the lower left corner of the screen is calculated as $-1 \times L / 4$. The Y coordinate is $-1 \times W / 4$. In AutoLISP, the expression to calculate the x coordinate is (* -1 (/ L 4.0)). Note that each expression is enclosed in parentheses.

Notice the sequence of opening and closing parentheses for the List functions in line 23, including the Setq function, which starts at line 23 and ends at the end of line 24. The Setq function assigns a list to the symbol Min and a list to the symbol Max.

In lines 25 and 26, the lists bound to Min and Max are assigned to the AutoCAD system variables Limmin and Limmax, which control the screen limits. After the screen limits are set, the AutoCAD Zoom and All commands are invoked in line 27 with AutoLISP's Command primitive.

Save the House.lsp file and either exit Edit (DOS) or toggle to AutoCAD (Windows). Then reload the HOUSE.LSP file into AutoCAD. Watch for error messages when the functions are loaded, and make corrections to the Houlse.lsp file if necessary.

Because you haven't exited the drawing since the last function was run, you don't have to rerun the House and Input functions because the values calculated by those functions are still assigned to variables. (If you exited the previous drawing, you'd have to rerun House and Input.)

Run the Drawlim function by entering **(drawlim)** at the command line. Watch for error messages, and make any necessary corrections to the House.lsp file. Also, check the screen limits to see that they suit the length and width you entered under Input. If not, correct the Drawlim function in the House.lsp file before continuing.

19.7 House Draw Function

Using Edit (DOS) or Notepad (Windows), add the following to your House.lsp file:

```
30: ;
31: (defun housedrw ()
32:     ; Draw walls using extruded lines
33:     (setq t (* -1 V))
34:     (command "elev" 0 t)
35:     (setq a (list 0 0) b (list L 0) c (list L W)
36:           d (list 0 W))
37:     (command "line" a b c d "c")
38:     (setvar "thickness" 0)
39:     ; Draw roof using 3Dface
40:     ; South side
41:     (setq a (list 0 0 0)
42:           b (list 0 (/ W 2.0) G)
43:           c (list L (/ W 2.0) G)
44:           d (list L 0 0))
45:     (command "3dface" a b c d)
46:     (command "")
47:     ; North side
48:     (setq e (list 0 W 0)
49:           f (list L W 0))
50:     (command "3dface" e b c f)
51:     (command "")
52:     ; West gable
53:     (command "3dface" a b e)
54:     (command "") (command "")
55:     ; East gable
56:     (command "3dface" d c f)
57:     (command "") (command "")
58: )
```

The Housedrw function begins at line 31 and ends at line 58, as indicated by the opening and closing parentheses. The eave of the house is to be at elevation 0. The side and end walls of the house are drawn as extruded lines, as illustrated in Figure 19.2. The thickness of the extrusion is calculated in line 33 and bound to the symbol t by the Setq primitive.

In line 34, AutoLISP's Command function invokes AutoCAD's Elev command, sets the current elevation to 0, and sets the thickness to the value bound to the symbol t.

Two dimension coordinate lists defining the plan corners of the house (see Figure 18.2) are bound to the symbols a, b, c, and d in line 35. The house walls are drawn by the expression in line 37. Note how the Close command, c, is enclosed in quotation marks so the AutoLISP interpreter doesn't interpret it as a symbol. In line 38, the Setvar primitive sets the current thickness to 0 since extruded lines are no longer necessary.

The remainder of the function uses AutoCAD's 3Dface command to draw the roof and gable ends. In line 46, the Command primitive, Command "", is invoked with a null (quotation marks with no space between them) value to exit the 3Dface command.

In lines 54 and 57, a null value is entered twice in order to exit the 3Dface command. This is necessary because only three points on the face were entered in the previous command. Try a three-point 3Dface using AutoCAD to verify this.

Save the program and either exit Edit (DOS) or toggle to AutoCAD (Windows). Reload the House.lsp file and run Housedraw. If the house plan isn't drawn, edit the House.lsp file, making the required corrections, and try again.

When you've debugged each of the functions, edit the House.lsp program and remove the semicolons preceding the function calls on lines 7, 8, and 9. The function calls in those lines will no longer be comments, and will therefore be invoked when the House function is run. Save the House.lsp file and reload the new file into AutoCAD. Then erase the house drawing from the screen and reload House.lsp. Run the House function by entering **(house)** at the command line. Notice the difference in operation?

19.8 Assignment

1. Add a user-defined function to the House.lsp file in order to request the viewing rotation angle of the house in the xy plane, and assign the value entered to the symbol rx. The function should then request the rotation angle from the xy plane and assign the value to the symbol rz. Then invoke the Vpoint command, which expects the following responses:

Command: **vpoint** <return> Rotate/<View point>: **r** <return> Enter angle from XY plane from X axis: This is the value assigned to the symbol rx. <return> Enter angle from XY plane: This is the value assigned to the symbol rz. <pick>

2. Modify the House function to draw 1'–0" eaves on the roof of the house.

20

AutoCAD in the
Windows Environment

Objective: To run multiple applications and transfer data from one application to the other. (For Windows 95, refer to section H.7 in appendix H.)

20.1 Working in Multiple Windows

AutoCAD for Windows works in the Windows environment, which allows you to open multiple applications. Boot AutoCAD and, when AutoCAD is loaded, hold down the <alt> key and press and release the <tab> key. Each time you press the <tab> key while the <alt> key is held down, the title of an open application is displayed on the screen. When the title of the application you want to run is displayed, release the <alt> key and the application will appear in the foreground. Toggle to Program Manager and then back to AutoCAD.

When you have multiple documents open, make sure to close all of them before turning the computer off. Close Windows by clicking on the control menu box (the dash in the top left corner of the window) in the Program Manager window. This allows you to exit to DOS and ensures that all Windows applications are closed. You can then safely turn off the computer without losing data.

Although you can have other applications open while working with AutoCAD for Windows, only one copy of AutoCAD 13 can be running in Windows 3.1 at any time.

20.2 Using Windows Clipboard

Windows Clipboard acts as a temporary storage area for transferring data between applications in the Windows environment. Clipboard can store only one image at a time, and each time a new image is sent to Clipboard the previous image is removed. You can use the following formats in AutoCAD to copy entities to the Clipboard:

Bitmap. Bitmap images are composed of a pattern of dots and the image cannot be scaled. There might be degradation in the quality of the image. Most Windows applications support bitmap images.

Vectors. This process transfers information to an AutoCAD drawing or an application that supports the Windows metafile format (WMF). When you paste the entities, the correct format is automatically used. Both formats contain screen vector information. Data is transferred without loss of resolution, and entities can be scaled. When you paste entities into AutoCAD, they're inserted into the current UCS as a block, and the prompts are the same as those for the Insert command, allowing you to scale and rotate the block. Although information transferred to AutoCAD in WMF format contains screen vectors, the objects are more difficult to modify than those in AutoCAD format.

Embed. When you embed part or all of an AutoCAD drawing in another document, a copy of the drawing is stored in the destination document. Embedded drawings can be modified. The embedded drawing, however, is no longer associated with the original drawing and, if the embedded drawing is modified, the original source drawing won't be affected.

Link. When you link entities between an AutoCAD drawing and another document, you connect the two applications. The link tells the destination document where to find the original drawing. Linked drawings are automatically updated as the drawing is modified.

20.2.1 Copying bitmap images to Windows Clipboard

You can copy the contents of an entire screen, including the menu bar, tool boxes, and status bar, from AutoCAD to Windows Clipboard bitmap format by pressing the <print screen> key on your keyboard. Try it now. To see if the procedure worked, hold down the <alt> key and press <tab> repeatedly until the Program Manager (or Windows Clipboard) title is displayed in a box in the middle of the screen. Then release the <alt> key to display the Program Manager window. Click on the Main Window and then double-click on the Clipboard Viewer icon to display the Clipboard Viewer window. If an image of your screen isn't visible, toggle back to AutoCAD and try pressing the <alt> and <print screen> keys together. Toggle to Clipboard Viewer. If an image of your screen still isn't visible, try pressing <shift> and <print screen> together and check Clipboard Viewer again.

The image will be transferred to Clipboard, and you can paste it into other applications. This will be discussed later in this chapter.

You can also transfer objects to other documents in bitmapped format by using the Cutclip and Copyclip commands, discussed in the following section. These commands copy images in vector format, but Clipboard stores the image in both bitmap and vector format so you can paste it into applications requiring a bitmap format.

20.2.2 Copying vectors to Windows Clipboard

You can copy vectors from AutoCAD to another application in AutoCAD and Windows metafile format with the following commands:

Cutclip. Deletes selected objects from the drawing and stores them in the Clipboard in vector format. Select Edit, then Cut, or choose the Cut icon (Figure 20.1) from the standard toolbar. AutoCAD will respond with `Select objects`. Select the objects using standard AutoCAD selection methods, draw something, and then try Cutclip. Toggle to Windows Clipboard Viewer to verify that the object is stored.

Copyclip. Copies selected objects from the drawing to the Clipboard in vector format. Select Edit, then Copy or choose the Copy icon (Figure 20.2) from the standard toolbar. AutoCAD will respond with `Select objects`. Select the objects using standard AutoCAD selection methods.

Copylink. Copies the current AutoCAD view to the Clipboard in vector format. Select the following from the menu bar: Edit <pick> Copy View <pick>. Toggle to Windows Clipboard Viewer to verify that the current view is stored. Copylink also lets you link applications, discussed in section 20.4.

20.3 Pasting (Embedding) Objects into AutoCAD

As discussed earlier, applications use different formats for storing information, such as bitmap, Windows metafile, and AutoCAD vector format. Windows Clipboard stores data in all the formats the application is able to transfer to the Clipboard. When data is copied from AutoCAD to the Clipboard, it's stored in all available formats. When the contents of the Clipboard are pasted (embedded) into AutoCAD, AutoCAD uses the format that retains the most information, with AutoCAD vector being the preferred format. If the information is stored in the Clipboard in bitmap format only, AutoCAD will accept the bitmap format. Draw two joined lines on the screen and then select the following:

Edit <pick> Copy <pick> `Select objects:` Select the two lines. <pick> `Select objects:` <return>

You can use the Paste command to insert entities into another document. Using the current drawing, for example:

Standard <toolbar> Paste (Figure 20.3) (or select Edit, then Paste) <pick> `Insertion point:` Drag the block to a desired point. <pick> `X Scale factor <1>/ Corner/XYZ:` <return> `Y Scale factor (default = x):` <return> `Rotation angle <0>:` <return>

Figure 20.1 Cut tool.

Figure 20.2 Copy tool.

Figure 20.3 Paste tool.

List the data for the block:

Object Properties <toolbar> List (Figure 6.33) <pick> Select objects: Select the entity that was pasted. <pick> Select objects: <return>

AutoCAD will list data for the entity. Note that it's a block with a name similar to A$CA7D1. You can edit embedded AutoCAD items with grips. For information on editing with grips, refer to section 20.5, later in this chapter, and appendix D, section D.2. If an embedded object is modified, the original drawing (where the object was created) won't be affected.

Although the previous lines pasted into AutoCAD were created in AutoCAD, you can create objects in any Windows application that supports OLE, copy them into the Clipboard, and then paste them into AutoCAD. For example, toggle to Program Manager and display the Accessories window. Then open Paintbrush or another draw program you're familiar with, and draw something. With Paintbrush, click on the Cut tool and cut the object to be pasted. Then click on Copy on the Edit menu to copy the selected object to the Clipboard. Toggle back to AutoCAD and choose Paste in the Edit menu to embed the object into AutoCAD.

20.3.1 Editing embedded information

You can modify objects embedded in AutoCAD from another application as follows:

1. Double-click on the embedded object.
2. Windows will open the application that created the object, with the object displayed. Modify the object and save the file if needed.
3. Selecting Update from the application's File menu.
4. Closing the application or toggling back to AutoCAD.

AutoCAD will now display the modified object. You can resize or move the object in AutoCAD by clicking once on the object. Then click on a corner grip of the objects frame and drag the frame to resize it. To move the object, select it and then move the cursor into its frame until the four-arrowed move cursor appears. Then click, hold, and drag the object to the desired location.

20.3.2 Embedding objects starting in AutoCAD

As outlined previously, you can embed objects created in another document into AutoCAD by opening the application, copying the information you want to embed into the Windows Clipboard, opening the AutoCAD drawing, and choosing Paste in the Edit menu. You can also embed an object starting from AutoCAD as follows:

1. Open an AutoCAD drawing.

2. From the Edit menu, choose Insert Object. The Insert New Object dialog box, illustrated in Figure 20.4, will be displayed. Choose an application, e.g., Paintbrush Picture, and press OK.

3. The application selected will be opened. Create the information you want to insert, and save the file if necessary.

4. Select Update from the application's File menu.

5. Close the application.

When you reopen AutoCAD, the object will be inserted.

20.4   Linking an AutoCAD Drawing

Open the Proj-16 drawing. Set the current working mode to model and click on the viewport with the 3-D view, making it the current viewport. This view was saved with the name 3D in chapter 16, section 16.2. Before you link to a view, make sure the view is named. If it isn't, AutoCAD will give it a name such as OLE1. The Copy View option in the Edit menu will remain grayed until the drawing is named. Before linked to the 3-D view, freeze the layer named Viewlyr1. If this view is on, you can include the viewport outlines in the linked drawing in some form. Choose the following to link the 3-D view:

Edit <pick> Copy View <pick>

The Copylink command will be echoed at the command line and the view transferred to the Clipboard. Now the view needs to be linked to another application, in this case the Windows Write program, as follows:

1. Hold down the <alt> key and press and release the <tab> key repeatedly until the Program Manager title is displayed, then release the <alt> key. Windows Program manager will be in the foreground.

2. Click on the Accessories window, bringing it to the foreground, as shown in Figure 20.5.

3. Double-click on the Write icon, as shown back in Figure 20.4. The Write program will be loaded.

4. Choose the following: Edit <pick> Paste Link (or Paste Special) <pick>, then exit AutoCAD.

The 3-D view will appear in the Word document at the location of the cursor.

20.4.1   Editing linked views

Edit the linked 3-D view as follows:

1. Double-click on the 3-D view in the Write document. Windows OLE will locate the originating program (AutoCAD), load it, and open drawing Proj-17. Make sure you're in model space and layer Viewlyr1 is frozen.

2. Click on the Front view, making it current. Save the drawing.

3. Hold down the <alt> key and press the <tab> key as required to return to the Write document.

4. Choose the following: Edit <pick> Links... <pick>. The Links dialog box (Figure 20.6) will be displayed.

5. Press the Update Now box. The 3-D view will be updated and replaced with a plan view of the front UCS.

If you save the current document and exit Write, the next time the document is opened in Write you'll be asked if you want to update the links (Figure 20.7). If you choose Yes, OLE will boot the originating program and the file containing the linked view. You might have to reset the UCS in order to get the proper view in the destination document. Toggle to the Write document, as described in the previous instructions.

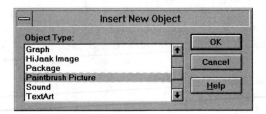

Figure 20.4 Opening an application.

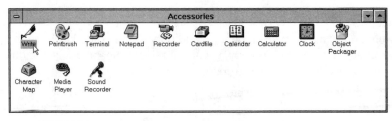

Figure 20.5 Accessories Window.

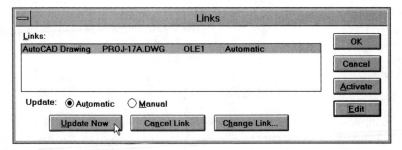

Figure 20.6 Links dialog box.

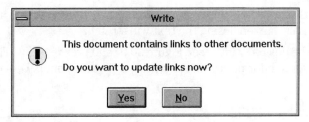

Figure 20.7 Updating links box.

20.5 Pasting Text from Windows Clipboard

You can import text from a Windows word-processing program into AutoCAD as follows:

1. Boot AutoCAD (if AutoCAD is already booted with Proj-16 loaded, begin a new drawing named c:\drawings\test).

2. Hold down <alt> and press <tab> and toggle to the Windows Program Manager.

3. Bring the Accessories window (Figure 20.5) to the foreground and open Notepad by clicking twice on its icon. Type some text into Notepad, then select the text by holding down the <pick> button on the mouse as you slide the cursor through the text. The selected text will be highlighted.

4. Choose Copy (or Cut) in Notepad's edit menu.

5. Toggle to AutoCAD. If you haven't already added text to the drawing and set the text height, do so now. Assuming the desired text height is 0.3 units, select the following:

Draw <toolbar> Single Line Text <pick> Justify/Style/<Start point>: Digitize a point anywhere on the drawing. <pick> Height <0.2>: **0.3** <return> Rotation angle <0>: <return> Text: **t** <return> Modify <toolbar> Erase <pick> Select objects: Digitize the text just entered. <pick> Select objects: <return>

Then select the Paste tool with the following:

Standard <toolbar> Paste (Figure 20.3) <pick>

The text will be copied to AutoCAD as paragraph text (Figure 20.8), with a text height (0.3) based on the last text entered into the drawing. You can edit the text with the Mtext editor, using grips. For information on using the Mtext editor, refer to appendix D, section D.4. You can change the location and space occupied by the text by using grips as follows:

1. Click three times on the small blue grip box on the top right corner of the pasted text (see Figure 20.8). A blue grip will appear at each corner of a box, enclosing the text.

2. Click on one of the grips, turning the grip from blue to red. As you move the mouse, the imaginary box enclosing the text will stretch.

3. Move the box to the desired width (see Figure 20.9) and press <pick>. Then press <esc> twice. For more information on using grips refer to appendix D, section D.2.

20.6 Importing/Exporting Files

AutoCAD objects can be exported (saved) in a variety of file formats and then imported into other applications. To export a file:

File <pick> Export...

The Export Data dialog box illustrated in Figure 20.10 will be displayed. Select a file type in the List Files of Type dialog box, and enter a filename. To import a WMF file to AutoCAD, choose the following:

File <pick> Import...

The Import File dialog box (Figure 20.11) will be displayed. Select a file to import and then press OK to import the file.

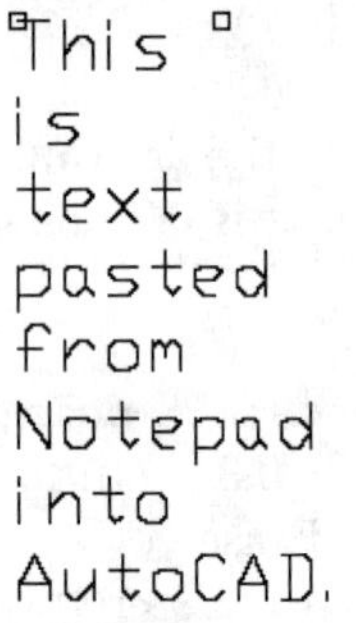

This
is
text
pasted
from
Notepad
into   **Figure 20.8** Text pasted into AutoCAD.
AutoCAD.

This is text pasted from
Notepad into AutoCAD.

Figure 20.9 Modified text.

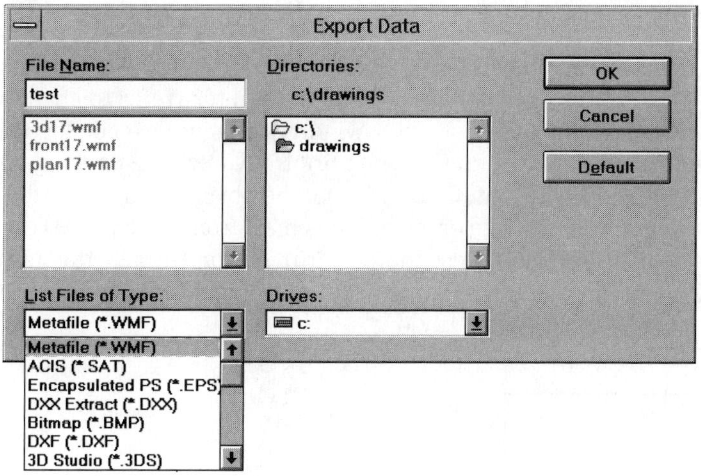

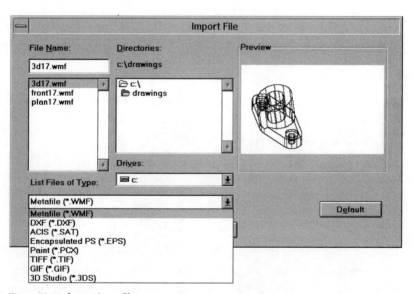

Figure 20.10 Exporting a file.

Figure 20.11 Importing a file.

20.7 Viewing, Printing, and Removing Linked and Embedded Objects

In order to plot or print embedded or linked objects in AutoCAD, you must configure AutoCAD to plot/print using a Windows system printer (refer to chapter 7, section 7.3). If AutoCAD is configured for a non-Windows driver, the embedded or linked object will be visible on the screen but won't print. If you view a drawing having linked or embedded objects with AutoCAD for DOS, the objects won't be visible.

To cut, copy, or clear a linked or embedded object from an AutoCAD drawing, place the cursor on the object and press the <return> button (usually the middle or 2) on the mouse to display the menu box illustrated in Figure 20.12. Choose the desired menu item: Cut, Copy, Clear, or Undo.

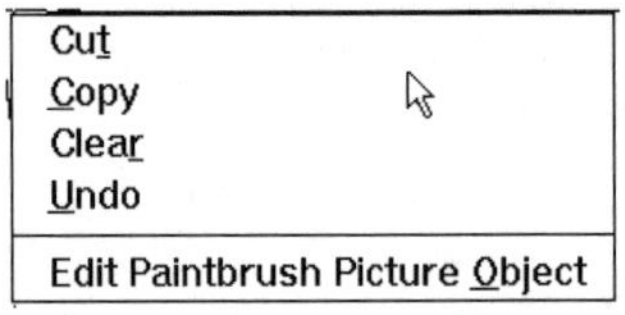

```
Cut
Copy              ▷
Clear
Undo
─────────────────────────
Edit Paintbrush Picture Object
```

Figure 20.12 Moving OLE objects.

A

Toolbar Menus

This appendix lists all the toolbar menus in AutoCAD, arranged as follows:

- Each main section addresses a separate toolbar, for example Standard and Modify. The toolbar is shown at the beginning of each of these sections.

- Sections within those main sections describe and illustrate each tool or icon in the toolbar. For example, New and Open (A.1.1 and A.1.2) are icons in the Standard toolbar (A.1).

- Subsections that don't have reference numbers represent pop-up icons (flyouts) you can invoke after choosing the main icon (the numbered section preceding the group of subsections). The appearance of the main icon defaults to whatever fly-out was last selected, so no icon is shown for icons with flyouts.

- When the actual icon/command name differs from the commonly used name for it, for example qsave for save or copyclip for copy, both names are listed in the section head—the descriptive name first, followed by the actual name in parentheses.

Table A.1, at the end of the appendix, lists all the toolbar menus and tools alphabetically and refers you to the correct section in the appendix.

A.1 Standard toolbar

A.1.1 New

 Creates a new drawing file.

A.1.2 Open

 Opens an existing drawing file.

A.1.3 Save (qsave)

 Saves the current drawing.

A.1.4 Print (plot)

 Plots a drawing to a plotter, printer, or file.

A.1.5. Spell

 Checks spelling in a drawing.

A.1.6 Cut (cutclip)

 Copies objects to the Windows Clipboard and erases them from the drawing.

A.1.7. Copy (copyclip)

 Copies objects to the Windows Clipboard.

A.1.8 Paste (pasteclip)

 Inserts data that has been copied to the Windows Clipboard.

A.1.9 Undo (u)

 Undoes the most recent operation

A.1.10 Redo

 Reverses the effects of the previous U command.

A.1.11 Tool windows

 Aerial view (dsviewer) Opens the Aerial View window.

 Draw toolbar. See section A.3.

Modify toolbar. See section A.4.

 Dimensioning toolbar. See section A.5.

 Solids toolbar. See section A.6.

 Surfaces toolbar. See section A.7.

 External Reference toolbar. See section A.8.

 Attribute toolbar. See section A.9.

 Render toolbar. See section A.10.

 External Database toolbar. See section A.11.

 Object Properties toolbar. See section A.2.

 Standard toolbar. See section A.1.

A.1.12 Select Objects

 Select w. Selects all objects inside rectangular window.

 Select c. Selects all objects within or crossing a rectangle.

 Select g. Selects all objects within a specified group.

 Select p. Selects the most recent (previous) selection set.

 Select l. Selects the most recently created (last) object.

 Select all. Selects all objects on thawed layers.

Select wp. Selects all objects inside a selection polygon.

 Select cp. Selects all objects within or crossing a selection polygon.

 Select f. Selects all objects crossing a selection fence.

 Select a. Switches to add selection mode.

 Select r. Switches to remove selection mode.

 filter. Creates a list of properties required of an object for it to be selected.

A.1.13 Group

 Creates a named selection set of objects.

A.1.14 Object Snap

 from. Snaps to a point relative to other geometry.

 end. Snaps to the closest endpoint of an object, arc, elliptical arc, ray, mline, or line, or to the closest corner of a trace, solid, or 3dface.

 mid. Snaps to the midpoint of an arc, elliptical arc, spline, ellipse, ray, solid, xline, mline, or line.

 int. Snaps to the intersection of a line, arc, spline, elliptical arc, ellipse, ray, xline, mline, or circle.

 app. Snaps to the apparent intersection of two objects (line, arc, spline, elliptical arc, ellipse, ray, xline, mline, or circle).

 cen. Snaps to the center of an arc, elliptical arc, ellipse, solid, or circle.

 qua. Snaps to a quadrant point of an arc, elliptical arc, ellipse, solid, or circle.

 per. Snaps to a point perpendicular to an arc, elliptical arc, ellipse, spline, ray, xline, mline, line, solid, or circle.

tan. Snaps to the tangent of an arc, elliptical arc, ellipse, or circle.

 nod. Snaps to a point object (node).

 ins. Snaps to the insertion point of text, a block, a shape, or an attribute.

 nea. Snaps to the nearest point of an arc, ellipse, spline, ray, xline, mline, line, circle, or point.

 quick s. In conjunction with other Object Snap modes, snaps to the first snap point found.

 non. Turns off Object Snap modes.

 ddosnap. Sets running Object Snap modes and changes the target box size.

 cal. Evaluates mathematical and geometric expressions.

A.1.15 Point Filters

 .x. Makes the x coordinate the next specified value.

 .y. Makes the y coordinate the next specified value.

 .z. Makes the z coordinate the next specified value.

 .xy. Makes the x,y coordinate the next specified value.

 .xz. Makes the x,z coordinate the next specified value.

 .yz. Makes the y,z coordinate the next specified value.

A.1.16 UCS

 dducsp. Selects a preset user coordinate system (UCS).

dducs. Manages defined user coordinate systems.

 ucs w. Sets the current UCS to the world coordinate system.

 ucs o. Defines a new UCS by shifting the current UCS origin.

 ucs za. Defines a new UCS by specifying the origin and direction of the positive z axis.

 ucs 3. Defines a new UCS by specifying the origin and direction of the positive x and y axes.

 ucs ob. Defines a new UCS based on a selected object.

 ucs v. Defines a new UCS with the xy plane parallel to the screen.

 ucs x. Rotates the current UCS about its x axis.

 ucs y. Rotates the current UCS about its x axis.

 ucs z. Rotates the current UCS about its z axis.

 ucs p. Restores the previous UCS.

 ucs r. Restores a saved UCS as the current UCS.

 ucs s. Saves the current UCS to a specified name.

A.1.17 View

 ddview. Creates and restores views.

 vpoint 0,0,1. Sets the 3-D visualization viewing direction from a point in space on the north (top) side of the object.

vpoint 0,0,–1. Sets the 3-D visualization viewing direction from a point in space on the south (bottom) side of the object.

 vpoint –1,0,0. Sets the 3-D visualization viewing direction from a point in space on the west (left) side of the object.

 vpoint 1,0,0. Sets the 3-D visualization viewing direction from a point in space on the east (right) side of the object.

 vpoint 0,–1,0. Sets the 3-D visualization viewing direction from a point in space in front of the object.

 vpoint 0,1,0. Sets the 3-D visualization viewing direction from a point in space behind (in back of) the object.

 vpoint –1,–1,1. Sets the 3-D visualization viewing direction from a point in space on the southwest (sw) side of the object.

 vpoint 1,–1,1. Sets the 3-D visualization viewing direction from a point in space on the southeast (se) side of the object.

 vpoint 1,1,1. Sets the 3-D visualization viewing direction from a point in space on the northeast (ne) side of the object.

 vpoint –1,1,1. Sets the 3-D visualization viewing direction from a point in space on the northwest (nw) side of the object.

A.1.18 Redraw

 Redraw. Refreshes the display of the current viewport.

 Redrawall. Refreshes the display of all viewports.

A.1.19 Pan

 Moves the drawing display into the current viewport (flyout).

A.1.20 Zoom In (zoom 2x)

 Zooms the display to two times the current view.

A.1.21 Zoom Out (zoom .5x)

 Zooms the display to half the current view.

A.1.22 Zoom Window (zoom w)

 Zooms an area specified by two opposite corners of a rectangular window.

A.1.23 Zoom

 Increases or decreases the apparent size of objects in the current viewport.

A.1.24 Space

 tilemode 1. Returns to tiled viewport mode and restores the most recently active tiled viewport configuration.

mspace. If a floating model viewport exists, this switches to model space.

 mview. If no floating model viewport exists, this creates a floating viewport and turns on existing viewports.

 pspace. Switches to paper space.

A.1.25 Help (or ?)

 Displays online help.

A.2 Object Properties Toolbar

Layers

Color control

Linetype

Object creation

Multiline style

Properties

Inquiry

A.2.1 Layers (ddlmodes)

 Manages layers.

A.2.2 Color control (ddcolor)

 Sets the color for new objects.

A.2.3 Linetype (ddltype)

 Loads and sets linetypes.

A.2.4 Object creation (ddemodes)

 Sets properties for new objects.

A.2.5 Multiline style (mlstyle)

 Defines a style for multiple parallel lines.

A.2.6 Properties (ddmodify)

 Controls object properties.

A.2.7 Inquiry

 list. Displays database information for selected objects.

 id. Displays coordinates of a location.

 area. Calculates the area and perimeter of objects or of defined areas.

 massprop. Calculates and displays the properties of regions or solids.

 dist. Measures the distance and angle between two points.

A.3 Draw Toolbar

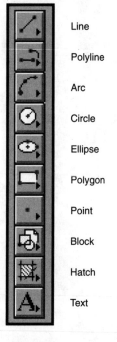

	Line
	Polyline
	Arc
	Circle
	Ellipse
	Polygon
	Point
	Block
	Hatch
	Text

A.3.1 Line

 line. Allows you to draw 2-D or 3-D lines by specifying endpoints.

 xline. Creates infinite lines commonly used as construction lines.

 ray. Creates semi-infinite lines commonly used as construction lines. A ray has a specific start point and extends to infinity.

A.3.2 Polyline

 pline. Creates a 2-D polyline.

 3dpoly. Creates a 3-D polyline of straight-line segments.

 mline. Creates multiple parallel lines.

 spline. Creates a quadratic or cubic spline curve.

A.3.3 Arc

 Creates an arc with icons for optional inputs (flyout).

A.3.4 Circle

 circle. Creates a circle with icons for optional input: center, radius, center, diameter, 2P, 3P, and TTR (flyout).

 donut. Draws filled circles and rings.

A.3.5 Ellipse

 Creates an ellipse or elliptical arc (flyout).

A.3.6 Polygon

 rectang. Draws a rectangular polyline.

 polygon. Creates an equilateral closed polygon.

 solid. Creates solid filled polygons.

 region. Creates a region object for a selected set of existing objects.

 boundary. Creates a region or a polyline of a closed boundary.

A.3.7 Point

 point. Creates a point objects

 divide. Places evenly spaced point objects or blocks along the length or perimeter of an object.

 measure. Places point objects or blocks at measured intervals on an object.

A.3.8 Block

 ddinsert. Inserts a block or another drawing.

 block. Creates a block definition from a set of objects.

A.3.9 Hatch

 dbhatch. Fills an enclosed area with an associative hatch pattern.

 psfill. Fills a 2-D polyline outline with a Postscript pattern.

A.3.10 Text

 mtext. Creates paragraph text.

 dtext. Displays text on the screen as it's entered.

 text. Creates a single line of text.

A.4 Modify Toolbar

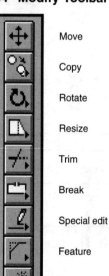

Move

Copy

Rotate

Resize

Trim

Break

Special edit

Feature

Explode

Erase

A.4.1 Move

 Displaces objects a specified distance in a specified direction.

A.4.2 Copy

 copy. Duplicates objects.

 offset. Constructs an entity parallel to another circle, line, or curve entity.

 mirror. Creates a mirror image of an object.

 mirror3d. Creates a mirror image of an object about a plane.

 array. Creates multiple copies of an object in a rectangular array.

 array. Creates multiple copies of an object in a circular array.

 3darray. Creates a 3-D rectangular array.

 3darray. Creates a 3-D circular array.

A.4.3 Rotate

 rotate. Rotates objects to a new position about a base point.

 rotate3d. Rotates objects about a 3-D axis.

 align. Moves and rotates objects to align with other objects.

A.4.4 Resize

 stretch. Moves or stretches an object.

 scale. Enlarges or reduces selected objects equally in x and y directions.

 lengthen. Lengthens an object.

 point change. Changes the properties of existing objects.

A.4.5 Trim

 trim. Trims objects at a cutting edge, determined by other objects.

 extend. Extends an object to meet another object.

A.4.6 Break

 Erases part of an object, or splits an object in two (flyout).

A.4.7. Special edit

 pedit. Edits polylines and 3-D polygon meshes.

 mledit. Edits multiple parallel lines.

 splinedit. Edits a spline object.

 ddedit. Edits text and attribute definitions.

 hatchedit. Modifies an existing associative hatch block.

A.4.8 Feature

 chamfer. Bevels the edges of objects.

 fillet. Fillets the edges or objects.

A.4.9 Explode

 explode. Breaks a compound object into its component parts.

 union. Creates a composite region or solid.

 subtract. Creates a composite region or solid, subtracting the area of one set of regions from another and subtracting the volume of one set of solids from another.

 intersect. Creates composite solids or regions from the intersection of two or more solids or regions.

A.4.10 Erase

 Removes objects from a drawing (flyout).

A.5 Dimensioning Toolbar

Linear dimensioning

Aligned dimensioning

Radial dimensioning

Angular dimensioning

Ordinate dimensioning

Baseline dimensioning

Continue dimensioning

Center mark

Leader

Tolerance

Align dimension text

Dimension style

A.5.1 Linear dimensioning (dimlinear)

Creates linear dimensions.

A.5.2 Aligned dimensioning (dimaligned)

Creates an aligned linear dimension.

A.5.3 Radial dimensioning

 dimdiameter. Creates a diameter dimension for circles and arcs.

 dimradius. Creates a radial dimension for circles and arcs.

A.5.4 Angular dimensioning (dimangular)

 Creates an angular dimension.

A.5.5 Ordinate dimensioning (dimordinate)

 Creates ordinate point dimensions using x or y coordinates.

A.5.6 Baseline dimensioning (dimbaseline)

 Continues a linear, angular, or ordinate dimension from the baseline of the previous or selected dimension.

A.5.7 Continue dimensioning (dimcontinue)

 Continues a linear, angular, or ordinate dimension from the second extension line of the previous or selected dimension.

A.5.8 Center mark (dimcenter)

 Creates center marks or center lines for circles or arcs.

A.5.9 Leader

 Creates a leader line with annotations.

A.5.10 Tolerance

 Creates geometric tolerances.

A.5.11 Align dimension text (dimtedit)

 Edits dimensions with options: Specify Location, Home/New, Rotate/Oblique.

A.5.12 Dimension style

 ddim. Creates and modifies dimension styles.

 dimedit. Edits dimension text and extension lines.

A.6 Solids Toolbar

Box

Sphere

Cylinder

Cone

Wedge

Torus

Extrude

Revolve

Slice

Section

Interference

AME convert

A.6.1 Box

 Creates a 3-D solid box (flyout).

A.6.2 Sphere

 Creates a 3-D solid sphere.

A.6.3 Cylinder

 Creates a 3-D solid cylinder (flyout).

A.6.4 Cone

 Creates a 3-D solid cone (flyout).

A.6.5 Wedge

 Creates a 3-D solid with a sloping face, tapered along the x axis (flyout).

A.6.6 Torus

 Creates a donut-shaped solid.

A.6.7 Extrude

 Creates a unique solid primitive by extruding an existing 2-D object.

A.6.8 Revolve

 Creates a solid by revolving a 2-D object about an axis.

A.6.9 Slice

 Slices a set of solids with a plane.

A.6.10 Section

 Uses the intersection of a plane and solids to create a region.

A.6.11 Interference

 Finds the interference of two or more solids and creates a composite solid from their common volume.

A.6.12 AME convert (ameconvert)

 Converts AME solid models into AutoCAD solid models.

A.7 Surfaces Toolbar

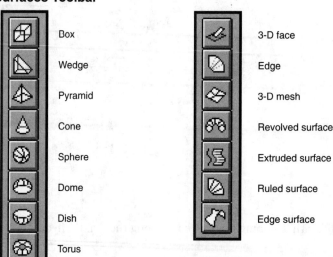

Box		3-D face	
Wedge		Edge	
Pyramid		3-D mesh	
Cone		Revolved surface	
Sphere		Extruded surface	
Dome		Ruled surface	
Dish		Edge surface	
Torus			

A.7.1   Box (3d box)

 Creates a 3-D wireframe box.

A.7.2   Wedge (3d wedge)

 Creates a 3-D wireframe wedge with the sloping face tapered along the x axis.

A.7.3   Pyramid (3d pyramid)

 Creates a 3-D wireframe pyramid.

A.7.4   Cone (3d cone)

 Creates a 3-D wireframe cone.

A.7.5   Sphere (3d sphere)

 Creates a 3-D wireframe sphere.

A.7.6   Dome (3d dome)

 Creates the upper half of a spherical polygon mesh.

A.7.7   Dish (3d dish)

 Creates the lower half of a spherical polygon mesh.

A.7.8   Torus (3d torus)

 Creates a toroidal mesh that's parallel to the xy plane of the current UCS.

A.7.9   3-D face (3dface)

 Creates a 3-D face.

A.7.10   Edge

 Changes the visibility of 3-D face edges.

A.7.11   3-D mesh (3d mesh)

 Creates a 3-D polygon mesh object.

A.7.12 Revolved surface (revsurf)

 Creates a rotate surface about a selected axis.

A.7.13 Extruded surface (tabsurf)

 Creates a tabulated surface from a path curve and a direction vector.

A.7.14 Ruled surface (rulesurf)

 Creates a ruled surface between two curves.

A.7.15 Edge surface (edgesurf)

 Creates a 3-D polygon mesh from four adjoining edges.

A.8 External Reference Toolbar

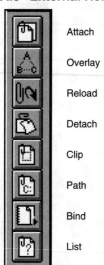

Attach

Overlay

Reload

Detach

Clip

Path

Bind

List

A.8.1 Attach (xref attach)

 Attaches an external reference to a drawing.

A.8.2 Overlay (xref overlay)

 Overlays an xref so it doesn't appear in a parent drawing that references the child drawing containing the xref.

A.8.3 Reload (xref reload)

 Reloads one or more xrefs.

A.8.4 Detach (xref detach)

 Detaches xrefs from a drawing, erasing all copies of the specified xref.

A.8.5 Clip (xref clip)

 Inserts and clips an xref, removing a portion of the xref from view to fit a defined viewport.

A.8.6 Path (xref path)

 Edits the path name of an xref.

A.8.7 Bind

 xbind. Binds all dependent symbols of an xref to a drawing.

 xbind block. Binds specified block objects in an xref to a drawing.

 xbind layer. Binds specified layer objects in an xref to a drawing.

 xbind ltype. Binds specified linetype objects in an xref to a drawing.

 xbind style. Binds specified text styles in an xref to a drawing.

 xbind dimstyle. Binds specified dimension styles in an xref to a drawing.

A.8.8 List (xref list)

 Lists an xref's path and the number of xrefs attached to the drawing.

A.9 Attribute Toolbar

Define attribute

Redefine attribute

Edit attribute

Edit attribute globally

A.9.1 Define attribute (ddatdef)

 Creates an attibute definition.

A.9.2 Redefine attribute (attredef)

 Redefines a block and updates associated attributes.

A.9.3 Edit attribute (ddatte)

 Edits the variable attributes of a block.

A.9.4 Edit attribute globally (attedit)

 Changes attribute information independently of its block definition.

A.10 Render Toolbar

Hide

Shade

Render

Scenes

Lights

Materials

Materials Library

Render preferences

Statistics

A.10.1 Hide

 Regenerates a 3-D model with hidden lines suppressed.

A.10.2 Shade

 Displays a flat-shaded image of the drawing in the current viewport.

A.10.3   Render

 Creates a realistically shaded image of a 3-D wireframe or solid model.

A.10.4   Scenes

 Manages scenes in model space.

A.10.5   Light

 Manages lights and lighting effects.

A.10.6   Materials (mat)

 Manages rendering materials.

A.10.7   Materials library (matlib)

 Imports and exports material to and from a library of materials.

A.10.8   Render preferences (rpref)

 Sets rendering preferences.

A.10.9   Statistics (stats)

 Displays rendering statistics.

A.11   External Database Toolbar

Administration

Rows

Links

Select objects

Export links

SQL editor

A.11.1 Administration (aseadmin)

 Performs administrative functions for external database commands.

A.11.2 Rows (aserows)

 Displays and edits table data, and creates links and selection sets.

A.11.3 Links (aselinks)

 Manipulates links between objects and an external database.

A.11.4 Select objects (aseselect)

 Creates a selection set from rows linked to text selection sets and graphic selection sets.

A.11.5 Export links (asexport)

 Exports link information for selected objects.

A.11.6 SQL editor (asesqled)

 Executes structured query language (SQL) statements.

A.12 Miscellaneous Toolbar

Mesh

Insert multiple blocks

Oops

Shade

Sketch

Trace

A.12.1 Mesh

 Creates a planar mesh of m,n size.

A.12.2 Insert multiple blocks (minsert)

 Inserts multiple instances of a block in a rectangular array.

A.12.3 Oops

 Restores erased objects.

A.12.4 Shape

 Inserts a shape.

A.12.5 Sketch

 Creates a series of freehand line segments.

A.12.6 Trace

 Creates solid, filled, or open continuous lines.

TABLE A.1 Alphabetical List of Toolbar Menus and Tools

Tool toolbar	Appendix section
3-D mesh	A.7.11
3-D face	A.7.9
administration	A.11.1
align dimension text	A.5.11
aligned dimensioning	A.5.2
AME convert	A.6.12
angular dimensioning	A.5.4
arc flyout	A.3.3
attach	A.8.1
Attribute toolbar	A.9
baseline dimensioning	A.5.6
bind flyout	A.8.7
block flyout	A.3.8
box	A.6.1, A.7.1
break	A.4.6
center mark	A.5.8
circle flyout	A.3.4
clip	A.8.5
color control	A.2.2
cone	A.6.4, A.7.4
continue dimensioning	A.5.7
copy flyout	A.4.2
copy	A.1.7
cut	A.1.6

TABLE A.1 (Continued)

Tool toolbar	Appendix section
cylinder	A.6.3
define attribute	A.9.1
detach	A.8.4
dimension style flyout	A.5.12
Dimensioning toolbar	A.5
dish	A.7.7
dome	A.7.6
Draw toolbar	A.3
edge	A.7.10
edge surface	A.7.15
edit attribute	A.9.3
edit attribute globally	A.9.4
ellipse	A.3.5
erase	A.4.10
explode flyout	A.4.9
export links	A.11.5
External Reference toolbar	A.8
External Database toolbar	A.11
extrude	A.6.7
extruded surface	A.7.13
feature flyout	A.4.8
hatch flyout	A.3.9
help	A.1.25
hide	A.10.1
inquiry flyout	A.2.7
insert multiple blocks	A.12.2
interference	A.6.11
layers	A.2.1
leader	A.5.9
lights	A.10.5
line flyout	A.3.1
linear dimensioning	A.5.1
linetype	A.2.3
links	A.11.3
list	A.8.8
materials library	A.10.7
materials	A.10.6
mesh	A.12.1

TABLE A.1 (Continued)

Tool toolbar	Appendix section
Miscellaneous toolbar	A.12
Modify toolbar	A.4
move	A.4.1
multiline style	A.2.5
new	A.1.1
object creation	A.2.4
object group flyout	A.1.13
object snap flyout	A.1.14
object Properties toolbar	A.2
oops	A.12.3
open	A.1.2
ordinate dimensioning	A.5.5
overlay	A.8.2
pan	A.1.19
paste	A.1.8
path	A.8.6
point flyout	A.3.7
point filters flyout	A.1.15
polygon flyout	A.3.6
polyline flyout	A.3.2
print	A.1.4
properties	A.2.6
pyramid	A.7.3
radial dimensioning flyout	A.5.3
redefine attribute	A.9.2
redo	A.1.10
redraw flyout	A.1.18
reload	A.8.3
render	A.10.3
render preferences	A.10.8
Render toolbar	A.10
resize flyout	A.4.4
revolve	A.6.8
revolved surface	A.7.12
rotate flyout	A.4.3
rows	A.11.2
ruled surface	A.7.14
save	A.1.3

TABLE A.1 (Continued)

Tool toolbar	Appendix section
scenes	A.10.4
section	A.6.10
select objects	A.11.4
select objects flyout	A.1.12
shade	A.10.2
shape	A.12.4
sketch	A.12.5
slice	A.6.9
Solids toolbar	A.6
space flyout	A.1.24
special edit flyout	A.4.7
spelling	A.1.5
sphere	A.6.2, A.7.5
SQL editor	A.11.6
Standard toolbar	A.1
statistics	A.10.9
Surfaces toolbar	A.7
text flyout	A.3.10
tolerance	A.5.10
tool flyout	A.1.11
torus	A.6.6, A.7.8
trace	A.12.6
trim flyout	A.4.5
UCS flyout	A.1.16
undo	A.1.9
view flyout	A.1.17
wedge	A.6.5, A.7.2
zoom	A.1.23
zoom window	A.1.22
zoom in	A.1.20
zoom out	A.1.21

Plot Drawing Scale Factors

Scale	Scale factor	Scale	Scale factor
Drawing units = meters (decimal)			
1:1	1000	1:30	33.33334
1:1.5	666.6667	1:40	25
1:2	500	1:50	20
1:2.5	400	1:100	10
1:3	333.3334	1:200	5
1:4	250	1:250	4
1:5	200	1:300	3.333334
1:10	100	1:400	2.5
1:15	66.66667	1:500	2
1:25	40		

Scale	Scale factor	Scale	Scale factor
Drawing units = millimeters (decimal)			
1:1	1.0	1:30	0.033
1:1.5	0.6666667	1:40	0.025
1:2	0.5	1:50	0.02
1:2.5	0.4	1:100	0.01
1:3	0.3333334	1:200	0.005
1:4	0.25	1:250	0.004
1:5	0.2	1:300	0.0033
1:10	0.1	1:400	0.0025
1:15	0.0667	1:500	0.002
1:25	0.04		

Drawing units = feet (architecture)

¹⁄₁₆" = 1'0"	0.00521	½" = 1'0"	0.0417
³⁄₃₂"= 1'0"	0.0078125	¾" = 1'0"	0.0625
⅛" = 1'0"	0.0104	1" = 1'0"	0.0833
¼" = 1'0"	0.0208	1½" = 1'0"	0.125
⅜" = 1'0"	0 .03125	3" = 1'0"	0.25

Drawing units = feet (engineering)

1" = 1'0"		100" = 1'0"	
1.5" = 1'0"	0.0833	150" = 1'0"	0.000833
2" = 1'0"	0.0555	200" = 1'0"	0.000555
2.5" = 1'0"	0.0417	250" = 1'0"	0.000417
3" = 1'0"	0.0333	300" = 1'0"	0.000333
4" = 1'0"	0.0278	400" = 1'0"	0.000278
5" = 1'0"	0.0208	500" = 1'0"	0.000167
10" = 1'0"	0.0167	1000" = 1'0"	0.000083
15" = 1'0"	0.0083	1500" = 1'0"	0.000055
20" = 1'0"	0.0042	2000" = 1'0"	0.000042
25" = 1'0"	0.0033	2500" = 1'0"	0.000033
30" = 1'0"	0.0028	3000" = 1'0"	0.000028
40" = 1'0"	0.0021	4000" = 1'0"	0.000021
50" = 1'0"	0.0017	5000" = 1'0"	0.000017

AutoCAD Scale and Text Heights

TABLE C.1 AutoCAD Scale and Text Heights—Imperial Units

			A. Drawing units: Feet (AutoCAD decimal units)						
			³⁄₃₂" Text		⅛" Text		³⁄₁₆" Text	
Drawing scale	Hatch	Ltscale	Txt	Dimscale	Txt	Dimscale	Txt	Dimscale
⅛" = 1'0"	8.00	6.00	0.75	4.17	1.00	5.56	1.50	8.33
³⁄₁₆" = 1'0"	5.33	4.00	0.50	2.78	0.67	3.70	1.00	5.56
¼" = 1'0"	4.00	3.00	0.38	2.08	0.50	2.78	0.75	4.17
⁵⁄₁₆" = 1'0"	3.20	2.40	0.30	1.67	0.40	2.22	0.60	3.33
⅜" = 1'0"	2.67	2.00	0.25	1.39	0.33	1.85	0.50	2.78
½" = 1'0"	2.00	1.50	0.19	1.04	0.25	1.39	0.38	2.08
⅝" = 1'0"	1.60	1.20	0.15	0.83	0.20	1.11	0.30	1.67
¾" = 1'0"	1.33	1.00	0.13	0.69	0.17	0.93	0.25	1.39
⅞" = 1'0"	1.14	0.86	0.11	0.60	0.14	0.79	0.21	1.19
1" = 1'0"	1.00	0.75	0.09	0.52	0.13	0.69	0.19	1.04
1.5" = 1'0"	0.67	0.50	0.06	0.35	0.08	0.46	0.13	0.69
2" = 1'0"	0.50	0.38	0.05	0.26	0.06	0.35	0.09	0.52
¼ size	0.33	0.25	0.03	0.17	0.04	0.23	0.06	0.35
½ size	0.17	0.13	0.02	0.09	0.02	0.12	0.03	0.17
Full size	0.08	0.06	0.01	0.04	0.01	0.06	0.02	0.09

TABLE C.1 (Continued)

B. Drawing units: AutoCAD architectural or engineering units

Drawing scale	Hatch	Ltscale	3/32" Text		1/8" Text		3/16" Text	
			Txt	Dimscale	Txt	Dimscale	Txt	Dimscale
1/8" = 1'0"	96.00	72.00	9.00	50.00	12.00	66.67	18.00	100.00
3/16" = 1'0"	64.00	48.00	6.00	33.33	8.00	44.44	12.00	66.67
1/4" = 1'0"	48.00	36.00	4.50	25.00	6.00	33.33	9.00	50.00
5/16" = 1'0"	38.40	28.80	3.60	20.00	4..80	26.67	7.20	40.00
3/8" = 1'0"	32.00	24.00	3.00	16.67	4.00	22.22	6.00	33.33
1/2" = 1'0"	24.00	18.00	2.25	12.50	3.00	16.67	4.50	25.00
5/8" = 1'0"	19.20	14.40	1.80	10.00	2.40	13.33	3.60	20.00
3/4" = 1'0"	16.00	12.00	1.50	8.33	2.00	11.11	3.00	16.67
7/8" = 1'0"	13.71	10.29	1.29	7.14	1.71	9.52	2.57	14.29
1" = 1'0"	12.00	9.00	1.13	6.25	1.50	8.33	2.25	12.50
1.5" = 1'0"	8.00	6.00	0.75	4.17	1.00	5.56	1.50	8.33
2" = 1'0"	6.00	4.50	0.56	3.13	0.75	4.17	1.13	6.25
1/4 size	4.00	3.00	0.38	2.08	0.50	2.78	0.75	4.17
1/2 size	2.00	1.50	0.19	1.04	0.25	1.39	0.38	2.08
Full size	1.00	0.75	0.09	0.52	0.13	0.69	0.19	1.04

C. Drawing units: Engineering (feet) (AutoCAD decimal units)

Drawing scale	Hatch	Ltscale	3/32" Text		1/8" Text		3/16" Text	
			Txt	Dimscale	Txt	Dimscale	Txt	Dimscale
1:3000	250.00	187.50	23.44	130.21	31.25	173.61	46.88	260.42
1:2500	208.33	156.25	19.53	108.51	26.04	144.68	39.06	217.01
1:2000	166.67	125.00	15.63	86.81	20.83	115.74	31.25	173.61
1:1500	125.00	93.75	11.72	65.10	15.63	86.81	23.44	130.21
1:1250	104.17	78.13	9.77	54.25	13.02	72.34	19.53	108.51
1:1000	83.33	62.50	7.81	43.40	10.42	57.87	15.63	86.81
1:750	62.50	46.88	5.86	32.55	7.81	43.40	11.72	65.10
1:600	50.00	37.50	4.69	26.04	6.25	34.72	9.38	52.08
1:500	41.67	31.25	3.91	21.70	5.21	28.94	7.81	43.40
1:400	33.33	25.00	3.13	17.36	4.17	23.15	6.25	34.72
1:300	25.00	18.75	2.34	13.02	3.13	17.36	4.69	26.04
1:200	16.67	12.50	1.56	8.68	2.08	11.57	3.13	17.36
1:100	8.33	6.25	0.78	4.34	1.04	5.79	1.56	8.68
1:50	4.17	3.13	0.39	2.17	0.52	2.89	0.78	4.34
1:25	2.08	1.56	0.20	1.09	0.26	1.45	0.39	2.17
1:20	1.67	1.25	0.16	0.87	0.21	1.16	0.31	1.74

TABLE C.2 AutoCAD Scale and Text Heights——SI Units

A. Drawing units: Meters, English measurement system set

Drawing scale	Hatch	Ltscale	2.5-mm Text		3-mm Text	
			Txt	Dimscale	Txt	Dimscale
1:10	0.25	0.19	0.03	0.14	0.03	0.17
1:20	0.51	0.38	0.05	0.28	0.06	0.33
1:30	0.76	0.57	0.08	0.42	0.09	0.50
1:40	1.02	0.76	0.10	0.56	0.12	0.67
1:50	1.27	0.95	0.13	0.69	0.15	0.83
1:100	2.54	1.91	0.25	1.39	0.30	1.67
1:200	5.08	3.81	0.50	2.78	0.60	3.33
1:250	6.35	4.76	0.63	3.47	0.75	4.17
1:300	7.62	5.72	0.75	4.17	0.90	5.00
1:400	10.16	7.62	1.00	5.56	1.20	6.67
1:500	12.70	9.53	1.25	6.94	1.50	8.33
1:750	19.05	14.29	1.88	10.42	2.25	12.50
1:1000	25.40	19.05	2.50	13.89	3.00	16.67
1:2000	50.80	38.10	5.00	27.78	6.00	33.33
1:5000	127.00	92.25	12.50	69.44	15.00	83.33

B. Drawing units: Millimeters, English measurement system set

Drawing scale	Hatch	Ltscale	2.5-mm Text		3-mm Text	
			Txt	Dimscale	Txt	Dimscale
1:1	25	19	2.5	14	3.0	17
1:2	51	38	5.0	28	6.0	33
1:3	76	57	7.5	42	9.0	50
1:4	102	76	10.0	56	12.0	67
1:5	127	95	12.5	69	15.0	83
1:10	254	191	25.0	139	30.0	167
1:20	508	381	50.0	278	60.0	333
1:50	1270	953	125.0	694	150.0	833
1:100	2540	1905	250.0	1389	300.0	1667
1:200	5080	3810	500.0	2778	600.0	3333
1:250	6350	4763	625.0	3472	750.0	4167
1:300	7620	5715	750.0	4167	900.0	5000
1:400	10160	7620	1000.0	5556	1200.0	6667
1:500	12700	9525	1250.0	6944	1500.0	8333
1:750	19050	14288	1875.0	10417	2250.0	12500

TABLE C.3 AutoCAD Scale and Text Heights—SI Units

A. Drawing units: Meters, Metric measurement system set

Drawing scale	Hatch	Ltscale	2.5-mm Text Txt	2.5-mm Text Dimscale	3-mm Text Txt	3-mm Text Dimscale
1:10	0.25	0.19	0.03	0.01	0.03	0.01
1:20	0.51	0.38	0.05	0.02	0.06	0.02
1:30	0.76	0.57	0.08	0.03	0.09	0.04
1:40	1.02	0.76	0.10	0.04	0.12	0.05
1:50	1.27	0.95	0.13	0.05	0.15	0.06
1:100	2.54	1.91	0.25	0.10	0.30	0.12
1:200	5.08	3.81	0.50	0.20	0.60	0.24
1:250	6.35	4.76	0.63	0.25	0.75	0.30
1:300	7.62	5.72	0.75	0.30	0.90	0.36
1:400	10.16	7.62	1.00	0.40	1.20	0.48
1:500	12.70	9.53	1.25	0.50	1.50	0.60
1:750	19.05	14.29	1.88	0.75	2.25	0.90
1:1000	25.40	19.05	2.50	1.00	3.00	1.2
1:2000	50.80	38.10	5.00	2.00	6.00	2.4
1:5000	127.00	95.25	12.50	5.00	15.00	6

B. Drawing units: Millimeters, Metric measurement system set

Drawing scale	Hatch	Ltscale	2.5-mm Text Txt	2.5-mm Text Dimscale	3-mm Text Txt	3-mm Text Dimscale
1:1	25	19	2.5	1.0	3.0	1.2
1:2	51	38	5.0	2.0	6.0	2.4
1:3	76	57	7.5	3.0	9.0	3.6
1:4	102	76	10.0	4.0	12.0	4.8
1:5	127	95	12.5	5.0	15.0	6.0
1:10	254	191	25.0	10.0	30.0	12.0
1:20	508	381	50.0	20.0	60.0	24.0
1:50	1270	953	125.0	50.0	150.0	60.0
1:100	2540	1905	250.0	100.0	300.0	120
1:200	5080	3810	500.0	200.0	600.0	240
1:250	6350	4763	625.0	250.0	750.0	300
1:300	7620	5715	750.0	300.0	900.0	360
1:400	10160	7620	1000.0	400.0	1200.0	480
1:500	12700	9525	1250.0	500.0	1500.0	600
1:750	19050	14288	1875.0	750.0	2250.0	900

Troubleshooting Hints

D.1 General Hints

1. Always make backup copies of important drawing files, but remember that diskettes are volatile storage devices and data can easily be lost. Make two backups of very important data, and store each backup in a different location.

2. AutoCAD normally places its temporary files in the file directory containing the drawing. If you use a floppy diskette for your drawing directory, you'll need space on the diskette for the drawing file plus the backup file and AutoCAD's temporary files. If the drawing size is greater than one third of the diskette capacity, you might not have room.

3. If you must use a floppy diskette for your drawing directory (often necessary in a classroom situation), set the temporary file location to the hard drive. First create a subdirectory on your hard drive by toggling to Windows File Manager, as outlined in chapter 1, section 1.2.1. Then make a subdirectory, as outlined in chapter 1., section 1.2.4, using an original name such as c:\tempdraw, and then close the File Manager. (In DOS, enter the following at the DOS prompt: **c:\> md c:\tempdraw**.) Boot AutoCAD and choose the following:

Options <pick> Configure <pick>

The Configuration menu, illustrated back in chapter 7, section 7.1 will be displayed. Select 7, Configure Operating Parameters, to display the Operating Parameters menu. Then select 5, Placement of Temporary Files, and specify the file location on the hard drive to store the temporary files, e.g., c:\tempdraw.

4. You can set AutoCAD to automatically save at specified intervals by using the Preferences dialog box (refer to Figure 6.2 in chapter 6). Don't forget to click on the Automatic Save Every box to turn it on. You turn the Automatic Save feature on or off in the Configure Operating Parameters menu (refer to chapter 7, section 7.1.7).

5. If you aren't using AutoCAD on a network, turn file locking off (item 11 in the Configure Operating Parameters menu). Refer to chapter 7, section 7.1.7.

6. If file locking is on (see item 5) and AutoCAD crashes, you might not be allowed to open a locked file. AutoCAD will specify the locked file. To unlock the file, choose the following:

File <pick> Management <pick> Utilities... <pick>

The File Utilities dialog box, illustrated in Figure D.1, will be displayed. Press the Unlock files... command button to display the File(s) to Unlock dialog box. Select the locked file(s), which will have a file extension ending with K (.DWK, .MXK, etc.).

7. If you work in S.I. units, you might want to change the measurement units to metric in the Preferences dialog box (Figure 6.3). The setting will become default, so remember to change the units back to English if you work in Imperial units on a drawing. You must set the units prior to opening a new drawing.

8. If you want to use the DOS menu structure in AutoCAD for Windows, type **menu** at the command prompt and press <return>. The Menu dialog box illustrated in Figure D.2 will be displayed. In The List Files of Type box, choose *.MNU, then locate the acadfull.mnu file in the acadr13\support directory. Press OK and AutoCAD will load the file creating the .MNC and .MNS files. You can return the standard Windows menu by setting the List Files of Type specification to *.MNC and *.MNS, and then choosing the acad file.

Figure D.1 File Utilities dialog box.

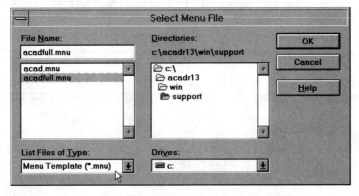

Figure D.2 Setting the Acadfull menu.

9. Many commands that request filenames use dialog boxes by default. If you'd rather have an ordinary prompt, enter the following:

Command: **setvar** <return> Variable name or ?: **filedia** <return> New value
for FILEDIA <0>: **1** <return>

If Filedia is set to 1, you can request a dialog box by entering a tilde, ~, when Auto-CAD requests the filename. Setting Filedia to 0 enables automatic use of dialog boxes. Selecting the Type It box allows you to enter data at the command prompt.

10. If your menu disappears, you can recall it by entering:

Command: **menu** <return> Menu file name or . for none: **acad** <return>

11. If AutoCAD rejects a point you're selecting and reports that it's outside the limits, you can turn limits checking off by entering:

Command: **limits** <return> **Off** <return>

12. The Zoom Vmax command lets you zoom out as far as possible without a drawing regeneration.

13. If you press the <return> key or <pick> button to digitize a point and Auto-CAD doesn't accept the point, press the <backspace> key a few times. Then try entering the point again. You might have inadvertently pressed another key prior to pressing <return>.

14. If you plot a drawing and your noncontinuous lines are plotted as continuous lines, you probably didn't set the Linetype scale (Ltscale) properly. It's easy to forget this when inserting drawings into another drawing (see chapter 12, section 12.8.1).

15. If parts of your border aren't plotting, enter the actual sheet size when entering plot data (for example, enter 11×8.5 inches for an A-size sheet rather than selecting AutoCAD's A size).

16. If something on your drawing doesn't plot and everything around it is plotting, check if the item not plotting is on layer Dimaso. Layer Dimaso is created for Auto-CAD's associate dimension control points and items on that layer don't plot.

17. When working on a large drawing:

- Set Linetype Scale (Ltscale) to a large value so all lines appear as continuous. This will speed up drawing regeneration and also simplify screen picks. Alternatively, set all linetypes as continuous. Then prior to plotting, set the desired linetypes.

- Leave all hatching until the end to speed up drawing regeneration.

- Freeze layers that don't need to be displayed, and thaw them prior to printing.

- If the drawing contains a lot of text, enter **Qtext** at the command line and specify On. Prior to plotting, turn Qtext Off. When Qtext is on, AutoCAD displays text and attribute objects as a rectangular box bounding the text area.

- Turn Fill off to speed up drawing regeneration, and turn it back on prior to plotting.

18. To make two lines meet perfectly, use the Fillet command with a radius of 0.

19. The Lengthen command changes the length of objects and the included angles of arcs (in DOS, select Modify, then Lengthen):

Modify <toolbar> Lengthen <pick> Delta/Percent/Total/DYnamic/<Select object>:

If you select an object, AutoCAD will show the length and included angle (where applicable). The following options are available:

Delta. Allows you to enter an amount to increase the length by.

Percent. Sets the length by a specified percentage of the object's original length, e.g., 0.5 would reduce the length to 50% of its original length and 1.5 would increase the length by 50%.

Total. Sets the total length by the object to the value entered, or defines the angle of an arc.

Dynamic. Lets you drag the object's length to the desired value.

20. The Edge option to the Trim and Extend commands allows you to define the trim or extend line at another object's implied edge, e.g., where the objects would intersect an imaginary boundary line of an object.

21. The UCS option to the Trim and Extend command allows you to trim or extend an object based on its apparent intersection with a UCS plane.

22. Use the Undo command extensively if you're experimenting on a drawing. If the experiment doesn't work out, Undo the set of commands. Remember that Undo files aren't saved after you exit the drawing. If you're doing a complex procedure, complete the procedure correctly before exiting the drawing. If the procedure isn't correct, you can undo and retry it, providing the sequence of commands was done during the current drawing session.

23. If you're experimenting, use Undo to set a marker. You can then undo to that marker:

Command: **undo** <return> Auto/Control/BEgin/End/Mark/Back/Number>:

Entering **Mark** places a mark at the current location. Entering **Back** takes the drawing back to the last mark. Entering a number specifies the number of preceding operations to be undone.

24. If AutoCAD displays the message "Disk almost full" when you're working with a floppy diskette, you can free space by using the Undo command as follows:

Command: **undo** <return> **control** <return> **none** <return>

25. If an object on a layer doesn't have the layer's color or linetype, you might have set color and/or linetype by object with the Object Creation Modes dialog box (refer

to Figure 6.6 in chapter 6). To turn color back to By Layer, choose the following in the menu bar:

Data <pick> **Object Creation...** <pick>

Choose Color... in the Object Creation Modes dialog box and then set the logical color to BYLAYER in the Set Color dialog box (see Figure 6.7 in chapter 6). To fix entities that were drawn with the wrong color, see the next hint.

26. If you have entities with their color or linetype set to By Object, you can change them to By Layer as follows:

Edit <pick> **Properties** <pick> Select object: Digitize the entities to be changed. <pick>

A Modify dialog box similar to that illustrated in Figure 16.39 (depending on the object selected) will be displayed. Change the color or layer to BYLAYER.

27. If you have entities you don't want to accidently change when working in detail on a drawing, place those entities on a separate layer(s), and then lock the layer in the Layer Control dialog box (see Figure 6.9 in chapter 6).

28. You can use the Rename command to change the name of blocks, dimstyles, layers, linetypes, text styles, views, UCSs, or viewports.

29. You can use the Purge command in the Data menu to remove unused blocks, dimension styles, layers, linetypes, multiline styles, shapes, and text styles from the drawing database. You can invoke Purge at any time (unlike with earlier versions of AutoCAD).

30. Minserted blocks cannot be exploded.

31. The Explmode system variable controls whether Explode supports nonuniformly scaled (NUS) blocks. Setting Explmode to 0 doesn't explode NUS blocks, and 1 (the default) explodes NUS blocks.

32. Exploding an object might change the color and linetype (also see hint 25, earlier in this section).

33. You can smooth out circles, arcs, and fillets on the monitor by setting Viewres to a larger value (try 500). The higher Viewres, the slower the regeneration in a complex drawing.

34. You can use the Scale command to rescale an entire drawing. For example, to change a drawing from inches to millimeters, set the screen limits to suit the larger metric drawing (multiply them by 25.4), and choose the following (in DOS, select Modify, then Scale):

Modify <toolbar> Scale <pick> Select object: Place a selection window around the entire drawing. <pick> Select objects: <return> Base point: **0,0** (or the lower left corner of the drawing if it isn't 0,0) <return> <Scale factor>/Reference: **25.4** <return>

35. You can often reduce the size of a drawing file considerably by creating a Wblock using the name of the drawing for the filename. When asked for the block

name, press <return>. Use an insertion point of 0,0, and use a selection window to select the entire drawing. Don't Wblock a drawing when you're using user coordinates (UCS). If you do, the current UCS becomes the WCS and all UCSs, named views, and viewport configurations will be deleted from the wblocked file.

36. If the paper space icon is replaced by a broken pencil icon, set the UCS to World.

37. If you're in paper space (see chapter 13, section 13.1), you can't toggle to model space by clicking the PAPER toggle button in the status bar until you've opened a viewport. If you select View, then Floating Model Space, you'll be requested to open a viewport.

38. You can scale linetypes according to drawing units by setting Ltscale as outlined in chapter 6, section 6.7.1. In this case, the same linetype might look different in each viewport in paper space, depending on the scale of that viewport. To rectify this, see the next hint.

39. In paper space, you can scale linetypes to look uniform in all viewports (even if they have different scales), as follows:

Options <pick> **Linetypes** <pick>

If Paper Space Linetype Scale has a tick mark in front of it, paper space linetype scaling is enabled. This sets linetype dash lengths based on paper space units, even for entities in model space.

40. Noncontinuous pattern linetypes often appear continuous around the vertices of a 2-D polyline. To set the dashes to appear as a continuous pattern, enter the following:

Command: **plinegen** <return>

Enter **1** to enable or **0** to disable linetype continuity throughout the entire length of 2-D polylines.

41. To change the display of existing noncontinuous pattern polylines, choose (in DOS, select Modify, then Properties...):

Object Properties <toolbar> Properties <pick> Select objects: select the 2-D polyline to be changed. <pick> Select objects: <return>

The Modify Polyline dialog box will be displayed. Select the LT Gen box and press OK.

42. You can create construction lines extending over an infinite distance with the Ray command (refer to appendix A, section A.3.1), which draws lines from a finite starting point extending to infinity, and also with the Xline command (see appendix A, section A.3.1), which draws infinite lines in two directions. Because rays and xlines are normally used only for construction lines, don't place them on a layer that can be frozen when the ray and xline are no longer required.

43. When plotting to a printer, AutoCAD scans your drawing from top to bottom, sending the data to the printer as horizontal strips. Consequently, a drawing without a border can often be printed more quickly than one with a border. If the border isn't necessary, for example on a test plot, put it on a different layer and turn the layer off prior to plotting.

44. You can save plotter settings for a drawing to file and retrieve them from the file the next time you print the drawing. To save the settings to file, set the desired plot settings in the Plot Configuration dialog box (see Figure 7.1 in chapter 7). Then choose Device and Default Selection..., which displays the dialog box illustrated in Figure 7.2. Press Save Defaults to File... and enter the filename, which is often the same as the drawing name. The file extension in the dialog box is PCP. Retrieve the plot settings by choosing Get Defaults from File... in the Print/Plot Default Selection dialog box. If you use the same settings for a number of drawings, create standard plot files you can retrieve as required.

45. The Saveasr12 command (entered at the command prompt) saves the drawing in AutoCAD R12 format, but 3-D solids will be decomposed to polylines and arcs.

46. The Group command allows you to relate two or more objects so they're named and selected as a group. You can explode groups to degroup them. Exploding doesn't affect blocks or attributes in the group. For example, chapter 16, section 16.3.2 shows the Divide and Measure commands being used to divide a line by placing nodes at the division points. The nodes are placed in the previous selection set and can be erased with Erase Previous. If the nodes are accidentally removed from the selection set, it could be a chore to erase them individually. You can place them into a group immediately after they're created as follows (in DOS, select Assist, then Group Objects):

Standard <toolbar> Object Group <pick>

The Object Grouping dialog box illustrated in Figure D.3 will be displayed. Enter a name (31 characters maximum) for the group in the Group Name box and press the New < command button. AutoCAD will continue with:

Select objects: **p** (previous) <return> Select objects: <return>

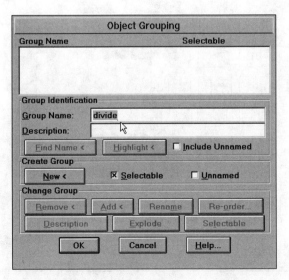

Figure D.3 Object grouping dialog box.

Turn the Selectable button on, which allows you to select the group by clicking on one item in the group. Press OK to exit the dialog box. Note the other options to Add, Remove, Rename, etc. You can later erase the group as follows:

Modify <toolbar> Erase <pick> Select objects: Click on one item in the group. <pick> Select objects: <return>

You can also select groups by using their group name and the Select Group tool and Select Objects flyout (see appendix A, section A.1.12).

47. The Attdisp command allows you to turn the visibility of attributes (see chapter 12) on or off.

48. The Find File... command button in the Select File dialog box (refer to Figure 5.23 in chapter 5) displays the Browse/Search dialog box, illustrated in Figure D.4. This box uses thumbnail images of drawing files to facilitate locating a desired drawing. Image boxes containing an × don't have thumbnail images available, and might have been created with an earlier version of AutoCAD.

49. The Ameconvert command converts AME solids to AutoCAD (R13) solid objects, with some changes to the object.

50. With AutoCAD for DOS, an Aerial View window is displayed when you choose Aerial View in the Tools menu (see the following hint).

51. With AutoCAD for DOS, you can enter a help screen on the Accelerated Display List Driver by entering:

Command: **dlx** <return>

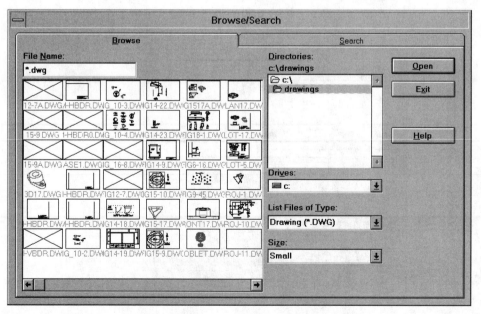

Figure D.4 Drawing directory browse box.

When the help screen is open, look up aerial view (av) to see how to display the Aerial View window (hint 49) and how to use it.

52. With AutoCAD for DOS, enter **dlxtext** at the command prompt to toggle a pop-up text window. Try it and then press F1.

D.2 Using Grips

Grips are discussed in chapter 3, section 3.5.2. This section contains more applications for grips. Load AutoCAD and draw the circle and two lines illustrated in Figure D.5. Then pick a point on the right line and the circle. Both entities will be highlighted and small blue boxes, *grips*, will appear on the entities. You then can manipulate the highlighted entities by using the grips. If the grips don't appear, set the Grips system variable to 1 and retry the preceding:

```
Command: grips <return>
New value for GRIPS<0>: 1 <return>
```

The cursor will have a small target box at its intersection, indicating that the Grips system variable is set to 1. Move the target box onto the grip on the right side of the circle, as illustrated in Figure D.6, and press <pick>. The grip will fill in, becoming hot (red), indicating that it will serve as the basis for editing. The first grip mode is Stretch. Move the cursor to the right and the circle will stretch. Press <return> to complete the stretch.

Choose Undo in the toolbar. Now make the grip at the top of the line hot and stretch the highlighted line as illustrated in Figure D.7. Press <return> to complete the command.

Undo the last command, and pick a point on the left line to highlight it. Now make the grip at the top of the lines hot and stretch it as shown in Figure D.8. Both lines will stretch since the hot grip was on both entities.

Undo the last command, and stretch the right line as illustrated in Figure D.9. Since the line is stretched from its midpoint, it moves with the hot grip rather than elongating or shortening. The options at the command line are as follows:

```
Command: **STRETCH**
<Stretch to point>/Base point/Copy/Undo/eXit:
```

The default option is <Stretch to point>. You can select a point with the cursor or by entering coordinates of the new point on the keyboard. To specify a base point other than the base grip, enter **base** or **b**. To copy the entity, enter **copy** or **c**.

Undo the last command, and make the grip at the top of the lines hot. Then press <return>. The option at the command line is now Move. Move the entities as shown in Figure D.10 All highlighted entities will move together.

Undo the command. Make the same grip hot again and press <return> <return>. The option is now Rotate. Try the Rotate option as illustrated in Figure D.11.

Undo the command. Make the same grip hot, and press <return> <return> <return>. The option is now Scale. Scale the entities as illustrated in Figure D.12.

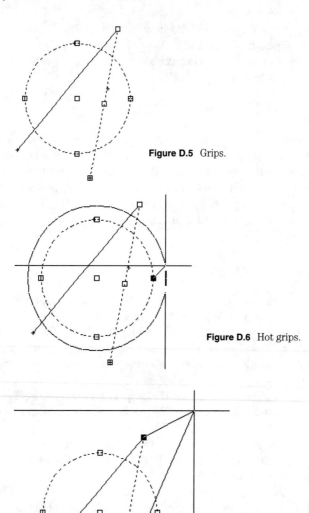

Figure D.5 Grips.

Figure D.6 Hot grips.

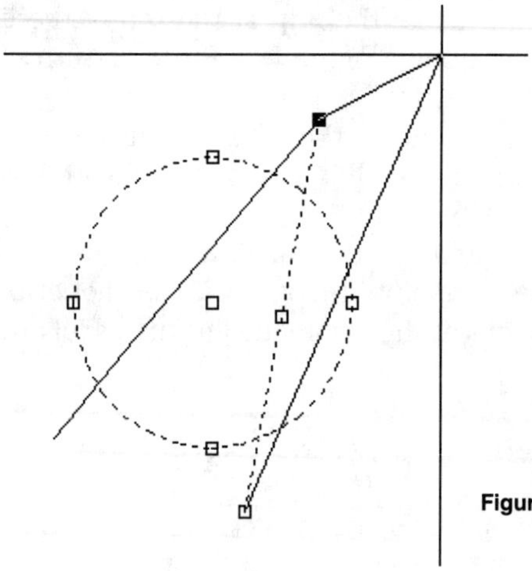

Figure D.7 Stretching a line.

Undo the command, make the grip hot, and press <return> <return> <return> <return>. The option is now Mirror. Mirror the entities as shown in Figure D.13.

Undo the command, and make the grip at the peak of the two lines hot. Then enter **b** (base) to select a different base point, and pick the grip at the midpoint of the line on the right side as the base point. Stretch the lines as illustrated in Figure D.14. Compare this Stretch to the one in Figure D.9. The hot grip at the top of the connecting lines will link the two lines together.

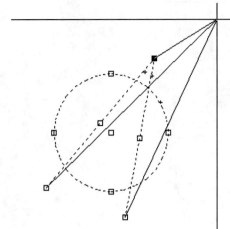

Figure D.8 Stretching a system of entities.

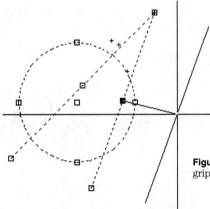

Figure D.9 Stretching a line by a midpoint grip.

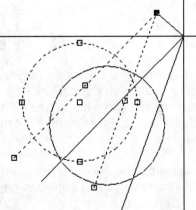

Figure D.10 Move option.

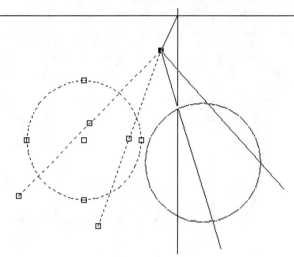

Figure D.11 Rotate option.

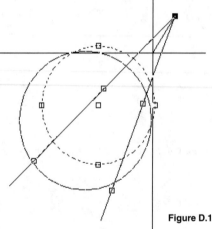

Figure D.12 Scale option.

Undo the last command. Now try Scaling the entities with the hot grip at the midpoint of the line on the right side, as illustrated in Figure D.15. Compare this with scaling using a controlling grip at the top of the two lines, shown in Figure D.12.

Undo the last command, then anchor the line on the right side by pressing the <shift> key as you pick the two grips at the end of the line on the right side, shown in Figure D.16. Then use the controlling (hot) grip at the midpoint of the line on the left to stretch the entities. The anchored line won't stretch, but the line on the left side will.

You can use the Ddgrip command to modify the color and size of grips. Also, the grip on an inserted block is usually the insertion point. Enable the grips inside the block by setting the enabling button in the Ddgrip dialog box.

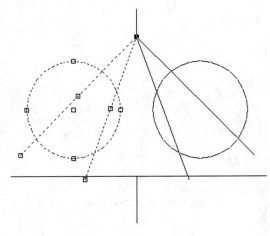

Figure D.13 Mirror option.

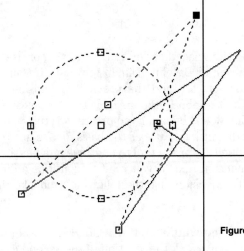

Figure D.14 Stretching linked entities.

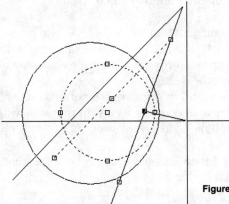

Figure D.15 Controlling grip and scale option.

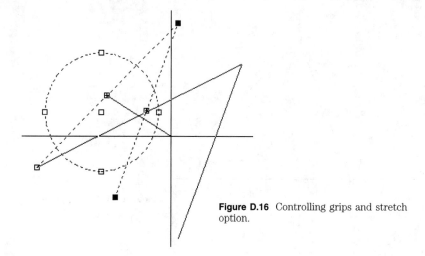

Figure D.16 Controlling grips and stretch option.

D.3   Dimensioning Hints

1. You can continue a dimension placed earlier in the drawing or use it as a base-line with the Continue Dimension or Baseline Dimension tools. If Continue Dimension or Baseline Dimension is selected and the previous dimension was a linear dimension, AutoCAD will prompt `Second extension line or Return to se-lect`. If the previous dimension wasn't linear or you pressed <return>, AutoCAD will prompt you to select a linear dimension to use as the basis for the next dimension.

2. When you use the Continue Dimension tool to continue a dimension, AutoCAD automatically inserts the dimension text. If you want to continue a dimension but don't want to use the default dimension, use the following to invoke the Continue command:

Command: **dim** <return> Dim: **continue** <return> `Second extension line origin or return to select:` Pick the location of the second extension line, or see hint 1 in this section. <pick> `Dimension text <default>:` You can press <return> to use the default, text or enter another value. <return>

3. AutoCAD stores all dimensioning system variables to a style name, except for dimasho and dimaso. Dimasho controls whether dynamic dragging is on when you edit and insert dimensions, and dimaso turns associative dimensioning on/off. You'll probably want to leave dimaso on (the default).

4. You can use the dimstyle command to compare the current text style with another set of text styles. For instance, to compare a current text style with the Standard style, enter (note the use of tilde, ~, in the following):

Command: **dimstyle** <return> `?/Enter dimension style name or RETURN to select dimension:` **~standard** <return>

AutoCAD will show any differences between the two styles.

5. If you have certain text styles that you use often, create a prototype drawing(s), set the dimension styles you require (refer to chapters 3 and 4) save them with an appropriate name, and save the drawing(s). Then when you open a new drawing, set the appropriate prototype drawing by clicking on the Prototype... command button in the Create New Drawing dialog box (refer to Figure 1.15 in chapter 1). You can then select the appropriate dimension style from the drop-down Current box in the Dimension Style dialog box (see Figure 3.8 in chapter 3).

6. You can easily modify dimensions with the Ddmodify dialog box. Refer to chapter 16, section 16.10.11.

7. You can create stacked dimensions by setting the units as follows:

Dimensioning <toolbar> Dimension Style (Figure 4.7) <pick>

The Dimension Style dialog box (see Figure 9.10 in chapter 9) will be displayed. Press the Annotation... command button to display the Annotation dialog box (refer to Figures 9.3 or 14.10). Then press the Units... command button to display the Primary Units dialog box, illustrated in Figure D.17. Select Architectural (Stacked) or Fractional (Stacked), depending on the units you're working with. When stacked units are used, the fraction 3/4 appears as ¾.

D.4 Entering Multiline Text

You can enter multiline (paragraph) text with the Mtext command. For example, enter the following (in DOS, select Draw, the Text):

Draw <toolbar> Text (Figure D.18) <pick> `Attach/Rotation/Style/Height/ Direction/ <Insertion point>:` Pick a point where you want the start of the text to be. <pick> `Other corner:` Pick the other corner of a rectangle to be about 1.5 in square. <pick>

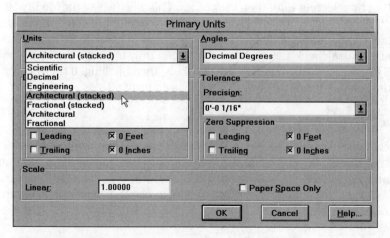

Figure D.17 Setting stacked dimension units.

Figure D.18 Text tool.

The Edit Mtext dialog box illustrated in Figure D.19 will be displayed. Enter the text illustrated by pressing <return> after the period at the end of each line. The start point of the rectangle that defines the text boundary is important because it also defines the insertion point for the paragraph text. Options in the Mtext dialog box are:

Stack. Creates text that's aligned vertically as fractions.

Import. Displays the Import Text File dialog box, which allows you to select text from a text file to be inserted into the text boundary.

Properties. Allows you to change properties such as the text style, height, direction, attachment point, width, and rotation.

Attribute options available in the dialog box are:

Overline. Turns on overlining for new text or selected text.

Underline. Turns on underlining for new or selected text.

Browse. Displays the Change Font dialog box.

Color. Specifies a color for new or selected text.

Height. Specifies the height for new or selected text.

In these commands, two corners of a rectangle are selected. This rectangle defines the space the paragraph text will occupy, i.e., the text wrapped onto the next line when it meets the right side of the boundary. If you want to define only the width of the boundary, enter **w** and specify a width value.

You can edit paragraph text by using the Properties tool (see Figure 9.7 in chapter 9) or by selecting Edit, then Properties. This will display the Modify Mtext dialog box, illustrated in Figure D.20, which provides a number of edit options, such as Edit Contents... and Insertion point.

You can also check the spelling of text in a drawing with the Spell tool (see appendix A, section A.1.5). In DOS, select Tools, then Spelling. If there's no spelling error, the command will appear to not have been invoked.

D.5 Using AutoCAD's Help

You can invoke available help in AutoCAD (or any other Windows application) by pressing the F1 key, pressing the Help button (see appendix A, section A.1.25), choosing Help in the menu bar, or pressing the Help command button in a dialog box. The following gives a brief overview of how to use the Help menu (Figure D.21) in the menu bar:

Help (menu bar) <pick> How to use Help <pick>

The Contents for the How to Use Help window, shown in Figure D.22, will be displayed. Items that are green and underlined are topics on which you can get information by clicking on the item. To learn what the buttons at the top of the window mean, scroll the contents list up until Help Buttons is on the screen, and then click on it. (If you don't know how to scroll, click on the topic titled Scroll Through a Help Topic.) The Help Buttons screen is shown in Figure D.23.

To find help on how to use a command or a dialog box, exit the current Help screen and select Contents from the Help menu (refer back to Figure D.21), press the F1 key, or press the Help tool. The Contents help window, shown in Figure D.24, will be displayed. Click on Toolbars, as shown, to display the Toolbars Help window illustrated in Figure D.25.

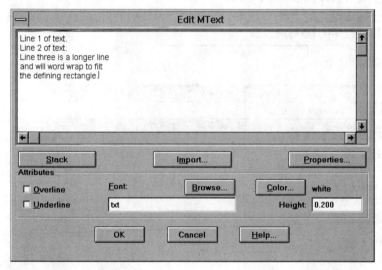

Figure D.19 Mtext dialog box.

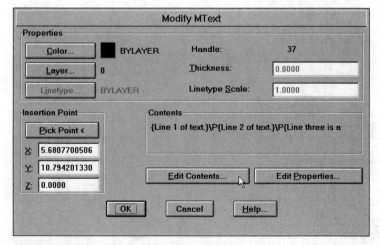

Figure D.20 Modify Mtext dialog box.

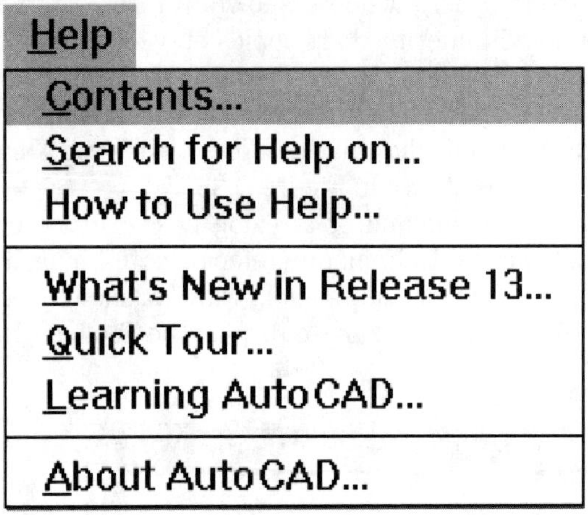

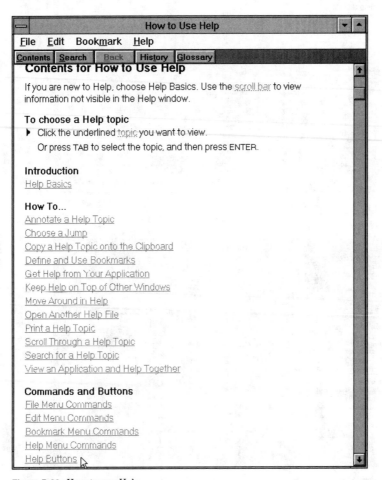

Figure D.21 Help menu.

Figure D.22 How to use Help.

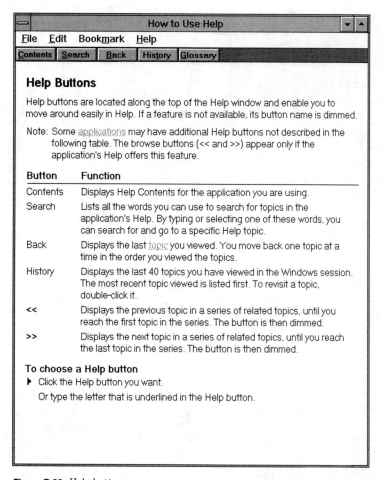

Figure D.23 Help buttons.

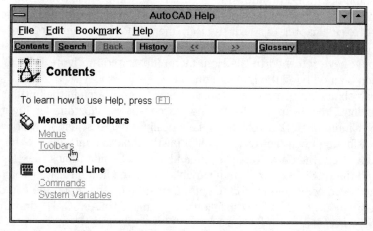

Figure D.24 Contents help window.

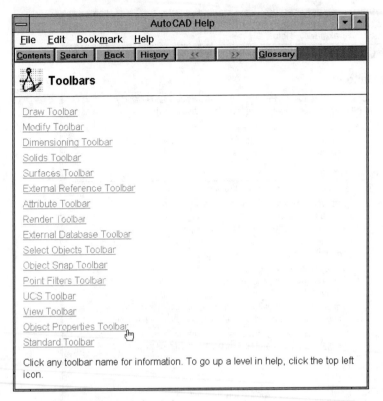

Figure D.25 Toolbar menu help window.

To find help on the Object Properties tool, select it in the list, as illustrated in Figure D.25. The Object Properties tool's help window, shown in Figure D.26, will be displayed. Click on the Properties tool to display the DDMODIFY help window (see Figure D.27). Select Line in the list to get help on modifying lines. The DDMODIFY Modify Line help window, shown in Figure D.28, will be displayed. You can display the same help window by choosing Help... from the Modify Line dialog box (refer to Figure 14.25 in chapter 14). Exit the Help menu and draw a line in AutoCAD, select Modify to display the Modify Line dialog box, and press the Help... command button. You should have returned to the Help menu illustrated in Figure D.28. Look up information on modifying the Line command.

You can obtain information on a topic by clicking on Search in the buttons bar in the Help window. Press Search to display the Search window, illustrated in Figure D.29. To get information on UCS, scroll the alphabetically ordered selection window until the topic is visible and then click on it, highlighting the topic and moving it to the Show Topics window. Click the Show Topics command button. Similar topics, like the UCS command and the UCSFOLLOW system variable, are listed in the Related Topics window. Click the Go To command button to get information on the topic. You can display the same help window by choosing the following commands in AutoCAD's drawing window:

View <pick> Press the F1 function key, then select Set UCS in the Help screen (Figure D.30), as shown.

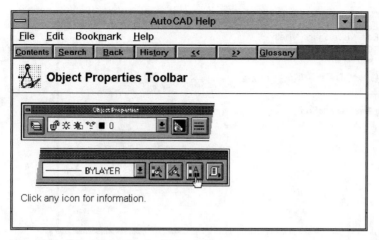

Figure D.26   Object Properties tool help window.

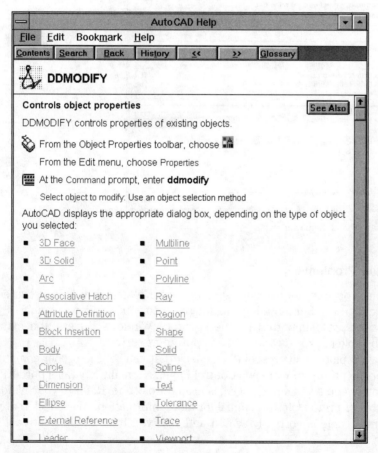

Figure D.27   DDMODIFY help window.

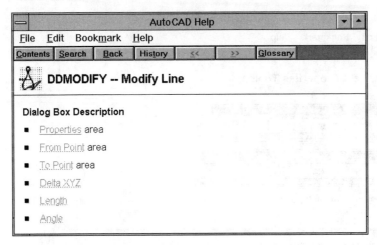

Figure D.28 Modify Line help window.

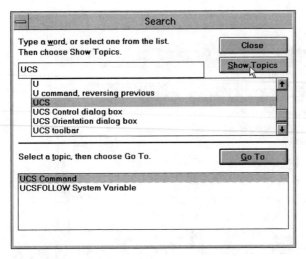

Figure D.29 Search help window.

D.6 Printer/Plotter Problems

1. The procedure for installing system printer/plotter drivers is discussed in chapter 7, section 7.3. For more information, refer to your Windows manual. If your plotting device isn't supported by the standard Windows drivers, the manufacturer might be able to provide you with an appropriate driver.

2. If your plotter isn't responding, check that you set the proper communications port for the printer in Window's Control Panel. Normally a parallel port, LPT, is used for printers and a serial port, COM, is used for plotters. Refer to your Windows manual and your printer/plotter manual for more information. Also check that your plotter/printer cable is correctly seated and that you have the correct cable for your plotter.

3. Truncated plots are often caused by an improper paper size setting in AutoCAD for your plotter/printer, or an incorrect plotting scale. Use AutoCAD's plot preview option prior to plotting (see chapter 7, section 7.3).

4. If you're plotting from paper space and the plot appears out of scale, the drawing might actually be in model space (see chapter 13, section 13.1.4).

5. If the plot is oriented incorrectly on the paper, check that you set the rotation angle correctly, or that the sheet's x and y sizes are entered correctly for your plotter/printer (see chapter 7, section 7.3).

6. If your pens are skipping, slow down the plotter speed.

7. Problems with line weight, missing arrowheads, pens not lifting from the paper between text letters, etc. are usually due to mixing units when specifying pen sizes and dimension units, e.g., MM dimension units and inch pen sizes (refer to chapter 7, section 7.3).

8. Maintain your printer/plotter properly to prevent many printing/plotting problems before they happen.

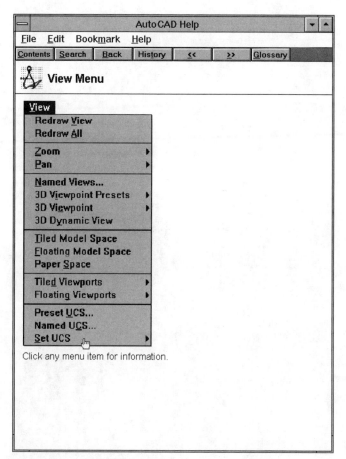

Figure D.30 View help screen.

E

Border.mnu Menu+

```
***MENUGROUP=BORDER
***POP0
[Osnap]
[Center]center
[Endpoint]endpoint
[Insert]insert
[Intersection]intersection
[Midpoint]midpoint
[Perpendicular]perpendicular
[From]from
[None]none

***POP1
[Easy1]
[Line]line
[Circle]circle
[Border]pline \w 0.2;0.2
[Erase W]erase w
[Erase L]erase l;;
[Oops]oops
[--]
[Acad-Mnu]menu acad
[Plot]plot
[Save]save
[Quit]quit

***POP2
[Title Block]
[->Metric]
[A Size]limits -5,-5 280,215 zoom a +
insert c:/drawings/am-hbdr;0,0 1 1 0
[<-B Size]limits -5,-5 430,280 zoom a +
insert c:/drawings/bm-hbdr;0,0 1 1 0
[->Imperial]
[A Size]limits -0.2,-0.2 11,8.5 zoom a +
insert c:/drawings/ai-hbdr;0,0 1 1 0
[<-B size]limits -0.2,-0.2 17,11 zoom a +
insert c:/drawings/bi-hbdr;0,0 1 1 0
[--]
```

```
[Insert]insert
[Move]move
[Erase]erase
[Ltscale]ltscale
[Undo]undo

***POP3
[Attach]
[->Xref]
[Attach]xref attach
[Detach]xref detach
[Reload]xref reload
[Bind]xref bind
[<-Change path]xref path
[->Block]
[Insert]insert
[<-Explode]explode
[->Edit]
[Move]move
[Erase]erase
[Ltscale]ltscale
[<-Undo]undo

***POP4
[Full Size]
[->Metric]
[A Size]layer make border1;;limits 0,0 255,185 zoom a +
line 0,0 255,0 255,185 0,185 c insert c:/drawings/title1;255,0 +
1 1 0 \\\\\\\\\\\\block b2;0,0 c 0,0 255,185;;$p4=BORDER.ma $p4=*
[<-B size]layer make border1;;limits 0,0 380,240 zoom a +
line 0,0 380,0 380,240 0,240 c insert c:/drawings/title1;380,0 +
1 1 0 \\\\\\\\\\\\block b2;0,0 c 0,0 380,240;;$p4=BORDER.mb $p4=*
[->Imperial]
[A Size]layer make border1;;limits 0,0 10,7.25 zoom a +
line 0,0 10,0 10,7.25 0,7.25 c insert c:/drawings/title1;10,0 +
0.039 0.039 0 \\\\\\\\\\\\block b2;0,0 c 0,0 10,7.25;;$p4=BORDER.ia $p4=*
[<-B Size]layer make border1;;limits 0,0 15,9.5 zoom a +
line 0,0 15,0 15,9.5 0,9.5 c insert c:/drawings/title1;15,0 +
0.039 0.039 0 \\\\\\\\\\\\block b2;0,0 c 0,0 15,9.5;;$p4=BORDER.ib $p4=*

**ia
[Scale]
[->Archit.]
[1/8"=1'-0"]limits 0,0 960,696 insert b2;0,0 96 96 0 zoom a +
layer set 0;;$p4=BORDER.POP4
[1/4"=1'-0"]limits 0,0 480,348 insert b2;0,0 48 48 0 zoom a +
layer set 0;;$p4=BORDER.POP4
[1/2"-1'-0"]limits 0,0 240,174 insert b2;0,0 24 24 0 zoom a +
layer set 0;;$p4=BORDER.POP4
[3/4"=1'-0"]limits 0,0 160,116 insert b2;0,0 16 16 0 zoom a +
layer set 0;;$p4=BORDER.POP4
[1"=1'-0"  ]limits 0,0 120,87 insert b2;0,0 12 12 0 zoom a +
layer set 0;;$p4=BORDER.POP4
[<-1:N     ]limits 0,0 \insert b2;0,0 \\0 zoom a +
layer set 0;;$p4=BORDER.POP4

**ib
[Scale]
[->Archit.]
[1/8"=1'-0"]limits 0,0 1440,912 insert b2;0,0 96 96 0 zoom a +
layer set 0;;$p4=BORDER.POP4
[1/4"=1'-0"]limits 0,0 720,456 insert b2;0,0 48 48 0 zoom a +
layer set 0;;$p4=BORDER.POP4
[1/2"=1'-0"]limits 0,0 360,228 insert b2;0,0 24 24 0 zoom a +
```

```
layer set 0;;$p4=BORDER.POP4
[3/4"=1'-0"]limits 0,0 240,152 insert b2;0,0 16 16 0 zoom a +
layer set 0;;$p4=BORDER.POP4
[1"=1'-0"  ]limits 0,0 180,114 insert b2;0,0 12 12 0 zoom a +
layer set 0;;$p4=BORDER.POP4
[<-1:N     ]limits 0,0 \insert b2;0,0 \\0 zoom a +
layer set 0;;$p4=BORDER.POP4

**ma
[Scale]
[->Metric m]
[1:10]limits 0,0 2.55,1.85 insert b2;0,0 0.01 0.01 0 zoom a +
layer set 0;;$p4=BORDER.POP4
[1:20]limits 0,0 5.1,3.7 insert b2;0,0 0.02 0.02 0 zoom a +
layer set 0;;$p4=BORDER.POP4
[1:50]limits 0,0 12.75,9.25 insert b2;0,0 0.05 0.05 0 zoom a +
layer set 0;;$p4=BORDER.POP4
[1:100]limits 0,0 25.5,18.5 insert b2;0,0 0.1 0.1 0 zoom a +
layer set 0;;$p4=BORDER.POP4
[1:250]limits 0,0 63.75,46.25 insert b2;0,0 0.25 0.25 0 zoom a +
layer set 0;;$p4=BORDER.POP4
[1:300]limits 0,0 76.5,55.5 insert b2;0,0 0.3 0.3 0 zoom a +
layer set 0;;$p4=BORDER.POP4
[1:400]limits 0,0 102,74 insert b2;0,0 0.4 0.4 0 zoom a +
layer set 0;;$p4=BORDER.POP4
[1:500]limits 0,0 127.5,92.5 insert b2;0,0 0.5 0.5 0 zoom a +
layer set 0;;$p4=BORDER.POP4
[1:1000]limits 0,0 255,185 insert b2;0,0 1 1 0 zoom a +
layer set 0;;$p4=BORDER.POP4
[<-1:N     ]limits 0,0 \insert b2;0,0 \\0 zoom a +
layer set 0;;$p4=BORDER.POP4

**mb
[Scale]
[->Metric m]
[1:10]limits 0,0 3.8,2.4 insert b2;0,0 0.01 0.01 0 zoom a +
layer set 0;;$p4=BORDER.POP4
[1:20]limits 0,0 7.6,4.8 insert b2;0,0 0.02 0.02 0 zoom a +
layer set 0;;$p4=BORDER.POP4
[1:50]limits 0,0 19,12 insert b2;0,0 0.05 0.05 0 zoom a +
layer set 0;;$p4=BORDER.POP4
[1:100]limits 0,0 38,24 insert b2;0,0 0.1 0.1 0 zoom a +
layer set 0;;$p4=BORDER.POP4
[1:250]limits 0,0 95,60 insert b2;0,0 0.25 0.25 0 zoom a +
layer set 0;;$p4=BORDER.POP4
[1:300]limits 0,0 114,72 insert b2;0,0 0.3 0.3 0 zoom a +
layer set 0;;$p4=BORDER.POP4
[1:400]limits 0,0 152,96 insert b2;0,0 0.4 0.4 0 zoom a +
layer set 0;;$p4=BORDER.POP4
[1:500]limits 0,0 190,120 insert b2;0,0 0.5 0.5 0 zoom a +
layer set 0;;$p4=BORDER.POP4
[1:1000]limits 0,0 380,240 insert b2;0,0 1 1 0 zoom a +
layer set 0;;$p4=BORDER.POP4
[<-1:N     ]limits 0,0 \insert b2;0,0 \\0 zoom a +
layer set 0;;$p4=BORDER.POP4

***AUX1
;
***AUX2
$P0=*
***BUTTONS1
;
***BUTTONS2
$P0=*
```

Notes: The menu as shown is for AutoCAD for Windows; for AutoCAD for DOS, remove italized items. Also, the reader must create the following drawing files: title1, am-hbdr, bm-hbdr, ai-hbdr, and bi-hbdr (outlined in chapter 12).

Contour.bas Program

```
10 CLS:KEY OFF
20 PRINT TAB(25);:PRINT "CONTOUR CALCULATION PROGRAM":COLOR 7,0:PRINT
30 PRINT "The output for this program is printed on a lineprinter.
   Turn the lineprinter on NOW."
40 PRINT:COLOR 0,7:PRINT "Press any key to continue":COLOR 7,0
50 C$=INKEY$:IF C$="" THEN 50
60 LPRINT TAB(10) "ELEVATION";TAB(25) "X-DIST.";TAB(40) "Y-DIST"
100 CLS:INPUT "Distance between rows of grid ";DROW
110 PRINT:INPUT "Distance between columns of grid ";DCOL
120 PRINT:INPUT "Enter number of rows in grid ";NROW
130 PRINT:INPUT "Enter number of columns in grid ";NCOL
140 PRINT:INPUT "Enter contour interval ";UNIT:PRINT
150 DIM EL(NROW,NCOL)
160 FOR I=1 TO NROW
170     FOR J=1 TO NCOL
180     PRINT "Enter elev. of row";I;"column";J;": ";:INPUT EL(I,J)
190     NEXT J
200 NEXT I
210 FOR I=1 TO NROW
220     FOR J=1 TO NCOL-1
230     ELL=EL(I,J):ELR=EL(I,J+1)
240     IF ELL=ELR AND ELL<>INT(ELL) THEN 340
250     IF ELL=ELR THEN XDIST=DCOL*(J-1):YDIST=DROW*(I-1):
   ELEV=ELL:GOSUB 500:IF J=NCOL-1 THEN XDIST=DCOL*(J):
   YDIST=DROW*(I-1):GOSUB 500
260     IF ELL<ELR THEN LO=ELL:HI=ELR ELSE LO=ELR:HI=ELL
270     ELEV=INT(LO+.99)
280         WHILE ELEV<=INT(HI):IF ELEV=HI AND ELR>ELL AND J<NCOL-1 THEN 320
290     XDIST=(ELEV-LO)/(HI-LO)*DCOL:YDIST=DROW*(I-1)
300         IF ELL<ELR THEN XDIST=XDIST+DCOL*(J-1) ELSE XDIST=DCOL*(J)-XDIST
310         GOSUB 500
320         ELEV=ELEV+UNIT
330         WEND
340     NEXT J
350 IF I=NROW THEN 480
360     FOR J=1 TO NCOL-1
370     ELB=EL(I,J):ELT=EL(I+1,J)
380     IF INT(ELB)=INT(ELT) THEN 470
390     IF ELB<ELT THEN LO=ELB:HI=ELT ELSE LO=ELT:HI=ELB
```

```
400      ELEV=INT(LO+1)
410          WHILE ELEV<=INT(HI):IF ELEV=HI THEN 450
420          YDIST=(ELEV-LO)/(HI-LO)*DROW:XDIST=DCOL*(J-1)
430          IF ELB<ELT THEN YDIST=YDIST+DROW*(I-1) ELSE YDIST=DROW*(I)-YDIST
440          GOSUB 500
450          ELEV=ELEV+UNIT
460          WEND
470      NEXT J
480 NEXT I
490 END
500 LPRINT TAB(10) ELEV;TAB(25) XDIST;TAB(40)YDIST
510 RETURN
```

AutoCAD DOS Menu Tables

Menu	Section in appendix
File	G.1
Assist	G.2
View	G.3
Draw	G.4
Construct	G.5
Modify	G.6
Data	G.7
Options	G.8
Tools	G.9
Help	G.10

G.1 File Menu

New...	Opens new drawing file
Open...	Opens existing drawing file
Save	Saves current drawing without exiting
Save As...	Saves current drawing; you specify a filename
Print...	Opens Plot Configuration dialog box
External Reference >	Displays external reference command options
Bind >	Display Xref bind options
Import >	Displays import file options
Export >	Displays export file options
Management >	Utilities, Audit, and Recover
Exit	Exits AutoCAD

G.2   Assist Menu

Undo	Undoes last command
Redo	Redoes an Undo
Object Snaps >	Displays object snap selection menu
Point Filters >	Displays coordinate point filters (.x, .y, .z, .xy, .xz, and .yz)
Snap	Toggles snap on/off
Grid	Toggles grid on/off
Ortho	Toggles ortho on/off
Select Objects >	Displays object selection modes (window, crossing, etc.)
Selection Filters...	Displays Object Selection Filters dialog box
Group Objects	Creates a named selection set of objects in a group
Group Selection	Controls group selection (Pickstyle 0 or 1)
Hatch Selection	Controls hatch selection (Pickstyle 1 or 3)
Inquiry >	Displays Inquiry menu
Cancel	Cancels current command

G.3   View Menu

Redraw View	Redraws current viewport
Redraw All	Redraws all viewports
Zoom >	Displays Zoom options
Pan >	Displays Pan options
Named Views...	Saves and restores a named view
3D Viewpoint Presets >	Sets a viewing direction using image tiles
3D Viewpoint >	Sets a viewing direction
3D Dynamic View	Creates a perspective view of a model
Tiled Model Space	Sets Tilemode to 1 (model space)
Floating Model Space	Sets working space to model space
Paper Space	Sets working space to paper space
Tiled Viewports >	Creates viewports in model space
Floating Viewports >	Creates viewports in paper space
Preset UCS...	Sets a UCS using image tiles
Named UCS...	Saves and restores a named UCS
Set UCS >	Displays UCS options

G.4   Draw Menu

Line	Draws multiple line segments
Construction Line	Draws a line that extends to infinity in two directions
Ray	Draws an infinitely long line that has a finite start point
Sketch	Draws freehand lines
Polyline	Draws a polyline
3D Polyline	Draws a 3-D polyline
Multiline	Draws a multiline
Spline	Draws a spline curve through given points

Arc >	Displays arc menu options
Circle >	Displays circle menu options
Ellipse >	Displays circular and arc ellipse options
Polygon >	Draws a polygon or 2-D solid
Point >	Display point menu options
Insert >	Inserts a single or multiple block, or shape
Surfaces >	Draws 3-D surfaces
Solids >	Draws 3-D solid models
Hatch >	Boundary hatches objects
Text >	Displays text menu options
Dimensioning >	Dimensions objects

G.5 Construct Menu

Copy	Creates a copy of a selected object
Offset	Creates a copy of a line or curve, parallel to it at a specified distance
Mirror	Mirrors a selected object about a specified axis
Array >	Creates a rectangular or circular array of a selected object
Chamfer	Bevels an edge between two lines or surfaces
Fillet	Constructs an arc between two lines, arcs, circles, or surfaces
Region	Creates a 2-D closed area from closed shapes
Boundary	Creates a boundary composed of objects
Union	Combines solids or regions
Subtract	Subtracts solids or regions
Intersection	Creates a solid from the intersection of two solids or regions
Block	Creates a single object from compound objects
Attribute...	Displays Attribute Definition dialog box to associate text with a block
3D Array >	Creates a 3-D rectangular or circular array of a selected object
3D Mirror	Mirrors a selected object about a 3-D axis
3D Rotate	Rotates a selected object about a 3-D axis

G.6 Modify Menu

Properties...	Controls properties of existing objects
Move	Moves an object
Rotate	Rotates an object
Align	Translates an object in 3-D space
Stretch	Stretches a portion of an object
Scale	Alters size of an object
Lengthen	Changes length of objects and the included angle of arcs
Point	Creates a point object
Trim	Trims a portion of an object extending past a boundary
Extend	Extends a line, arc, or polyline to meet a boundary
Break >	Breaks an object at selection points
Edit Polyline	Edits polylines
Edit Multiline...	Displays a dialog box to edit a multiline

Edit Spline	Edits a spline curve
Edit Text...	Edits line text
Edit Hatch...	Changes the angle and spacing of a hatch
Attribute >	Edits attributes
Explode	Breaks a compound object into component parts
Erase	Removes an object from the drawing
Oops!	Restores erased objects

G.7 Data Menu

Object Creation...	Sets properties for new objects
Layers	Manages layers
Viewport Layer Control >	Manages layers in viewports
Color	Sets the color for new objects
Linetype...	Creates, loads, and sets linetypes
Multiline Style...	Creates or modifies a multiline style
Text Style	Creates or modifies a text style
Dimension Style...	Creates or modifies a dimension style
Shape File...	Loads a shape file
Units...	Displays Units Control dialog box
Drawing Limits	Sets drawing screen limits
Time	Displays the date and time statistics of a drawing
Status	Displays drawing statistics, modes, and extents
Rename...	Changes the name of objects
Purge >	Removes unused named references from the database

G.8 Options Menu

Drawing Aids...	Displays Drawing Aids dialog box
Running Object Snap...	Sets a running object snap
Coordinate Display	Sets the coordinate display mode
Section...	Sets object selection mode
Grips...	Controls grip options
UCS >	Sets UCS icon
Display	Sets options for solids, attribute display, point style, and text
Linetypes	Sets linetype scale and generation
Preferences...	Displays System Preferences dialog box
Configure	Configures AutoCAD
Dialogue Box Colors...	Configures dialog boxes
Render Configure...	Configures AutoCAD render modes
Tablet >	Configures tablet modes
Log Files >	Displays session, audit, and xref log files
AutoSave Time	Sets time interval for automatic saves
System variables >	Lists or sets system variables

G.9 Tools Menu

Applications...	Loads AutoLISP and ADS files
Run Script...	Loads script files
External Commands	Shells to DOS
Aerial View	Displays Aerial View window
External Database >	Links drawing to external databases
Hide >	Redraws object with hidden lines temporarily removed
Shade >	Displays Shade menu
Render >	Renders solid objects
Slide >	Saves and views slides
Image >	Saves and views rendered images
Spelling...	Checks spelling in a drawing
Calculator	Evaluated mathematical and geometric expressions
Menus...	Loads a menu
Reinitialize...	Reinitializes the input/output ports, digitizer, display, and program parameter file
Compile...	Compiles shape files and PostScript font files

G.10 Help Menu

Help...	Displays online help
Search for Help On...	Searches for Help topics by keyword
How to Use Help	Explains how to use the online Help system
What's New in Release 13	Shows new functions in Release 13
About AutoCAD...	Displays information about this version of AutoCAD

Using AutoCAD with Windows 95

H.1 Windows 95 Environment

Windows 95 is a graphical operating system similar to Windows 3.1; it's designed to run 32-bit Windows programs such as AutoCAD 13 for Windows. It will also run Windows 3.x and DOS software. Windows 95 can run multiple simultaneous applications more smoothly than Windows 3.1. You can even have multiple copies of AutoCAD 13 for Windows running at the same time, each working on a different drawing. Windows 95 includes built-in peer-to-peer networking and will interface easily with most existing local- and wide-area networks, allowing you to share your AutoCAD drawings much more easily. This appendix will outline some of the procedures for working with AutoCAD 13 in the Windows 95 environment, where there's a difference between the procedure used with Windows 3.1. It is not intended to be a thorough introduction to Windows 95.

When Windows 95 is loaded a desktop similar to that illustrated in Figure H.1 is displayed. The *task bar* is the program launcher and switcher, as well as a status bar. You'll use the Start button (see Figure H.1) to launch applications, open documents, and make settings, and you'll use the buttons to the right of the Start button to open programs or folders and switch tasks.

H.2 Preparing a data diskette

You must format new blank diskettes before you can use them. Note that if you format a disk after data has been stored on it, the data will be lost. To prepare a new blank unformatted data disk for use, do the following:

1. Choose My Computer from the desktop by moving the mouse to its icon and pressing the <pick> button on the mouse twice quickly to display the My Computer dialog box, illustrated in Figure H.2.

2. Select the disk drive for the diskette to be formatted by moving the mouse onto its icon in the dialog box and pressing the right button on the mouse once. Right-clicking on the icon will display the command menu shown in Figure H.3.

3. Choose the Format option by clicking once on it to display the Format dialog box, shown in Figure H.4.

4. If the drive and disk capacity in the Capacity box isn't correct, click on the arrow to the right of the Capacity box to display a drop-down box, and select the proper drive and disk capacity for the floppy disk. The capacity of a 3.5-inch high-density disk is 1.44MB and the capacity of a 5.25-inch high-density disk is 1.2MB.

5. In the Format Type and Other Options boxes, choose the appropriate options from the following:

Quick. Erases all files on formatted disks. Use this when you have a previously used diskette and want to delete all of the data on the diskette.

Full. Does a full format. Use this for a new unformatted diskette.

Copy System Files Only. Makes the disk bootable without formatting. This isn't necessary for a data diskette.

Label. Lets you name the diskette.

No Label. Clears an existing label from the diskette.

Display Summary When Finished. Causes a dialog box to display information such as the space available and identification of any bad sectors.

Copy System Files. Formats the diskette and makes it bootable. This isn't usually necessary for a data diskette.

6. Press the Start button in the dialog box to format the diskette. When the format is complete, press Close to exit the dialog box.

H.3 Working with folders and diskettes

Refer to chapter 1, section 1.2.3 regarding the use of directories and subdirectories. In Windows 95, directories and subdirectories are referred to as *folders*. The easiest way to work with folders in Windows 95 is to use Windows Explorer. Load Explorer by clicking on the Start button in the lower left corner of the desktop (see Figure H.1). Then move the cursor up on the Start menu to Programs and then left into the Programs menu. Place the cursor on Windows Explorer, as shown in Figure H.5, and press the <pick> button. The Explorer screen, illustrated in Figure H.6, will be displayed. You can use Explorer to perform almost any Windows 95 system task, such as adding printers, making Control Panel settings, running programs, and creating and managing folders (directories) and documents (files).

To view the contents of a diskette, click on the diskette's icon, e.g., 3½ Floppy (A:), in the Explorer window, as shown in Figure H.6. The contents of the diskette will be shown in the Contents box (App-H, H-1, etc.).

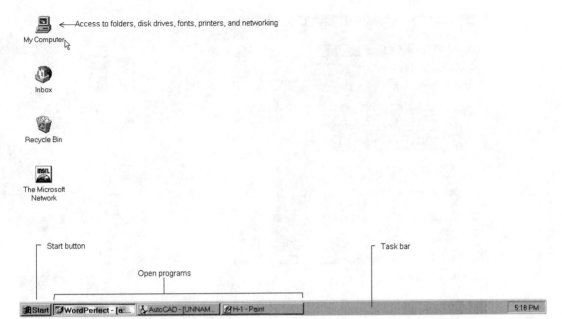

←——Access to folders, disk drives, fonts, printers, and networking

My Computer

Inbox

Recycle Bin

The Microsoft
Network

Start button

Task bar

Open programs

Start | WordPerfect - [a:... | AutoCAD - [UNNAM... | H-1 - Paint | 5:18 PM

Figure H.1 Windows desktop.

Figure H.2 Selecting a diskette.

Figure H.3 Formatting a diskette.

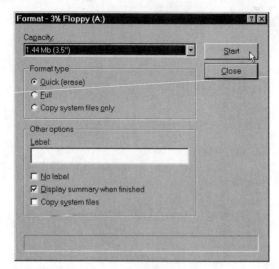

Figure H.4 Format dialog box.

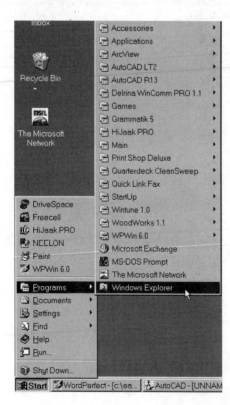

Figure H.5 Loading Explorer.

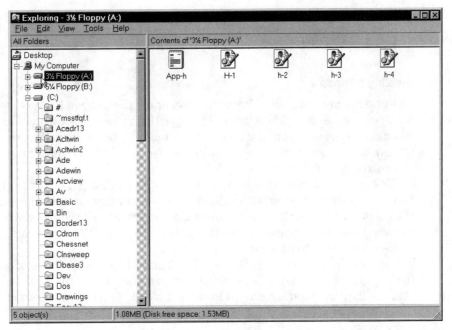

Figure H.6 Using Explorer.

Folders (directories) are displayed as icons of file folders. A folder icon with a + in a box to the left of it has subitems (subdirectories) that aren't shown. For example, to view the contents of folder Acadr13 (see Figure H.6), click on the plus sign in the box to the left of it. Noting that the folder has further subitems, click on the + beside Win. Display the contents of the Sample folder by clicking on its icon, as illustrated in Figure H.7. The + in the box beside the expanded folders is replaced by a – sign. Click on the – to collapse the folder.

H.3.1 Creating a new folder

You'll create a new folder (subdirectory) named Drawings in the root directory of drive C:, as follows:

1. Open Explorer and click on the drive C icon (refer back to Figure H.6) to change to the root directory of drive C (or whichever drive you want to use for the Drawings folder).

2. Click on File in the menu at the top of the Explorer window to display the File menu.

3. Move the cursor down the File menu onto New and then move horizontally to the right to Folder, as shown in Figure H.8. Press the <pick> button.

4. Windows 95 will create a new folder named New Folder, shown in Figure H.9. The name New Folder is highlighted and boxed, indicating you can rename it. Type **Drawings** from the keyboard and press <return>.

H.3.2 Manipulating a Window

The title bar at the top of a documentation or application window includes buttons for changing the size of the window. Figure H.10 illustrates the title bar for Explorer. You can use the – button to minimize the window. When you click on the minimize button, the window will be *iconized* in the task bar at the bottom of the screen, as shown in Figure H.11.

Click on the iconized window in the task bar, Exploring-(C) in Figure H.11, to restore the window. The button to the right of the minimize button in Figure H.10 is the maximize button. Click on it to maximize the screen to its largest size and change the icon to two rectangles. Click on the same button (with the two-rectangle icon) to restore the screen to its previous size.

Use the Close button with the × (see Figure H.10) to close the application or folder. If you want to rerun Explorer, you must restart it from the Start menu. Notice that the Explorer icon is removed from the task bar when the application is closed.

H.4 Starting AutoCAD

To start AutoCAD R13 for Windows, click on the Start button, shown back in Figure H.1, to display the Start menu. Move the cursor into the menu to Programs to display

Figure H.7 Viewing a folder.

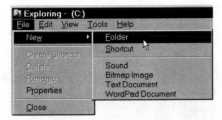

Figure H.8 Creating a new folder.

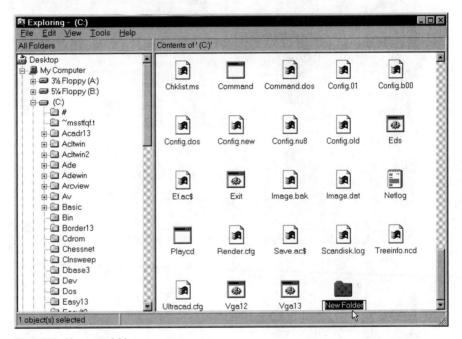

Figure H.9 Naming a folder.

Figure H.10 Windows title bar.

Figure H.11 Iconized window.

the Program menu (your list will be different because you have different programs on your computer). Then move in the Program menu onto AutoCAD R13 (your folder might be called AutoCAD 13, ACAD13, CAD13, etc.) to display the contents of the AutoCAD 13 folder, as illustrated in Figure H.12. Locate the AutoCAD 13 program icon in the folder with the mouse and press the <pick> button. AutoCAD 13 for

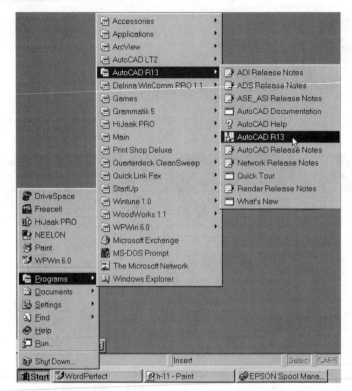

Figure H.12 Starting AutoCAD.

Windows will now load. Continue as outlined in chapter 1, section 1.3.1. You can start AutoCAD 13 for DOS as follows:

1. Click on the Windows Start button (see Figure H.1).

2. Choose Shut Down... in the menu to display the dialog box illustrated in Figure H.13.

3. Press the Restart the Computer in MSDOS Mode radio button, as shown.

4. Press the Yes command button.

Windows will be removed and the DOS prompt will be displayed. Enter the name of your AutoCAD batch file at the prompt and press <return>, e.g.: C:\> **acadr13** <return>. Continue in chapter 1, section 1.3.1. After exiting AutoCAD for DOS, type **Win** at the DOS prompt to reload Windows.

H.5 Copying a File in Windows

You can use Explorer to copy files in Windows either after exiting AutoCAD or while it's still loaded. Load Explorer as outlined in section H.3 (refer back to Figure H.5) to display the Explorer window, illustrated in Figure H.6. Then follow this procedure to copy Proj-1.dwg from the Drawings folder to a diskette in drive A:

Click on the Drawings folder icon in Folders list (in the box on the left side of the Explorer window) to open the folder and display its contents in the Contents box (on the right side of the Explorer window). You can change the icons in the Contents box by selecting large icons in the View menu, as illustrated in Figure H.14. Try the other options.

Place the cursor on the Proj-1 icon in the Contents box, press and hold down the <pick> button, and move the cursor into the Folders list. The cursor will carry an image of the icon with it. Place the cursor onto the 3½ Floppy (A:) icon (shown back in Figure H.6) and, when the icon's name is highlighted, release the <pick> button. The Proj-1 file will be copied into 3½ Floppy. This is called *dragging and dropping* a file. You can drag and drop files into any folder.

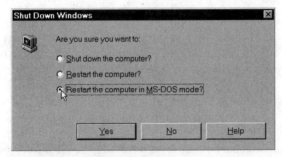

Figure H.13 Existing to DOS.

Figure H.14 Setting the icon image.

H.6   Renaming a File in Windows

You can rename files (and folders) in Explorer using the mouse's right button. Place the cursor on the file to be renamed, e.g., Proj-1, and press the right button of the mouse, displaying the menu in Figure H.15. Click on Rename in the menu. The name of the folder is highlighted, but you can change it. If you don't want to change the name, press <esc>.

H.7   AutoCAD in the Windows 95 Environment

Read chapter 20. For the applications in this section, working with Windows 95 is similar to working with Windows 3.1. (If you're knowledgeable about OLE, AutoCAD 13 supports only OLE1.) Following chapter 20, section 20.1, load Windows 95 Clipboard by clicking on Start and locating Clipboard Viewer in the Accessories menu, as shown in Figure H.16.

When Clipboard is loaded you can minimize it, for instance to return to the Auto-CAD window, by clicking on the window's minimize button (–), as shown in Figure H.10. Once minimized, you can restore the Clipboard window by clicking on its icon in the command bar (see Figure H.11). Try it. Note that Paint is also located in the Accessories menu.

You can also toggle between open applications using <alt>–<tab>, as outlined in chapter 20, section 20.1. A box will appear in the middle of the screen with an icon for each of the open applications and files. Each time you press <tab> while holding down the <alt> key, a rectangular box toggles to the next application icon and the name of the application or open file in the application is shown at the bottom of the box. When the application you want to view is highlighted, release <alt> to display the window for that application.

The Paste command in Windows 95 invokes PasteLink. To paste an AutoCAD object, select Edit and then Paste Special.... The dialog box in Figure H.17 will be displayed, but it will have a Picture option in the As: box. Choose Picture and then OK.

H.7.1   Linking an AutoCAD drawing

Open Proj-16 in AutoCAD, as outlined in chapter 20, section 20.4. Set the current working mode to Model and 3D View as the current viewport. Use the Copy View command to begin the link. Open Windows Wordpad (located in the Accessories

Figure H.15 Renaming a file.

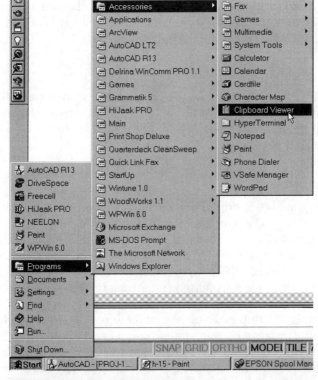

Figure H.16 Starting Clipboard.

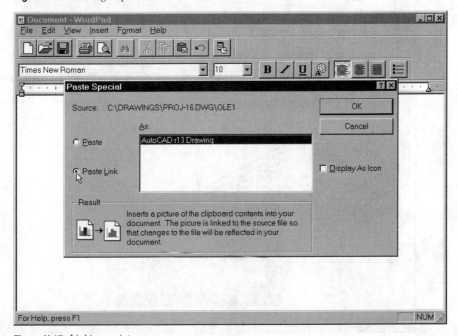

Figure H.17 Linking a picture.

menu, see Figure H.16) to use the link facility. In Wordpad, choose Paste Special... in the Edit menu to display the dialog box illustrated in Figure H.17. Press the Paste Link radio button, as shown. Press the OK button.

H.7.2 Editing linked views

To edit the linked view, double-click on the linked image in Wordpad. If AutoCAD isn't opened, right-click on the linked image to display the menu shown in Figure H.18, and click on the item shown. AutoCAD will open. Modify the drawing as described in chapter 20, section 20.4.1.

H.8 Installing a Printer

AutoCAD 13 has a good set of printer drivers, and you'll probably be able to select your printer in the Printer Configuration menu. If your printer isn't listed, try to get a driver from the manufacturer and install it from the AutoCAD Configuration menu. If you use a system printer and need to modify paper size options from those available in AutoCAD's Plot menu, you'll have to change the settings through Windows, as follows: Click on the Windows Start button (refer back to Figure H.1), Settings, and then Printers.

Windows will display a Printers dialog box on the screen with an icon for each of the printers currently installed on your system, plus an Add Printer icon. If you want to install a new printer, choose the Add Printer icon and follow the procedures in the Windows Add Printer Wizard. If you want to change the settings (paper size, etc.) for an existing printer, click on the printer's icon with the right mouse button. A menu

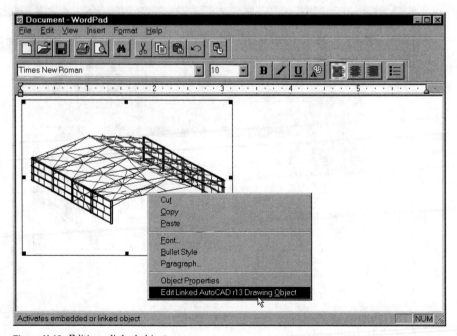

Figure H.18 Editing a linked object.

similar to the one shown back in Figure 11.15 in chapter 11 will be displayed. Choose Properties from the menu, choose Setup in the Properties dialog, and then make the necessary settings to the dialog box. Press OK to exit each dialog box. The new settings will apply to the system printer in the AutoCAD Print dialog box.

H.9   Using AutoCAD for Windows 95

AutoCAD for Windows 95 is distributed as Release 13c4 (or later). This version of AutoCAD meets the Windows 95 compliance requirements, such as long filenames, mail enabling, and OLE2 support. Additional commands, useful for 3-D modeling, are:

Solview. Creates floating viewports with orthographic projection in order to lay out multi- and sectional view drawings or three-dimensional solid and body objects.

Soldraw. Generates profiles and sections in viewports created with the Solview command.

Solprof. Creates profile images of three-dimensional solids.

These commands will simplify the process outlined back in section 17.10 of chapter 17 to create profile images of 3-D models. I was working with a beta edition of the software while writing this book and was unable to invoke the commands. For more information on the commands, use the AutoCAD help option (refer back to section D.5 in appendix D).

The Windows 95 version of Release 13 supports OLE2 (object linking and embedding). Windows 3.1 supports only OLE1. One of the differences between OLE1 and OLE2 is that, when you edit embedded objects (refer back to section 20.3 in chapter 20) by double-clicking on the embedded object in the host application (i.e., a word-processed document), another windows containing AutoCAD doesn't apear. You remain in the host window (your document) and AutoCAD and the host application negotiate an arrangement to display AutoCAD menus and toolbars in the host document. Then you can modify the embedded object with the AutoCAD toolbars and menus. This applies only to editing embedded objects; when you edit linked objects (refer back to section 20.3 in chapter 20), AutoCAD is opened in a separate window.

Index

@ symbol, 22, 23

A

Aerial View window, 66-69, 302-303
  changing image size, 68-69
  using Locator tool to pan, 68
  using Locator tool to zoom, 68
  using pan with, 67
  using zoom with, 66-67
alarms, error, 112
American National Standards Institute
  (ANSI), 97
angular dimensioning, 57-58, 143
Annotation command, 50, 65, 103, 141,
  299
Arc command, 25-27, 47-49, 60
architectural units, 19, 216
Array command, 134-136, 243
associative dimensioning, 105, 201-203
Attdef command, 175-176, 223
attributes, 175-190
  border blocks, construction, 176-184
  creating, 179-180
    blocks, 182
  editing, 184
    definitions, 181-182
  title block
    construction, 176-184
    headings, 178-179
AutoCAD
  configuring, 109-112
    alarm on error, 112

allow detailed device configuration,
  110
automatic save feature, 112
default plot file name, 112
digitizer, 111
exit to main menu, 110
file locking, 112
initial drawing setup, 112
operating parameters, 112
plotter, 111
show current configuration, 110
temporary file placement, 112
video display, 110-111
icons, 8
loading, 17-18
operating systems and, xx
program, xix-xx
starting, 8-14
AutoCAD device interface (ADI), 109
AutoLISP, 341-348
  functions, 341
    drawing limits, 346-347
    Drawlim, 346-347
    Getdist, 344
    house, 343-344
    Housedrw, 347-348
    Setq, 344, 346
    user-defined, 342-343
  input, 344
  primitives, 342
    Defun, 343, 344
    List, 346